# STORMY PETREL

# STORMY PETREL

*The Life and Work of Maxim Gorky*

by DAN LEVIN

APPLETON-CENTURY

New York

APPLETON-CENTURY
AFFILIATE OF
MEREDITH PRESS

Library of Congress Catalog Card Number: 65-14403

MANUFACTURED IN THE UNITED STATES OF AMERICA FOR MEREDITH PRESS

VAN REES PRESS  •  NEW YORK

# ACKNOWLEDGMENTS

MUCH of the research for this book was done in and through the facilities of the University of Chicago Library; additional research was done in the New York Public Library, through the interlibrary loan division of the Cleveland Public Library, and in the Library of the Gorky Institute of World Literature and the Lenin Library, both in Moscow.

I got valuable insights from talks with various Soviet scholars and men of letters. If the conclusions I came to, about the kind of man Gorky was, his basic beliefs, the nature and meaning of his writing, and his death, differ sharply from theirs, I know they will understand my sincere effort to interpret the man and to write the truth about him as I see it.

For those who may wish to consult the sources of material in the book, a bibliography and a typescript of footnotes, keyed to a marked copy of the book, are available in the University of Chicago Library.

# CONTENTS

# STORMY PETREL

# BOOK I

## Orphan of the Burning Heart

## CHAPTER 1

IN 1868, seven years after the liberation of the serfs in Russia, Nizhni Novgorod (Lower Novgorod) was a slatternly but busy little city, at the confluence of the Volga and the Oka, about 225 miles east and slightly north of Moscow.

Founded about the year 1200, in territory of pagan Mordvin tribes, it was probably a colony of the original Novgorod (Great Novgorod), then a power in northwest Russia, head of a strong free merchantry, Moscow's rival. Myth and folktale link Nizhni Novgorod with the legendary hero, Ilya Muromets, who bestrode first the Great Novgorod region, then that of Kiev. Just as in ancient Greece, where Athena the Owl and other bird-divinities peopled the early imagination, Nizhni Novgorod recalled the hero-bird Starling, the Mordvin, friend and helper to Nightingale-Robber, whom Ilya Muromets conquered—a symbolic recollection, no doubt, of the winning and settling of the region. Possibly the solid merchants who set out afoot from Novgorod's Church of Holy Sofia, on pious pilgrimage to Jerusalem, tarried to found a trading post on their river route to the Orient; and armed conquest, by combined Novgorodian, Kievian and Rostovian princes, followed.

Another local celebrity was Woodpecker, a wizard, consulted by Starling on occasion; and low hills on the far side of the Volga—toward Asia—would thenceforth be Woodpecker Hills. They reminded the conquering prince of the heights above Kiev, cradle of Russian Christianity, and he therefore founded the city; religion secured, in legend as in life, what had been won by commercial penetration and armor.

The other great figure of Russian hero-legend, Vasska Buslayev, also hailed from Novgorod. He was the hero of reckless good nature, freedom of action, wild friendship of equals. When Ivan the Terrible, in 1570, was making Moscow the single great power, he extirpated the merchantry of Novgorod, Ilya's and Vasska's own, in a slaughter that went on for weeks at a rate of five hundred to a thousand a day. But by this time the namesake city, Nizhni Novgorod, had long been a bastion of medieval commerce in the hinterland.

It lived and prospered, as trade came up the Volga from Persia via Astrakhan. After the period of Tartar invasion and rule in Russia, and the violent dynastic wars of the early seventeenth century, its *kreml* (the fortress of the frontier town) fell into disuse—it became the town jail. Crafts developed: silversmithing, iconography, ceramics; businesses of all kinds added to the old rugged Novgorodian tradition: shipping, construction, carpentry, furniture, dye shops for textiles.

It was a middle-class town, a town of business. No son of its middle class could renounce his heritage with impunity.

The birds, once divinities, still thronged the woods bordering the city, on both sides of the Volga. Besides the nightingales, the starlings, and the woodpeckers, there were, among others, goldfinches, bullfinches, siskins.

A decade before this story opens, a census showed Nizhni Novgorod having a population of 30,789, including 17,927 males. By far the biggest single group—as might be expected—were the *meschanye*: burghers, including shopkeepers, small businessmen, and craftsmen, the latter being classified in guilds. These numbered 4,823.

A much smaller and more select category (472) was that of the *kuptsy*, or merchants. These were the coming class in the new Russia that seemed emerging: entrepreneurs, builders of factories, shipping magnates. But the meschanye were certainly slated to be the guts and backbone of the new Russia, especially if now, without slavery, it developed as other countries of Europe had done.

Clergy numbered 2,331. A total of 636 were listed as "gentry" (gentlefolk, rather than "nobility"). There were 1,155 "shop workers." "Yardpeople" (house serfs) came to 1,065. There were 2,440 *kantonisty* (the illegitimate children of soldiers, raised and educated by the Tsarist government at various centers, of which Nizhni Novgorod was one, to become soldiers).

A troublesome category, in a class-and-caste society in troubled transition, was that of *raznochintsy*—those from various *chins*, or official classes; they numbered 840, and must have included lawyers, doctors, newspapermen, writers, and others who represented newfangled professions.

Beggars are not listed, nor prostitutes, nor are rag-and-bone pickers.

Nor are derelicts and bums, whose main place of congregation was a street by the river front named, fittingly, Million Street; and whose number would grow, in the depression that would follow the Turkish War of 1877.

There were 254 stone houses and 2,089 wooden ones. Of the total of 2,343 houses, 2,282 were identified by the census as private dwellings. Most people carried on their occupations where they lived.

There was a Cathedral of the Blessed Nativity, with four cupolas; thirty-five churches; eight monasteries. Two of the churches (one of them that of the Archangel Michael) were considered "beautiful"; others, such as that of St. Barbara, were more humble. The skyline of Nizhni Novgorod, as freighters, barges or paddle wheelers carrying passengers approached up the Volga, was low-lying, featuring the gold-skinkling cupolas of the churches. As the ships drew nearer, the rows of dun-colored, green-colored, white-colored houses appeared. One street, Uspensky—street of "the going into eternal sleep," in honor of the Blessed Virgin, Mother of God—was noted as a street of dirty-reddish stone houses.

The corner house on Uspensky Street and its inner yard were also the dye shop ("the business") of the Kashirin family, a family of the meschanye.


The head of the Kashirin family and business will be known here as Grandpa. A short, tough, angry man, red-haired and red-bearded, a serf freed long before the Emancipation, he had in his youth pulled barges on the Volga, straining his wiry guts along the shore on a rope tied to the barge, cutting his bare feet on stones, chanting that mournful and majestic "Volga boat song," charming symbol of the Old Russia.

But with vigor, cunning, determination, he had raised himself to another class, in the fifties and sixties. He became the foreman of a large dye shop in Nizhni Novgorod. By this time he was married to a plump, lively local girl, of great character, full of the religious poetry of the folk. As a child, Akulina too had wandered the Volga, begging with her mother, a serf freed when she became crippled and thus incapable of strong work. She will be known as Grandma. There were eighteen children born; three survived.

"If all would've lived," Grandma would later tell her grandson, "we would've been a whole streetful. But the Lord took a liking to my blood, he took and took the kids, for angels. And I'm sad, but happy too."

With his two surviving sons, Mike and Jake, Grandpa Kashirin at last set up his own dye shop, the business. The third child who survived was a daughter, Barbara, buxom, intelligent, and attractive.

Next door, while they were still on Kovalikha Street, before Grandpa founded the business, lived young Maxim Peshkov. Born in Siberia, the son of a soldier, he had run away from his father's cruelty and for a time led the blind to town markets. Soon, however, he learned the trades of carpentry, cabinetmaking, and upholstering, in Nizhni Novgorod. One day, when Grandma and her daughter Barbara were picking berries in their garden, he vaulted the low fence and asked Grandma for her blessing. She was stunned. The young man had no standing, while Grandpa now owned four houses and was a shop foreman. But . . . a child born out of legal wedlock would bring tragedy.

Grandma hired a priest to marry them, but Grandpa found out. He leaped into a horse-drawn cab, club in hand, his sons with him, one carrying a rifle. Inspired by a favorite saint, Grandma had cut through the shaft of the carriage, and they went into a ditch. By the time they managed to reassemble and get to the church, the marriage had taken place. Mike made a rush for young Peshkov, who threw him down the church steps, spraining his arm. "What God has given me, I will keep," he told them.

Grandpa finally forgave—as much as a man of his bitter temper could—the gay, intelligent and audacious bridegroom. The couple came to live in the attic of the Kashirin family. There, on March 16, 1868, their son was born. He was named Alexey Maximovich (the middle name for his father, Maxim, in accordance with Russian custom) Peshkov. His birth was entered in the register of the church of St. Barbara.

But Barbara's violent and jealous brothers were afraid her husband would be taken into the dye firm. They pushed Peshkov into a hole in the Volga ice, then stamped on his fingers as he tried to scramble out; but they were too drunk to be efficient, and went away too soon. He managed to climb out, and refused to tell the police who had nearly drowned him. For this he was blessed by Grandma; in the Kashirin clan it was an axiom, the police must never be brought in. For Mike and Jake, it would have meant Siberia. Peshkov took many weeks recovering. Then he took his wife and his small son and went to Astrakhan to live; it seems he got a job there as manager of one of the ship wharves, with an additional commission: to build the triumphal arch for the Tsar's coming visit.

Astrakhan, an old and historic port at the Volga's mouth, was the juncture of Russia and Persia, multilingual and full of color. Through it moved big shipments of herring and caviar, and with them came, even more frequently than elsewhere in Russia, the cholera plague.

The little boy, Alexey, fell ill. He seemed to remember his father cheerfully and constantly nursing him; then his father disappeared, and his place was taken, after a while, by a gay, kind, exciting, funny woman with a bulbous nose—his Grandma, whom he did not remember. Soon after came the first full, rounded conscious memory, of a scene which is always one of life's crises, and which in this case must have had a powerful influence on the forming mind.

He faced it, at the age of four, clutching the hand of his grandmother. Many years later he would describe it, in the opening sentences of a book which is one of the world's enduring classics of autobiography.

In a close, half-dark room, on the floor, under a window, lies my father, dressed in white and unusually long; the toes of his bare feet are strangely distended, the fingers of his gentle hands, resting on his breast, are also curled; his gay eyes are covered tight by the blackened discs of two lead coins, his kind face is dark and scares me with its bared teeth.

His mother, half-naked, in a red skirt, is on her knees, interminably combing the dead man's hair. The little boy notes that the comb she uses is the one with which he himself enjoyed scraping watermelon seeds. She talks to the dead man without stopping, her eyes swollen and seeming to melt, as tears well from them without stopping. The grandmother weeps in cadence, and pushes the little boy forward toward his father, but he only clings to her.

Then his mother cries out, falls to the floor, Grandma rushes to her and gets on her knees beside her, and they seem to thresh about on the floor. The terrified boy hides in a corner. The second half of the traumatic scene ends with the wail of a child: his little brother has been born, prematurely.

Then, a rain-drenched cemetery. The little boy, Grandma, the sexton, two gravediggers, the coffin, two shovels.

Looking down into the muddy hole in which his father's coffin has been sunk, the boy sees two frogs on the yellow coffin lid. As the shovels pour wet earth down into the hole, the frogs try frantically to climb the walls of the grave, but they can't make it. The earth pours down, the grave is filled.

Leaving the graveyard, Grandma asks Alexey why he isn't crying. "I don't want to." "You don't? Well, you don't have to," she answers gently.

They ride in a horse-drawn drozhky down a broad, filthy street lined with dark red houses. Alexey asks Grandma, "Can those frogs ever crawl out?" "They won't, God be with 'em," she assures him. God, it occurs to him then, comes more frequently and familiarly into Grandma's conversation than He ever did in his father's or mother's.

The next scene is a few days later, on a paddle-wheel steamboat bound up-Volga from Astrakhan. It stops at Saratov, and there a sailor comes into the tiny cabin and takes away a small white box. In it is the body of Alexey's baby brother, Maxim, who has died on the trip. His mother and Grandma go ashore to bury the little fellow. The dazed boy also goes ashore, gets lost, is put back aboard by kindly passengers, having been recognized by the sailor who carried out his baby brother. Until he sees Grandma again, he believes he has been abandoned, in the collapse of everything.

The trip continues. At its end is Nizhni Novgorod. Grandma and the boy spend most of the time on the deck together. She becomes a favorite of the sailors, who make fun of her but admire the tales she tells, the folk ballads she recites.

Once he sees that Grandma, staring out over the Volga, is crying. The tears are of sorrow and happiness—joy at the world, grief at the grief in it. When Nizhni Novgorod appears ahead of them, she laughs in delight like a girl. "How beautiful it is! See the churches—they're swimming!" With shouts, confusion, and heartsick anxiety in the dazed boy, the paddle wheeler comes to dock, and aboard comes the whole motley Kashirin clan, led by red-bearded Grandpa.

This is where Alexey will grow up. Here his mother abandons him, and he is brought up by Grandma, and a violent Grandpa, and violent uncles, in a harsh Russia just staggering out of medieval times.

## CHAPTER 2

"THERE began" for him, "and flowed on, at terrible speed, a thick, colorful, inexpressibly strange life."

Most of the vast land still sprawled in the archaic past—a "dark" peasantry (muzhiks) living brutish lives, working the soil with antiquated tools, banded in their immemorial communes, adoring their "Tsar-Daddy," ninety per cent illiterate, still paying quitrent or day labor to amortize their emancipation, which had inflamed hope without making things dramatically better; those driven from the land beginning to drift to the cities, joining the urban poor; and beside them, a failing and bewildered gentry, shorn of the slave labor on which their security had rested.

But as the countryside dreamed on, in travail and stagnation, the haphazard cities—like Nizhni Novgorod—grew: struggling, dirty, somber, yet full of that "thick, colorful, inexpressibly strange life."

There were hives of the slum poor, and in-betweens struggling on the rungs of the economic ladder. Wealth was rare, for capital was lacking, but a few new merchant princes were creating themselves, and by the next generation would have wastrel sons to carouse in taverns. Most of the cast was composed of those mentioned in the census (or omitted): small shopkeepers, stevedores, carpenters, painters, dyers . . . army men, women kept by merchants or officers, hired help, day laborers . . . police agents . . . beggars, prostitutes, derelicts . . .

Into this life "the Peshkov brat"—this was how he saw himself looked upon—was thrown. He had come at an unfortunate time of dramatic downward change in the Kashirin family's fortunes. This compounded the traumatic changes caused by his father's death.

Instead of being the loved only son of a coming man, manager of a ship dock, he was an orphan dependent on his grandfather, an aging, embittered man who had two grown sons for whom he could not provide. For the Kashirin Firm was going down.

Many such home industries were perishing. The hand-run dye shops of Nizhni Novgorod had been doomed as far back as the 1840's, by the coming in of mechanized textile plants which included dyeing vats. In 1847 there had been 136 hand-worked dye shops; by 1866, two years before Alexey's birth, the Kashirins' was one of five that remained. Year by year the odds mounted. The firm could not survive. Grandpa had emerged too recently from the lower classes; he had no room for play; he had no backing; his sons were uneducated (he had risen too late to help them). The Kashirins were becoming "declassed."

The child Alexey did not understand this clearly, but felt all of it excruciatingly. It marked him forever. He would become one of those hurt, rebellious, burning children of the middle class who had lost their class, and therefore bitterly rejected it. Great things and terrible things—great deeds, great crimes, great songs—have often come from this unfortunate social layer.

"Poverty is everything," Grandma told Alexey. And with poverty went cruelty, violence.

The characters of those first growing years, in a household which now teetered on anarchy's edge, and soon on poverty's, stamped themselves in him. They would be his models of what people were, and what their fate was.

There were the foolish, violent, emotion-clouded uncles, Mike and Jake, and their pathetic children, and Mike's wife whom he beat secretly and ferociously, and who would die in childbirth; Gregory, the faithful foreman of the failing dye shop, with cataracts forming on his eyes; Tsigannok ("Gypsy"), huge, too faithful handyman, who would be crushed under a crossbeam the uncles laid on him to save horses; and, above all, tyrannical Grandpa, who whipped his grandson into unconsciousness and illness, kicked Grandma in the chest, and beat his daughter on the head until her hairpins were driven into her flesh.

All this was the fury of frustration, the fury of a man facing a life's defeat. In Grandpa there was something noble, too; there was much he really understood. He knew he was cruel to others because he was cruel to himself. But the boy's love for him was almost altogether coated with dread, and much of the rebellion growing in him would take the form of rebellion against Grandpa.

There developed in him, quite early, a preoccupation with the question of the nature of God. Grandma's God was clearly not Grandpa's. Grandpa, approaching his ikon corner warily, seemed to pray before God as before a tough magistrate or an angry creditor. "Judge me, God," he prayed, "by my faith, not by my works, which surely could not weigh in my favor," and, "Quench the passions burning in my soul, for sorrow overwhelms me; I am accursed."

But Grandma's God was nothing of the kind, and her relation to him was entirely different. Lying under a heavy blanket, eyes wide, Alexey watched and listened to Grandma at her prayers, before her ikon of the Mother of God of Kazan. She knelt, one hand on her breast, the other at intervals making the sign of the cross. The greenish moonlight, through the ice traceries on the window pane, kindled her dark eyes with phosphorescence, and showed clearly her kind face with its large nose. Her silken nightcap glistened like wrought metal. Her dark dress cascaded from her shoulders, spreading out on the floor. All this, many years later, he would describe, just so. It was a character-forming scene, a scene never to be forgotten.

After the more formal prayer, Grandma talked to God, heart-to-heart. She pointed out to Him—though of course He knew!—that her own sinning was through stupidity and not ill will. She asked Him, affectionately and confidently, to forgive the faithful.

Alexey took to Grandma's God. He asked her to tell him about Him. She agreed, but took care first to sit up straight and straighten her kerchief. When she spoke about God, it was in a special way, her voice rather hushed, drawing out the words, keeping her eyes closed.

The Lord sits on a knoll, among the meadows of Paradise, on an altar of sapphires, beneath silver lindens, and those lindens bloom the whole year round; there is in Paradise no winter, or autumn, and the flowers never wither, they just bloom without stopping, in the joy of having God's favor. And near the Lord the angels fly in throngs—like snow falling, or bees swarming—or like white pigeons flying from heaven to earth and back to heaven—telling God everything about us people. . . . And to everyone He deals out according to their deeds—to this one grief, to that one joy. And everything of His is so good, that the angels enjoy themselves, fluttering their wings and singing to him over and over, "Glory to you, Lord, glory to you!" And He, dear one, only smiles at them—as if saying, "All right, that's enough."

Still, it was Grandpa who taught him to read; only this would make him able to rise again, from the hopeless lower-class life to which, by the family's failing economic position, he now seemed fated. For text, Grandpa used at first the old Slavonic psalter, then the Old Testament, mainly the Psalms. From there, Grandma, who was illiterate, took over—and Alexey learned by heart the "Lives of the Saints" in ballad form, and other religious folk ballads.

This was his early training.

As he grew and began to run the streets, he sensed more sharply a cruelty in the life around him. It seemed to him bred into the very play of the children, who tortured or baited roosters, dogs, cats, Jews, helpless drunks, and other unfortunates.

Once Grandma took Alexey to haul water from the town pump. They came on five townsmen beating a peasant—trampling him, "dragging him as dogs might drag another dog." Grandma dropped her pails and used the yoke to beat them away. Then she tended the peasant, who held his torn nostrils in muddy fingers while blood spurted into Grandma's face and onto her breast. She could not repress an outcry, and a fit of trembling. The boy stood watching.

An especially painful experience was to see Gregory, Grandpa's old shop foreman, still straight and handsome, but now quite blind, going the beggar's rounds. A tiny gray woman led him. She would stand under a window and pipe, "Something for the poor blind, for Christ's sake." Gregory himself stood with lips pressed tight, his broad beard touching his stained, folded hands.

Alexey would dash in, crying, "Gregory's out in the street!" Grandma would go out and talk with Gregory, and would laugh and stroke his beard, but he would only speak a few monosyllables. Sometimes she called him into the kitchen and fed him. When she chided Alex for avoiding the good man, the boy asked: "Why did Grandpa send him away?"

"Grandpa?" She paused, then hardly audibly, she made this prophecy: "Remember what I tell you—God's grievous punishment will come upon us for it. God's punishment..."

And her words were not off the mark. Ten years later, after she had gone to her death, Grandpa was making the beggar's rounds himself, his mind broken, whining under windows, "Show some pity, cooks, just a morsel of meat pie, a little morsel. Ekh—you!"

Grandma too would die begging. All his dear ones would become sacrifices to what he could not help seeing as a callous, cruel way of life.

He had not been born an underdog, but being orphaned made him feel he had become one. There was considerable reality in this, besides the emotional reality; and the fall of the Kashirin fortunes brought the two realities even closer. His background, and the shock of the tragic change, would make him thoughtful, sensitive, and articulate, in a way that the true-born underdogs, in a land like Russia, could seldom be.

In these years concern for the underdogs haunted the cultured Russian's imagination. It was a main theme of Russian literature. But so sharp were the lines of caste and class, so restricted the chances for a higher education, that no voice from among these underdogs themselves had yet been clearly heard.


Hurt and bewildered by the rugged cruelty of the streets, the little boy lay in bed, waiting for Grandma to roll in beside him, after she finished her long and intimate discussion with God. He asked himself, to the murmur of her voice: What kind of man was my father? Where is my mother?

Then he imagined his mother living among the robbers, robbing the rich for the poor, and being scolded sternly by the Mother of God, in the language of one of Grandma's ballads:

> Not for you to gather, greedy slave,
> All the world's gold, all the world's silver.
> Not for you, soul covetous, to cover
> With all the world's wealth your nakedness.

But his mother answers the Mother of God:

> You forgive me, most holy Mother of God,
> Take pity on my little sinful soul.
> Not for myself did I rob the whole world,
> But for the sake of my son, my only one! ...

This was the folk culture of Russia, the fief of Byzantium, singing a medieval song, in a land being dragged reluctantly, painfully, toward the modern world. Cruelty and tears were its signs; its obsessions, Good and Evil, the conflict of sin and holiness. These would be the obsessions of his life; these, and bitter orphanhood.

Grandma kept a starling with a broken wing and a wooden leg she had fashioned for it to replace the one ripped off by a cat. To the boy, when overcome by frequent melancholy, the poor starling seemed a symbol for himself.

In the boy an implacable protest was forming, an endless dissatisfaction, yearning for a different reality. It might take the form of religious mysticism, or of physical violence, or of moral and intellectual revolt.

Once a scarred, wild convict was being led through town, in chains, to exile. The boy stood in the milling crowd. Suddenly the convict yelled to him, "Come on, lad, come for a ride with us!" The boy almost leaped forward to meet the wild invitation.

There were many signs of the family's fallen state. Grandpa, having divided the already doomed business, under pressure, between his incapable sons, sold the house on Uspensky Street and moved into two dim cellar rooms, with Grandma and Alexey. There had been an old nursemaid —no middle-class family was complete without one; now she was gone. Grandma had taken to quiet drinking.

Alexey's mother returned, briefly, still a strong and proud woman, but battered by life. She tried hard, for a time, to make a life worth living for her boy. She rented a room of her own in a warehouse cellar. Standing on a stool, Alexey saw a grim landscape: a factory gate, flanked by lanterns, "gaping open like a toothless old beggar's mouth"; swarms of tiny people crawled in, and later were "spewed out." At nightfall, a dingy reddish light pulsed down from the factory, illuminating the stack.

He wore castoff clothes: a pair of his mother's shoes, a coat made out of an old jacket of Grandma's, trousers patched to fit. "Ace of diamonds," the street kids called him—that being the convict's mark. He fought in the street, often (at least in memory) against odds; in later years, when hard pressed, he spoke of life as "a fist fight."

For some months Barbara—"Iron Barbara"—managed to send her son to school. The young priest who gave the religious lessons kept sending him home because he had no Bible. But one day an unusual bishop, Khrisanph, a scholar and humanist, visited the school.

He was small, hunchbacked, and looked like "a wizard." He was the first of several wizards who entered Alexey's life. (Perhaps the most famous would be Tolstoy, and Lenin.) But Bishop Khrisanph was the only wizard who was wholly good and kind.

Calling me over in my turn, he asked: "How old are you? Is that all? How tall you are! Been out in the rain a lot, eh?"

Asked to read his favorite Bible story, young Peshkov explained he had no Bible. The bishop suggested he might have heard some things from it. "Know the Psalms? Good. And the prayers? There you are! And the lives of the Saints? In ballads? Well, you seem to be up on the subject."

While the priest, red-faced, stood to one side, the bishop had Alexey recite—Alexis, Man of God, then King David, then several Psalms.

When the good wizard had left, blessing all in the name of Father, Son, and Holy Ghost, the young priest said from now on Alexey was to help him with the lesson.

With Grandma listening, meanwhile, he was reading *Robinson Crusoe* —traditionally one of the first adventures for Russian boys—and Andersen's fairy tales.

But no better period could set in. The family was going down. Grandpa now made the rounds of friends and acquaintances with sob stories, getting money from them. Barbara left; then, after bearing an illegitimate child, which was given away, she remarried, badly. She returned again to her parents' nondescript flat, with a baby brother for Alexey—Nicky. Nicky did not last long. He died "unnoticed, like a faint star extinguished by the dawn." Soon Barbara herself faded, consumed by tuberculosis.

Alexey was already helping out, as a ragpicker. On holidays and early mornings he went through streets and backyards with a sack, collecting rags, paper, bones and scrap metal.

When Barbara died, Grandpa decided there had been enough school. Into the world—"Among People"—Alexey was sent, two days after the funeral. He was nearly eleven.

He never forgave Grandpa. Actually there was probably little choice; the whole story of Grandpa and Alexey is complex, never honestly told, full of ambivalent emotions. One feels that the boy had reached an emotional point of no return. He *was* an abandoned orphan, thrown by a cruel mean Grandpa into the world. He would, from now on, structure his life in accord with this image.

In fact, the whole story that now unfolds, of his rise from poverty and struggle against the lower depths, is an artistically "made" story. In reality it is, at least partly, a story of a boy's rejection of the life of the meschanye, of the lower middle class, of the place in life to which his Grandpa clung and wanted him to cling. The middle class of Nizhni Novgorod probably had enough solidarity—the middle class usually has—to find a place somewhere for a bright, energetic boy of its own, and it is likely that Grandpa saw in him a hope for the entire family. He refused; it was a tremendous, deep-reaching decision.

It was Grandpa who got him his first job "Among People"—as a doorboy for a shoe store owned by a family connection. He slept on the stove, brushed the clothes and polished the boots of the whole household, heated the samovar, fetched wood, and washed the dishes. He enticed in no customers, was enraged by the crass morals he saw, revenged himself by dropping vinegar into his master's gold watch. He also upset boiling cabbage soup on himself, and lay in a hospital, hands bandaged. Then Grandpa managed to get him a job as handy boy for a draftsman (or architect), a distant uncle. He lived with the man's family, was miserable, endured his state through the winter. In the spring, he ran away.

He roamed the Volga's shore for some days, getting meals and shelter from the stevedores; finally, he was taken on as a mess boy aboard a Volga steamer, on the same run as that of his early childhood: between Nizhni Novgorod and Astrakhan.

He was hired thanks to Smoury, the chef on the paddle wheeler, a growling giant with a solid gold heart. The influence would be historic.

"Do you have a father or mother?" Smoury growled. "Do you know how to steal? No? Well, don't worry. They're all thieves here, they'll teach you."

But Smoury took it upon himself to teach the boy something different. In his cabin, stretched out in a hammock rigged up beside the icebox, he handed the boy a book and said: "Read!"

Under the moon, the old, reddish boat, with a white stripe on its funnel, moved through the silver river; and Alexey, sitting on a chest, read aloud: "The umbra pierced by a star shows that the dreamer has good relations with heaven and is free of vice and profanity." Smoury, a cigaret dangling from his lip, made appropriate comments. From astrology, they moved on to Scott's *Ivanhoe*; from Ivanhoe, to *Letters of Lord Sydenham*; from that peer, to Fielding's *Tom Jones*; from Tom, to *Harmful Insects, Their Extermination.*

When Alexey read "Taras Bulba," Gogol's classic romance of the Cossacks, and got to the part where Taras killed his son, the huge chef sprang out of his hammock, bent over, and bawled. Tears splashed from his cheeks to the floor as he snorted, "Oh my God, oh my God!" Then he roared at Alexey, "Read on, you rib of a devil!"

On read young Alexey. Beneath the moon, the boat moved on. Far out on the Volga, unexpectedly, the man already was forming—in the boy of twelve—who would write:

Each book was a rung in my ascent from the brutish to the human, toward an understanding of a better life and a thirst after that life . . . It is to books that I owe everything that is good in me.

It was not selective literary fare. Neither was the life of the paddle wheeler, plying the great unkempt river, selective. He was learning where he could, like a boy in a street fight, grabbing whatever was handy. Smoury helped him fix resolves of character, sometimes resorting to blows. He probably encouraged his idealized view of "good women." He taught him that the cruel and barbarous was the "Asiatic" in Russia, as against the "European," which valued books. He taught him that the written word was something holy; and that writing should be "true to life." These were fairly clear values, less difficult and mysterious than those of Grandma's religious ballads, which stated moral "truths" in which Good and Evil were strangely intermingled.

As for Grandpa's Novgorodian values—middle-class meanness and hypocrisy, scrambling for the ruble—he had repudiated them. He was an orphan, rising from nowhere, and Smoury was his first teacher. What had begun as mixture of myth and reality would become, by his determination, palpably and completely real.

# CHAPTER 3

THESE first years of Alexey Peshkov's life, and of his dawning consciousness, were also the last great years of a movement that had embodied all the quandaries, noblest hopes, and strivings, of nineteenth-century Russia.

The protest of Russia's intelligentsia against tsarism and mass poverty had unfurled steadily from the 1820's into the 1870's. It ranged from modest desire for agrarian and constitutional reform, through utopian socialism in the spirit of Fourier, Owen, and Saint-Simon, to apocalyptic visions of the utter destruction of the state and the return to the natural, rural, communistic man. It was a great, many-faceted, idealistic movement, that attracted most of the finest spirits in the land.

Its leaders were men like Hertzen, Chernyshevsky, Pisarev, Tkachev, Lavrov, Bakunin, Mikhailovsky. But actually its heroes and leaders, its faces and dreams, both gentle and fanatical, were too many and too varied to be summed up in a few names. Its most common belief was, probably, that history is the story of the struggle for human progress. Its special feeling, by and large, was that Russia, by its rural nature, and the existence of the peasant commune (the mir), was closer to the natural, or socialist, ideal than other lands; so that if only reform or revolution could free the peasants from their moribund darkness and downtroddenness, it might be possible to achieve a clean, prosperous, enlightened land without going through the misery, seen in the West, of forced industrialization and capitalism.

Its psychology was often religious; many of its men and women believed that they were dreaming of, and working for, a return to the real way of Christ. Even its iconoclasts were usually altruistic idealists; but, revering Darwin, Feuerbach, and other advanced thinkers, they based themselves, rationalizing, on "utility"—arguing that it was the selfish desire of each for the best and most pleasurable life that should impel all to the communal life, a sharing of all with all.

Perhaps its typical representative in literature was Turgenev's figure Bazarov, who sacrificed his personal life to science, preparing himself, in utter and mysterious devotion, for the coming overturn; for Russia was "On the Eve."

A movement nearly altogether of the intelligentsia—a unique word connoting education, liberalism, awareness of humanitarian ideals—it was freighted with a sense of guilt: guilt before the "dark" peasant masses, on whose backs, these sensitive people felt, they lived their fortunate, cultured lives. They were determined to repay a great "debt" to the people. In the wings of their consciousness, it seems—even of the atheistic ones like Bakunin—there stood the dream of a return to the communal brotherhood of early Christianity.

To the movement's banners, in each generation, came the educated young of Russia, especially from the now impoverished gentry, the lower ranks of the clergy, and nationality and minority groups such as Georgians and Jews. Its men and women staffed the government-sponsored zemstvos or local councils, which attempted to improve rural conditions. It had its martyrs of devotion: between two and three thousand young men and women "went to the people" in 1873, walking hundreds of miles into villages and peasant communes to bring medicine and grammar, to work with their hands among the people, and sometimes to spread forbidden literature and persuade them to revolt. The surly, ingrown peasants invariably looked with suspicious fear at these "white-hands," most of whom didn't know which end of a cow to milk or how to drive a nail; they ignored them, or beat them up, or turned them over to the Tsar's police.

It had its martyrs of violence too, and these became prominent in the seventies—the very years in which Alexey Peshkov, unaware, was growing up—as zealots of the movement conceived the desperate notion that by killing hated officials, and in particular the Tsar, they could rouse the people to want freedom. Many lost their lives in such attempts, and the names of the terrorists were inscribed on the roll of honor of the movement—but also splitting and dooming it.

Overall, the movement had come to be known as the *Narodnichestvo*—the Populist movement. It warmed Alexey's childhood, without his being aware of it; by the time he was a grown young man, trying to organize a viewpoint, it would be rolling—its effulgence still lighting the Russian scene—into its sunset.

The break with home, even for an orphan, is seldom made in one clean try—especially if one is not yet thirteen.

Fired by the head steward for being too honest, Alexey got Smoury's farewell kiss and hug, then briefly returned to Grandpa and Grandma. For a while he and Grandma apparently went begging. Then he began to trap birds, which Grandma sold on market days (reluctantly, for she doubted God would approve). To her amazement, some birds brought a whole ruble.

Alexey roved the forests lining the Volga, snaring birds from red-bonneted goldfinch to the beautiful Apollo titmouse. He learned their songs, matched wits to get them into his cages, learned things about them that most people usually only learn, if they are watchful, about other people.

This was a very special relationship. It seems as if there was something primitive in his imagination, which actually made it easier for him, in some ways, to feel at one with birds than with people. Many years later he would write of these small creatures, "In their image it was that fairies, cherubs, seraphs, and all the angels were created by man, father of earthly beauty, to console himself."

Hard winter ended the bird trapping. He went back to work in the architect's household. A tailor's wife, nearby, lent him books—Stendhal, the Goncourts—and he also bought paperbacks on sale in a local bakery.

He grappled with words like "metaphysics," "chiliasm," "Chartist." He read about Attila, Tsar of the Huns, sheathed in steel, riding through ravaged lands, behind him the dark press of his warriors, calling, "Where lies Rome, the Mighty?" Rome was a city, but who the devil were the Huns?

As he recalled it, he asked his boss, then an army chaplain, then a young lieutenant; they all shrugged him off. Finally the local druggist, Goldberg, told him the Huns were nomads, but none were left; they had died out.

Joining the chef Smoury in the procession of those who influenced the growing boy, the druggist would adjust his glasses between thumb and forefinger, and drive in ideas "as if he were hammering tacks into my head." "Words, my lad, are like leaves. To discover why they are shaped this way and not that, we must study the growth of the tree. To understand words, my lad, we must know books. Man can be a flourishing garden only where every plant is both pleasing and useful."

He read secretly, after chores, in the attic; the boss's wife disapproved.

She very possibly did; but a legend was being constructed by the boy. The know-nothing middle-class denizens of Nizhni Novgorod were proud of their quiet, peaceful lives: "We don't know anything—glory to God!" And they hated to see a commoner reading. And the commoner (though in reality a distant nephew) was a homeless orphan, fighting against the middle-class world, to rise in spite of all of them. The transformation, from the boy who had been born into a substantial middle-class family, into a nameless orphan from below, was being completed. Helped by hard circumstance, he was molding his unfolding life into a work of art.

But there were also always those who realized the special zeal in the sad, gaunt boy, befriended him, and blessed him with books. The sense of their constant intervention, as part of the romance of his destiny, was one of the tools he used for that molding of his life into a work of art. Now there appeared a young woman, an officer's widow, who in his private daydream became known as "Queen Margot." She would provide for the adolescent boy both his first real sexual ideal and his first intense exposure to poetry.

Queen Margot lived in a nearby flat. She was beautiful and proud, her head held high, eyes unwavering, "as if she saw everybody from a distance." She rode horseback in a sweeping velvet steel-gray dress, shod in tan riding boots, hands in white gauntlets. She would use the knee of her soldier servant to vault deftly into the saddle, after petting the muzzle of her horse.

Like storied amoral medieval beauties (thence, "Queen Margot"), or a goddess, going where she pleased and choosing whom she pleased, she provided an ideal—which conflicted, however, with another ideal. When he saw her, once, in bed with one of her officer beaux, he was filled with admiration and *shame*. When she learned what was troubling the boy of thirteen, she assured him he too would learn how fine love was.

He believed her, but there was a conflict—between the ideal of the woman and the man free in love, and that of the "purity" of women, and the "holiness" of good men.

The sentimental view of women was strong in the Russian middle classes. Besides, he had seen some brutal examples, close up, of how men treated women. His goal of rising to a higher life, from the "animal" or "Asiatic" condition, had fastened to the idea of "pure" love, of a lofty chivalry. But finally, there was a special quality in him, deepened by Grandma's ballads, whose heroes were recluses and ascetics. This youth had been conditioned, part way, to be a holy man. The grown man would never quite forgive passion for infringing on the holiness of love.

This conflict would mark him. For some, the yearning for free sexual life is the spur to general social protest; for others, the ascetic ideal provides the spur. Each impulse also gives rise to art, veiling and transforming itself. In his case, both drives were strongly there, along with all the other reasons for protest. Its intensity and confusion were increased.

But these were the years of the preparation of protest. Queen Margot, too, started giving him books.

Thanks to her, he read the poems of Béranger, translated, and works of Russians: Tyutchev, Aksakov, Turgenev. The books "washed my soul, cleansing it of the refuse of beggarly and bitter reality." Over and over this statement will be repeated.

She also gave him Pushkin's poems to read, perhaps believing they would help him come to understand the nature of love. Their impression must have been very sharp. He would write it down, many years later, using a touching image that belongs properly to early childhood:

I read them through all at once, seized with that greedy feeling you experience when you come on an unknown beautiful place—you always try to run all around it at once. So it is after you walk a long time along mossy clumps of a marshy forest and suddenly there unfolds before you a dry meadow, all in flower and sun. For a minute you look at it spellbound, then happily run all over it, and every touch of your feet on the soft grass of the fertile ground delights you quietly.

Then, from somewhere deep, a grateful thought: "What happiness—to be literate!"

There was a curious significance in the loan of a book of Pushkin's poems, at this particular moment in Russian history, by a free and easy lady to an adolescent boy.

A Pushkin celebration had recently been held in Moscow. His statue was unveiled; Turgenev spoke, and Dostoyevsky.

This came at a time of rightward reaction. The impetus given by emancipation had been spent. The "dark" masses had not responded to Populist appeals. Mass poverty barred Russia's progress; for lack of progress, Russia seemed doomed to mass poverty. (This is still the dilemma of underdeveloped countries.) Successive generations of idealists had spent themselves; and their resort to terror had turned the moderates against them. A recoil took place, toward the emblems of the past—faith in the Tsar, in Russia's mission to unite the Slavs, in the Orthodox religion.

In the circumstances, the speeches of Turgenev and Dostoyevsky became statements of record, on behalf of retreating Left and on-charging Right, with Pushkin as a disputed symbol.

Turgenev's was a rearguard speech. He pointed out that Pushkin, a splendid lyric poet, had still been a poet of and for the cultured few, and urged literate Russia not to set Pushkin up as a permanent standard. "Let us hope," he added wistfully, "that in the not distant future even the sons of our common people, who now cannot read our poet, will understand what that name means: Pushkin—and that they will repeat . . . 'This is a monument—to our teacher.' "

This wistful hope for the commoners was the only way Turgenev dared to slip in the old dream of the Left: may the underdogs of Russia eventually rise to literacy and, therefore, perhaps to greatness . . .

Dostoyevsky, after a brief, unhappy contact with the revolutionary movement, for which he paid by doing time at hard labor in Siberia, had become the champion of tsarism and religious Orthodoxy. This conversion was probably the emotional spring of his best writing. Now he spoke to a whole troubled leisure class. He raised his horn and sounded the mystic blast of Pan-Slavism. He invoked Pushkin as the representative of the rootless Russian intellectual, who once sought refuge "in gypsy camps, and in the arms of wild women," and now, in socialism. "Humble yourself, proud man!" he called. "Find yourself in yourself!" Truth lay in humble communion with the people. Then Russia would become the harmonizer of the Aryan race, the civilizer of all Europe. "Let our land be poor, but Christ in a serf's garb has traversed it."

With awesome psychological intuition, he had put his hand on the sense of alienation of the Russian intelligentsia, and had guessed that it was the effort to heal this bleeding wounded that tempted them toward socialist revolution. He recalled them to self-examination, and then on to Orthodoxy, patriotism, and adoration of the impoverished peasant.

He carried the day. "A prophet!" the assembled intelligentsia shrieked.

Men threw themselves, sobbing, into each other's arms. "Victory!" thundered Dostoyevsky in a letter to his wife. "Complete victory."

It was June of 1880. Eight months later Tsar Alexander II was assassinated by the "fighting battalion" of the People's Will. This did nothing except fatally injure the hopes of Populism. The new Tsar was, understandably, tougher. Dostoyevsky seemed indeed a prophet.

But in an attic in Nizhni Novgorod, Alexey Peshkov—who later would be known as Maxim Gorky—was reading Pushkin. He seemed to have appeared, like a gangling, sad-eyed adolescent genie, in answer to Turgenev: "Here I am; the first of your commoners of the future."

## CHAPTER 4

THAT spring Alexey again ran off, to work again as a mess boy on a Volga paddle wheeler. When the navigation season ended, he returned, and was apprenticed by Grandpa to an ikon painter.

Into the ikon shop came Nikonites, self-castrated Skoptsy, Old Believers. And there were the ikon painters themselves, the dehumanized "God-daubers," daubing at their benches in the smoke of their cheap tobacco, singing lugubrious songs, the room heavy with stench of glue, varnish, rotten eggs.

At night they danced, circling around a huge woman. One of them died on a nearby cot, eaten by tuberculosis. "Patience," Grandma counseled, when he visited her and cried.

By now, the image of the orphan waif, rising from nowhere, had taken on not only literacy but eloquence. To the God-daubers he read the poetry of Lermontov. All dropped their work, and listened. Alexey's readings brought a richness—so he believed, and it must have been so— into their lives. On his name day, the ikon painters gave Alexey an exquisitely done ikon of Alexey, Man of God. The presentation speech:

What are you? Just a kid, a thirteen-year-old orphan; and I, a man about four times your age, speak your praises and commend you for standing with your face toward people and not aloof. Stay like that toward people and you'll be all right.

Thus was the people's knight given his accolade, at thirteen. The proof he never forgot is in the thrilling quality of the passage, written more than thirty years later. He could never do anything that might be construed as betraying the hopes of the old ikon makers, and many like them. This explains his last years, which seem strange to some, as well as anything can.

He worked again for the architect, as an underage overseer of carpenters, plasterers and laborers against theft of tools. (Surely the man wanted to help his distant nephew find a niche in the business world; as surely, by now, the boy's inner dream precluded any such accommodation.) Each year the crew erected the pavilions for the Nizhni Novgorod fair, a big thing in provincial Russia, which annually made the town solvent.

"I did not drink vodka and had nothing to do with women—books took the place of these two forms of intoxication for me." Books, at this time, were Gogol's "Dead Souls"; Dostoyevsky's "House of the Dead"; Scott, Dickens; Pushkin, Béranger, Heine; and above all, Flaubert's "Temptation of St. Anthony" and "A Simple Heart." The cultured Frenchman's longing for mystical, primitive ethical Christianity echoed strongly in the "red cave of the heart" of the declassed young Russian, determined to be one of the poorest of the poor.

He wanted to go still farther. He began to be drawn to Million Street, where Nizhni's debris assembled. His growing protest tempted him to identify with the down-and-outers, alcoholics, hoboes, derelicts, thieves, those whose overall designation was "barefoot bums" (*bosyaki;* literally, "barefooters").

I saw that life was criss-crossed with theft, like an old coat with gray threads. At the same time, I noted that these people worked on occasion with tremendous enthusiasm . . . And altogether they lived more festively than other people.

To sink would have solved many problems.

Somewhat contrary, though related, impulses were also at work. In a tavern, he listened to the singing of a drunken harness maker. "He filled the dim, bleary depths of the tavern with chords of silver . . . Even the drunks were silenced and sat with their heads bowed . . . Then a churchlike quiet descended over the tavern and the singer was like a benevolent priest who did not arraign but simply and with all his heart prayed for the whole family of mankind . . ."

This belief in the religious power of music would also endure; one by one, the emotional commitments of the man, and the writer to be, were being fixed.

He lectured a porter who abused a drunken prostitute. The man, furious, asked if Alexey pitied her. "Yes." "Would you pity a cat?" "Yes." A cat was sitting on the porter's lap. He picked it up by the tail, and bashed its head against the stone balustrade; its warm blood splashed Alexey. He threw the body at the lad's feet: "What are you going to do about *that?*"

They fought, "threshing about the yard like two dogs"; then Alexey sat in the grass, "nearly demented with inexpressible anguish," biting his lips to keep from bawling.

Repeated inexpressible, and often unexplainable, anguish drove him, on scowling autumn days, off the highroad into the forest, "past even the dimmest trails." Or, standing watching the Volga,

... I was overcome with a wish to liberate the whole world and myself, by some magical act, so that I and everyone would whirl with joy in a mass carnival dance, so that people would give their love to each other here on earth, so that they would live for each other, and their lives be courageous, exalted, and beautiful.

But I thought also, "I must do something for myself or it will be all over for me."

At not quite sixteen, he set off. This parting was the last. Grandma told him, "Remember this: God doesn't judge men; that's the devil's specialty. Well, good-bye." Wiping tears from her faded sunken cheeks she added, "We won't see each other again ..." From the steamer's rail he saw her on the dock, making the sign of the cross and with the other hand wiping her cheeks with a threadbare shawl.

And now the realization came to me that I would never know another person so intimately, and that no other would be so dear to me.

Kazan, down-Volga, was an old Tartar city, once capitol of the Golden Horde. In its university, Tolstoy had studied. Alexey intended to take exams and get a scholarship. If he had, his story would have been different. After the killing of the Tsar, the curriculum of Russian universities had been changed, to stress the classics and get the students' minds off politics and economics; and for the lower classes, there were few scholarships.

Still, it appears that if Alexey had been well prepared in mathematics he would have stood a good chance.

But instead he had to begin a marginal existence in the old Tartar city, picking up odd jobs as a stevedore on the Volga. At night, around rugged fires, the stevedores talked of life, defeats, injuries, women ... A *gymnazia* (high school) student, Pletnev, took him on as a roommate, in a dilapidated tenement. Two of the other rooms on their floor were occupied by prostitutes, the third by a mathematician who was proving God's existence mathematically; he died with the job half-done. Pletnev taught Maxim—as Alexey was now sometimes called, from his patronymic—sciences and grammar. They shared a cot, hot-bunking, for Pletnev worked nights as a proofreader.

One night the tenement was raided and some of the tenants arrested, charged with trying to start an illegal printing press. When Maxim reported this in the morning, Pletnev said: "Run, Maxim, quick as you can, to ———." Maxim "flew straight as a bird," delivered a mysterious message (the man pretended not to understand), and went away pleased at having carried out "my first piece of conspiratorial work."

Thus, naturally and without profound thought, the youth entered the struggle against the Tsar. The field was now held jointly by the Populists and a newer brand of revolutionaries—Marxists.

When the People's Will moved toward terrorism, a group had split off, calling itself "the Black Re-Division" (advocating a redivision of the rich black land of Russia). It was headed by George Plekhanov, a young intellectual, P. B. Akselrod, an idealistic Jew of farm background, and a young woman, Vera Zasulich, the heroine of an attempt to kill the police chief of St. Petersburg. They had all become impatient with Populism's theories, which seemed to run against the time's industrial grain, and recognized terrorism as self-defeating. They found in the writing of Marx and Engels what seemed to them a more realistic approach to history and revolution. This meant (in despite of their agrarian title) pinning greater hope on the industrial workers, accepting the seemingly hateful idea that Russia too would pass through capitalism before attaining socialism, and counting on what according to Marx was the inevitable flow of history. They gained followers among the intelligentsia who still believed in revolution.

Sometimes a few years make a great difference. It seems probable that Alexey Peshkov was just too young to have drunk the nectar of the Populist appeal when most intoxicating, to be nourished with the idea of becoming one of its next generation of martyrs.

One of the five who were hanged in the center of St. Petersburg, for killing Alexander II, Sophia Perovskaya, a member of the Great Russian nobility, had written to her mother: "My darling, I implore you to be calm and not to grieve for me ... I have lived according to my convictions, and it would have been impossible for me to do otherwise. So I wait here with tranquil conscience ..."

Grinevitsky, who had thrown the bomb, destroying both the Tsar and himself, had written, the night before:

"History shows that the luxurious tree of freedom needs blood to quicken its roots.... Fate has revealed for me an early death, and I shall not see our day, our hour of victory; and never shall I know the blazing light of our triumph. But I believe that by dying I am doing all that is in my power to do, and no one on earth can demand more of me."

Such sentiments of martyrdom are potent. There is no doubt that Alexey Peshkov knew these emotions. But he was steeling himself, as he grew, to beware of the quixotic. This seems to have been a victory of the reasoning power: he felt he had grown up amid inexorable and tragic sacrifices; but there was something wrong, rationally, with actually *seeking to become a sacrifice.*

It was also a matter of timing; he was still so busy struggling to live that he was not ready to look for an altar at which to offer himself. By the time he was, the altar was not there; or at least it was another altar, claiming to serve the same cause, but in the name of science and reason, instead of in the name of quixotic idealism and martyrdom.

Across a field, late at night, he followed the silhouette of the man ahead of him, toward a secret study circle. The circle was studying Adam Smith, with Chernyshevsky's commentary. Maxim found Smith's views on the strictly competitive nature of society no revelation: "Direct experience had engraved them on my flesh."

On another level of his life, he moved among the Volga stevedores. He needed both identities. Hired to help take out the cargo of a barge, laden with Persian goods, which had staved in its bottom on a submerged harbor rock, he experienced something that would become a guide, puzzling and deceptive, in his search for a philosophy of life: the ecstasy of furious physical activity.

Such rapture as I lived through that night I had never before experienced. My soul was inflamed with longing to live out my life in such half-mad orgies of activity. The waves surged around the barge, the rain

scourged the deck, the wind howled down the river, while in the gray
mist of the dawn, drenched men dashed about, half-naked, eager and
untiring, shouting, laughing, exulting in the power expressed in their
work...

The onset of such a joyous frenzy of energy appeared irresistible,
appeared capable of miraculously transforming the earth, covering, in one
night, the whole globe with palatial cities, as in fairy tales.

This vision would become central in Gorky. A perfectly straight line
runs from the despairing cry of Chekhov's gentle gentleman, Uncle Vanya:
"We must hasten, and work! Work!"—to the response of Gorky's frenzied
stevedores. The two images taken together are a clue to one of the emotional beliefs that shaped Russia's modern history: redemption by work.

He lived on still another level: hanging around a grocery store which
was a rendezvous for Kazan's young intelligentsia—the students of the university, theological seminary, veterinary school. He was trying to absorb
"culture," and break down the doors to their world. It was an unhappy
experience, and stamped him with an angry, hurt imprint.

The intelligentsia were men of advanced ideas, but also products of a
very class-conscious society. They considered young Peshkov—at least so
he keenly felt—an "unspoiled son of the people": a museum specimen. He
was welcome to hang around, but not to be talked with, on equal terms,
about Schopenhauer and Hegel, Nietzsche and Marx, Darwin and Mikhailovsky. "Keep your nose out of matters that don't concern you," one of
them told him.

It was a part of Russia's tragedy that many in the more fortunate classes
wanted to help the commoners, were even willing to adore the People,
but were mentally unable to accept those below them on terms of equality.
The boy Maxim would try to forgive; the man Gorky would save the
lives of many of them. But his basic emotional set could not help being
further solidified. He was an outsider, answering scorn for scorn. He was
"self-born." He must never forget that he was one of the disinherited.

He got a steady job in a basement bakery. His extra duties were to feed
the Yorkshire hogs of his boss; his extra vocation, to enlighten his fellows, reading aloud to them—while they kneaded their crullers—books
scrounged by him from his other life, among the intelligentsia. The comradeship of those who toiled in that pit, "like blind worms," would be
immortalized by him in "Twenty-Six and One," one of his prize stories.

All week the men looked forward pathetically to a day's drinking and carousing in the House of Joy. Maxim would go loyally with them, but not to drink or carouse. Both the men and the whores finally told him: "It's no fun with you around." The madam was angry; he discouraged trade. But she came to like Maxim, and even confided in him.

A personal moral chastity early became for Maxim a part of social idealism. It would stay with Gorky, along with a revulsion against the sanctioning of love by the "hypocritical convention" of marriage.

The House of Joy became a fixture as the locale of novels and stories he would write. It was one of his formative experiences.

A different kind of bakery was started by the grocery keeper. The profits would finance good works for the People. Maxim was to be the "supervising assistant"—to see that the master baker didn't steal. The master baker did, and Maxim didn't have the gumption to stop him. What was worse, he would bring his teen-age mistress in, lead her to a heap of flour sacks, and tell his young supervisor, "Take off about half an hour."

I left them, thinking how horribly different this was from the love portrayed in books.

He wandered shivering about the dark wintry town, peering into windows to observe people. At last he guessed the baker's dozen must be finished, and he could go back, where it was warmer. There he resumed reading Tolstoy. He was dreaming of setting up, with his fellow toilers of the first bakery, a Tolstoyan agricultural commune.

The local policeman began to trail him, and invited him for tea. The policeman's rosy wife slyly rubbed the lad's leg under the table; but this would do her no good. Meanwhile, the policeman himself, Nikiforich, explained to Maxim his doctrine of the Spider's Invisible Web.

An invisible thread, like a spider's, issues from the heart of his Imperial Majesty, the Emperor Alexander III . . . Everything is bound together by this thread. In this invisible strength the kingdom of the Tsar is held together for all time. But the scheming English queen is bribing the Poles, the Jews, and Russians too, to cut the thread wherever they can, saying they are doing it for the sake of the people.

Then Nikiforich suggested Maxim let him know what went on at night at the grocery keeper's.

The study circle now was discussing a book by Plekhanov. The slow current, and Maxim with it, was veering away from the Populist shore, toward the other, that of Marxism.

He had still other friends—an old weaver, Nick Rubtzev, and Jake Shaposhnikov, a consumptive carpenter who stormed at God. One night with them, one with the intellectuals. He was casting about, as anguish and bewilderment mounted. Pletnev was taken away to prison in St. Petersburg. On another tea visit, Maxim was propositioned by Nikiforich's wife —to become a police agent. Disgusted, he decided not to go there again, tea or no tea!

The Kazan world whirled faster, tearing asunder. His reading was filling him with contrary images, of humanity and vileness. Shaposhnikov died, miserably. Rubtzev, mourning him with Maxim, said: "Jake was wrong to use up his big heart reviling God . . . One should rather be furious with himself and repudiate this odious life." A pitched battle between drunken sailors leaving the House of Joy and workers ended with friend and foe being hauled toward the police station. Maxim and Rubtzev escaped over rooftops, and Maxim never saw his pal again.

News came of Grandma's death—a street beggar.


The Populist bakery was going bankrupt. In despair, Maxim started studying the violin. One night he caught the violin teacher rifling the bakery's cashbox; to keep from striking him as the man stood abjectly before him, oily tears dripping from colorless eyes, Maxim sat down on his own fists. Thus ended the music lessons.

He tried to fall in love, but nobody was interested. "I was in need of a woman's caress, or at least of a woman's friendly attention."

On December 12, 1887, he bought a revolver, went to a bluff over the garbage dump, and shot himself where he thought his heart was, puncturing a lung. The town's Tartar night watchman got him to a hospital in time. A suicide try is always something profound and mysterious. To understand it completely would be to understand the man completely, which is impossible. He himself would write about it, many years later, at a crucial moment in his career, when he was for the first time trying to understand himself better. For now, it is enough to point out that he was desperate enough, at the age of nineteen, to try to kill himself.

The wound healed, though later a tubercular process started; he would live fifty years with a bad lung. Kazan days were ending. A Ukrainian,

Romass—one of the last of the pure Populists—invited Maxim to come up-Volga. There Romass ran a general store as a peasant hamlet; and tried, in "bull sessions" with shopping peasants, to instill populist and socialist ideals. Maxim went.

The effort at local Populism ended bitterly—leaving Maxim with an unfaltering conviction about the cruelty of the Russian peasant; he would never be sentimental on this subject. He next worked his way on a Volga freighter to the Caspian, to a job at a Kalmuck fishery. Then came jobs as night watchman at various godforsaken railroad stops. There was brutality; there were drinking bouts and sex orgies—at which his role was to stand against a wall and sing folk songs for the revellers, trying to purify their sunken souls (his bass voice seems to have charmed them, but not into forgetting fundamentals); and, as usual, there was another tutor, an ex-divinity student, branded "politically unreliable": he coached the youth through History of the Inductive Sciences.

He often dwelt, persuasively, on the power, the beauty, of the mind. "After all, boy, reason decides everything. That lever, in time, will sway the world."

"On what pivot?" I asked.

"The people," he replied, with conviction. "Above all, you—your mind."

"I shared his conviction," Gorky wrote.

After Maxim had moved on to another whistle-stop, this man killed himself, leaving a friend instructions to sell his things and pay the landlord; to take most of his books, send those in Greek and Latin to a certain Kiev address, and his volumes of Herbert Spencer to "Oldhead" Peshkov.

## CHAPTER 5

WITHOUT ever passing through the portals of the University of Kazan, Maxim had gone through more than one "university"; and this higher education of his had taken place at a crucial time (and much of it, at a crucial spot) in Russian history. Those years of 1884 to 1888 were a divider: years of psychological and physical changeover. (By means of occasional rapids, turns, dramatic climaxes, the seemingly blind and senseless historic stream sometimes protests that it has direction and purpose.)

Police state measures had followed the assassination of Tsar Alexander II; there was some die-hard student agitation. In at least a few nobly frantic natures, the neurotic dedication of the terrorists was taken as a heroic model. One such was Alexander, or Sasha, the older of the Ulyanov brothers of Simbirsk—another Volga city. While pursuing an intense study of earthworms (he was a science student at the University of Kazan), he also began to work on explosives. In 1886, a clumsy plot to kill Alexander III failed. At the trial, young Ulyanov tried to clear everybody but himself. He was hanged.

The Ulyanov family was highly respected gentry; the father had reformed the school system of Simbirsk province, making education available to many commoners. Now the family was cut dead by middle-class Simbirsk; even "close friends" made excuses. The younger (aged sixteen) Ulyanov, who would be Lenin, was affected spiritually to an extreme degree by his brother's fate and the ostracism of his mother. Of course any future career for him in Tsarist society was also permanently blighted.

Through the intercession of a respected gymnazia teacher—named Kerensky—Vladimir (nicknamed Ilya) Ulyanov was reluctantly admitted to the University of Kazan to study law. This was in 1888, after Maxim Peshkov had shot himself, recuperated, and gone off with Romass to promote peaceful Populism up-Volga. The following year, for taking part in a student rally, young Ulyanov was dropped. He spent a summer reading Chernyshevsky's "What Is To Be Done?"—a crisply sentimental, naïve novel of sexual protest and social idealism based on Fourier's and Owen's communal theories. Then he went into the world, a man with burning wrath, fixed goals, an incisive and brilliant if arid mind, and a beguiling, even magnetic, surface personality.

Within fifteen years he would be a dominant figure in the Russian socialist movement—his image as the vindicator, by new paths, of his brother, the last terrorist martyr, probably helped mesmerize many. Operating mainly in exile, he would be well on his way to making that movement a tool of his own machine: a tight-knit conspiratorial elite, composed of men and women as pure in their understanding of Marxism, according to *his* interpretation, as the members of any fanatical religious order.

Maxim's—Gorky's—life and career would become intertwined with Lenin's, in an ambivalent and fateful way. But this was in the future:

he had not known the terrorist older brother, nor the avenging younger one, in Kazan. The older Ulyanov's execution, however, had been a sort of knell for the morally based but romantic, quixotic, disorganized protest of Populism—a movement all too human. The field had been cleared for "Marxism's iron logic." To say that ethics were to become unimportant would be oversimplifying; most of the Marxists were also moral idealists. But by the logic of the new creed, since they were only carrying out the commands of a mythical historical Will, morality had to become secondary.

The emotional changeover must have been profound. A whole structure of idealism had been shattered. (Maxim's suicide try was surely connected with this dead end; 1887 was, statistically, a banner year for suicides.) The nineties were approaching: Russia was entering an industrial boom, with all its dislocations; soon would come a great famine, in 1891; while the alienation of thinking, sensitive Russians from the Tsarist regime now encompassed several generations.

Portraits of the artist as a young man usually devote an early chapter to the first arrival of the hero in the great metropolis, to taste its glories and temptations, joust with kindred talents, find a place for himself in its glittering salons. This was not so for Alexey Peshkov, who would be Maxim Gorky. He must have entered Moscow, that first time, not only as an unknown, but as an unknown young tramp, aged twenty, deep in his role of being one of the land's disinherited, still teaching himself to read, not yet daring openly to think of himself as a writer even of the future. He must have slept on a park bench, then found a cavernous basement flophouse, where "in the shadows nameless bodies writhed and snored, with rags for bedclothes," and where his always acute sense of smell was struck by "acid odors of putrefaction."

A shaggy, obese ex-chemist sat cross-legged, mending trousers by candle butt, bawling an obscene hymn to the Virgin; there was a silver-haired ex-pianist; many other exes. A broken-nosed almost naked woman entered, dancing. They heaved her down, beside a man just "deceased"—who had lost hope and joined the true brotherhood of the Lower Depths. At this point in the mock service, poor Maxim's mind sought Queen Margot, "the sustaining dream of loveliness in my life."

He seemed to be swaying, pulled by a gravity, at the edge of the derelict life, fascinated by its freedom. It also seems clear that a strong moral code, instilled in childhood—"life is real, life is earnest"—always restrained him.

As if running from the gravitational pull, he fled Moscow, setting out to tramp Russia; headed, vaguely, home to Nizhni Novgorod. The sense that this is also a morality play, a ballet of Good and Evil, staged by a young man "constructing" himself—the temptation to disintegrate being opposed by the call of saintly, ennobling forces—grows as one sees him stop off, a pilgrim, at Yasnaya Polyana, home of Tolstoy, dean of the saintly life. The Count was away; the young tramp—the Countess made this clear—had no credentials.

The day when the two men would meet and know one another as equals (together with Chekhov: a formidable trio) was still more than a decade away.

He hoboed homeward, through central Russia, by foot and cattle car. Sometimes, in Jewish villages, he got work as what is still known as the "shabbas-goy," the gentile who is free to do the necessary chores on the Sabbath, in lieu of the pious Jewish householders and farmers. In one Russian peasant village, after being fed, he was pressed into service to read the prescribed prayers over a dead peasant throughout the night; nobody in the village could read and the priest was away. Sometimes he got bread by working on Cossack farms. To this phase belongs his story of the Cossack wife, taken in adultery, who is dragged naked down the village street tied to a horse; and the part not included in that story as written— that the knightly young Peshkov rushed to the rescue and was so battered by the enraged Cossacks that he had to be carted away to a hospital by a passing peddler.

When he arrived, in a cattle car (along with a shipment of prize bulls), at Nizhni, he had in his tramp's sack—this is the first overt acknowledgment—a notebook full of writings, including an epic poem, "The Song of the Old Oak": "Into it I had crammed every idea that had strayed into my head during the past hard and varied ten years." This must have been 1889, and he was twenty-one.

Called for military service but rejected (his bullet-holed lung), Maxim volunteered as an army engineer, to guard Russia's Pamir border against the heroes extolled by Kipling. He was turned down as "politically unreliable." Still in Nizhni, he started screwing up the courage to approach Korolenko, one of the most renowned of the old Populist writers, a sweet, idealistic man. He was getting ready to show Korolenko his secret writing, and get an opinion. In the meantime, he did paper work for a lawyer, Lahnin.

Just then he was picked up in a police raid on the flat of a friend with whom he was staying. Lodged in a tower of his hometown kremlin, he was brought before the police chief, a retired general who collected medals and was reading "The Theory of Electricity" (in French) and "Reflexes of the Brain." "You're not a Jew or a Pole, you're a writer," he told Maxim. "When I let you off, take your manuscript to Korolenko." He showed Maxim his medal collection, blowing dust off each, fondly. "Well, off with you. God bless you. Apply yourself to writing."

Ten years later, when Gorky—by then famous—was again in jail, he was told that the old general, who had followed his literary career with pride, had died, leaving him his medals. Gorky, touched, gave them to the Nizhni-Novgorod museum.

To Korolenko he went, at last, and thrust a bunch of manuscripts at the kindly, stocky man. Korolenko, scanning them, tried to be both gracious and sincere. "You use coarse expressions—because you consider them stronger?" Maxim said these were due to "my lack of time and opportunity to acquire a gentle vocabulary and finer sensibilities." Korolenko gently pointed out clichés, word slips. "All I wanted," Gorky would remember, "was release from this humiliating scene."

Korolenko sent the manuscript back in two weeks, with a penciled note: "It's not easy to estimate your powers ... but I think you have talent. Write about something you have actually experienced ... I'm no judge of poetry. Yours seems to be confused ... but I found some lines that are powerful and alive." The youth stared at the note: nowhere had Korolenko said anything about his *ideas*.

He tore the manuscript up. He would never write again. "What could it mean, I pondered, to write something I had actually experienced? I had experienced everything I had set down."

He sat of a night on the Volga's bank, brooding, when Korolenko came by and put a hand on his shoulder. He'd heard that Maxim had joined a study circle, headed by a Marxist who claimed Korolenko was trying to "galvanize the corpse of Populism." Now Korolenko said: "What's the rush to pick a creed? Materialism is becoming a fashion. Its simplicity makes it tempting. Its pull is particularly strong on those who won't take the trouble to think for themselves ... Every attempt at a rational explanation of life deserves a hearing."

Maxim's response seems to have been evasive. He was impressed by Korolenko's candor and gentle, thoughtful smile; "such comments on Marxism, however, were familiar to me." He did not contradict the older man, but asked instead how he managed to preserve his serenity in the ferment of the times.

Korolenko spoke earnestly, in reply, of the intellectual's lonely role, as the foundation of every new construction: Socrates, Bruno, Galileo, Robespierre, the Decembrists . . . Perovskaya, Zhelyabov (the terrorist-martyrs) . . . "along with everyone now starving in exile." They were life's vital force. He spoke of Prometheus, of Voltaire . . . When all the strivings and idealisms to defend the unjustly used were "heaped together . . . spark upon spark, it will become a conflagration that will purify earth of lies and filth and transform life."

Gorky never said as much, but these words became and remained a central part of his own vision.

As Maxim walked him home, Korolenko asked: "Writing again?"

"No."

"I am convinced of your talent," Korolenko said, trying to undo the harm of the first critique.

But Maxim was whirling in ferment again. Head crammed with Empedocles, visions of chaos, he wandered the Volga bank, seeing God, as on ikons, in a long white shirt, trailed by a naked woman, breasts streaming rays of gold. The kindly Armenian night watchman would lead him home by the arm: "Why go walk when you sick? Sick man, he be home in bed." On a legal application to be filled in for his boss, Lahnin, he scribbled instead:

> The night has no ending
> My torment is great.
> If I only could pray!
> If I knew the bliss of faith!

He went to a hunchbacked psychologist (a wizard again, but only garden variety), who said Maxim needed a girl who knew how to play. The young knight was "repelled"; but he was ripe, and the prescription was waiting, in a Nizhni basement apartment.

Olga Kaminsky had studied painting in Paris, then obstetrics, had been an actress, conceived a child, then picked up a husband. The husband is described by Gorky—he is unfair about it, probably because of guilt, though he certainly did not seduce Olga away from the man—as a Polish intellectual who lay on his back muttering: "The life task of a member of the intelligentsia should be the continuous accumulation of scientific goods for distribution among the masses."

As for Olga, her chestnut hair fell in curls over rosy ears and "framed her flushed young cheeks like a sumptuous headdress." She must have recalled Queen Margot—there is a similarity in the strokes of the brush—but Margot had the advantage of remaining an ideal.

The love-dazed youth dived from a barge for a swim, caught his foot in the lines, and nearly choked, dangling with head underwater. She visited him as he lay abed, and he confessed his love. She said, in effect: "No . . . not yet." It was enough. On thunderclouds, wings on his feet, he went off wandering over Russia again—the lower Volga, the Don, the Ukraine, the Crimea, Bessarabia, the Caucasus. He alighted finally in sun-shot Tiflis, got a newspaper job and took part in reddish discussion groups.

An eye-witness saw: ". . . A tall youth, broad-shouldered and of athletic build, with a broad coarse Russian face and long hair . . . Intelligent and thoughtful eyes expressed strength and determined will." This was, of course, the exterior.

There in Tiflis, urged by Kalyuzhny, a former man of the People's Will back from hard Siberian labor, he wrote his first published story, "Makar Chudra." It appeared in *Kavkaz* ("Caucasus"), a local daily, in September 1892.

Word came that Olga was back again from Paris, sans husband but with her child, asking about him. He charged back to Nizhni. She came to him, and they lived together in a semiconverted bathhouse, scandalizing the neighborhood. He earned their bread by newspaper work. He now wore a fine mustache.

He says "my wife"; and each of his relations with women was based on the companionate ideal. It has already been shown how abhorrent to him was anything like promiscuity, or even what in most cultures would be considered a normal and becoming sexual looseness.

If only they had been more compatible!


"At a poor man's wedding even the night is short," runs the proverb with sad, wise irony. I confirmed its truth through personal experience.


He disclosed to Olga, on the first night of their married life, his starry view of the relations of men and women.


"Do you mean that? Do you really believe that?" she asked as she lay in my arms, in blue moonlight.

Her rose-colored body seemed transparent, she exhaled a heady, bitterish smell of almonds. Her thin fingers thoughtfully played with a lock of my hair, she looked into my face with wide, anxiously open eyes, and smiled uncertainly.

"Oh, my God!" she cried out, springing to the floor, and began thoughtfully pacing the room from light into shadow, satin skin shining in the moon's light, soundlessly touching the floor with her bare feet. And, again coming up to me, stroking my cheeks with her palms, she said in the tone of a mother: "You should have begun life with a girl—yes, yes! Not with me . . ."

The bohemian life in the Nizhni bathhouse was widely bruited, and Korolenko urged Maxim to end it. As for troubled Maxim, "Her [Olga's] philosophy, I felt, was mostly gynecology; her obstetrics course served as her testament." She explained that God had suddenly disappeared, "like cigaret smoke, and with him my visions of sanctification in love." And besides, she fell asleep while he was reading her one of his stories.

It is true that the story in question, "Old Woman Isergil," is long-winded and rambling; but it contains what was probably his basic myth, that would sustain him. He was groping; and Olga was not interested in watching people grope.

He was fighting on several fronts. Archbishop Khrisanph—the dear wizard of one far-off day in school—had written a book, "The Religions of the East," and Maxim refused to accept its thesis, "that fear, anguish and grief constitute the substance of the world." One day it would seem more persuasive. Meanwhile, Olga attracted suitors, and hated passing them up. "Friends who considered themselves kind came to me with tales affecting my marital honor"—the lumbering phrase was supposed to be lightly sardonic.

But the final injury was to his humane instincts, over an old one-eyed Jew whom a policeman beat viciously. Maxim saw the old man going down the street, covered with dust, slow and majestic, "his large dark eye looking solemnly into the silent, sultry sky, while trickles of blood from his injured mouth ran into his white beard, dyeing the silver strands a bright red." He came home to share his emotions with Olga. Again she was startled. "What weak nerves you have! . . . A fine-looking man you call him; but how could he be with only one eye."

"She shunned," wrote Gorky, "all suffering as an enemy. Life was a series of wonderful tricks."

When they parted, they had lived together two years.

He went roaming Russia again, his spirit perplexed. Korolenko must have helped him make the break, to get him out of the bathhouse. A relationship had developed, warm but uneasy. Korolenko discouraged his poetry, praised his prose. "You're not a romanticist, you're a realist, understand?" Korolenko had never been so wrong. He suggested Maxim go away and marry a nice bright girl. "I told him I would rather not discuss that"; but he would do just that.

Through Korolenko, he got a job as a columnist on a paper in Samara, down-Volga—the "Gazette." Also through Korolenko, he made his literary breakthrough.

"Chelkash" was his first story which Korolenko could really admire. "Not a bad thing, in fact a fine story, all hewn out of one block ... The best thing about this is that you value the individual as he is." Korolenko was coeditor of the important magazine "Russia's Wealth" (*Russkoe Bogatstvo*), and saw to it that "Chelkash" appeared there, in 1895, as the lead story, by Maxim Gorky—Maxim the Bitter.

## CHAPTER 6

THINGS he himself wrote many years later have served as the main guide through Alexey Peshkov's orphan childhood and youth, until he became the writer Maxim Gorky. They are essential for the genesis of the man and artist, but they have their drawbacks: no one, looking back on his early years, can avoid constructing them into a work of art.

At this point, however, new sources appear—Gorky's early work, written when he was still the orphan Peshkov, just becoming Maxim Gorky. These first preserved writings are splendidly and naïvely self-revealing. Clearly visible are the very springs on which Gorky's emotional life, and therefore his art, will be mounted.

That early epic poem, "The Song of the Old Oak," was lost, apparently destroyed by him himself after the unfortunate criticism of Korolenko. Only the opening line is known: "I came into the world to disagree."

Boyhood's hurt and anger, and the resulting obsession with the questions of God, sin, and justice, came through in a very early story. An old hillman of the Caucasus prepares to kill, in vengeance for his son. He prays:

Lord ... you know why I came here, and I know. Don't hold me back, Lord ... For you know, too, how I loved my son, Vahno, and you saw how he lay on the ground, all in blood ... You saw all this and you did not hinder anyone then. Don't hinder me now, Lord! You are just, and always will be just; and when I, an old man, will come to you—and that will be soon—you will judge me, as having been just! Tomorrow is your holy day—and you must forgive me!

Aside from probably being a close mimicry of Grandpa Kashirin's prayers, this speech is the projection of the orphan child's dream of violent revenge for injuries and hurts.

Such violent hurt and anger will wear away or tear apart a young heart, unless an object outside the self can be found, in whose behalf to use these emotions. As soon as the young Peshkov knew he could write coherently, he began to struggle for a way out from his self-consuming hurt and anger, and the self-pity which often masks these two. The best escape of this kind is through social idealism. And, by his twenties, out of his experiences, romantic reading, and the Russian situation around him, he constructed such a way out—a guiding myth—and cast it in the form of two allegories. These are basic to everything.

In the very first of them, a strange note is sounded, which shows how clearly the very young man saw the kernel of illusion in the grain of social idealism, even while choosing this escape. The insight is troublesome. And his response is one which will mark his whole life and art. It is the gnostic response—to take the beauty of the lie over the ugliness of truth, and by sheer determination, if at all possible, convert the lie into the truth, so that a new truth is born, and the wicked old truth becomes a lie. And now for the story, about "The Siskin Who Lied and the Woodpecker, Lover of Truth."

The woods of a certain unidentified land are filled with songs heavy and hopeless, sung by the various birds led by the crow.

> K-r-r-r! In battle with a doleful fate
> For lowly us there's no salvation.
> Looking all about we see
> Pain and sorrow, dust and ashes.
> K-r-r-r! Terrible the blows of fate.
> He who's wise will bow before them.

Suddenly there comes the bold reply of an unknown songster.

> I hear the cawing of the crows
> Confounded by the cold gloom's fear.
> I see the fog—but I don't care—
> Because my mind is brave and clear.
> Whoever dares, come follow me!
> This fog from live souls must take flight!
> We'll kindle hearts with reason's fire
> And crown the whole wide world with light!

The birds are struck, but before they will believe the new champion, they need his pedigree. He is interrogated by a proud-looking goldfinch— "goldfinches, as is well known, do not have songs of their own." By what right does this drab, small siskin (in the bird family, the siskin is indeed a small, plebian-looking relative of the goldfinch) sing so bold a song?

The siskin draws himself up to his full height (presumably, about two inches), and declares:

I base my right on an unshakeable conviction in the higher calling of birds, as the final, most complex and wise act in the creation of Nature . . . The path that we must take is unknown to me, but I am certain that we must go forward. *There*, ahead, lies a land worthy of being our reward for the toil which we endure on the way. There is eternal, unextinguishable light, there are unheard-of wonders . . .

On!—to the land of happiness! where a mighty victory awaits us, where we will be the lawgivers of the world and the rulers of it, where we will be the rulers of everything . . . On!—to that wonderful—"Forward"!

Inflamed, the birds cry: "Forward!"

"Permit me," the woodpecker breaks in.

Then, like a highly educated pedant, he destroys the birds' enthusiasm for the little siskin's lyric vision. It is necessary to bow to the might and wisdom of Nature. Facts show that ahead, in that "Forward!," lurks the bird trapper. Even if the birds avoid his nets, they will only reach another field, then a village, then a field . . . and, the world being round, will inevitably return to this same thicket . . . "No one can fly higher than himself."

The woodpecker concludes by demanding punishment for the siskin for trying to fool them into thinking he has such a high opinion of them.

The birds look at the siskin. They see tears drip silently from his eyes, and decide he must be crying over his guilt before them.

The birds fly off silently, gloomily.

He was not satisfied; the story ended too badly. Within a year he wrote it again. The heroic legend of "The Flaming Heart of Danko" is a revered item in the Soviet Union today, while the pathetic legend of the siskin is obscure.

The legend of Danko occurs in a story interesting as a whole, because it takes in three main facets of Gorky's yearning: for communal inter-dependence (a human family), for sexual freedom, and for heroic overall liberation. This is the story of "Old Woman Isergil"; it is the one the young writer was reading to Olga Kaminsky when she fell asleep.

Old Isergil is a gypsy woman, who has lived and loved. Reclining on the Black Sea shore, with night oncoming, clouds overhead, Moldavian gypsies camped, singing, nearby (these romantic settings, which he had experienced, were a stock in trade of Gorky's early stories), she tells her secret wisdom to young Maxim.

Old Isergil tells three stories—a legend, a story from her biography, and a second legend—and each is vital in tracing the genesis of Gorky.

A hero is born—son of a mortal woman and an eagle. He is so arrogant and so independent of the needs and desires of others that he is condemned by the Tribe to live endlessly. His punishment was "in himself": it was "to be left free." After a thousand years he becomes clusters of drifting fog on the steppe. At the end the outcast comes to the Tribe, in agony, and begs for death; but he cannot die.

The story, its theme as old as pre-Homeric legend, ends with the Moldavians, united and interdependent, singing in chorus, against the Black Sea.

"The noise of the waves could not be heard for their voices."

Next comes Isergil's story of past amours, and of reckless heroes she has known. "When a man loves great deeds, he can always do them, and can find where they can be done ... If people understood life, everyone would want to leave behind him his shadow on it, and then life would not devour people without a trace ..." This last image, of life as a devouring beast unless people are strong enough to tame it, recurs many times in Gorky's later work. Its origin was clearly in statements by Grandpa Kashirin.

Finally, Isergil tells the quiet, listening youth the story of Danko. She points out blue sparks—phosphorescence—flying over the steppe, as if someone were striking matches, which the wind then extinguished. These are the fragments of Danko's heart.

In the old days lived a people encompassed on three sides by an impassible forest, on the fourth by a steppe. Hard times came. The people (the Tribe again, or the birds in the wood) were driven by others (undefined) into the swamps in the depth of the forest. One youth of the Tribe, Danko, said: "Arise, let's go into the forest, and pass through it, for it has an end—everything in the world has an end. Let's go. Heyah!"

The parallel with the siskin is exact, and the birds in the more homely legend are the people in this, the more heroic one.

"Lead us!" they said. And Danko led them. (Here is the one real difference between the legends; by the time the second was written, he was living with Olga, heroically defying society.) Storm. Thunder. Darkness in the forest. They rebelled, accused Danko of misleading them. The myth is that of Prometheus, but the story is also that of Moses, and so Grandpa must again be credited with an assist.

"What can I do for people!?" Danko cried, stronger than thunder (the combined exclamation and question is typical—self-questioning becomes, in the same instant, a hortatory cry).

Suddenly Danko tore open his breast, tore out his heart, and lifted it high. It burned brighter than the sun. "Let's go!" he cried. They charged after him. The forest opened, and they reached a sea of sunlight and clear air, on the steppe. He cast a joyous glance at the free earth, and fell dead. The people failed even to notice that beside his body still flamed his brave heart. Only one observant man (unidentified) noticed, and, afraid of something, stepped on the heart. It gave off sparks, and died out.

"That's where they come from," said Old Isergil, "those blue sparks on the steppe, that appear before the storm."

Thus ends the Legend of Danko's Flaming Heart.

Old Isergil then falls asleep. The boy covers her old body (with his own cloak, no doubt), and lies down himself. "On the steppe it was quiet and dark. Across the sky clouds crawled, slow and lonely ... The sea noised hollowly and sadly."

She could sleep for eternity, Old Isergil, satisfied that her work was done; she had made it possible for the orphan boy to state to himself one of the most satisfactory of dream wishes, and on the highest, most heroic level. Whether she actually lived and said these things is beside the point.

In this second, heroic form, the twice-told legend—of the leader who

sacrifices himself in the desire to lead the Tribe into a yearned-for, unknown "Forward"—would provide the psychology and the idealism for
Soviet Russia. The young would be inspired by it, to join the Communist
movement, to die for their country, to do whatever was called for in the
ideal's name . . . It became the underlying legend. This is what is meant
when it is said that Gorky was the father of all Soviet literature, and that
it is impossible to understand the psychology of early Soviet man without
understanding the early writing of Gorky.

Beneath the allegorical legends lay quandaries, and these, too, he wrote
out in allegorical form. They show the same perplexed yearning and need,
the same young moralist on the path toward some as yet undefined
"Forward," or some as yet unformed conviction.

All over Russia this mysterious path was opening. The Populist seeds
had brought up grain; social idealism had begun to pass into revolutionary
organization; Lenin had already set his single-tracked course. Dead ahead,
a decade away, lay the year of the first Revolution, 1905.

Feeding the quandaries was an unresolvable anger at life. Such anger
logically leads to violence, against oneself (and this he had tried) or, more
normally, against others. The story of "The Cabby" (*Izvoshchik*, driver
of a horse-drawn cab) is that of a man who commits murder.

Thanks to the murder, he becomes an affluent citizen; but one day, a
tiny cabby manikin—like the one who appeared to Mann's Doctor Faustus
—appears. "Look with a clear eye," he advises the man, "at life. What order
is there? No right dealing, no love."

Perched on the bedpost, the demon cabby (like a figure out of Hieronymus Bosch's dreamworld) proceeds: "How can I judge you, when I am
a man too? How can I judge you, when there's no Law in me either?"

The murderer shakes off the apparition, but his character deteriorates.
He lives as if dead.

When the demon cabby appears again, it is clearer that he is Satan, a
perverse good angel. He advises the man to cry out: "There's no Law in
me!" Maybe people will hear, realize this is their plight too, and he will
be a sacrifice toward something better.

So the theme takes shape: the need to reject the old—which is Lawless,
without an inner path—and to find a Path and a Law. It is an old religious
theme. If this is kept in mind, all the later career and art of Gorky come
into focus.

The man is elected to office. All fawn on him. All are blind. No one can tell Good from Evil.

He gets up suddenly among them, and starts his confession. "You do not know me! ..." Consternation; a call for the police. But he goes on decisively:

"There is no Law in me, and my heart has died. Guard your hearts from destruction, root law in them. Do not be indifferent, for indifference is fatal to man's soul." The demon cabby yells encouragement: "That's the way! ... You should have done this long ago. Now you will suffer. And suffering is good. Now you will bear a cross—and that is the first need in life."

It was a dream; the man awakes. Why a cabby? he keeps asking himself ... Why indeed?—unless because the Russian horse cabby, that all-familiar figure of those days, had suddenly come as the symbol of the cabby that drives the soul, where it knows not, by routes unknown, to destined goals, without its yea. Gorky, it is clear, had no idea.

This crudely written story, packed with only half-suspected emotional drives, full of borrowings from Gogol, Dostoyevsky and Tolstoy, has something none of them had—and which they all wanted—a natural, inbred, religious outlook. The morality in it is completely internal; the only help received is from Satan (God's emissary). The confession wells up in spite of everything society can do. This is not an intellectual effort to attain a religious feeling; it is the real, demonic thing.

For Tolstoy, a man of the world, the religious view of life, which he urged on others, could be only partial. For Gorky, it was his whole life: to find a new Path, a new Law, was his whole ambition.

By the time Gorky knew Tolstoy, he was refusing to admit these things about himself; or rather, they had become transmuted into social passion. This would infuriate Tolstoy.

There was, besides, romanticism, rich but mellifluous, the poet's unfailing mark:

> Farewell! I've lifted sail.
> I grasp the tiller with a sigh.
> And with the gulls' sharp call
> And the white foam-swell
> With all by which earth signs farewell
> To me, I cry ... Farewell!

This is the other side of "Forward!"

This quality, too, will remain, growing gnarled as it is bruised by the rough antinomies of life, by the bewildering conflict of Good and Evil. Its long, reluctant death, and its transfiguration, are also a big part of Gorky's complex story.

# CHAPTER 7

THE young Gorky was fumbling his way out of the underworld of symbolic and allegorical figures—an old oak, a siskin and a woodpecker, a boy with a burning heart, a tiny devil who is the angel of conscience—toward "real" characters. The process was unusually slow and hard, life's drastic early experiences having compounded the inborn conflict between active, leaping idealism and poetic dreaminess. And when the first real figures came, they were invested with all the perplexities, the moral preoccupations, and the unresolved anger, amounting to fury.

His first, and long unpublished, novel was called "Orphan Paul." Its hero is an orphaned waif; his heroes will all be orphaned waifs, or men who are early orphaned. There is a loved prostitute, who is kind to Paul after he tries to kill himself.

There is mounting rage and desperation, for Paul cannot change his position in life or her character. There is brutal murder, trial, sentence to penal labor. Setting off, chained, he asks to visit her grave; he is refused. So it ends.

For its first half, the narrative has a startling, fresh, rugged clarity: "Here is someone describing from inside the life of a whole silent class!" Then an emotional upheaval seems to fill the work with turgid ink; the end is melodramatic violence, an excuse for letting out anger and self-pity recklessly.

From the legends and allegories, and that early novel ending in hopeless violence, the emotional road seems to have forked, and he tried both branches. One led to the unfortunates and lowly of Russia, who lived under its law; the other was that of those who rebelled, and lived frankly without a law. The choice, seen in that way, appears very sharp.

The one road led to hermits and beggars and "holy wanderers," characters moral and humble, who either failed to affect the heartless condition of reality, or fell its sacrifice. These characters, and this whole frame of mind, were near and dear to him. The other branch, at that moment in Russian history, led to the barefoot bums of Russia, and its Lower Depths —and to fame.

The two roads did not really run so far apart. The distance between them was only one of protest and rebellion.

He himself was their link, like a Hermes who traversed the physical and spiritual roads of this lower Russia, meeting over and over these two kinds of wayfarers, finding an identity with both, loving the one kind but sensing their hopelessness, being repelled by the other kind but admiring their rebellion, and trying to see in them a hope.

For this latter kind of "hero" Russia was ready. For the former, the moral and humble, no culture and no society has ever been ready, though sometimes people are charmed in spite of their disdain.

To take first the humble, unfortunate and lowly, who nearly always are also the "good"—there is the story of "Grandpa Arkhip and L'ion'ka." They are two of the wandering beggars along old Russia's "holy" roads; Grandpa does petty thieving when he can. They are not bums, but people whom the famine of 1891 drove off the land, grandfather and little grandson.

"My wise little one!" (Grandpa exclaims to the boy.) "Rightly you said—everything's dust . . . cities, and people, and I and you—just dust. Ekh you, L'ion'ka, L'ion'ka . . . If you could read and write! . . . You'd go far . . . And what'll become of you? . . ."

And, again, he tells L'ion'ka sadly: "The world's a beast. It will swallow you at a gulp."

Their beggar chant is: "Lords, for the sake of Jesus Christ . . ."

There in the distance is a village church, with its five cupolas, painted red, flooded with the rays of sunset and glistening rose-gold through the green of trees: a description conveying all the enchanted, sad, beggarly beauty of old Russia.

L'ion'ka is very much like little Alexey Peshkov; Grandpa Arkhip very much like Grandpa Kashirin in his last manifestation, that of a beggar. And years before Alexey had gone begging with Grandma.

Grandpa steals a little girl's kerchief. L'ion'ka bitterly calls him an old thief, cries out that he wishes Grandpa would die. Thunder punctuates the scene; Nature is alive, and condemns the humble. There is double tragedy, double burial of the two pathetic beggars by neighboring Cos-

sacks. "They scattered earth on the mound and put a stone cross on it."
And thus is immortalized, in its impoverished simplicity, a story of Russia
without rebellion.

He was very close to this story; yet its pathos led nowhere.

Another example is the justly famous "Twenty-Six and One." It is
about twenty-six poor devils of bakers, in an underground bakery; without
question this was the underground bakery of Kazan.

The windows are barred. They are given half-rotten tripe to eat. From
morning to night they knead dough and roll it. The stone underground
chamber is swelteringly close. "Dreary and sickening was our life within
its thick, dirty, moldy walls."

A lovely young girl sometimes opens their cell door and jokes with
them. She becomes an ideal, their faith in the existence of an innocent
goodness. But a handsome ex-soldier, who works next door in a better-
paying, airy bakery, visits them and boasts of his sex exploits. A tragic
temptation makes them stake their common faith on a bet: that he cannot seduce the little embroidery girl.

When faith and hope are shattered, they crowd around her, reviling her.
She is mute, shivers, then spurns them, and walks off—"erect, beautiful,
proud." They go back mutely to their damp stone basement.

The story contains a wealth of longing. These are not rebellious, defiant
heroes—no Dankos—but those who walk, and work, with heads bent . . .
yearning. Protest is barely felt. It is an extremely delicate story.

It is characteristic that Tolstoy could praise only this, of all Gorky's
stories he knew, without reservation. True, it stands up artistically as do
few of the others. But its note is quiet and hopeless regret. Tolstoy was
comfortable with it; except for himself, he couldn't help preferring the
humble.

These humble characters of Gorky's are "good"; and this opens a broad
and complex problem. Literature is said to be a repository for moral values;
but actually, it usually models its heroes on those of its surrounding society,
who live on the prevailing moral level. "There is not a crime I did not
commit," Tolstoy had written in his "Confession," "and for all that I was
praised."

It is hard to create central figures far above the prevailing moral level,
without losing the drama and conflict so important to literature, and the
reader's sense of identity with the characters. And if, in defiance of these
facts of life, a "good" character is created, he is usually acceptable only
if he is shown as inferior in some important way. An essay by Aldous

Huxley on this very subject, centers on Gorky's story "The Hermit"—another of his good and humble creations, a man "who does not put us to shame, because he is manifestly a half-wit." This guarantees that "at least, the reader will be able to feel himself superior to the virtuous character."

The same problem is in the Twenty-Six. They are inferior to the reader because of their low condition—or rather, their hopeless acceptance. They are doomed sacrifices. All their morality will win only a condescending tear, a condescending smile.

So to keep portraying the humble, good and moral meant to accept inferiority and defeat; this road was intolerable.

The other road, of protest, would be fateful. It would make Gorky, first, "the hobo who became a writer," then "the Stormy Petrel of the Revolution," and finally the founding figure of Soviet literature.

A step on that road was the first published story, "Makar Chudra." Among gypsy vagabonds, a violent tale is told of two highly improbable and romantic lovers, stolen from Pushkin. All the romantic trappings and the need for violence of the early efforts cling to the story; it is a chrysalis.

But by the second story, "Chelkash," the one Korolenko admired, the figures break clear; their protest, in Russian society, is recognizable and real.

Chelkash is a young delinquent of a great port city, Odessa. He is daring, amoral, aggressive, a leader, has a certain code of nobility. When the inferior delinquent he has enlisted to help rob a cargo ship shows how badly he wants the money they stole—enough to try to kill his buddy from behind—Chelkash throws the money in his face. This is a knight of old in modern rags; the knights were also primarily delinquents, but with an inbuilt code of behavior.

"Malva" has been called "a female Chelkash." A gang girl in embryo, in a fishing village, without a care for the future or morality, she gives herself to whoever wins her liking or pity. She too has her inbuilt code. A female knight of the sands, she is a tramp but not a bird of prey.

As the stories went on, a line was crossed, from youthful delinquents to barefoot bums. It was a line of morality, but never sharp; the capacity for morality always remained.

Two bums stroll down hobo lane, an eagerly listening Maxim beside them. One says to the other: "I, brother, think there are two different kinds of souls. Depends on how life breathes on it" (literally, "on her": the word "soul" is feminine in Russian). "... If it breathes gently—the soul's all right, happy, and light, but if it breathes like September, the soul

will be gloomy, limp. It's not up to the man. What can he do? He grows
by himself, and the soul grows..."

And the two bums stroll into the hobo sunset, like Russian Chaplins,
singing:

> Ekh, chase away, wind, the storm clouds
> Unravel, you, grief and yearning
> So that clear may shine the little sun
> So that I may live, a fine young man
> Ekh, careless and free—happily
> Ekh, free and happily...

Did the bums sing it? Or did it come from within Maxim? If the soul
is character, is character fate? If society can be changed, will character
change? Or, does character need to be changed first, to change a man's
fate? Which must or should come first? He clearly has no idea.

But that which is yearningly desired is a free and happy life. That is
always clear.

"Konovalov," written in 1896, is possibly the fullest statement by Gorky
of the barefoot-bum life and what it meant for him. Its figure, Konovalov,
works (between drinking binges) in the Kazan bakery.

The bakery is thus the historic meeting point of the world of the barefoot bums and of the humbly good—the Twenty-Six. The same pathos
surrounds its description. The intimate bond, in fact the identity, of the
humble and moral with the amoral and proud is laid bare. The difference
is—protest.

"Without some kind of love," says Konovalov, "a man can't live; for
that even his soul is given him, so that he can love..."

"If a man never had anything good in his life," says Konovalov, "then
he won't believe anyone."

Konovalov is very real. From him might have emerged a realistic working class hero, but this was not to be. Gorky had to reject the barefoot
bums, those rebels without a Cause. He had to find a hero who had a
Cause. He did it for the sake of morality and goodness.

"Why am I alive on earth," says Konovalov, sitting on the curb outside
the bakery, "and who on it needs me, if you want to look at it?... I live,
and yearn... Why?... No one knows... I don't have an inner path—
do you understand."

This desperate need for an inner path, a Law, would soon lead Gorky
to Tolstoy; then, to Lenin.

Maxim tries to explain. It's not Konovalov's fault. His aimless, rootless life is caused by circumstance, economic condition. But Konovalov disagrees. Something is wrong *inside,* he insists. People like him are not included in any order of things. "A special reckoning is needed for us, and special laws—to root us out of life! Because there's no usefulness in us, but we take up space in it, and stand in the way of others."

Is the final responsibility society's, or the individual's? The talk is supposed to be between young Maxim and Konovalov. It is really an internal debate, within Maxim.

The story lights up, too, Gorky's nascent conviction about poetry. Konovalov, looking into the night sky, sighs, and says merely: "Ekh—how good!" Gorky, recalling this, writes, "Like everything, poetry too loses its holy simplicity when a profession is made of poetry." He compares the artificial beautifying of nature by poets with the "holy simplicity" of true poetry that wells from Konovalov's character and his life.

This would always be how Gorky felt about poetry. The truest poetry was the unwritten poetry in life itself. If anyone dared *write* poetry, it must be the purest cry of his soul. This is a radical view; but Wordsworth and others have felt the same way about poetry.

"The problem is not life," says Konovalov, "but man. Man has to be rebuilt from the start." This would become Gorky's main theme.

It would also be the theme of the Russian revolution; just as it had been the theme of the Populist dreamers. Gorky bridged the gap.

Konovalov disappears. Maxim meets him years later, a barefoot bum, an "ex-man," laboring on a temporary construction job near Odessa. They crawl into a hole for the night, and Maxim lies watching the dying campfire, thinking of Konovalov's pointless fate. "Thus are we all (like the campfire) ... If only we might catch fire and blaze more brilliantly."

This image of blazing sparks (reflection of Korolenko's inspiring speech by the Volga bank) would be with Gorky constantly. In a play of a few years later, "Children of the Sun"—when he already moved in the glow of a faith—is a duet which answers, exactly, that yearning sentence at the campfire.

To call this "romantic protest" is to say little. At the core of the barefoot bums is a mystery, just as in the hermits and beggars. They are symbols of dissatisfaction with life itself—but they seem to be dissatisfaction with the structure of Russia. The difference, so vital, is a nuance; he was always dimly aware of it, but never quite saw it.

Those who thrilled to his stories must also have been swept up by this ambiguous protest; and by religious idealism, to which sensitive Russians had been conditioned—to see the splendor in the lowly.

In these stories is no glorification of evil. The violence of these ex-people is mainly to themselves. The lament for the good always goes on inside. In only one story the bum commits murder; and it is clear that this is a terrible thing. In another, the bum is on the brink, but is saved from the immoral deed by the sorrow of someone else, whom he comforts instead.

In fact, underneath all of them is the old, old theme, so alluring—the innate goodness of man.

It was this that took the imagination and conscience of literate Russians; for if these creatures had such moral sense, such inborn yearning for goodness, as this man, one of them himself, claimed so eloquently, how dare they be kept in such an abject state? The romantic adoration of cultured publics for the free and lawless life did the rest; he was carried to fame.

Symbols these creatures all were of an outcast state of the heart; but they took the shape of outcasts and rebels of society.

Only in a very few of the early stories was Gorky able to face life *within* society. The Volga seemed to serve as a medium through which it was possible to handle a less romantic reality while still expressing his moral and religious protest and yearning. One such story is "On a Raft."

The loaded clouds slowly crawl above the drowsy river; it seems as if they keep dropping lower and lower; it seems as if in the distance their gray tattered edges have touched the surface of the swift spring waves, and that there, where they touch the waters, an impenetrable wall of clouds has risen to the skies, forming a protective barricade for the flow of the river and the path of the raft.

It was really a protective barricade. Gorky, like Russia, was still rural in deep ways, though he had been absorbed into the urban. The river was a rampart, and an assurance—like the birds, forests and roads, but mightier—that nature was more, and more permanent, than his limited but bitter experience.

The same kind of rampart the Mississippi must have been for young Mark Twain. In the famous passage in *Huckleberry Finn* that begins, "It was a monstrous big river down there . . ." he describes the first signs of dawn:

... The first thing to see, looking away over the water, was a kind of dull line—that was the wood on t'other side; you couldn't make nothing else out; then a pale place in the sky; then more paleness spreading around; then the river softened up away off, and warn't black any more, but grey ...

That was Twain looking back on the Mississippi, long years after. One day, long years after, Gorky would look back on the Volga of youth, and would seem to continue that description of early morning Twain had begun; and the great likeness, and unlikeness, of the two men and their two countries lie in the descriptions:

... Ever more swiftly swirled the fog off the meadows ... and then bushes, trees, haystacks began to take form. Sunlight flooded the meadows, looking like streams of gold along the riversides. The sun, by a mere look into the still waters under the bank, made the whole river seem to rise up toward it, as it mounted the sky and blessed the bare, chilled earth with warmth and joy and drew from it sweet autumn fragrances. In the air's transparency, earth looked limitlessly vast. Everything seemed to be afloat in space ...

Each river is the mirror of the perceiving heart. Twain's, more artful, is also clearly nearer to our times, centered on the humans who experience the river, and on the objective world. Gorky's is more primeval, and more passive. It is basically still a medieval and religious description: the "streams of gold" are an ikon image; so is the "blessing" of the earth. It looks into a romantic vastness, the limitless beyond. Twain's is down to earth, and becomes more so as his famous paragraph goes on (with dead fish lying around, and "the song-birds just going it!"); while in Gorky's, the whole world finally floats into space.

But still, there was a great likeness between Huckleberry Finn and Alexey Peshkov—between the boy Twain created, who was a part of himself, the part he sloughed off in real life, and the boy that Gorky altogether was. There was a resemblance in the two rivers, and what they meant. Many felt, early, these resemblances.

But we are on a raft on the Volga, banks hidden by night, "the raft gliding over the waters swiftly and noiselessly ..."

In the stern, at an oar, stands a youth of twenty-two, Dmitry, the son of the raft's owner; and the gnarled, mean hired hand, Sergey, is at the tiller. Far ahead, at the prow, hidden by night, stand Dmitry's father and Dmitry's wife, who is his father's mistress.

The raft hand probes the painful story. The youth is one of those to whom sex is repulsive; it conflicts with the otherworldly religion he imbibed as a child. His father arranged the marriage. On the consummation night, the youth told her—as he now tells Sergey, forcing out the story—"I, see here, can't husband with you, Maria ... I'm a sick man, feeble. And I didn't, see here, want to marry at all ... It's just filth, and sin ... And children, too ... For them you have to answer to God."

The girl wailed, then cursed him. He told her he would have wanted to go to a monastery.

The raft hand, outraged, mocks the youth: "Lummox! What is it a girl needs? A monastery, sure? ... How many laws you've broken! ..."

Dmitry replies, quietly and stubbornly: "The law, see, Sergey, is in the soul. One law for all: don't do that which is against your soul, and you won't go ill on earth."

"Soul" is old-fashioned, but here is a modern golden rule. It is beyond what Tolstoy, for example, achieved—for he was still tied to dogma and the existing society.

The raft hand keeps needling. The youth at last cries out that he'll go away. "Soulless ones! ... To run from you is the only way to be saved! Why do you live? Where is there God for you? ... Do you live in Christ? ... But there are people elsewhere, whose souls live in Christ, and contain love, and yearn for the world's salvation ... I saw them. They called me. I'm going away to them. The book of the Holy Writings they brought me ... I'll leave you, you mad wolves—you live off each other's blood. Anathema on you!"

In the prow of the raft stand the two lovers. The father, a husky man who loves life (he roars at those in the stern to enjoy letting out his bass voice), stands at his oar, in a red shirt; three paces away is the woman, smiling as she glances at the wide-chested figure of her beloved. She is barefoot, clad only in a wet clinging sarafan. They are hungry for each other, full of passion and affection. Meantime, "Beneath the raft the water purls thoughtfully. On the left, somewhere far off, cocks begin to crow. Almost imperceptibly swaying underfoot, the raft swims forward ..."

But, as the river day dawns, their minds snag on the thought of her husband, her lover's son. While he lives, their love must always stay in the shadow of guilt. He approaches the idea of doing away with the youth: "... And then with you—to Siberia, to the Kuban ... And we'd pray off our sin before the Lord ..." She sighs. They draw back from the idea, and turn to the hope that Dmitry is sickly. Perhaps ...

The spring sunrays shower the water, playing on it, rainbow-colored. The wind blows, everything shudders, taking on life and laughter. The dark-blue sky among its clouds smiles to the sun-painted water. And the clouds are now behind the raft. Before the raft shines a clean, bright sky, and the sun, still cold, of morning. "In the air swam the saplike smell of earth, of just-born grass, and the resinous aroma of pine cones ..."

And that is the story; not a "slice of life," but a whole, and wholly internal, vision of it.

Over and over this vision will be repeated.

# CHAPTER 8

SAMARA—1895–6. A tall, broad-shouldered, stooped young man may be seen walking the Volga city's broken streets, peering into taverns and river steamers. He has gone into a flamboyant phase: dark bohemian cape with floppy wings, wide Cossack trousers of blue calico, soft Tartar boots decorated with green, red, yellow leather, over his trousers a Russian blouse with narrow Caucasian belt; carrying a thick knotty cane; long strands of blond hair hanging from under a soft black hat with rain-drooped broad brim.

He does a column for the Samara "Gazette," muckraking the local administration, using a curious pen-name: Yegudiil Khlamyda. (It will make sense later.) At night he is writing the stories that are bringing recognition.

In his cellar flat he has works by Shakespeare, Hugo, Byron, Goethe, Schiller, Maupassant, Dickens, Thackeray, Stendhal, Mérimée, Gautier, Flaubert, Balzac, Baudelaire, Poe, Verlaine—all in translation, for he never learned a foreign language; and the Russian symbolists ("decadents"), whom he considers morally bad, while admiring their use of language and even understanding, more than he will admit, their disenchantment.

The "Gazette" carried excerpts from Nietzsche's "Thus Spake Zarathustra," and one can guess how they get there. Nobody has read Nietzsche without being influenced; there is no doubt Gorky was influenced—especially by the appealing and dangerous theory of the necessary illusion, but also by the pregnant idea of the need for man to grow a softer, more human "second nature." But in any case, he was far from being a product of Nietzsche's philosophy.

The real molding influences had been drastic events of real life. Besides, his idea of "living for the good of others" was that very Judeo-Christian morality Nietzsche scorned. Gorky's protest was on behalf of the weaklings of life. They were to be admired if they became rebels; otherwise, they were to be defended. His strongest yearning—to make the traditional but violated morality be real—is always clear. Indicative was his decision, in Samara, to learn what the Jews really were and stood for. To this end, he started studying Hebrew, under a consumptive watchmaker. Lieberman, cheeks hectic with the phthisic flush, was too brilliant to stop talking and listen to questions; Gorky never learned Hebrew.

It was in Samara, too, that he met a small brunette girl with big eyes, Ekaterina Pavlovna Vozhina, a gymnazia graduate and a proofreader on the "Gazette"—a bright Russian girl of the type Korolenko had recommended. She became his legal wife in 1896; a son, Maxim, was born to them. She was a Populist radical, and when the Social–Revolutionary Party was formed out of the remains of Populism, this would be her political allegiance.

Marriage was galling to him; one need only look at the photographs. As for Ekaterina Pavlovna, she was a tough little woman, with great staying power—and his life was not fated to be severed from hers, either in marriage or out of it.

He himself was wavering between Korolenko and the Marxists. On the "Gazette" he tilted with the Marxist columnist of the rival "News." When he moved back to Nizhni, to be a reporter on the local "Leaf," he carried out what Korolenko called "moral sanitation"—championing poor and orphan children, attacking corruption, urging homes and education for those "on the bottom." He was also talking about revolution; so was everybody else. The difference between Korolenko and the Marxists was in theory and methods; that a revolution was needed, and probably on its way, was common belief.

Gorky became ill with tuberculosis in 1896. A Marxist newspaperman, Posse, had admired Gorky's stories. When he heard about the writer's desperate health and lack of cash, he tapped a literary fund, and also got a magazine to take Gorky's story "Konovalov" and send a 150-ruble advance. On this Gorky went to the Crimea, to a sanatorium.

When he returned to Nizhni, he was arrested and sent to jail in Tiflis. Documents had piled up in the Department of Police about seditious "readings." One had been given before students of Kazan's Seminary (this was the same Peshkov boy the Seminary students had snubbed).

Posse pulled wires, and Gorky was allowed to come back to Nizhni "under surveillance." The terms of surveillance were still loose, and a writer was something special; he seems to have been able to move freely.

A final crisis, before his final breakthrough to fame, came when he again fell ill, again with no money. Posse tried to find someone to bring out a collection of his "Stories and Sketches." Most publishers still looked down at the upstart—not really of the intelligentsia. Two ex-Populists, now Social Democrats, tyros in publishing, took a chance. The book came out in 1898. For the first time in Russian trade-book history, an author's work began to sell in the tens of thousands. It reached one hundred thousand copies—a staggering figure, in a population eighty-five per cent illiterate.

Real money came from them on; he spent it on orphans he "adopted," charity shelters, moochers, revolutionary students, the new Social-Democratic Party, then its bolshevik faction. He himself used what he needed; he instinctively considered money evil.

The hobo years were behind, and the temptation to be one of the derelicts who lived like the birds of the air, or in holes. He had gone through a love affair, and into marriage; he had done his youthful writing, and now—as the century prepared to turn—was suddenly the most widely admired young writer in Russia. World fame was on its way. Because of his life and subject matter, he was not just a celebrity but a cause.

Yet he himself still needed to find a Cause.


Although literature's main current—the classic—had always been pessimistic about human nature and fate, the eighteenth and nineteenth centuries had already produced many writers with visions of a New Jerusalem. Socialist theory had deepened the strain. Nor was the insight into the lowly and outcast unknown—nor even religious identification with them as the chosen.

But Gorky brought to the times—and the particular mental state of Russia—a strange and striking mixture: his biography, as if he himself was the proof of his theme; the religious undertone; the folk poetry; and a special élan. And also in his vehement protest was a special arrogance. The

Russian idealist psychology was given to extremes. Gorky's dream-figures, reverberating in such minds and hearts, could well give back an amplified sound: "We have been naught—we shall be all."

The deeper conflicts, so stark in the early allegories, and even in these very stories that brought fame, were dimly perceived by him, not at all by his public.

He himself was conscientiously and modestly forming his view of art, and his place in it. Art was the means for "the education of man's mind and emotions, and the ennoblement of life." Moral guidance had long been the acknowledged purpose of literature for Russia, as well as in most countries and ages. This was the great "civic tradition." ("Be a citizen!" Nekrassov, "The People's Poet," had urged idealistic Russians; all else was vanity.) The young Gorky had assigned himself, rationally and modestly, to carry on that tradition.

But underneath stirred the quandaries and shaking doubts. He wrote another allegory: a "dialogue" of Reader and Writer. The Writer declares he must "help man understand himself, raise his faith in himself, wage war against vulgarity in men, provoke in their minds shame, wrath, courage, and do everything that will make them nobly strong and capable of imbuing their life with the holy spirit of beauty." The Reader whistles him a song about a blind man leading the blind: "How can you be a guide when you don't know the road?"

This poignant image, blind leading blind, will recur often.

In this inner state, in the last few years of the century, certain mysterious emotional decisions must have been made. Their course may be traced in still another allegory—a famous one. He first wrote it in 1895. Four years later, he revised one sentence, and added another. Then this prose poem, "The Falcon," in heavy romantic fustian, became a historic marker on the path of the Revolution.

A mortally wounded falcon falls to a ledge beside a smug, safe garter snake. It still wants to soar. The garter snake suggests the brave bird might crawl to the edge and fall over: maybe the wind will lift its wounded wings. The falcon does so, falls, and is dashed to death on the rocks by the sea below. The garter snake then meditates: "Why this pride? Why their reproaches? So as to cover up the madness of their desires? And to cover up, by means of these, their ineptness for the business of living? Strange birds!"

In a few startling strokes, Gorky gives a whole psychological explanation of the revolutionary. It was the only such clear statement he ever made. But he put it in the mouth of the garter snake—lowly, safe, despised.

The mysterious inner process, and the changes ... Originally, the last eulogy of the brave mad bird was: "... You will always bathe in the sky, the free sky, where there is no measure to the wing spread of the free bird, flying upward." Gorky was twenty-seven. Four years later, these lines were replaced by: "In the song of the brave and strong spirit you will always be a living example, a proud call to freedom, to light." And a last line was added, the key: "The madness of the brave we sing!"

"The madness of the brave!"—the leap over the precipice will cover up all ineptness for the business of living, resolve all quandaries. The line became a marching slogan, young Russians repeated it in hushed and throbbing voices; it helped raise a whole generation pledged emotionally to whatever would come, and whoever would come.

Storm was coming. And Lenin was coming.

The young man Gorky, so hurt early in life, but with so much idealism, with a deep religious preoccupation with morality, had risen from life's depths. In joy, and with great energy, but still carrying all his inner conflicts and quandaries, he went on—to search for friends dedicated to goodness and beauty, to make a useful place for himself in Russian life and letters, to find a man who would be an ideal of both wisdom, morality, and strength; to clarify his mysterious internal yearnings and to point them toward an external goal.

# BOOK II

## *Flight of the Stormy Petrel*

## CHAPTER 9

FAME had typed him as "the barefoot bum who became a writer," and for a short time he played the part of the crude young man from nowhere, putting on, for people who didn't know him well, a swashbuckling vocabulary, especially in correspondence. It was his gauntlet: "I am the Orphan of the Burning Heart; take me or leave me." Actually, it was a shield against snubs and snobbery.

This pose clung to him when he sat down, in November of 1898, to write a decisive letter. It was to Chekhov. His motives were plain, and mixed as motives usually are. He was fighting for a place in the sun; and he also wanted to find a man to admire and be a dear friend. His forthright determination was clear; and also the genuineness and trepidation under the pose of the half-literate bumpkin.

The approach was made possible by one of Gorky's new publishers, to whom Chekhov apparently remarked that he would like to read Gorky's book. Forthwith came the letter, couched in the picturesque idiom proper for a self-taught orphan. It informed Chekhov that the book was being sent and then plunged at once farther:

Frankly speaking—I'd like to make clear to you the sincerest hot love that I unrequitedly have nursed for you from the time I was just a shaver, I'd like to express my joy before your wonderful talent, sorrowful and seizing the heart, tragic and gentle, always so beautiful and subtle. Ekh, the devil, take it—I squeeze your hand—the hand of an artist and a heartful, melancholy man, it must be—yes?

There was enough in that letter to let Chekhov know the young man wanted friendship; but to make sure, there was a postscript: "Maybe you

will wish to write me? Simply—'Nizhni, Peshkov,' or else, care of the
Nizhni-Novgorod Leaf."

Chekhov's response, warm and genuine, made it possible for the young
man to stop playing the bumpkin and write his next letter in more normal
Russian. In it he told Chekhov what it had meant to him to read Chekhov's
play, "Uncle Vanya"—the passage is self-revealing and touching. He also
asked Chekhov's opinion of the stories in the book he had sent him.
Chekhov wrote back: "What opinion? An indubitable talent and even a
real, large talent."

He mentioned defects: lack of restraint ("When a man spends the least
possible number of movements over some definite action, that is grace.
One is conscious of superfluity in your expenditure"), and a forced, uncertain depiction of the intelligentsia. Here he put his finger on a source
of long confusion and hurt.

The letters became frequent. Chekhov referred to "coarse" language,
and Gorky took it to heart; Chekhov hastened to reassure him: "Nothing
is less characteristic of you than coarseness; you are clever and subtle and
delicate in your feelings." He singled out two of Gorky's stories (one of
them, "On a Raft") as masterpieces.

The reply showed the young man had been waiting to find someone to
whom to open his heart with all its grievances and its childish need for
affection:

You say that I didn't rightly understand your words about coarseness—
let it be! Let it be that I'm delicate and talented, and—let the devil take me!
In my delicacy and talentedness I won't believe even if you tell it to me
still again, and a second time, and ten times. You say that I'm clever—here
I had to laugh. This made me both gay and bitter. I—am stupid, as a steam
engine. From the age of ten I have had to stand on my own feet. I had
no time to study, I could only gulp life, and work, and life warmed me
with blows of its fists, and stoked me with everything good and bad,
finally got me warmed up, got me started, and here I go, flying. But there
are no rails under me. I feel with a freshness, and not weakly, but I am
not able to think, and somewhere ahead a crash awaits me . . .

Chekhov, grandson on both sides of slaves, had become a doctor; he
was a fringe man, therefore, not of the established intelligentsia. He had
struggled with poverty, with the stifling circumstances of small-town life,
and with tuberculosis which would bring premature death. Real fame had
come too late—with his plays for the Moscow Art Theatre—but he turned

most of his bitterness inward. Young Gorky came to him in fullness of heart, offering and asked friendship, impetuously, clumsily, shyly; Chekhov's acceptance was generous, modest, and even shy.

By March of 1899 the friendship by correspondence had ripened enough for Gorky to visit Chekhov at his Yalta *dacha* (summer home) in the Crimea, and Chekhov wrote a friend: "In outward appearance he is a barefoot bum, but inside he is a man of taste—and I am glad." Chekhov even took on himself the task—sometimes taken on by an older brother, or an uncle—of helping polish the rough diamond: "I want to introduce him to women, believing they will be useful to him, but he bristles up, like a porcupine." (He had a little wife waiting in Nizhni Novgorod, and by his marriage he had put away defiance of the conventions; or had he? In this uncertain state of mind, he probably didn't know what to do with Chekhov's kind proposals—so he bristled.)

After that visit, Gorky felt able to ask shyly whether Chekhov wouldn't send him a memento of friendship—such as an inscribed watch. Chekhov duly sent a watch, inscribed: "To Peshkov from Chekhov 1899." Gorky wrote him: "I want to walk down the street and yell, 'And do you know, you devils, that Chekhov gave me a watch as a present!' "

To Gorky, Chekhov lived on a rare moral and intellectual level, to which he aspired. This sense of Chekhov's role as a guide is clear in every word of Gorky's about him. There were limits—unavoidable for one like Chekhov—beyond which the older man could not bestow affection. But then, Gorky's need for it was insatiable—he was the orphan nonpareil.

Chekhov's dour, gently mocking but actually devastating view of Russian life confirmed what Gorky felt so hurtfully, and his understatement was an astringent. When Chekhov said an honest man in Russia was regarded with suspicion, like a thief, he was saying dryly what Gorky wanted to cry in fury and outrage.

Chekhov was free of the quirks of the intelligentsia—such as snobbery. (The best friend of his youth, and still dear, was Isaac Levitan, a Jew, the most sensitive artist of Russia—also a doomed tubercular.) Gorky's awareness, too, that Chekhov's tuberculosis, unlike his own, was not arrested, called to the younger man's emotions. And the austere beauty of Chekhov's writing worked on him powerfully. Chekhov set severe limits in his art, and thus there was no rivalry with one like Gorky who had no limits and needed to acquire some: a rivalry which would set in fiercely for Gorky with Tolstoy. Chekhov could only help him.

What came about seems actually to have been a rather precious relationship—of a young friend, a nephew, even a younger brother, to an older. The younger man was able to, or thought he could, encourage the older one, so prone to disheartenment, always threatening to write no more. And how much Gorky accepted and trusted Chekhov is shown by the fact that he was able to read to Chekhov a poem—the wonderful beginning of a poem—about Vasska Buslayev. He read it to no one else.

Vasska Buslayev was perhaps the most Russian of the legendary Russian heroes: the Novgorodian strong boy who loved his mother, a great braggart who performed fantastic feats, mostly for the hell of it, who stood up for the commoners, but was a great mischief doer (*ozornik*), who flailed wildly doing whatever came into his head, flouting even God in his playfulness, an eternal boy, dying finally through heedlessness, after a pilgrimage to Jerusalem.

Gorky seized on him, the latent wonder of Russia; and Vasska's monologue—prologue to what was to be an epic—is one of modern social idealism's more splendid lyrics.

> Hey-ah!—If I only had all that strength!
> I'd give a hot breath and melt the snow everywhere!
> Round the whole earth I'd go—plow it all up!
> I'd go around a whole age—I'd found towns all over,
> Build churches all over, plant gardens all over!
> The earth I'd beautify like a young girl,
> And I'd hug her like my bride,
> I'd lift her to my breast—carry her to the Lord:
> —Hey, Lord, just look at her—
> Look how Vasska's dolled her up!
> You? Heck—You just threw her like a stone into the sky,
> But me, I made her into a dear emerald!
> Hey look, Lordie—look and be happy,
> Seeing her burn, green, in the sun's rays!
> I'd give her to you for a present,
> But that wouldn't be right—I want her myself!

Chekhov said, and Gorky recorded his words,

"That is good ... Very real, human. Precisely in this is the 'sense of all philosophy.' Man made the world habitable, he will even make it comfortable for himself." Tossing his head stubbornly, he repeated: "He will."

Since Gorky was thrilled at how well Chekhov understood his poem, it is fair to agree that this was what Gorky, too, wanted—a world comfortable for humans. And this is the aim and his lyric is its fair statement, of the communist dream: no Platonic Republic of supermen; no bohemia; it is the acme of the conventional. Its only condition is: For all.

Chekhov then asked Gorky to read Vasska's boast again. He heard it through, looked out the window, and said: "The last two lines .., aren't needed. They're *ozorstvo*" (what an ozornik does: mischief or spoilage for its own sake, impulsive action without moral justification).

He had spotted the one weakness, and this is a flaw that runs through most of Gorky's life—the fascinated regard of the man of high morality for the ozornik, the man without moral scruple, who wins regardless of means. (It is the most human of flaws; and without ozorstvo, the traditional Russian hero is hardly complete.)

The story of all Gorky's poetry is painful. Even after fame, and all through life, the snobbery of the "professional poets," the Establishments of Right and of Left, made him unable, or too sensitive, to publish his poetry. Instead, he sneaked it into his novels, essays, stories and plays. Thus, the splendid Vasska monologue appeared only after twenty-five years, tucked into his essay on Chekhov. The last two lines, which Chekhov criticized, are still there, a mark of his stubborn desire to hang on to what was true to himself, and at the same time to record faithfully his relations with Chekhov.

He wrote Chekhov:

Speaking frankly—I would like you to point out my shortcomings to me from time to time, give me advice and in general treat me like a comrade who requires teaching.

He added that he found he could not say this to Chekhov, but had to do it in writing. That he could even do it in writing shows how much trust had been developed and how much reserve had broken down.

He got advice. In Chekhov he found what he had needed badly, someone kind and altruistic, with impeccable taste, and dispassionate. From him he was able, psychologically, to learn. He would never again have a critic both disinterested and close, both kind and penetrating.

It was Chekhov also who, later in 1899, led him to Tolstoy.

The man who stamped Russian literature with his mark, as if for all time, had also become a kind of moral hearth, to which all seekers—fakes included—came. There was a legend of St. Leo; and there was also a real, powerful, most complex old man—and a nobleman.

About fifteen years earlier, a very young man who did odd jobs and hoboed around the country had sent the great man and writer a letter, asking if he could grant him and some pals a bit of land, that they could cultivate as "Tolstoyan" farmers. There was, of course, no reply.

Five years after that, the same young man, still tramping Russia, still looking for someone to admire and to be his model, showed up at the hearth place, Yasnaya Polyana itself. The Countess Sophia, Tolstoy's wife, gave the young bum rolls and coffee in the kitchen, told him Tolstoy was away at a monastery, and remarked that all kinds of shady rascals were always trying to meet Lev Nikolayevich. She was very genteel; young Peshkov got the point, agreed with her, and went on his way.

Ten years passed. The fame of the new writer, Gorky, "the writer who had been a barefoot bum," was all over Russia. And Chekhov, now a friend, wrote to him that he had talked about him with Tolstoy.

He praised you very highly and said you were a "remarkable writer." He likes your "Goltva Fair" and "On a Raft," but he does not like your "Malva." He said: "You can invent anything you like, but you cannot invent psychology. In Gorky one comes across sheer psychological inventions; he describes what he has never felt." So much for you! I told him the next time you were in Moscow we would come together to see him . . . Tolstoy has been asking about you for a long time; you arouse his curiosity. He is evidently impressed.

So the door, which he had stormed in vain when a nobody, opened graciously when he was a somebody, and a friend of Chekhov's. Gorky must have had some bitter reflections about this. He did not forget easily— in fact, he never did.

One day in January of 1900 Tolstoy wrote in his diary: "Gorky called. We had a fine talk. And I liked him. A genuine man of the people."

This, Tolstoy would always insist Gorky be. It would be hard for him to swallow the fact that Gorky was famous, that his image was not that of the traditional Russian muzhik, and that it called forth in whole masses emotions alien to those Tolstoy insisted were the true path.

For Gorky, that first meeting, in Tolstoy's study, was not comfortable. Tolstoy attacked his work, and at one of its weakest points, the psychology of sex. The old sensualist had no way of knowing, when he started, that the authentic young peasant, "with pugnacious nose, Asiatic cheek-bones, and a big body, all bone and muscle," was a prude. He soon found out.

A young woman in one of Gorky's stories—one of his worst, about the intelligentsia—was improbable, Tolstoy said. How could a young and healthy girl be sexually indifferent? Why? Gorky wrote, "I was depressed by his tone, quite disconcerted, so crudely and harshly did he endeavor to convince me that shame is not natural to a healthy young girl."

Then he tangled with the despotic old man about literary opinions. Gorky dared to say he thought Gogol was influenced by Hoffmann, Sterne, and possibly Dickens. Tolstoy gave him a quick glance, and asked: "Did you read that somewhere? No? That's not true. Gogol hardly knew Dickens. But you've really read a lot—watch out, that's harmful. Koltsov ruined himself that way."

This kind of condescension was hard to forgive. Yet Tolstoy's comment showed real insight. If anyone is close to the religious folk lyricism of Koltsov, it is Gorky. His spirit recalls at once that of the complexly naïve man who sang:

> Open wide, you forests dark and deep,
> Flow apart, you rivers hastening.
> Become dim with dust, little road, highway mine,
> Bring me tidings, guide, O my singing bird.

The whole exchange hurt, and made him feel Tolstoy's interest in him was mainly ethnologic. And what hurt as much was the obscene language, the attitude toward women!

But as he was leaving, Tolstoy suddenly embraced him, kissed him, and said: "You...are a real peasant! It'll be hard for you among the writers, but don't fear anything, always say what you feel, let it come out crude—that's nothing! Wise people will understand."

And, strangely, the relationship grew.

Gradually, to Gorky, the coarse words began to seem natural and simple coming from Tolstoy's "shaggy lips." Gorky began to be reassured; he no longer thought Tolstoy talked that way because he thought it was the only language Gorky understood.

He even got so he could enjoy, in a way, Tolstoy's approval of the sexual. One day as he walked up the Crimean coast to visit Tolstoy—thus far had the friendship developed—he came on the great writer, "a smallish old man with a soft Crimean hat on his head, winking with one of his piercing gray eyes." He was winking at a cooing pigeon making love to its dove in the middle of the road. "A wise old man, winking knowingly."

He sent Tolstoy a letter: "Please send me your picture, if you are in the habit of doing so. I beseech you, let me have one . . . I bow low to you, M. Gorky." Tolstoy sent it, and "grasped his hand with friendly feeling." He added that he liked Gorky's writings, but had found Gorky better than his writings. "You see what a compliment I am paying you; its main value is in its being sincere."

In reply there came a whole credo:

Many thanks, Lev Nikolayevich, for your portrait, and for your fine and kind words about me. I do not know whether I am better than my books, but I know that every writer must be higher and better than his writings. For what is a book? Even a great book is only a dead, black shadow of the word and only a hint at the truth, whereas man is a depository of the living God. By God I understand one's untamable yearning for self-perfection, for truth and justice. Therefore even a bad man is better than a good book. It's so, isn't it?

I deeply believe that there is nothing better than man on earth, and I even say, paraphrasing Democritus: Only man exists, the rest is a point of view. I have always been and shall be a man-worshipper, only I cannot express it with adequate force.

He ended by bowing low, and firmly grasping Tolstoy's hand. The young "peasant" had made his declaration of independence, and even of war; it was clumsy, but clear. Yet, "I am terribly anxious to call on you again." From now on they would be Beloved Enemies: a difficult relationship, between the man Gorky came to see as a Godlike wizard, who did not love God, and the man Tolstoy came to see as the moral "spy" of a strange folk divinity. Part of the time Chekhov would be there, fortunately, to make things go tolerably smoothly.

The "old wizard" was a crucial experience; but there were other phases —also intense and prophetic—of the young Gorky's life and work, in these years of first fame. He had completed and published his first major novel.

## CHAPTER 10

"FOMA GORDEYEV," dedicated to Chekhov, is probably the first modern Russian novel, a book of great vigor, epic feeling and startling naïveté. It claims to describe the rebellion of a young merchant prince, whose father rose to power "when on the Volga fortunes were being made with storybook speed." Actually it reflects the confused anger of a young declassed upstart, Gorky.

Ignat Gordeyev, Foma's father, is a powerful transposition of wish—a burly dream portrait of all the confident amoral men so unlike Gorky's own dimly remembered father.

Strong, handsome, and far from dull, he was one of those people who are always and in everything accompanied by succcess—not because they are talented and fond of hard work, but more because, wielding enormous reserves of energy, they along their way do not manage to—in fact are not capable of—pondering over their choice of means and know no other law but their personal desires.

Parallel to Ignat, and emerging full length only when he dies, is Jacob Mayakin, his business partner, godfather to young Foma. He is harsher, falsely pious, meaner, though with the same power, earthy wisdom and conservatism as Ignat. This man, who justifies himself to his godson by the Book of Job and the Psalms of David, is clearly Grandpa Kashirin, transposed to a higher class.

At root, then, this is the story of the very young Alexey Peshkov's struggle against the view of life and place in life his tough Grandpa Kashirin must have tried hard to impose on him; his violent refusal was probably the mainspring of his lifelong protest, and his art.

One more main character gives the book a booming sound, not a person but a river, the Volga, "wide-breasted," with her ships, her flanks "adorned in gold and green velvet."

Against this background the reader follows the growth, groping anger, rebellion, of Foma Gordeyev, miscast among the intellectuals of a Volga town which is clearly Nizhni Novgorod. A real wastrel merchant prince might have felt uneasy, but arrogant awareness of power would have brought out different behavior. These are really the feelings of the sensitive upstart Gorky, injected into the skin of the merchant prince.

Among his father's and godfather's bargemen Foma is happier; he rejoices in furiously helping to load a freighter. (In the joy of physical action, the introvert and the People can unite.)

His first sexual experience, reticently told, is with a peasant woman of thirty, Pelagea, who carries bags of grain aboard the Volga-plying freighter of his father's fleet. He ends with a sense of "the loss of something precious," but also of new manliness. He sends her away roughly, then follows her out on deck, and she takes the youth on her lap and places his head on her breast.

And as she talks to him of fleeting life and the need for love, one realizes suddenly she is Old Isergil, who gave the youth (who would be Gorky) Danko's flaming heart—only rejuvenated from sixty to thirty.

Less fortunate is Foma's experience with a sophisticated socialite back home, who wants him to play her "game of love." He finally cries: "The beauty of an angel God gave you, but where is your heart?" This ends it, but later he defends her honor when a rich scoundrel refers to her as a "cocotte." Foma grabs his whiskers and pulls him around, making him dance. To a friend who has watched the whisker-pull in amazement, he explains: "I consider her good—then it has to be, she is good." This kind of romantic idealism was basic to the young Gorky; its loss would be a wrench, and its memory would follow, twining itself about his later constructions.

Foma adds: "I am a simple man—a wild man. I am not unfortunate; I merely have not got used to living." This recalls not only Billy Budd, but also the garter snake's insight: that the "madness of the brave" covers up ineptitude for living.

All the main findings about life that Gorky had come to are here displayed: the kingship of work, the violent rejection of the mean middle-class life, of "chasing the ruble," the bitter finding that the "good" are usually weak, that the "bad" are strong ... The novel is a showcase of his figures and themes ... Thus, there is old Anany Shurov, who took away his son's wife and sent his son to a monastery (probably the original of the father of "On a Raft"). Old Anany tells Foma: "Sin ... teaches." Again, old Anany tells Foma: "The strong man gets forgiven— for the weak there's no forgiveness." In such homespun thinking, and the brutal facts of life that he experienced around him as he grew, was the origin of Gorky's reluctant admiration of strength—not in any German philosophy.

His friend now introduces the knightly but timid Foma to some young women "who know how to live," and soon four couples are picnicking, with cognac, by the river, their pleasure raft moored to the bank. Foma's girl is a tall stately brunette; in Gorky's few fine love scenes, it will always be this girl. Here she is Alexandra (Sasha), and she loves money for gifts. She tells him frankly: "It is possible to love this way—yes."

At dark, the party becomes a drunken brawl except for Foma, who is sulking. The revellers stagger around on the raft; Foma grows furious, and chops the stake that moors it. He experiences a wonderful feeling as the raft, with its drunken burden, moves off toward submerged rocks. "Something heavy and dark" seems to flow out of his breast. They start screaming—"Save us! . . . You're drowning human beings!" "Are you really human beings?" Foma screams after them.

Sasha manages to jump off the raft, and he drags her ashore. The raft hits a small island, and nobody drowns. But a glimpse has been gotten of a terrible inner anger, and of the fact that it is driven by insecurity, feelings of inferiority, inability to cope with a life of stark rivalry— a glimpse of the engines of revolution.

Old Mayakin complains that Russia is confused. "People have been led to think they can do anything . . . Give them freedom then, let them run from side to side, go wild; soon they'll grow weak, poor things, their hearts are rotted out . . . Then they'll be caught [like birds!] by capable, real people—people who are capable of being the real masters of life." These masters will tell the poor caught birds: "Silence! Or we'll shake you from life like worms from a tree."

To this terrible vision—was it originally Grandpa Kashirin's?—of the triumph of a hateful, hated strength, over ineffectual, lawless people, Gorky would hold for many years. Its fulfillment would constitute his own tragedy.

Foma and Sasha ride the Volga, to the music of a hired orchestra, drinking champagne. But in his fits of introspection, he demands: "Who are you?" Then, "Who am I?" She fights back: "Take what you want from me, but don't crawl into my soul." But he cannot stop being a reformer.

Sasha kisses him farewell (the way Malva kissed the lover she was discarding), and goes off with a less introspective master. Foma goes wild with drink and women. He cries out to people: "See how you live. Aren't you ashamed?" And they reply: "And how should one live?"—the old quandary. Mayakin, outraged, cuts off Foma's bank draft. "We laid the foundations of life!" he pleads with Foma. "We laid ourselves into the earth in place of bricks! Now we need to build further . . . The path was laid by the fathers and we must walk it! . . ."

Mayakin's daughter, Lyuba, a poor idealist who believes in books, tries to explain to her father the other path: "So that all may be happy . . . All need freedom . . . just like air . . . And, in everything, equality! . . ." Mayakin is satisfied she is a fool. "How can all be equal, when each wants to climb higher than the others?"

The final scene takes place on a merchant ship of Mayakin's fleet, the *Ilya Muromets*—named for that smashing, slashing hero of deep Russian legend. It is the annual get-together of the new moneyed rulers of deep Russia.

Gathered are "thirty men, all solid citizens, the flower of the local merchantry." They include a man who started his climb by operating a string of whorehouses; another who, twenty years ago, stood trial for arson; and similar solid figures. They kneel in prayer on the ship's deck, before turning to Polish vodka, oysters and meat pies; and they sing the "Persian March" along with the hired military orchestra. Mayakin rises for a ringing eulogy of the merchant class, who have sown the Volga with ships, built Russian trade and power—upholders and builders of order and life, bearers of culture. All raise their wine cups, and Mayakin leads the "Hurrah!"

"And we are the first people of life and the real masters of our society," Mayakin adds, with a scathing look at the renegade, his godson, Foma Gordeyev, who has come aboard, though not invited.

Foma stands up, drunk among the drunken merchants, and makes his reply: "You bastards . . . It's not a life you've made—but a jail . . . Not order you've created—but chains you've hung on man . . . Stifling, strait, no place for a free soul . . . Man is perishing. You soul-destroyers!"

His nearly incoherent, actually joyous frenzy mounts, but he cannot clarify his accusations; he can only multiply them, and the insults.

"It's not life you're building, but a privy! . . . Do you remember God? The five-kopeck piece is your God! . . . Blood-drinkers! You live by the strength of others—you work by the hands of others! Not in fire but in boiling dirt will you be boiled. For ages your agony will not end!"

At last they recover their senses, jump him, tie him up, then mock him. His surrender is abject, his humiliation pathetic. "I wanted to say the truth . . . to heal you . . ." (These are almost the very words of the poor siskin.) He is empty, as if a boil had burst.

Mayakin sternly tells him there is no forgiveness (no forgiveness except for the really strong!). Then he states his own victorious philosophy: he who wants to get some good from life is not afraid to sin. God appointed man to build life, and didn't give him much reason . . . that means he won't look too hard for faults, " 'cause He's holy and much-merciful."

Foma disappears. Years later he comes back from the Urals, beaten, despondent, sort of half-witted. Merchants mock him, sometimes, on the street: "Hey you, prophet!" The novel ends in abject defeat. The great cleansing outbreak of violent protest came to nothing. Words are not enough.

"Foma Gordeyev" was brought out in installments in the new magazine *Zhizn* ("Life"), organ of the new Social-Democrat Party of Russia, from whose leadership Lenin was already driving the first Russian Marxists, Plekhanov, Akselrod, Zasulich. It was late in 1899.

Chekhov felt parts were "splendid," though he had reservations about the whole. "Of Gorky will come a big writer."

It remains his best novel. There is confused but honest self-examination. Politics and a Cause were closing in; they would make self-examination impossible. It contains a crude but determined effort to look into the dynamics of social change in Russia. It is therefore a modern social novel; and Foma is a modern, real hero. Except in ripe, disillusioned, angry old age, Gorky would never again create a full-length living figure—only states of mind and symbols.

Things like fame, marriage, friendship with Chekhov and Tolstoy, solved nothing internal; and in writing "Foma Gordeyev" he had exposed his problems to himself.

The dead end of the barefoot bums, which had brought fame, he had rejected; and the climax of "Foma," giving vent to his protest in depth, had shown he had no direction—a steam engine, flying, with no rails under it. Desperation was, as usual, around the corner.

"The Three of Them," published in 1900, immediately after "Foma," was part of a psychic retreat, or at least a holding action, in the shelter of Nizhni Novgorod, of the security of marriage, and of a return to base, in his subject matter, to urban classes more like his own. "Foma" had been a transposition; this novel was franker (it may actually have been begun earlier).

Its orphan hero, Ilya, is raised by a grandfather who is a holy hermit (modelled on a hermit in a legend of Grandma Kashirin's, a figure that meant much to Gorky). Then the boy is taken to town, and given over to a hunchbacked uncle (Grandpa Kashirin, like Proteus, in one of his many forms). He grows up with a pal equally hurt by fate, and a girl friend who has fallen into prostitution.

The story promises much, and Ilya could be a splendid lower-class hero. But from the time he goes to work in a store, thus entering the class of burghers (the meschanye), a terrible anger begins to tear the story's fabric asunder. Finally, there is murder, then, at a business banquet, violent confession combined with denunciation: "It's no use for you to talk of God, no! ... Why do you betray one another, rob one another? ...Deceivers, devils! ... You deceive God and yourselves! ..." Then, the violent, hopeless rebel, chased by the outraged burghers and police, runs with all his force into a stone wall, head-on, destroying himself.

Not only the whole wild ending, but the handling of the theme of crime, showed again the religious and moral core of the young Gorky's protest. For him, the motive of crime was spiritual agony caused by the social suffering inflicted by a depraved society. The hero was originally good and happy. Dostoyevsky's hero murdered from a spiritual agony and evil supposed to be embedded fatally in human nature itself. This ancient notion, to which Dostoyevsky gave such currency in modern literature, Gorky refused to admit; and the simple evidence of life insists it is not the whole truth. Gorky's footing was far from sure; but the ground he held was high. This is one reason his work has remained important, no matter how disillusioned and battered he and his high estimate of man finally became.

But the very depth of this moral issue, so central for Gorky, took his work beyond the usual possibilities of social realism. He could not develop further in this direction, as an artist; "Foma" and "The Three of Them" were as far as he could go. He would have to turn, pick up the symbolic thread, and follow wherever it took him. But he could not, then, possibly see this.

The hero smashing his head against a wall, full tilt, meant that the artist and the man were again at a dead end. Casting about, Gorky fell back on compassion, in a story about a whorehouse bouncer, "Red Vasska," whose main job is to keep the girls in line by torture. When he is mangled in an accident, one of the girls he used to torture the most cruelly insists on taking care of him. He lives, somehow, or half lives, and manages to mumble a proposal of marriage; she shrieks with laughter. Red Vasska mumbles: "Ekh you! What do you understand? . . . A villain . . . Do you think—a villain, and that's all? Do you think—it's easy, if a villain? . . ."

As Vasska is carted off, at last, to a hospital, he begs forgiveness of all the girls. The one who had taken care of him says she will wait for him. The reader cannot help doubting their lives will be any different . . . but . . . there is hope . . .

This is the "conversion ending." Imported from the literature of religion, it had already been used by Tolstoy, Dostoyevsky, Korolenko. But from Gorky's "Red Vasska," where it was applied to the plebeian urban scene, perhaps for the first time, this sentimental device would pass on to be a seal upon "proletarian literature."

The "Song of the Blind" is another story of compassion. The writer has entered a tavern filled with the poor; a blind mendicant sings, in traditional wailing folk meter, with a halt in the middle of each line.

> Oy, show pity—on us the poor blindies.
> There's no work at all—we can do-o-o.
> There's no seeing—in our little eyes.
> Oy, they cannot see—God's dear li-i-ight . . .
>
> Show pity on us—kindly people.
> Help us, whoever—believes in God.
> Blind eyes and—a soul that's blind.
> Help us, whoever—believes in God.

One of the listening men shoves a coin toward the woman. She sits immersed in her song, hands on her chest, blind eyes shut. "She felt for the coin with her hand, took it in her fingers, quietly struck it against the table, and laid it back on its former spot." The man who had put it there "sighed, shook in his place, and again lowered his head."

The writer can no longer stand his emotions. He pays for his beer, and goes out. "There in front of me is the wide straight road into the distance, toward the setting sun; along its sides motionless stand old sad birches, just as if listening for something; not one twig shivers on them. A night bird soundlessly sweeps by me in the air. Black, it appears just as unnoticed as appear remembrances in the soul, and disappears in the murky distance."

Remembrances in the soul—remembrances of the fate of Grandpa and

Grandma, conditioning so many other remembrances, making so much of life seem a remembrance of the soul.

Such things, however, bite away protest, get in the way of the madness of the brave. This story was published in 1901. Gorky planned to include it in a 1903 collection, but did not; this is worth noting, for just then, 1902–3, was the time of the fateful personal turn. It was never reprinted during his life.

Social outrage was mounting again in him; it vied with compassion as he sought a direction in which to go. Experience had shown him that protest and not humility was wanted and admired. Songs of the poor blind were not proper for the Falcon, who would be the Storm-Messenger. What was moral was the call to action; this was his crystallizing belief. All it needed was an object, a clear Cause. This lay just below the horizon, as the sun came up—on blind and angry alike—in the new century.

# CHAPTER 11

EARLY in the winter of 1899–1900 a writer from Moscow, Teleshov, stopped at Nizhni Novgorod on his way somewhere. Walking down a street, he passed a tall young man with long hair, carrying books under his arm. The young man's face impressed itself, and his stooped walk, and his clear gaze.

The next day Teleshov happened to read in the local paper (the "Leaf") a letter to the editor, signed Maxim Gorky. It asked the citizens of Nizhni Novgorod to help organize sleigh rides on the river for the children of the poor, and to send to his apartment skates, wristbands, money. Teleshov went to the address given. He was met at the door by the same young man. Gorky took his hand—"and his own hand was big and strong"—and led him in, called his wife Ekaterina Pavlovna, introduced them, then went to another room and returned with a child in his arms, wrapped in a warm blanket. "This is my Maximka, my son," he said with pleasure. He pulled from under the blanket Maximka's little hand, and gave it to Teleshov to shake.

When they settled down to tea and chat, Teleshov told Gorky about a circle of writers he had formed, who met at each other's apartments, read each other's works, talked about literature, society, life. Gorky was obviously attracted: "How comradely you live, as writers should."

Chekhov had long urged him, as part of the polishing process, to get to the big cities; but Gorky had clung to Nizhni Novgorod, where a letter would get to him, as he had let Chekhov know, if it was simply addressed "Nizhni—Peshkov." "His childhood and youth," writes a biographer, "had been stamped with Nizhni-Novgorod impressions, and it must have meant much to him to have risen from the lower depths to the position of an important figure in the very same city."

"His appearance," Teleshov recalls, "was striking. He was tall, wiry, somewhat stooped; long hair, thrown back, coming almost to his shoulders, small light mustaches but with chin clean-shaven, wise, deep eyes and occasionally, in a moment of special friendliness, a charming smile, hardly noticeable. In his speech the letter 'o' stood out, as with many Volga-dwellers, but this 'o' sounded softly, hardly noticeably, giving his speech a certain special independence and simplicity, and his voice was soft, chesty, pleasant. He dressed customarily in black linen blouse, belted with a thin cord, and wore high boots."

The sleigh rides for the children of the poor were part of an annual yuletide celebration Gorky had created in Nizhni. He had also organized a popular subscription to build a roomy lodging for barefooters and other adult unfortunates; and had helped set up scholarships for local boys to go to universities. For the children of the slums, he organized holidays and pageants, collecting and handing out shoes, shirts and trousers, books and food.

For Gorky's Christmas celebration the children were gathered in the halls of the Nizhni-Novgorod Kremlin. Ekaterina Pavlovna sewed shirts and blouses from the donated goods. The boots the kids got were often brand-new felt ones. Even the kids from the tough Konavino district were loyal to Gorky, and no brawls or pickpocketing were reported.

"Save me," he wrote to Teleshov the following winter, "or I am lost. The success of last year's yuletide, gotten up for 500 children from the slums, captivated me, and this year I worked up a yuletide for 1000. Wow, I bit off a lot. And it's too late to retreat. I ask, I beg, I shout— help the tattered, hungry children, the dwellers in the slums! Please, gather everything anyone will give: two arshins of calico and a five-penny piece, half an arshin of corduroy and old boots, a pound of candy and a cap— we'll take anything. Anything. I only hope my enterprise doesn't get into the papers..."

And later, he wrote again:

"For the money, for the books—thank you, dear pal. May it be known to you that you donated 50 pairs of pants." He then dunned Teleshov for copies of the latter's popular Christmas story, "Mitrich's Yuletide."

The same spirit led him to the strangest of the men who helped him organize the children's Christmases. He was Savva Morozov, head of the biggest textile plant in Russia, a powerful industrialist who had never gotten over his bitterness at having to go into his family's business instead of going on to be a chemist. Gorky accosted him. They had beer, mixed with water, together in a Nizhni tavern. Morozov at once wrote out an order for five hundred arshins of cloth for the Nizhni-Novgorod tykes. This was only the beginning of a powerful emotional and personal relationship, that led both men to a progressively fiercer involvement in the social storm—and Morozov, soon, to ruin and death.

From Christmas trees for slum kids to more dangerous things was not a long step in Holy Imperial Russia; but Gorky had to give more reasons for arrest than unauthorized community fund activities. Meantime he whirled on, in his self-created stream—art and life, personal and increasingly political, friendships that ran the gamut, from Chekhov, through "adopted" orphans and a tavern-singer he tried to get into the town's best church choir, to Savva Morozov . . . fervid belief in human ennoblement, deep underlying disquiet.

He started to get to the big cities, too. With Teleshov's invitation, direct from a Moscow writing group, besides Chekhov's introductions, he must have decided he could really brave the metropolis in whose depths he had once camped, an unknown young bum. This time he must have been startled to find how his fame had gone ahead of him: "The tramp who became a writer," now also "The Falcon," spokesman of the madness of the brave. There were no movie stars then, and he was already becoming what was probably the closest thing. Crowds gathered on the street: "That's Gorky!" . . . "Nice going, Falcon!" . . . He was upset by the adulation, sometimes behaved outrageously, sometimes ran into strange apartments to get away from the autograph seekers.


The start of the century must have been—so felt many who lived in it and then memorialized it—an exhilarating period of ferment and groping in Russian literature.

The lines that led left and right, to social significance, futurism, religious mysticism, had not yet fully untangled; in fact, "pure" and "civic" art, long at war, had temporarily drawn closer. Chekhov's "Cherry Orchard" and "Uncle Vanya," which seemed to embody despair and quietism, contained implicit protest too, whetting new dreams. In Moscow and St. Petersburg, young men from the lower intelligentsia, who had risen to awareness and literary ambition, were expressing themselves in poetry and prose, in rivalry with those who had a heritage of status—the so-called symbolists, really end-of-the-century romantics, who worked hard at creating a religion of art and sex, so as to burn with a gemlike flame.

Revolution, undefined but romantic and stirring, was the word, even for some of the aristocratic young people, but especially for the young people from below. Revolutionary impulses and impulses of art ran together, on a road that had not yet come to a final fork.

There was a place ready for Gorky in Teleshov's circle of young writers. He leaped in, with all his great energy, his winning enthusiasm, his passion for helping everybody in sight, being friends with everybody, bringing everybody together. With his background, it seemed that he represented much more vigor, much less inbred inhibition to action, than any of the others. What others mused about, he did.

Teleshov's group called itself *Znanye* ("Knowledge"). This banner was already, at least part way, that of a union of art with a sense of social awarenesss. It seems fairly clear that it was, even before Gorky, a group of the "outs"; the more sophisticated "ins" of the literary world had their own evening get-togethers; and their work was the staple of the powerful literary journals.

The "Knowledge" group met to read poetry once a week (on Wednesdays) in Moscow. It included not only poets, and was not even confined to writers. Isaac Levitan, the artist, Chekhov's friend, was appparently a charter member. The writers, besides Teleshov, included Chirikov and Bunin. Soon after Gorky started coming, he became, by force of his personality and, inevitably, his new fame, a driving force in the "Poets of Knowledge." At the "Wednesdays," as their meetings became widely known, "young authors read their unpublished things in an intimate milieu," writes Teleshov, and exchanged views on them. Later, driven by Gorky's verve, "Knowledge" began to publish.

Soon Gorky brought in Leonid Andreyev. He had read a story of Andreyev's in an obscure magazine, went out and found Andreyev, and clasped him as a friend. Andreyev began reading his new work at the

"Wednesdays." Next Gorky appeared dragging Stepan Gavrilovich Petrov, who used the pen name Skitalets ("a wanderer," who can find no place in life). He was a fantastic character in his own right, who had worked with Gorky on the Samara "Gazette." He saw himself as the spirit of wrath: "I am both the sword and the flame!" In the group, however, he seemed to define himself as Gorky's thunderous shadow.

Kuprin, a powerful realistic writer, joined the group. Serafimovich, whose novel "Iron Flood" would become a Soviet classic, was brought by Gorky into the "Wednesdays"; so was Golushev, a professor of gynecology, art historian, orator, literary critic. And then, as a key member, another of Gorky's multivarious friends, another Volga character, Feodor Chaliapin, the greatest bass voice of the age.

"Chaliapin," writes Alexander Kaun, "was then at the height of his power and charm, his peasant naïveté not yet spoiled by success and facile victories over feminine hearts." Teleshov recalls how he would burst into the "Wednesdays," shouting: "Brothers, I want to sing!" Usually he was his own accompanist, but once he phoned Rachmaninov: "Sergey, I've *got* to sing! Take a *likhach* [a special drozhky driver with a fast horse] and gallop to the 'Wednesdays.' We'll sing all night." Sergey came galloping, and Fedya sang all night. The authors forgot their manuscripts. They sat watching the close-cropped head of Rachmaninov, his long fingers fluttering over the keyboard, and Chaliapin, tall and slender (this is surely an exaggeration by Teleshov), in high boots and black fur hat, his face severe and spiritualized. "Never and nowhere was he so enchanting, so fine," Teleshov writes.

Once Gorky dragged a batch of them from the "Wednesdays" to hear Chaliapin sing Rubinstein's "Demon," the opera based on Lermontov's tale, at the Imperial Opera. Gorky had harangued his Volga pal about the meaning of the Demon—that tortured soul who dies because, for love of a mortal, he has violated his demonic nature. According to another friend of Gorky's, Tikhonov, who tells the story of that evening, Chaliapin's "Demon" at first stunned the audience, though it finally enthralled them: instead of falling in love headlong, he starts with rage, for he knows he is dooming himself; he goes into it with eyes open, driven by mysterious and whelming emotions. Said Bunin, finally, learnedly: "That's right—there is such a variant of Lermontov's play." Gorky said: "But Chaliapin is following Milton, whom he hasn't read."

Chaliapin lived the Demon that night; Gorky would live it his whole life.

Sometimes older writers showed up at the "Wednesdays"—Zlatovratsky, Mamin-Sibiriak; rarely, Chekhov and Korolenko. The gang met at various apartments, including Gorky's on Martinskoy. There was camaraderie. They kidded each other by bestowing on each other the names of streets —hitting off, more or less subtly (usually less), their particular quirks. Andreyev, whose stories were scary, like Poe's, was Wagon Cemetery. Zlatovratsky was first Old Gates of Triumph, later Patriarch Pond. Goltsov, editor of the literary magazine "Russian Thought," was first Maiden Lane, later Granny's Hick Burg.

The name Gorky got, "for his barefoot bums and heroes of the Lower Depths," according to Teleshov, was the address of a certain Moscow square known as Cunning. This shows that the "Wednesdays" gang had spotted in Gorky the character of Luka, the holy wanderer, who is the center of a chapter soon to come.

Chekhov was hurt when he learned he "hadn't been tapped"; he too wanted an address.

Skitalets imitated Gorky's black blouse and high boots, only he wore his belt lower. Andreyev and Chaliapin added long tight-fitting jackets with wide skirts and standup collars. Gorky was the glass of fashion and the mold of form.

By the late spring of 1900 Gorky even had the "Wednesdays" come down with him to Yalta, in the Crimea. There he lived high on a hill, "in an apartment full of writers, young people, women," according to Teleshov. "I don't know when he belonged to himself," Teleshov adds.

With Gorky in Yalta at this time lived Lahnin, the lawyer for whom Gorky had worked a decade ago—one of the six great influences on him that he lists. Lahnin, now a stooped elderly man, showed his onetime apprentice "touching respect and love." From Gorky's it was a short walk to Chekhov's. It was at this point, too, that the Moscow Art Theatre troupe came to Yalta, that Gorky met them through Chekhov, and that Gorky began to write "The Lower Depths." This also must have been when he met Maria Feodorovna Andreyeva—though she does not appear in the big photograph of the Art Theatre troupe with Gorky taken that summer.

## CHAPTER 12

WITH the introduction of young Gorky to the dedicated band of the Moscow Art Theatre, and of the Moscow Art Theatre to the phenomenon of Gorky, the way was opened for a series of vigorous plays. One—the first conceived and the second completed—has lasting quality. It is the most symbolic, the least realistic, of the lot. He was not a realistic writer.

The Art Theatre was really an art theater, not a commercial one. Its men and women were alive to the currents of national life. Although few were revolutionaries, they all participated in the widespread feeling that Russia was "on the Eve" of great change. The Art Theatre had made itself the vehicle for Chekhov, and with his "Sea-Gull"—still, today, its emblem —had established itself as Russia's foremost dramatic group. Now Chekhov, displaying in life the same iron sense of moral discipline as in his plays, insisted on bringing the Art Theatre and Gorky together, to obtain for the younger man the early fame and forum that had been denied to himself.

The group met Gorky in the spring of 1900 at Chekhov's Crimean dacha, where Chekhov was ill of the tuberculosis that a few years later finished him. "Write a play," Chekhov had insisted. He "coaxed and exhorted [Gorky], volunteered to read the script, and assured him that even if his first production should fail, the harm would not be great."

Later, "he bombarded Stanislavsky, Nemirovich-Danchenko, his own wife—Olga Knipper—and other actors, with letters, suggestions, complaints, and appeared more concerned than when his own works were being produced. And with what triumphant joy he greeted the success of his protégé."

The Art Theatre's members were prepared to be impressed by Gorky, and they were. Olga Knipper wrote, years later: "Like a rocket he flew from somewhere into our quiet intelligentsia life, and stirred us with his tales of an unknown life."

Nemirovich-Danchenko, the codirector, pictured Gorky as:

A quizzical impetuosity, directed inward. Along with a calm exterior, an enormous store of unspent power ready to hurl itself down the first road prompted by intuition. A keen and precise eye from under a frowning brow, a swift appraisal and sorting out of observations. Concentration, cogitation, and a quick discard of what is obvious and outworn. Side by side with the good taste of modesty, an elemental faith in his self, or at least in his Weltanschauung. An agreeable singsong bass, a Volga "o" accent, and an enchanting smile that caressingly embraces you all at once. A peculiar, angular gracefulness of movements.

In that first meeting, he told Nemirovich-Danchenko the plan of "The Lower Depths." By the spring of 1901 he was far along in both that and another play, *Meschanye*, which it was decided to put on first.

That "enormous store of unspent power" sufficed for many other activities, carried on simultaneously; and it rode over such interruptions as arrest and jail. This second arrest, and what followed, are matters for a later chapter; but when Gorky finally got back to Nizhni, late in 1901, he had to stay put there, again under surveillance. Nemirovich-Danchenko journeyed there to have Gorky read the *Meschanye* script to him.

Production was supposed to be a sure thing, but Gorky clearly was not so sure. He wrote jokingly to a friend: "I passed my preliminary exam with honors for the rank of dramatist (Watch out, William Shakespeare!)," then added that when he started reading he had to work hard "to hide from Nemirovich-Danchenko the funny circumstance that my voice quavered and my hands shook."

By the spring of 1902 he was also able to read two acts of "The Lower Depths" to Nemirovich-Danchenko. Then he was exiled by the police again, to the whistle-stop of Arzamas. There he entertained Andreyev, and introduced him to a local priest who was making a lifelong fight to have the town put in a pipeline so its water supply would not be polluted. The priest and Gorky had become chums, holding long discussions while the police agents assigned to Gorky squatted in the bushes under the window. Andreyev left impressed and envious at Gorky's capacity for friendship with all kinds of birds. In Arzamas, between sessions with the priest, Gorky finished "The Lower Depths."

By then *Meschanye* was being put on in Moscow.

It is important that the first play to which Gorky was impelled was "The Lower Depths." It was Stanislavsky and Nemirovich-Danchenko who thought it better to avoid arousing more controversy around the controversial subject of Gorky and his barefoot bums, by first establishing him as a dramatist with a middle-class theme.

The one, "The Lower Depths," grew from his whole romantic involvement with the escape and protest of the derelicts of society. It was the belated last of a line. *Meschanye*, however, was his return to a galling, bitter theme of earlier youth: the mean life of the Russian lower middle class, the Meschanye—the class to which he had been born.

He had dealt with this theme in "Foma Gordeyev," but not directly, changing the Kashirin family into the family of a merchant prince. Now, in this first-produced play, he tried to meet it head-on. He would approach it again and again, always infuriated, as if pawing the ground. It always centered on a household much like the Kashirin household.

The violence of Gorky's rejection of the gray life of the meschanye mars this first play beyond repair. He must have felt so violently precisely because this would have been his natural level, by the "norms and forms" of that day's Russia.

But the most important thing about this play is that here we first meet Nil, the hero of Russia's future: the new image Gorky saw, to replace the violent and defeated Foma Gordeyev. Nil—"Nothing"—is one who came from below, who must make himself what he is to be. He is self-born, as it were—like his maker.

To Stanislavsky, Gorky wrote directions: "Nil is a man calmly confident in his strength and in his right to reconstruct life and all its norms and forms in accord with his, Nil's, understanding of it: And his understanding of it arises from a healthy, hale feeling of love for life, whose shortcomings arouse in his soul only one feeling—a passionate desire to do away with them."

This, then, is a historic figure—the original of the "New Man" of Soviet literature. He has been called "the first real revolutionary of the modern Russian stage." He is surely the foundation of the stereotype of the proletarian hero. But his primary service was to provide a model (as certain timely literary creations do) for countless young Russian lives.

The model Stendhal gave young Frenchmen, which influenced many generations, was the eager, ambitious, talented climber from the provinces, triumphing in the metropolis. Hemingway's model for Americans was the seeker of sexual freedom and other proofs of virility, preferably abroad. The model Gorky gave Russians, in Nil, was that of a devoted, moral, even ascetic, fanatical young social reformer. He is corny and overblown.

Yet one who looks at Nil with sympathy will see, beneath the corn, the elements of a hero older and more genuine than either of the others. If he seems smug and foolish, this is only partly his fault, and partly because of recent conditioning in favor of preying or dangling young men, and consequently to scorn anyone who doesn't prey or dangle. The stronger and more promising heroes of American literature have been, like Nil, dedicated men. This is the main line of heroes, whether religious or Promethean.

What Nil became, in time, is hardly Gorky's fault. The conditions of Russia made many of those who modelled themselves on him crude fanatics. To damn or mock Gorky's vision would be like holding Augustine—an earlier rebel, reformer, and idealist, who projected a Christian hero—responsible for the "heroes" of the Inquisition.

Nil arrives from work, face smudged with smoke, smeared with soot, hands also dirty, in a short leather jacket, oiled till it shines, belted, and in high dirty boots. He declares: "I love to live. I love noise, work, gay simple people."

The jacket, oiled till it shined, and belted, and all the other paraphernalia, physical and mental, would become, and still are today, a stock in trade of Communist heroes on the Soviet stage, like the American cowboy's boots, holster, six-shooter, Stetson, specious purity, and drawl. This portrait of a man is drawn by keeping the hands over the eyes to shut out any psychological insight.

In contrast to Nil are the meschanye, Philistines all, though some struggle: the father and mother, image of hateful immersion in the petty life of trade; frustrated, book-reading daughter; weakling of a son.

Father: "Pitiless ones! . . . What have you done? But we—lived . . . worked . . . built houses . . . for you . . . committed sins . . . maybe many sins . . . for you!"
Son: "Did I ask you . . . to do all that? . . ."

In this picture of middle-class life there is no special insight, as in the portraits by Arthur Miller, for example, or the early Odets. Gorky exceeds them only in how violently he hates it.

*Meschanye*—variously translated, in despair, as "Smug Citizens," "The Philistines," or "The Petty Bourgeoisie"—was staged in the fall of 1902 in Moscow. At first it was refused a license, but Nemirovich-Danchenko managed to get the censor to permit performances for subscribers of the Art Theatre only.

The censor cut out such phrases as: "The master is he who toils . . . remember that . . ." and "I see nothing pleasant in that I and other honest people are commanded by swine, fools, thieves . . ." On opening night, to make sure nonsubscribers didn't get in—and plenty did—the chief of police had uniformed cops acting as ticket collectors. Nemirovich-Danchenko finally ordered the cops out of the theater (and they went!). The same police chief, incidentally, had shortly before ordered a Moscow newspaper to cut out an advertisement for a sale of apples, because "something else might be understood by apples." This will give an idea of the atmosphere of Moscow in the fall of 1902, into which Gorky's play was dropped by the enthusiastic Art Theatre.

The play then toured the provinces, having to be cleared by each local censor. In Bialostok, during the performance, according to Lenin's paper, *Iskra* ("The Spark"), there was a demonstration. Civil guards went in and began beating the demonstrators; then the police and the crowd fought in the street. "One worker was killed," said *Iskra* quietly.

In Moscow itself the applause was moderate, and the play doesn't deserve more. But it wasn't the play. *Gorky* by this time was much more, out in the streets, in Moscow, St. Petersburg, and the provinces. He had been "The Barefoot Bum Who Became a Writer"; then, "The Falcon." Now he was "The Stormy Petrel." The new, wild, stirring identity had come literally on wings of song—to be precise, "The Song of the Stormy Petrel," a turgid prose poem of about three hundred and fifty words, with heavy onomatopoetic effects.

In Russian the name of that quaint, strange bird, the stormy petrel, is literally "messenger of the storm." Thus Gorky became, in one sweep, the Hermes of the coming Revolution.

> On the sea's hoary plain
> the wind gathers up the clouds.
> Between the clouds and the sea
> proudly wheels a Stormy Petrel
> like black lightning.
> Now scraping the waves with his wings
> now like an arrow shooting to the clouds
> he cries out, and
> the clouds hear the joy in the brave cry of the bird.

Thunder. The waves whine with rage. The bird flies madly, like a demon, through the darkening scene, laughing at the clouds, sobbing with joy. Blue flashes of lightning on the sea, like snakes of fire ...

"The Storm! Soon the storm will break!"—cries the Stormy Petrel. "Let the Storm break more strongly!"

It comes off badly, judged by literary standards; but so do most gospels. The emotions and ideas it roused, and their effect, must have already been there, tensed, in the state of mind of its hearers: breakdown of faith in the existing government, passionate sense of revolt against whatever was, passionate undefined idealism. The "Song" merely served as a mechanism to let them spring.

The liturgical beat, allied with an effect of sonorousness close to pompousness, is a main distinguishing mark; as if the song is an assurance, liturgically given, that the revolutionary yeast will rise. The madness of the brave will win some terrible, wild, unimaginable victory.

There is no need to explain the symbols. All know already what the Stormy Petrel is, what the waves are; all feel the clouds in their breasts; know exactly what Storm it is; all accept the Petrel as its messenger and guide, though if asked who and what, all would probably give different answers: the revolutionary leader (undefined), the revolutionary writer, Marxism, Populism, the affirmation of the Rights of Man, the Social-Democratic Party, its Lenin faction—any combination of these is the Stormy Petrel.

It is all symbolism, incipient mass action, like trumpet notes or a hymn: it calls, and the rest is within. This is melodrama, close to hysteria—with a nebulous but idealistic moral theme. We are in the gospel realm of fantasy based on moral protest, the stirring up for release of potent, undifferentiated emotions. It can lead to anything, depending on who then channels these emotions.

It became "the fighting poem of the Revolution." Written by an amateur who hardly knew what he was doing, it helped rear a generation of professionals. One man would write: "It was reprinted in every city, it was distributed in copies run off in hectograph and on typewriters, it was copied out by hand, it was read and re-read in workers' circles and in circles of activists. It is possible that the editions of the 'Stormy Petrel' in those years attained several millions. There is no doubt that . . . these fighting poems, 'The Stormy Petrel' and 'The Falcon' . . . had no less a revolutionary influence on the masses than the proclamations of the various revolutionary committees of party organizations; in fact the very party organizations not infrequently published these calls by Gorky and distributed them widely among the masses."

Another man of that next generation—Kalinin, one of the very few "old bolsheviks" who somehow survived the purges—called the prose poem "the herald of 1905." He wrote: " 'The Stormy Petrel' of Gorky gave expression to the general state of mind, the desire to fight against the autocracy and its norms and forms."

Whether the Song really influenced the working masses directly is doubtful; but it certainly strongly influenced those who were already crying, or emotionally ready to start crying, "The masses are rousing!" in order to rouse the masses. It fortified the madness of the brave.

This madness of the brave was, to a degree, the psychology of the whole revolutionary movement, but it was preeminently the psychology cultivated by Lenin. The emotions awakened by this bombastic poem served his plans as no professional bolshevik organizer could. Lenin would seize that chaotic youthful outburst and never let go. Years later, when the "storm" of 1905 had broken and failed, leaving a trail of disillusionment, he would use that raw early anger of Gorky's—which Gorky by then had outgrown—to pep up new and undisillusioned legions toward new brave madness, and to warn them against any compromise or moderation: "Let the cowardly liberals motion with their heads at the oncoming storm, let these limited meschanye put all their 'mind and feelings' into awaiting new elections—the proletariat is preparing for struggle, in friendship and vigor it goes to meet the storm, rushes into the very thick of battle. Let the storm break!"

Lenin had long determined to divide the world into warring extremes, by destroying the middle. Gorky's confused intent, in that fateful prose poem, was still nebulous; the storm for him was an elemental movement of all idealistic people. But, though the men had not yet even met, Lenin's gravitational force was already being exerted. The work, like the life, of the angry, mixed-up dreamer, was already being edited by the consummate, ruthless politician, whose own dream had hardened into surrealistic determination.

Gorky was becoming, unconsciously, a tool. Soon he would be and for five fateful years would remain such, consciously and willingly. What nobler and more saving thing is there for a rebellious dreamer than to be the tool of a mighty, idealistic Cause?

But he was not yet thinking of himself as a tool when he conceived and when he was writing "The Lower Depths." Closely following the line of time makes this clear. He was not even yet the Stormy Petrel when, in 1901, he began putting his passion and anger into that play; though by the time it was staged—late in 1902, having been moved back so *Meschanye* could come first—the fateful mental turn had been made.

He was already yearning for a cause, and a man who embodied it; but he was not yet committed. He was no longer capable of the kind of self-analysis, and therefore of real characters, that was possible in "Foma Gordeyev"; but the yearning, the fury, the poetry, the symbols, in "The Lower Depths" are his own.

This play was a climax and a terminus, in a way for him and in a way for Russia. It was conceived and presented in years of the crossroad; in weird extreme trappings, it offered the last image of the idealistic protest that had been, in full pathos and knightliness. But the seething emotions in it, and some bitter and even cynical implications, helped build the momentum that hurtled Russia into the next stage: the stage in which humanitarian appeal was replaced by "iron logic"—another word for the desperate acting out of implacable commitments to fixed goals, vision by action, reason by will.

All that is analysis and hindsight. He himself, in "The Lower Depths," was back for a last stroll among the superfluous, the hopelessly rebellious, the spiritually and materially dispossessed, among whom, but for the grace of Books, he would have ended; and where part of his heart would always stay, for they are also, somehow, the real seekers.

# CHAPTER 13

"THE LOWER DEPTHS" is a strange, troublesome, undramatic drama; a confused sermon, a moral allegory which by its nature almost defies any form. It was given barely enough form by an artistic device Gorky must have learned from Chekhov. Chekhov had found that the essential truth of characters is illuminated when they talk themselves out while seeming to talk to one another; much of his dialogue is really parallel monologues.

Gorky's characters, in "The Lower Depths," are largely allegorical figures, most of whom speak in parallel monologues, in the name of Ruined Hopes and Man's Inhumanity to Man; while Luka, that enigmatic, wandering saint or swindler, wise hermit or liar, speaks for . . . the confused unanswered mystery in Gorky. The vivid bizarre setting, "a basement, resembling a cave," a night lodging for barefoot bums, serves to anchor a cloudy message in universal symbol. Chekhov's technique, draped over these creatures, makes the onlooker think he is getting a glimpse of human interiors; it also saves Gorky from choking on his own emotions; and by giving the illusion of movement—the spotlight passing from one figure to another—it preserves enough tension to keep the inherently static play alive.

Bubnov, the ne'er-do-well seller of caps, calls the attention of Kleshch, unemployed ironworker, to Kleshch's wife, Anna, dying on the plank that is her bed.

Bubnov: "... Your wife would like—"

Kleshch: "There's plenty who'd like all kinds of things."

Satin, a once-educated pimp, says: "Work? Make work pleasant for me, and maybe I'll work ... When labor is pleasure, life is good; when labor is duty, life is slavery."

As Luka, the old holy wanderer, is led in, he declares: "To me—all's the same. I respect crooks too. For me, there's good in every flea: all are black, and all of 'em hop ... There you are, Dearie, where can I settle in?" Here, in mendicant wanderer's garb, is the Beloved Enemy: part Grandma's holy hermit, part Count Lev Nikolayevich Tolstoy, and the most yearning part—and the most cynical—the real Gorky.

Says Luka, stretching his legs: "And still—you're People. No matter how you pretend, how you wriggle, you were born a man and you'll die a man ... And ever, I see, people are becoming smarter, ever more serious ... And though they live ever worse, they ever want things to be better ... They're stubborn."

By now close listening has revealed it is all one voice, speaking through these creatures' voices, saying two entirely different things, and trying desperately to blend them.

One statement is like that of the existentialists. Man's life is anguished, meaningless. The solace of religion is rejected. No exit. This seems the theme. But a countertheme, implied with muted passion, is the old nineteenth-century one, that Man is the greatest: he can do anything. These threads cross and recross; and the play is woven. The means used are liturgical. The characters are a chorus.

Using these creatures was a dazzling stroke. In the lowest, the highest is seen. And if man's possibilities are so great, his state so low, then the system must be changed, and man will change. This is the new resonance:

the twentieth century in the nineteenth century's arms. There being no organized army, these ex-men of Gorky's lead the way, like Brecht's salvation army, or Shaw's in *Major Barbara:* doomed and pathetic host. "But there is, there must be, a real living answer," is the unspoken refrain. Those seeing, or even reading, "The Lower Depths" are expected to supply the answering line themselves: "...Social change... Social revolution..."

Familiar Gorkian themes assemble, adding their voices to this dialogue of the two centuries. For example, the concept of a lawless life; and of not being needed, of being superfluous.

Nastya (the prostitute, who reads romantic novels): "I'm superfluous here."

Bubnov (calmly): "You're superfluous everywhere... and so are all the people on earth—superfluous."

As in a church, we can hear the spectator sounding his own response: "Let us create a world in which I do not feel superfluous."

This echoing effect that he manages to set up by the first act's end is widened into choral effect in the second, the play's finest act. The male lodgers are playing cards. Bubnov and Krivoi Zob sing:

> The sun rises and sets
> But my prison is dark.
> Day and night, around the clock,
> They stand guard at my window.

This plaintive lyric, by anonymous Populist martyrs or simpler criminals, came from deep Russia. Skitalets, Gorky's friend, is given credit for bringing it from the interior; he sang it, playing on his *gusli*, at the "Wednesdays." It was new to the metropolitan public when through the play it became famous.

In the card game, the Tartar, the play's most quixotic character, keeps asking Satin not to cheat. Suddenly the dying Anna breaks in, with pathetic accusation: "I can't remember when I wasn't hungry. I trembled over every morsel of bread... All my life I trembled... All my life I went in rags... all my unhappy life... what for?"

Luka (second solo voice, suddenly): "...You'll have rest there!... Endure a while. All, dear one, endure..." Bubnov breaks in with the next lines of the "Prisoners' Song":

> Guard me as much as you want to,
> Even without you I won't run away...

Then Krivoi Zob and Bubnov (the choir) complete the verse:

> I so want to be free—ekh!
> I can't tear my chains...

The polyphonic use of contrasts—Chekhov's sophisticated technique against the primitive folk pathos of the song—creates at this point a fine lyric sense: one feels he is seeing-hearing a fragment of a strange, static but darkly glittering church masterwork.

Two events then go to the heart of the play's elusive theme. Luka is the center.

First, the Actor (another of the ex-men) reveals himself. He is one who lost confidence, and this is fatal in life. Drink has wiped out his beloved lines of poetry. Luka explains it's possible to cure drunkenness; there's a free hospital. The Actor eagerly asks where. Luka has forgotten. But he urges the Actor to refrain from drink, endure... And later, when healed, he'll start to live again...

The Actor: "Can I, really?" Luka: "Why not! Man—can do everything ...if only he wants to..." The Actor (as if awaking): "You're a dope!"

Luka next assures Anna that her agony will pass. God will receive "His slave, Anna... Death to us is like a mother to little children." Anna: "But maybe...maybe I'll get well?" Luka (laughs): "For what? For agony again?"

Vasska Pepel, young thief and vagabond who yearns to be something better (he is a compound of Chelkash and Alexey Peshkov), has been listening intently. Now he says bitterly to Luka: "Brother...you lie well. Go ahead, lie."

So "What is truth?" is the play's question; and deep and tangled, for the author, is the answer. Luka has said things that rouse hope, but then can't deliver; while in reconciling Anna to death he took away hope. Therefore his "truths" do not help, but actually do harm. They are immoral. They are lies.

Contrast with Luka the Siskin, who "lied" so as to inspire the birds to seek a free, better life. He failed. But the hope he tried to convey was not really a lie; if they only had tried, it could have become the truth.

So truth is relative; it is in the mind, it depends on moral intention and moral effect. Almost at once, Vasska demands of Luka if there is a God; Luka smiles cunningly, hems, finally says: "You believe, and there is; you don't, and there ain't."

Anna dies. The Actor, coming in drunk, tells Luka joyously he has remembered the forgotten lines:

> Sirs! If to holy truth
> The world its way can't find,
> Honor the madman, then, who spills
> Gold sleep over mankind!

This seems to be a recommendation of despair: humanity needs the Beautiful Lie. It is probably not what Gorky meant; this study will return to these four lines, so important for gauging the mentality of the man who was the carrier of the Communist dream. But they do seem to say that the real truth is too dire to be supportable; that therefore the "true path" is . . . illusion.

If this is it, then the way is open to any madman or demagogue with his "gold sleep." Then anything is justified, life's actual problems resolved by means of a Beautiful Lie. Once this is done, any fanatical religious movement can form (one was forming, already, around the banner of Lenin). What younger men, unable to think for themselves, would do in the name of the Beautiful, the Noble, the Justified Lie, Gorky could not know. This is the path to tragedy.

And immediately, the Actor, looking at the dead Anna, says: "I am the path to the rebirth, as said King . . . Lear." Then he calls to Luka: "Come here, my faithful Kent!"

Kent was Lear's truthteller. Luka is clearly, most of the time, a truth-teller, and a truth evoker—but the truth that exists hurts and may do harm; therefore it is a lie.

In the third act, Luka reminds them that Christ commanded us to show pity. He tells of befriending two thieves, who then worked beside him honestly all winter. This proves "Prison won't teach good, nor will Siberia . . . but Man will . . . Yes. Man can teach Good . . . very simply."

The next lines, an unexplained jump, show that Gorky has never moved from his one concern—the one concern of his whole life: the relation of the Good and the True. Kleshch responds to Luka's story about teaching good, with: "Where's Truth? Here's Truth. No work . . . No strength . . . It's impossible to live—there's the truth!" He turns on Luka: "You, old man, console everybody . . . I'll tell you—I hate everyone. And this Truth—let it be damned! Understand? Understand them. Let it be—damned!"

That the true and good seldom correspond is a real and awful problem.

But to make utter war on Truth in the name of Goodness, so that neither can again have a meaning until the world is remade . . . Here rejection and fury run, fatally bitter, into the river of protest, giving a lethal content to the future of the Communist revolutionary movement. This is known as "hardness." Could protest have grown hard enough to be realistic, but not to be deadly?

All this is in the play—all the "seeds of tomorrow," idealistic and amoral, pious and tragic.

Luka has decided to go to the Ukraine, having heard of a new faith starting there. "People are always seeking, always wanting—whatever's better . . ." Vasska asks: "Do you think—they'll find it?" Luka: "People? They'll find it. Whoever seeks—finds . . . Whoever strongly wants—finds."

As if reverberating to Luka's yearning, Vasska tries to get Natasha to go away with him, they can start anew. She refuses to believe him. Meantime Kostilev, the owner of the night-shelter, quizzes Luka: So Luka can't stay long in one place? Luka: "They say that even water can't flow under a stone fixed in its place." Kostilev: "But a man, unlike a stone, needs his own place." Luka: "But what if someone's place is—everywhere?"

So Luka is really the holy hermit, from Grandma's ballads, wandering the earth. A mystic person—immortal creative curiosity, the immortal and pious human spirit. He is more than "Man," or at least different. He is, in part, Gorky's love of Tolstoy, refuting his rejection of Tolstoy; and he is Gorky's yearning; and Gorky's poetic dream of a wise old age. Says Luka: "I want to understand this business of being human."

Gorky himself insisted Luka was a charlatan; but the heart has its own reasons. Luka is extremely complex—as complex as his maker.

Kachalov, one of the Art Theatre's stars, described Gorky, in Moscow in September of 1902, reading "The Lower Depths" in a crowded room before the Art Theatre company and many others: Chaliapin, Andreyev, Chirikov are mentioned. This was probably a meeting of the "Wednesdays."

"When he began to read the scene," Kachalov wrote, "in which Luka consoles Anna on her death-bed, we held our breaths, and a wonderful stillness reigned. Gorky's voice trembled and broke. He stopped, remained silent for a moment, wiped a tear with his finger, and tried to resume his reading, but after the first few words he stopped again and wept almost aloud, wiping his tears with a handkerchief. 'Ugh, devil,' he mumbled, smiling with embarrassment through his tears, 'well written, by God, well done.' "

When Luka says a man's place may be everywhere, Kostilev replies: "Then he's a vagabond . . . a useless man." And, if a man really wants to be a Wanderer—a "strange" man—then he should keep quiet, live in a forest, pray for all men's sins . . . "And you—what kind of Wanderer are you . . . You don't have a passport . . ."

Luka doesn't have a passport; the Siskin also didn't have credentials; Gorky didn't have the pedigree expected of a holy man, a prophet, who could show the right path. Count Tolstoy did. In Luka, the ancient "strange" man of Russia, Gorky was stating his own right to be a prophet.

The exchange also explains, much better than Gorky's many confused explanations, why he wandered Russia in his early years: the image of such a holy wanderer was set before him, by Grandma, early; translate it into real life, in the real conditions of Russia, and you have, as Kostilev shrewdly insisted, a vagabond.

This is not the theme of social revolution, but of holy meditation and wandering, the great alternative. Both drives are in Gorky: rebellion, and holy wandering. This is why when seen from one angle Luka is a fraud, from another, Gorky's deepest projection.

Whatever drama is in the play is only a framework for these moral issues at its heart. This becomes even clearer once the third act has closed with a brief flurry of violent action. After that, there is no drama left; the last act is there mainly so two important things left unsaid may be said: two moral statements.

As the remaining down-and-outers ruminate, the Tartar speaks of Luka: "He was a good man . . . he had Law in his soul." Baron: "What Law, grand duke?" The Tartar: "Don't do harm to any man—there's the Law."

Let this stand, alongside the words by the unhappy boy of "On a Raft" ("don't do that which is against your soul"), as Gorky's belief, and also as the ethical ideal of the Soviet society his confused, yearning works helped bring into existence: it is identical with the Christian ethical ideal.

And then, there is Satin's famous statement, of which the last two lines have gone ringing down various corridors:

When I'm drunk . . . I like everything . . . (looks at the Tartar, who has knelt in prayer to Allah) . . . He's praying. Splendid! A man can believe or not believe . . . that's his affair. Man is free . . . Man—there's the

Truth. What is Man? . . . Not you, not I, not he . . . no. It's you, I, they . . .
in one . . . Do you understand? . . . In this—the beginning and the end . . .
Only man exists, everything else is the work of his hands and his brain!
Ma-an! . . . It sounds . . . proud! Man! We have to respect man. Not be
sorry for him . . . not to love him through pity . . . to respect him! . . .

Why Satin? Gorky himself said that in Satin's mouth the lordly speech
sounded "pale" and "strange"; but that there was no one else into whose
mouth to put it. This only makes more sharply clear Luka's role. With
him gone a-holy-wandering, much of the writer's deepest personality
has gone. And Vasska, the young vagabond, is in jail.

So Satin is a sort of devil's choice; but not a bad one. He undoubtedly
originated for Gorky, at least subconsciously, as Satan. The devil was
for him (as in heretical Eastern Christian thinking) often the advocate of
Good. He would intuitively reach for Satan, to make the last, important
statement about Man.

The play staggers to its close. The "Prisoners' Song" again—to the
rescue! The Baron comes in to announce that the Actor has hung himself.
Satin closes the play: "Ekh! . . . spoiled the song . . . Fool! . . ."

Chekhov must have been puzzling over his friend Gorky, and the fact
that in the guise of realism his best work was an intensely personal expression of religious symbolism. He wrote to Gorky, after reading "The
Lower Depths," saying that his work reminded him of Strindberg. Gorky's
delighted, flustered reaction showed he knew whereof Chekhov was
speaking.

But the Moscow Art Theatre, excited over participating, through
Gorky's play, in life on the other side of the tracks, was determined to
use on it all the meticulous superrealism of which Man is capable. They
gave it everything. Kachalov played the Baron; Stanislavsky himself, Satin;
Moskvin, Luka; Luzhsky, Bubnov; Vishnevsky lived the part of the Tartar
for weeks before presentation. To help Olga Knipper, Chekhov's wife,
prepare to play Nastya the streetwalker, Gorky offered to bring a girl
"of this sort" over to stay with the Chekhovs. He also carefully showed
Olga how to roll her own cigarets, using cheap *makhorka*. Kachalov
visited the Moscow dens, and studied especially the life of "Baron" Buk-
holz, a bum Gorky had known and who was supposed to be the basis
for the Baron. Stanislavsky took part in an excursion the whole group
made to Rogues Market in Moscow. The inmates were interviewed, notes
taken on speech, stance, appearance, hopes, dreams, social outlook. Sketches

were made of the room. Stanislavsky wrote: "I felt like Dante going through all the sections of Purgatory."

And so this morality play, this rather turgid, symbolic liturgical drama, was staged in Moscow December 18–31, 1902, by means of the most exacting realism, producing what must have been a weird, romantic blend.

Its opening performance "thrilled and stirred" the middle class audience. "The public called out, without end, the directors, the artists, and Gorky himself." The play then swept world capitals. When it was published in St. Petersburg in 1903, the first edition of forty thousand went in two weeks; by the end of the year seventy-five thousand copies had been sold. Gorky's new American publishers could now state that his fame surpassed Tolstoy's.

## CHAPTER 14

MEANWHILE, out of the "Wednesdays," with Gorky going full steam, had grown a cooperative publishing firm, "Knowledge." To commemorate its start, the central spirits sat for a photograph. There they are (left to right): Skitalets (the "tiger from the furrier's," Gorky called him), in long black pull-over, college-kid moccasins, and a pince-nez, hand hooked in his belt; the chunkily elegant, swarthily handsome Andreyev, semibeatnik, in debonair boots; long-haired Gorky, full beatnik, chin on his folded fists, pressing them down on the little table around which they are grouped; Teleshov (ever the gentleman); Chaliapin, with his rustic-sophomore grin ("anybody who's a pal of Alexey Maximovich Gorky is a pal of mine"); Bunin (another gentleman, and uneasy: "Is this really my crowd?"); and high-domed Chirikov, standing (a quarter of a century later, in bitter exile after the bolshevik take-over, he would call Gorky "the Smerdyakov of the Russian Revolution"—that being the oily flunky of "The Brothers Karamazov," who carried out evil for his tortured master).

The "Knowledge" anthologies and collections made a real mark on the Russian literary scene. Nondecadent writers got a chance, and the public got a viewpoint. The first issue included Andreyev, Bunin, Veresaev, Garin-Mikhailovsky, Gorky, Gusev-Orenbursky, Serafimovich, Teleshov

—three hundred forty-five pages for a ruble. There were no profits; the authors were the shareholders. All this was pure Gorky.

The first issue announced distribution of surplus: 1,000 rubles for a fund for higher education for women; 1,000 for the society of teachers, specifically for housing for (abandoned) children; 1,000 for the society for protection of public health, for building a children's home; and 500 for a public reading room in a Moscow suburb. In the nature of these beneficiaries, too, the fine non-Italian hand of Gorky can be seen.

"Alexey Maximovich," said Teleshov, "was a man of broad initiative, able to carry that initiative into life and to choose for it the proper people."

Forty of the "Knowledge" collections and anthologies came out, including issues devoted to contemporary writers, to scientific and popular-scientific books, to foreign writers (Zola was one). Pyatnitsky, the cooperative firm's business manager, did begin to press for mixing in less high-flown material; there may have been bigger financing problems than the idealistic Gorky imagined. (Later, according to Kaun, Pyatnitsky would deal very sharply with Gorky, who would be deprived of the money he had sunk into the publishing firm. "He was a poor judge of people," Kaun says of Gorky. His estimate does not necessarily contradict Teleshov's. The idealist usually wins—for others.)

"Knowledge" even put out cheap reprints, which Gorky tried to market in small towns, through local zemstvo organizations, to bypass the price jack-up by commercial distributors. In magazine format, also, selections from the anthologies went on sale in the cities, and were bought in unprecedented numbers. The commercial magazines, which featured the more established and sophisticated symbolists and decadents, protested that "Knowledge" was "depressing the taste of the public." Gorky explained to his friends that "the most attentive and serious reader of the day was the literate worker, the literate peasant-democrat, searching for answers." Teleshov says of Gorky at this time: "Whatever he spoke about, his words breathed simplicity and deep conviction. It was clear that his views and hopes comprised the very substance of his nature."

The "Wednesdays" themselves went on. Skitalets would bring his gusli —the ancient portable harp of the Volga soothsayers and glory bards. Between manuscripts, he would twang it and sing folk songs and ballads. One was the "Prisoners' Song"; another, the "Song of Stenka Razin and the Persian Princess."

Andreyev was appointed chairman for a banquet, for some good cause or other, and of course he brought the "Wednesdays" gang in to help him organize it. They did indeed. Skitalets, never one for half measures, leaped onto the rostrum, and roared at the startled public a "New Poem" (he and Gorky probably wrote it together):

> My God is not your God; your God forgives,
> But my God avenges! My God chastises!
> My God will bring you thunder and judgment...
>
> I hate you deeply, ardently,
> All of you—toads in a rotting pond!

The police came. The newspapers that reported the incident were shut down. The chiefs of the "Wednesdays" were hauled into court. Andreyev nearly went to jail.

Teleshov also gives an account of that famous "Wednesdays" meeting at which Gorky read "The Lower Depths," the place packed with writers, newspapermen, the directors and members of the Art Theatre, doctors, lawyers, scholars, artists. They sat on the window sills and stood at the open doors, from where they could hear though they could not see.

Gorky, says Teleshov, read the part of Luka with great enjoyment and emotion. Sometimes his voice broke, sometimes he had to stop to wipe away tears. When the words came: "Give Anna peace, she's lived a very hard life," whereupon Gorky stopped and wept openly, the listeners felt these words "were meant to refer to all Russia." Such was the mood, and Gorky was its embodiment.

The bad as well as the good, the "Wednesdays" shared together. On his comrades Gorky inflicted the reading of "Man," that incredible prose paean, which said so much he so ardently believed, and said it so badly. Chekhov remarked about it that Gorky sounded like a young Volga preacher intoning scripture through his nose.

In an hour of discouragement, when all whirls in chaos, "I call up before me the mighty image of Man."

Man! It is as if a sun is born in my breast, and with its brilliant light beckons it slowly—forward!—and higher!—You tragic wonderful Man!

I see his proud form and brave, deep eyes, and in them, the rays of fearless Thought, that mighty power which in moments of tiredness creates gods, in epochs of robustness hurls them down.

He goes, watering with his heart's blood his hard, lonely proud path, and he creates out of this scalding blood—imperishable flowers of poesy...

The flowers of poesy, the heart's blood, and the exclamation marks marched on ... and on ... The whole scene of the reading is recorded by Tikhonov, who was present. At last Gorky stopped, and the group sat in quiet embarrassment. "This has a deep significance," finally commented the loyal Andreyev. Bunin, whose opinion Gorky very much wanted, refused to give one. Politely he asked how Gorky had come to write the poem. Gorky told them—the account is far better than the poem. Again he asked Bunin for a comment, again Bunin dodged. Finally Gorky said: "You're right: I still write crudely, Ivan Alexeyevich [Bunin] ... crudely ... And maybe ... I still don't write what I should ... Maybe ..."

When he "belonged to himself," at night, presumably, or en route by train somewhere, this winning extrovert, the friend and bringer together of all, the Santa for slum children, the Revolution's Falcon and Stormy Petrel, ebullient threnodist of "Man," fermenter of groups and enterprises, was writing poems of a different nature:

> Everywhere on earth Death spills
> The fat smell of those she kills.
> Life lies in her bony paws
> Like a sheep in an eagle's claws.

And:

> Our life is like a waiting at a station
> Before departure to the world of darkness.
> The less luggage that you carry with you
> The easier and more convenient for you.

Given his views and hopes, moral guidance had to be joined by moral action. The writing of those first two plays had been rudely interrupted by a stay in jail; this is the place for that story.

By early 1901, his dossier at the Department of Police was groaning with demerits: a trip to St. Petersburg to take part in a meeting to celebrate the liberation of the peasants, after which he behaved, in a restaurant, "in a revolutionary manner"; taking part in the demonstration of the students in front of the Kazan Cathedral (Cossacks rode into the crowd, and one of the intelligentsia got his head broken); writing a proclamation about it; finally, acquiring (together with Skitalets) a mimeograph machine, which was put to use in a Nizhni-Novgorod suburb to grind out proclamations to the workers.

That did it. Gorky was arrested in his home town, and again put into its bastille.

All kinds of people tried to help, including Stanislavsky. But it was Tolstoy who got him out. Old Jehovah Sabaoth had many faces, and it was as a kindly, sweet, graceful old member of the nobility that he spoke with Prince Oldenburgsky, the Tsar's brother-in-law; and in a similar spirit he wrote the acting Minister of Interior, Prince Svyatopolsk-Mirsky, who himself was both literate and a liberal.

Serene Highness: The wife of A. M. Peshkov (Gorky) and his friends have requested me to intercede with whomever I can for the prevention of his murder before his trial, and probably without trial, through being kept, while sick and consumptive, in the Nizhni-Novgorod jail which, I am told, is horrible in its anti-hygienic conditions. I know Gorky personally and love him not only as a gifted writer esteemed throughout Europe, but also as an intelligent, kind, and attractive man. Although I have not the pleasure of knowing you personally, I somehow believe that you will take an interest in the fate of Gorky and his family, and will come to their aid in as much as it is within your power.

Please do not disappoint my expectations...

Gorky was released in a month. His letter of thanks to Tolstoy shows both real gratitude and embarrassment.

A condition was that he had to get out of Nizhni Novgorod. A doctor's certificate was obtained (there were plenty of left-wing doctors) stating that his bad lung had flared up, and asking that he be permitted to choose the Crimea as his place of "exile." This was granted, and also a brief stop-over in Moscow on the way. But at this point the student generation (probably with an assist by the Social-Democratic Party) decided the time had come for a demonstration.

Boys and girls together converged on the Nizhni railway station, chanting protests, singing *"Dubinushka,"* the "Cudgel Song" (the Volga boat song, but to a fast new tempo, meaning protest), passing out leaflets on the platform and in the waiting room:

We have gathered here to accompany the famous and beloved writer M. Gorky and to express our bitter disapproval at his being sent out of his native city. He is being sent out only because he spoke the truth and pointed out the improper things in Russian life... We in Russia are forbidden to speak the truth, to say that the people live poorly... Officials rob and strip the people ... Students are beaten by nagaikas [Cossack whips] ...

The plans of the young enthusiasts had a truly Russian sweep. They would line the path of Gorky's exodus, from Nizhni through Moscow, and all the way to the Crimea, with demonstrations just like this at every whistle-stop. It would be a long triumphal procession.

Trepov, the Moscow police chief, here proved himself a man of decisive action. He had Gorky pulled off the Nizhni-Novgorod train (Ekaterina Pavlovna and little Maximka were allowed to go on to Moscow), and put him on another train which was switched to nearby Podolsk. When Gorky failed to arrive in Moscow, a delegation from the "Wednesdays," led by Chaliapin, set off for Podolsk. There in the Ladies' Room of the train station they found their hero.

They talked the guard into letting Gorky go to a nearby restaurant with them. The police sent the restaurant manager to make them all register (name, occupation, address, "Don't call us, we'll call you"), but Chaliapin signed grandly for all of them: "Artist of the Imperial Theatre"; while police agents busily went through their fur coats which were heaped on chairs in the next booth. A German visitor, translator of Gorky's works, was with the "Wednesdays" group, and protested when he saw this going on, but they assured him it was normal procedure in Russia.

When they all got back to the station, says Teleshov, the city of Podolsk was out in force. The "Wednesdays" group, including their Artist of the Imperial Theatre and Gorky, were led back into the Ladies' Room, where they "felt uncomfortable," until the Moscow–Sevastopol express came in, on which was Gorky's family. He was pushed on, had just time to yell to all of Podolsk and the faithful delegates of the "Wednesdays": "Comrades! We'll soon all call each other 'You' " (the familiar *tih* of pals, instead of the formal *vih*), and the train took off, nonstop and at top speed for the Crimea.

Such was the mood; such the uneasy situation of "gentlemanly" repression; such Gorky's fame, the image he represented.

In the Crimea were Chekhov and Tolstoy. There began, for the rest of that year, the deepest part of the relationship, from which emerged, many years later, most of the splendid pages of Gorky's "Recollections."

The friendship with Tolstoy, which now became a fact, was the achievement for Gorky of a dream, and like all dreams it could not stand examination without becoming something else—wonderful, precious, to be mourned long after, but not a way of life, and not a salvation.

He had come looking for a saint, and humility (as Grandma's ballads had made clear) was the first of the saintly virtues. He found a most complicated and arrogant man. This arrogance was rank impiousness. And further findings were even more drastic. They are discussed in a later chapter of this study, as one of the immortal works of literature; for Gorky was able to bring himself to shape them, and was capable of shaping them into a magnificent essay, only after many years.

As for Tolstoy, he looked in Gorky for the idealized peasant, God-loving, God-fearing, and found a flailing rebel, prudish, penetrating, spouting up bits of modern weltschmerz, his own and culled from the Goncourts, Balzac, Nietzsche, Gogol, Baudelaire, Heine, Verlaine, together with a heretical reading of the Old Testament, the Testaments of Christ, and all kinds of other testaments which the great old man didn't know or would like to have ignored... writing turgid prose in which beat a new kind of bird that the old wizard was too sharp not to spot but which threatened the ruin of his own private Establishment... And yet, he was inwardly convinced, essentially that God-loving, God-fearing peasant was there, and this tantalized and baffled him...

Like Japanese wrestlers they circled the bristling theme of God and its twin, Death. (Until Gorky came, it had been Tolstoy's private preserve.) The penetrating, fascinated regard Gorky bent on Tolstoy was too knowing, he saw too much—he was a "spy" (this the old man himself called him) into Tolstoy's relations with the eternal.

"Sometimes it seemed to me," Gorky wrote (he kept notes of their talks, and this infuriated the master), "that the old wizard played with death, flirted with her, and tried somehow to fool her: I'm not afraid of you, I love you, I await you. And all the time he peers at her with his little sharp eyes, demanding: and what are you like? And what comes after you, what further? Will you destroy me entirely, or will something remain that will live?"

This kind of spying was outrageous!

The old wizard hit back. He told Gorky "The Lower Depths" was no good (Gorky read it to him, and Tolstoy was especially displeased with the character of Luka—who was partly Tolstoy himself). "Foma Gordeyev" was no good. All Gorky's characters were invented, all his emotions were false to life. Gorky should write only things like "Goltva Fair" —simple and truthful. ("Goltva Fair" was a real peasant pastiche: a scene at a village market, charming and hearty vignettes of Ukrainian peasants, Jews, gypsies, trafficking, striking bargains, swapping horses, getting the better of one another, complete with drinking and singing—a Brueghel-esque picture, the kind Brueghel did when the night demons let him alone.) Oh, how Tolstoy would have liked Gorky to leave off yearning for the complex and eternal. He was not only poaching; he was contradicting Tolstoy's formula for man and man's happiness.

To his diary and friends, then and years after, the old wizard confided his angry uncertainties over Gorky:

Generally speaking, fame, popularity, is a dangerous thing. One of its harmful effects is that it prevents one from treating celebrities simply, Christian-like. Gorky, for instance, pleases me greatly as a man, yet I cannot treat him with complete sincerity: his fame does not let me. He seems to me to be not in his right place. And this fame is harmful for himself too ...

And again:

Read Gorky after dinner, and strange!—an unkind feeling toward him, with which I struggle ... He is like Nietzsche, a harmful writer ... A large talent, but absence of any religious convictions whatsoever ...

At times, however, he seemed to prefer Gorky even to Chekhov. "I see here now and then Chekhov, an utter atheist but a kindly soul, and Gorky who has considerably more *fond*, even though he is overpraised."

Shortly before his death, in 1909, he wrote in his diary: "In the evening I read Gorky. He knows the dark people ... But the psychology is absolutely arbitrary and unjustifiable, in the for the most part heroic feelings and thoughts which he lends his characters; besides, the environment is exceptionally immoral."(!) And, again: "...Finished reading Gorky. Nothing but imaginary, artificial, tremendous, heroic emotions ...But a big talent."

Once, with a sigh, he remarked: "I suppose he is saying what is on people's minds."

He couldn't really give up on Gorky. And once, during the time when they were seeing each other often, there was a parting scene that is one of the crowns of literature—written by Gorky, many years later—and of human relations. It begins with a sudden question by Tolstoy: "Why don't you believe in God?" Gorky's simple reply was: "I don't have faith,

Lev Nikolayevich." "That isn't true," Tolstoy told him. "You are a believer by nature." Then followed one of the most eloquent statements ever recorded, of the meaning of faith and of love. Then came Gorky's humble acknowledgment, within himself: "And I, not believing in God, look at him for some reason carefully, a little fearfully, I look and I think: 'This man—is godlike.' "

This is found at the very end of the letter Gorky wrote to Korolenko, and never finished or sent, when he heard of Tolstoy's death.

The paths were parting. By 1902 Gorky had moved too far into another field of gravitation—in his quest for a model, a formula, a salvation, an answer to all queries.

# CHAPTER 15

IN the fateful year of 1902 Gorky finally chose one from among the directions.

That incessant yearning for a law and a path had always underpinned all his fervent activity. Without it, he was prey to the preoccupation with death. Tolstoy's offer of a passive religion, in the spirit of the traditional gospels, he had rejected. He had seen Tolstoy at close range: the man was great, and a great writer, but his religion was concocted for others, and he himself did not believe. Chekhov's despair cleared the past: he had "killed realism." Ahead lay only a few choices: the religion of art, which the symbolists and pseudo mystics professed, which he not only considered shallow but from which by class snobbery he was excluded; or the road of the old Populists, now become the Social Revolutionaries (SR's); or the bolshevism of Lenin. There must have been an agonizing inner pause, while the furious many-sided outer activity spun on.

In a novel written many years later, Gorky would portray a young idealist who chose the road of the SR's, and died senselessly after throwing a bomb that destroyed a petty official. This was the young Gorky who might have taken the other fork of the road, motivated by his religious and over-idealistic bent, toward romantic terrorism, violent self-destruction. "There but for the grace of Lenin go I."

Lenin was in Paris, but his janissaries controlled the Moscow unit of the

Social-Democratic Party. They were enthusiastic, active people—enthusi-asm and hyperactivity were to be the marks of Lenin's party. Their pro-gram must have seemed, to Gorky, a constructive effort to educate and rouse the workers, dedicated and romantic enough, but without the des-perate suicidal heroics of the SR's. He had no way of knowing that these same people, conditioned by Lenin's insistence on a military-type, con-spiratorial party, an iron instrument of the will at its top, would soon create a tragic mold for bolshevik thinking. (They were already moving away from the main, more democratic, revolutionary stream.) He had not met Lenin; he wanted, at least, to meet Lenin's comrades.

The scene of his first meeting with the bolshevik "center" of Moscow has been preserved, and in remarkable detail—if we trust the veracity of Tikhonov (pen-name: Serebrov), a fresh and biting writer who was a companion of Gorky's then, and whose association with Gorky went on for many years. We can place the very hour of the fateful conversion, of the movement of Gorky's yearning, romantic imagination into the magnetic field of Lenin.

Ironically, that year—1902—was the very year in which for the first time some of the Social Democrats abroad, among them Martov, the future "menshevik" leader, became dimly, scarily aware that Lenin might not be the democratic leader they had hoped for. The eye opener was an experience at the Second Congress of the Social-Democratic Party. There Lenin, in a bit of brilliant and unscrupulous political infighting, pinned on his opposition the title "mensheviks"— "those in the minority" within the Social-Democratic movement—although they actually had a majority; and on his own faction the title "bolsheviks"—"those in the ma-jority"—despite their being actually in the minority. These reversed desig-nations would be vital: they probably damaged the cause of the more liberal revolutionaries beyond repair. They were accepted uneasily but gracefully by Martov and Lenin's other opponents, who hated to make a scene.

The rendezvous arranged between the wildly famous young writer, the self-born spirit of the Revolution, its Stormy Petrel, and the Moscow Committee of the Social Democratic Leninists, was to be at the office of a woman dentist. It was Gorky who asked for the meeting. (It was usu-ally he who sought out people: Korolenko...Chekhov...Tolstoy... Andreyev...Morozov...) He and Tikhonov drove there together, Gorky with his head and face wrapped in a shawl, a huge wad of cotton dressing stuffed against his cheek. He was simulating toothache, and also keeping his face covered; police agents customarily followed him, and wherever he appeared crowds formed; and the dentist's office was at a busy intersection.

They got out of the horse-drawn cab on the way, to look at notices posted on the wall of the Strastnoy Monastery, among which was one informing them that the rendezvous was safe. Then they told the cabby to drive on. They ascended to the office together; the cabby was told to wait. In the dentist's office, a group of young people awaited Gorky. His appearance caused grins; he looked like a tall bundled-up granny. Tikhonov was present, he says, throughout the first scene.

"Does your tooth hurt very much?" their hostess, the dentist, asked, smiling. She was a husky brunette, says Tikhonov, "as women dentists should be."

Gorky stumbled, "Well ... see ... the authorities have fenced me in so ... there's nothing for it ... they're tough!" He coughed nervously.

All stood around awkwardly. A tall, young intellectual, wearing pince-nez with a ribbon, came in, the head of the committee, late—naturally. He was reminded, after another awkward pause, that he had a speech to read, and he did so: "Alexey Maximovich! ... I have been asked ... that is, instructed ... to welcome you in the name of the Moscow Committee of the Social Democratic, Russian ... in a word, from the M.C. We all love you and await ... Ilyitch [Lenin] also loves ... awaits ..." He got more confused.

Gorky pressed his hand warmly, by now aware that these young zealots were more flustered than he was. He suggested they all sit. Conversation picked up. They opened a meeting of the committee, with Gorky as honored guest. The dentist-hostess took Tikhonov out, and they agreed she would guard the entrance while he would go down to his cab and act as lookout. When he got to the cab, the driver started to quiz him about who had come to the dentist. Tikhonov guessed the man was a police spy.

In an hour Gorky came staggering out, highly excited, coat undone, hat on the back of his head, his bandage and shawl hanging loose. Tikhonov chided him, and whispered he thought the cabby was a spy. Gorky only laughed: "You'll soon go crazy with spies! ... you ought to join the SR's!"

Then, as they drove on, he kept shouting: "Fine lads! Fine lads! Strong people! They know what they want! They want a lot. I bet they'll get it ... I can't tell you everything. Don't be hurt ... I gave my word."

No doubt thanks to the cabby, Gorky's visit to the dentist went duly into the police records, along with an exultant letter by one of the young "splendids" (code name: Natasha) to the Leninist Center in Paris just before the whole Moscow batch was arrested:

... He [Gorky] made on all of us a wonderful impression. Our meeting bore an almost official character. I was so happy to hear that his sympathy is all on our side. Of "Liberation" [the organ of Peter Struve's Liberals] he read only the first issue, and doesn't want to see trash like that any more, and he doesn't sympathize with the Socialist-Revolutionaries, the only publication he considers worthy of respect, talented and intelligent, is Iskra [Lenin's paper—the voice of his fraction of the Social-Democratic Party], and our organization he considers the strongest and most solid. He very much wants to get better acquainted with our direction, all our publications and our practical work, and since his sympathy is solely with us, he also wants to help us however he can: in the first place, of course, with money ...

So it began. Without knowing the content of Lenin's thoughts—any more than did the splendid lads and lasses themselves—the still-young yearner, in the midst of fame, turned to the group that seemed both bold and organized, less quixotic than the SR's, more active by far than the staid Liberals (who included so many of the condescending upper intelligentsia).

The desire to help, "in the first place, of course, with money," was gratified at once. His own funds, even as a successful writer, would hardly have gone far, though he turned these over too. But there was, as has been seen, among Gorky's multitude of curious friends the wealthy industrialist Savva Morozov, the frustrated chemist, a man searching for a something in life, and probably for power.

Before the end of that same year, Gorky had brought together Savva Morozov and Krassin, Lenin's "finance minister"—later, until he chose exile, the finance minister of the Soviet Union. Morozov pledged two thousand rubles a month to Lenin's faction; and this was to be a major part of the funds on which Lenin's Iskra was kept going. It was not all Morozov would do for the bolsheviks. But his relation with Gorky forms surely one of the strangest recorded pages of friendship. The now headlong Gorky found in Morozov the kind of gambler with life on whom his imagination could fasten (another barefoot bum but in a grandiose setting); while Morozov found in Gorky the path to his dangerous game, which made life livable.

"To the end of his life," writes Tikhonov, "Gorky preserved the capacity for falling in love with people who showed him something extraordinary. This enchantment with Savva was one of the strongest and longest."

It has already been seen how often Gorky's love for varied people expressed itself in match-making, bringing together people who ordinarily did not fit together: Skitalets and Bunin, the "Knowledge" bunch and Chaliapin, the Moscow Art Theatre and the barefoot bums, Tolstoy and Andreyev, Andreyev and the rustic priest of Arzamas, Teleshov and the slum kids of Nizhni Novgorod...

Now he brought together not only Morozov and the bolsheviks, but also Morozov and the Moscow Art Theatre. Morozov began to support both. In the Art Theatre he worked, too, in shirt sleeves, painting scenery; but he did more than that. Nemirovich-Danchenko said, "Morozov took on himself all the material worries, built us a theatre, helped create a 'comradeship of artists.'" Stanislavsky spoke of his selfless work, "without false ambition or personal advantage."

Many thought otherwise. They believed Morozov and Gorky had teamed to take over the Art Theatre. Tikhonov clears Gorky, but not Morozov.

It is hard to tell when Tikhonov is really quoting, when dramatizing in direct speech what he guessed, himself writing the story of Savva Morozov and Gorky. He portrayed Morozov as fantastically complex, a worthy partner for Gorky. But his complexity moved in the sign of furious ambition.

A man of practical affairs, who bid against the Americans and British on the world cotton market, with mines and factories in Moscow, the Urals, and south Russia, and a hydroelectric plant in the planning stage, he saw Russia's potential throttled by a stupid dynasty. He dreamed of vast possibilities. His raging heart wanted power. Casting about, he saw the chance of buying not only the Moscow Art Theatre but something far more powerful, the bolshevik movement of Lenin. To this Gorky was his entrée.

"Power!" Tikhonov has him roar. "I need power! I am a boss. I have the best factory in Europe!...Do you know what that means?—Russia!...Turkey!...Persia!...The East!..." He is cynical about the bolsheviks, but is convinced Russia is a land of extremes, its people instinctively following extremists.

A wild conversation in Morozov's apartment, between the industrialist and Gorky, is "reproduced" by Tikhonov in direct quotes, with himself allegedly sitting in the next room until he feels he must leave.

Gorky says he has been told, by the merchant Bugrov, that Morozov has boasted of "buying the Revolution."

"He lies. Whom do you believe? The merchants aren't a fraternity, they're a pack of wolves."

Gorky says, "Strange . . . your deeds are clear, but your thoughts you hide from me. Tell me finally, straight, what do you want from the Revolution?"

Morozov replies, "A strong power and order."

"For this there's the Autocracy."

"It's rotted through."

"Then go to the Liberals."

"Whelps. They can't even bark . . . Russia can only be rebuilt from below."

Gorky (reports Tikhonov) strokes his mustache, wants to smile, thinks better of it.

"The Revolution's a dangerous thing," he warns Morozov. "It can slug you on the temple."

"My workers love me."

"For what, may I ask?"

"I'm better to them than the others."

"Not much."

Then Gorky asks him, "And what will you do with them after the Revolution?"

"I'll issue stock. I'll interest them in profits."

Gorky slams his wooden cigaret case down on the table.

"Bunk! Stupid ravings of Robert Owen!"

"He wasn't such a dumb industrialist," Morozov yells, but Gorky's bass shouts over his voice:

"But he ended stupidly! A spiritualist!"

"Spiritualism won't take me," shouts Morozov. "I'm an Old Believer."

Morozov is wandering in a fury about the dark room, stumbling against furniture. Gorky smiles—"he knew how to smile like a woman," adds Tikhonov—and then says: "Crazy guy! What did you get mad for?"

Morozov sits down, they pour another glass of wine. Morozov asks, "Do 'yours' need money? For a linotype? You've got another split going? Well, let Krassin send Uncle Misha, but not to my house, to the office . . ."

They argue again. Morozov pulls out a revolver, offers it to Gorky; then, no, he decides, he'll keep it. "When the time comes, I'll use it myself." The air of inevitable catastrophe was with Morozov always.

At this point Tikhonov—this may be all approximate fact or, more likely, informed fancy—leaves quietly from the next room. When he returns briefly, he sees through the open door Gorky pleading with Morozov, palms spread on his chest, neck thrust forward:

"Savushka. Understand. You're on the brink . . . You've got to get rid of the factory! I'm afraid for you."

However fanciful the scene, Gorky was surely gambling with his career in those days; and Morozov was staking three generations of a family business empire, and his life too, as it turned out.

On Morozov's desk were the autographed photographs of two men: Sergey Witte, the prime minister who wanted to make a modern capitalist state of Russia, and Maxim Gorky. He kept a Circassian bodyguard, complete with saber and shako. He haggled with cab drivers over twenty kopecks, then thrust three-ruble tips into their hands. A coffee-ring sent by Stanislavsky as a birthday present he hung around his neck, powdered sugar shaking off on the Persian rug. He employed fifteen thousand workers. He dealt on the market conservatively, because, he said, the workers and their families depended on him. He baited the mensheviks and the SR's with the name of Lenin, and told Krassin he was baiting his future friends; as for Lenin, he told the startled Krassin, to whom he was handing over big money for Lenin, "It's necessary to be friends with one's enemies."

Gorky insisted on a world where everything came full circle. No couples were too odd to match. He matched Savva Morozov with the Art Theatre, then with the bolsheviks, then took him around to Chekhov. And friends, in a curious way, the two became.

Morozov even took Chekhov out to his Ural plant for a holiday. (He had given both Krassin and Tikhonov jobs there.) Chekhov spent five days, during which he and Morozov hardly spoke, then his tuberculosis took a bad turn and he left.

"He scurries before the Revolution, like a devil before the dawn," said Chekhov of Morozov.

"He's smart, and talented, but in politics he's a hick doctor," said Morozov of Chekhov.

"Rich merchants always smell like a barber shop," said Chekhov of Morozov.

"He got his fame late, that's why he's a pessimist," said Morozov of Chekhov.

"If he has his way, he'll buy the whole intelligentsia for a plaything," said Chekhov.

"With his talent, if he only had direction..." wistfully said Morozov.

Gorky and Morozov together put on a drive to have a school in the Crimea named for Chekhov. When Chekhov learned the school's curriculum would include religion and prayers, he forbade them to bestow on him this honor. Later, when Chekhov had a bad relapse, it was Morozov who arranged his transportation to a sanatorium in Perm.

Morozov told Gorky how as a child he got the dirty shirt off the back of his more favored brother, whenever the brother graduated to a clean shirt. The grandfather had been a slave, and after emancipation built the factory. The father amassed further power. Savva Morozov now headed the dynasty, with the consent of the rest of the family.

He twitted Gorky for writing "Foma Gordeyev," which was really about the meschanye though it claimed to be about merchants—and not about *his* family, the true big Russian merchantry. Gorky said he was planning such a book—he had already told its story to Tolstoy, and Tolstoy had exclaimed: "You must write it!" He even had a name picked—"The Artamanovs."

(When he finally wrote it, more than twenty years later, the rise of a family like the Morozovs is there, but Savva himself is missing. Savva went too deep, within Gorky; he was one of his deep, mysterious symbols—quicksilver, not to be contained in what was supposed to be a "realistic" book.)

In the words of Teleshov, "the breath of the Stormy Petrel was in the air, and 1905 was approaching." Gorky's fame was high, his emotional commitments deep, his energy enormous.

Besides the "Knowledge" collections, he was editing, together with Maria Feodorovna Andreyeva, a bolshevik-line magazine. Andreyeva, a pretty and lively brunette, was the actress who had played poor, sweet Natasha, in the first staging of "The Lower Depths." The wife of a state councilor (an admiral, retired), and the daughter of a general, she had won Gorky, though probably he thought he won her, in 1901, during his trips to Moscow in connection with rehearsals for his first two plays and for the "Wednesdays."

His separation from Ekaterina Pavlovna, that tough, bright, petite, revolutionary girl, whom he called "an enraged canary," proved no joke; she broke down. His letters to her in this period range from the solicitous to the downright distraught. He was running with the revolutionary wave, the wave of self-expression. He was everywhere and everything; they would always be friends; he considered her a mother, a dear comrade. There was no formal divorce or separation; so of course there was no formal remarriage to Andreyeva. These were hypocritical sanctimonies of an obsolete and rotten order.

There is a flaming, hysterical quality to his whole life during these years, rising to the climax of 1905.


In that year, when a bolshevik girl could write about him to Lenin that "his sympathy is all on our side," Gorky started beating out a series of "social" plays. They were meant to be of service to the bolshevik cause. All are much like *Meschanye* which really stated more truthfully his inner anger at life.

He must have been carried away by the idea of illustrating the bolshevik thesis of the decadence and crumbling of the old order. But psychologically, it seems clear, these plays were largely a means of expelling his own inner maze, his desperate feelings. Striking at the vulgarity, weakness, unhappiness of the middle classes and intelligentsia was always a way for him to externalize, naïvely enough, the misery and yearning in his own nature—like a medieval craftsman crowding devils all over the walls of a cathedral, to get rid of them inside himself.

The first and best of these plays, "Summer Folk," is modelled clearly on Chekhov's "Cherry Orchard," but without Chekhov's character-magic. It centers on those who have entered the intelligentsia from below, and now own country "dachas" and waste their time on cards, idle talk, and love-making. "It is always twilight in men's souls," says one. "Life must be adorned," yawns another. "We just talk and talk without doing anything," says a third.

The chant of beggars intrudes: "A crust, good people, in the name of Christ..." One of the summer folk chases the beggars away.

"I have a feeling," says another of them, "that soon—sooner than we think—a different sort of people—brave, strong people—will take things over and sweep us away like refuse." This ominous vision, of alienation being ended by a ruthless outer force—"brave strong people," new masters of life—somehow bedeviled Gorky. It was prophetic.

Then one of the women suddenly exclaims:

We ought to be different—all of us. We're the children of cooks and laundresses, of wholesome working people, and we ought to be different ... These ties ought to fill us with a desire to improve and brighten and expand the lives of those, our kith and kin, who sweat in darkness and dirt from morning to night. Not for pity of them, not for charity's sake, should we seek to improve life, but for our own sakes, to escape an accursed isolation ... They sent us ahead to find a road leading to a better life for all; we went ahead and got lost ...

Here Gorky's play fills for a moment with his native moral poetry. But he had vowed to denounce these people, as part of his service to the cause; he had to make them as vacuous as possible again. Flicking a cigaret ash, one of the summer folk winds up the play: "It's all so unimportant, my friend. Everything. People are so evil. Pour me a glass of wine. So utterly meaningless, my friend."

The plays that followed deal dutifully with "other strata of the bourgeoisie," though with "new people" (indefinite but clearly honest workers) starting to appear. All are much like "Summer Folk," with less poetry, more tedium. Meant as class drama, social realism, all actually express mainly an inner rage and conflict, and the frantic desire to serve a Cause.

At this time, too, he wrote a labored allegory. It told, more succinctly than do the plays, Gorky's state of mind, his effort to divide the world into Good and Evil along the lines of Lenin, rejecting the great human in-between.

Red (Good) and Black (Evil) are fighting for the world. Red, blazing ever more brightly, like the sparks from bright fires of the future, wants "everything for everybody." Between them, abjectly and shamefully, scurries Gray, desiring only safety and comfort, ready to serve anybody, usually ending up by serving Black. Gray is "the eternal enemy of everything bright and bold."

On this particular myth of Gorky's some Soviet critics have fastened, as evidence that he was the same kind of man as Lenin, a man of extremes, ready to excommunicate and destroy the liberal, the moderate man of good will, even the wavering too-soft Communist. It is an effort to make two very dissimilar images seem alike.

The quaint and fanatic idea that Grayness (compromise, indecisiveness, moderation) should be hated even more than Blackness (that which is evil), one of Lenin's unfortunate legacies, was truly a curse to the whole revolutionary movement. Untold errors and tragedy stemmed from this false and romantic logic: that he who is not all the way with me is against me and worse than the worst of those against me. Lenin, and especially his true followers, were even capable of adding: he deserves to be killed.

Gorky was, in thought but even then not in deed, on the fringe of this hysterical notion for not quite five years, beginning about the time of that visit to the dentist's. The evidence of his life, and of that in his work which lives, is a disproof of the whole notion.

## CHAPTER 16

THE year 1905, "with the breath of the Stormy Petrel," was indeed approaching. To chronic social injustice was now added the stress of Witte's stepped-up industrialization. The disaffection of the thinking and idealistic part of Russia was nearly complete. Nicholas II's regime turned to scapegoats: the Jews.

"Crowded like herring within the restricted Pale of Settlement," says a scholar who knew the old Russia, "ousted from all productive occupations, limited in educational opportunities, abused and insulted in every way, the Jewish population naturally furnished a considerable proportion of the malcontents who saw their salvation in the overthrow of the Autocracy." Said the holy Tsar of the holy country, "The Jews deserve a lesson"; and "spontaneous" pogroms—the looting and killing of Jews by mobs—were organized by the ministry of the interior ... in Kishinev, then Gomel, Zhitomir, Simferopol, Bialostok, Odessa ... Babies were smashed at curbs, pregnant women ripped open and stuffed with feathers, nails driven into old men's nostrils.

Gorky belonged to the first generation in Russian history to break, in any number, with anti-Semitism. Hatred of Jews and discrimination against them were integral to the Tsarist government, the state church, and the traditional Russian mentality. The Jews were as much a touchstone in Russia as Negroes are in the American South today.

A story, "The Pogrom," written by Gorky for the benefit of the Kishinev victims, is probably the first unequivocal literary work in defense of Jews by a major Russian writer. He also wrote an article putting the real blame for Kishinev on bigoted newspapermen who poisoned the minds of readers. The Right-Wing press replied that it was Gorky's barefoot bums—his Chelkashes and Konovalovs—who actually carried out the pogroms. Both were right.

Gorky himself was straight on this issue all his life. Tolstoy and Chekhov were too; but he went beyond them in the excruciating suffering and shame that he felt at anti-Semitism. Even today, the record of his opposition to anti-Semitism makes it harder for anti-Semitism to become a decisive force in Soviet Russia.

Finding scapegoats in 1903 did not help the Tsar's Russia. The crisis of the moribund backward land only deepened. A gamble for foreign expansion, into Manchuria and Korea, brought war with Japan. Catastrophe —loss of the Russian fleet, of the Manchurian foothold, half of Sakhalin, world prestige—further disorganized the country. The years of 1904 and 1905 saw hunger, strikes, peasant riots, assassinations of officials by the SR's, uprisings in army and navy including the historic mutiny of the Black Sea cruiser *Potemkin*. A sense of coming apocalypse made many see visions in the sky. This supernatural sense would hang over Russia, intermittently, henceforth.

The very first scene of the first Russian Revolution, that of 1905, is largely the story of another of Gorky's strange friendships.

Workers of the Putilov and other munitions factories of St. Petersburg struck in January 1905. They prepared to march to the Winter Palace with a petition to the Tsar outlining grievances and asking for a constituent assembly:

These, Sire, are our main wants, with which we have come to Thee. Swear to order them fulfilled, and Thou wilt make Russia happy and glorious, and Thy name will be stamped in our hearts and the hearts of our descendants for eternity. But if Thou wilt not grant, wilt not respond to our prayer, we shall die here on this square in front of the Palace. We have no other place to go, and no use in going anywhere else. We have only two roads: either to freedom and happiness, or to our graves.

The procession had been organized by Zubatov, head of the Department of Police, who had got the happy notion of encouraging workers to form "official" unions so as to divert them from the revolutionary political ones. A priest in the service of the department, Georgy Gapon, was assigned to lead the procession; this he did. But this small and tense man was carried away, in the course of his duties, by the cause of the workers. How he met Gorky is not known; but Gorky was likely to meet anyone. These two men, Gapon and Gorky, were probably the key organizers of the great procession.

The march would end in a slaughter known as Bloody Sunday—and the history of the Revolution and the start of the fall of the Romanovs is usually reckoned from that date.

On that Sunday, January 22, 1905, as the workers, their wives and children prepared to march, a delegation of intellectuals—apparently organized by Gorky—went to see Svyatopolsk-Mirsky, now Minister of Interior, to get him to prevent an armed clash. He dodged them, being under fire at court as too liberal. Gorky's apartment became headquarters for Gapon, his priestly sidekicks, workers, revolutionaries, police agents and provocateurs, stray writers and intellectuals.

The marchers, an impressive procession, complete with crosses, holy images, portraits of the Tsar and his Tsarina, and babes in arms, approached the Winter Palace, and were faced by troops. The usual mix-up in orders took place, the soldiers fired, the Cossack cavalry charged, the snow was speckled with bodies and blood. It has been said often, not only by Gorky, that that volley, and that cavalry charge, destroyed for the Russian workers the Tsar's image.

The remnants of the procession fled, and Gapon ran to Gorky's apartment. Gapon was now a young man shocked into protest way out of line with anything dreamed of by Zubatov. The apartment was full of a motley assemblage of friends of Gorky, including Savva Morozov. Gorky would paint in his own slightly masked portrait, on that occasion, in a late novel: a tall, red-haired writer, smoking nervously. He gave Gapon a haircut, got him civilian clothes instead of his priest's robe, and took him to a meeting he had organized for that night. Gorky himself introduced the little priest. An onlooker described Gapon as he spoke, his pale face showing intense suffering, eyes burning, voice trembling. He read a letter he had composed to the workers: "Dear blood-welded brothers..." He rained curses on the Tsar, called on the workers to join the open revolutionary struggle.

The letter had been written on the spot, while the meeting was starting, by Gorky.

(Gapon, unlike many of Gorky's pals, then disappeared from Gorky's life, and from everybody else's. Many years later, after the bolshevik Revolution, he begged to be admitted into Soviet Russia; he got his wish, was quickly and secretly tried, and shot.)

Two days after Bloody Sunday Gorky was arrested, and put in the Peter-and-Paul Fortress of St. Petersburg, in the Trubetskoy Bastion—where had been kept the Decembrists, Bakunin, Chernyshevsky, Pisarev, and other Populists and revolutionaries. At noon the tower clock chimed a Byzantine hymn. (Twelve years later, chiming the "Internationale," the tower would house other occupants.)

The criminal acts charged against him included writing a declaration describing Nicholas II as a murderer and calling for "united struggle against the Autocracy"; issuing a proclamation calling on army officers to take off their uniforms and put down their arms; and, prior to Bloody Sunday, collecting funds for rifles, pistols and ammunition.

The government wanted a secret trial, Gorky's lawyers wanted it public. The support that came in from Western Europe was fantastic. A message of sympathy from Paris bore the names of the mathematician Poincaré, of Huysmans, Curie, Anatole France, Rodin, and even Briand. A society that included Clemenceau circulated a protest against Gorky's imprisonment. The Goethe Association in Germany and the Berlin *Tageblatt* circulated a release petition, signed by men like Hauptmann and Sudermann. Deputies of the Italian parliament asked their government to use its good offices "to save the life of Maxim Gorky." Czechs, led by Masaryk, met in Prague to "denounce the inhuman treatment and slaughter of peaceful citizens. Long live Maxim Gorky. Down with Tsarism!"

Only a few were so caddish as to point out that Gorky had been put in jail not for his art but for political activities. The German writer, Harden, enviously compared the relative lenience of the autocracy, which "permitted the young Gorky to sing his Songs of the Stormy Petrel undisturbed," with Prussian repression of all expression. But these carpers were overwhelmed.

The West saved him. "The Gorky case proved too messy a business at a time when official Russia was in dire need of financial and moral support from the outside world." The foreign press was assured he would not be shot or hanged. Then came a petition to free him on medical grounds (the ever-convenient tubercular process). Savva Morozov, on a weekend, with the banks closed, managed to scrape up ten thousand rubles bail. He was sprung.

It was while in the Trubetskoy Bastion that Gorky wrote "Children of the Sun," the only major work of those bolshevik-oriented years that was not a formula, and better than mediocre. Jail probably gave him a respite from the dazed emotional pace, and a chance to consider.

As for Savva Morozov, from this point on the bizarre and strong attachment faded, and its history is lost in tangled events and emotions. When he raised bail for Gorky, he was already in trouble. "His" revolution was starting, and soon "his" workers struck. His officials used violence, and Gorky refused to see him—a repudiation. His outraged family ganged up, and he was squeezed out of his empire, on grounds of psychological unbalance. "I've fallen between two stools!" he cried to Tikhonov.

In Geneva, Morozov still apparently turned over one more pile of money to Krassin. Then, after taking out a huge life insurance policy and naming the bolshevik faction as the beneficiary, he traced the outline of his heart on his skin with a chemical pencil, put that same Browning revolver he had shown Gorky against the outline's center, and fired. Gorky, as a youth, had messed up his suicide try; this man proved a professional at suicide.


While in Trubetskoy Bastion, Gorky petitioned the fortress' commandant to be permitted to write "a comedy." Permission was granted. He wrote the play, "Children of the Sun," there, in a month. As promised, he submitted it to the commandant, in the notebooks in which it was written; and as promised, these were delivered to him when, bail having been raised, he was released. Quaint were the rules of chivalry in that dim day.

He could never invent characters, and the same characters are here, as always, in his sorrowful, angry mind: again the mamma's boy afraid to leave the family nest; again the woman too idealistic and also stuck to the family . . . again the same cast. The rancor and pain he portrays was the rancor and pain he felt at the whole world.

But there is a lighter touch, and a clearer gaze. For one thing, in this play about the intelligentsia—for they are the "children of the sun"—love is allowed to hold its own against hate. And so, in at least one great moment, the play rises to a lyricism he seldom before, or after, attained.

"Fear of death," says Pavel (Paul), one of the men, "that's what hinders

people from being bold, beautiful, free people ... It frightens their reason ... But we, children of the sun, of the bright source of life, ... we
will conquer the dark fear of death. We are—children of the sun. It burns
in our blood, it is what gives birth to proud, flaming thoughts ... It is
the ocean of energy, loveliness and joy...!"

Liza: "Pavel, that's fine! Children of the sun ... That means—I too? ...
Say quickly, Pavel—yes? I too? ..."

Pavel: "Yes, yes! You too. All people!"

Liza then proclaims (one stanza the rise, one the despair, of her vision):

> On mighty glittering wings
> The eagle to heaven flies.
> Oh if only I could, I too,
> Like an eagle to heaven rise!
>
> But fruitless are my strivings,
> I, a daughter of sorrowful earth,
> And too long have these my soul's wings
> Trailed in the dust and in dirt ...

But at this point Vagin, who has been listening, suddenly breaks in with
the upswooping reply:

> Like sparks in the black smoke billow
> Of this life, we're alone—utterly!
> But we are its seeds of the future!
> We are fires of that which will be!
>
> In friendship we serve the bright temple
> Of freedom—where truth, beauty glow—
> So that into a proud flaming eagle
> Every poor blind mole may grow!

It is a duet fit for a fine opera, a valedictory to the martyr-populists,
and all the intelligentsia who sacrificed themselves or fell unheeded.

It also places the young Gorky where he belongs, among the purest
idealists. His "bright temple" is strangely like the famous one of Socrates,
which was topped by the cornice triangle of Virtue, Truth, and Beauty,
which are one. In Gorky's case, Freedom has replaced Virtue as the apex.
(Given Freedom, Virtue is assured!)

One more thing of interest: the "people," who surround the children
of the sun, are shown as primitive, even savage, and their power to destroy

the too tender intelligentsia is not necessarily a glorious power. There is
no false glorification, at least there was none as the play was given on the
Moscow stage in 1962. There was poetry, and an honest try at grappling
with life.


The Revolution was on, and the counter-revolution was on. The Tsar,
at Witte's urging and in Witte's wording, granted a constitution. The
strikes ended, and then began officially organized massacres of Jews, students, and others suspected of radicalism. Gorky was living with Maria
Feodorovna Andreyeva, his apartment guarded by two youths with revolvers in their hands. "They thought this up," he explained to Teleshov,
who visited him; he tossed his head, diffidently.

The fascist Black Hundreds killed a revolutionary, Bauman, at the celebration of the October manifesto granting a constitution. Gorky described
to Kaun the funeral held for Bauman, as he watched from his Moscow
apartment. "All Moscow marched after the coffin ... Here glimmers the
white head of Stanislavsky; there towers Chaliapin with his broad nostrils;
there is the painter Serov, there is Bryusov." It must have been an honor
roll of the thinkers, dreamers, intelligentsia; and the watchers watched
with high hopes. This must have been a high, if unrealistic, point of
Gorky's emotional certainty; one foot in the world of the generally idealistic marchers, one in Lenin's conspiratorial world, both worlds moving
forward on seemingly parallel tracks, full of directed energy, exhilaration,
determination ... the two sides of a single vision. It would never be that
way again.

Chaliapin rushed in, as Gorky still stood at the window; the Black
Hundreds had returned to the attack after the funeral procession ended,
and fighting was going on outside. Chaliapin was "ecstatic, dishevelled,
his hat way back on his head ... 'Ah, Alexey, do you see how fine it is,
never has there been anything so fine, do you understand? But no, you
could not understand that! Think: we have freedom, equality! Ah, my
God, how remarkable it is!' "

"Suddenly," Gorky added, "a volley crashed at the window panes, and
bits of glass showered all around us."

In December 1905, the St. Petersburg Soviet, under Trotsky, was making its stand. Barricades were raised, in both St. Petersburg and Moscow.
The Tsar's troops, including the Cossacks and the famous Semyenovsky
guard regiment, stayed loyal; artillery broke the revolt. Gorky was in-

volved in organizing support for the Moscow barricades. His room in St. Petersburg was searched. He moved fast, to Finland. Helsingfors students met him with: "Long live the free people of Finland!" He made speeches recklessly. Arrest was near. He got out of Russia.

His fame had moved ahead of him into the West. A Gorky evening was organized in Berlin. Gorky read "The Stormy Petrel" and "The Falcon." Rudolph Schildkraut read from Gorky's stories; Kachalov, from the Art Theatre, read Gorky's "Goltva Fair." At intermission, excited German Social Democrats, headed by Liebknecht and Kautsky, trooped backstage to offer their admiration.

"When Gorky was reading his Stormy Petrel," wrote Kachalov in his memoirs, "the Crown Prince could be seen watching with keen attention from the box nearest the stage; in the depth of the box shimmered the monocles, epaulets, tinselled collars of his resplendent suite."

Next on the triumphal route: the United States.


# CHAPTER 17


ALL through this phase of Gorky's life, including the trip to America, one gets the sense, truly, of a sea bird, say, a stormy petrel, flapping and hysterically flying, shrieking as if to call up elemental forces, or perhaps in fascinated horror over the illusion (which it knows is illusion) that these forces rising behind it are the result of its frantic flight and its frantic crying.

One also gets the sense, as the ocean liner plows the waves to America, bearing Gorky and his Maria Feodorovna, a Free Man and a Free Woman, that his flight is outracing time: outracing the understanding of people the world over as to what was really possible and likely in Russia, and of what was really happening in its revolutionary movement; that such understanding, the painful work of experience and thought, moves like slow ripples, concentric circles in the water, after the stones of events and personalities are dropped, while the keyed-up bird, the stormy petrel, races far ahead of the ripples. It is an experience in relativity of time.

For Lenin had already split the revolutionary movement, into "hards" and "softs"—the former group (Lenin's) staking all on a tough, conspiratorial elite of professional revolutionaries, who would manipulate the "unconscious" masses, the other putting its hopes on the rising "consciousness" of the masses themselves, with semiprofessional revolutionaries to be the revolution's midwife.

All agreed, as did liberals too, on the need to get rid of the stultifying Autocrat, but some dreamed of replacing him with constitutional democracy, while others (the hards) were already pioneering, often without being aware, the road of modern totalitarianism.

The split was final, and full of fate. Chaliapin's ecstatic outcry—"Alexey, do you see how fine it is, never has anything been so fine, do you understand? ... Think: we have freedom, equality!"—was already naïve baby talk, but of this Gorky had no idea, and neither did Maria Feodorovna. On their charmed ship, the *Kaiser Wilhelm der Grosse*, they approached the Statue of Liberty, entrance to golden America, where hotels did a thriving business in informal sex while any *known* sex informality was taboo.

America waited with open arms. "Revolution" was then not at all a dirty word. In patriotic American homes, in political circles, among influential business men, as well as among intellectuals, there was every sympathy with the Russian Revolution—it was far away, and very romantic, and so Russian. Mark Twain had even been telling Americans that our own country had begun through revolution, and that made everybody feel good.

A young American writer, Ernest Poole, conveyed what sounds like the authentic feeling of the time: "In Princeton I had hungrily read in translation Turgenev, Tolstoi, Dostoyevski, Gogol, Gorki, and other great Slav realists, and also American George Kennan's books on the early Russian revolutionists, books widely read all over our land."

When Red Sunday took place, Poole (like thousands of patriotic Americans) "hungrily" read the news stories, and Gorky's long dramatic wire to the Hearst papers, declaring: "The Russian Revolution has begun."

Meantime, in Russia, all factions had agreed that Gorky, then in Germany, should be the emissary of the Revolution to America. The bolsheviks, however, were the best infighters; Krassin could outmaneuver any half-dozen mensheviks or SR's. Besides, Gorky's heart was then, as has been seen, with the bolsheviks. ("Ilyitch awaits you ...") He had finally met Lenin, a shy, brief, happy meeting in a St. Petersburg apartment, in 1905. He had planned to make this man his next idol and now was following through.

So it was as an emissary of the bolsheviks, to raise money specifically for them, that Gorky came to America. That was fine with the American liberals who prepared to give him a triumphal welcome; they couldn't tell bolsheviks from mensheviks, Struve from Lenin, Breshkovskaya from Krupskaya, Gorky from Dostoyevsky—all were romantic Russian idealists and revolutionaries, prophets and fighters for democracy in that strange, wonderful, despotically ruled land.

In New York, Poole had helped organize the A Club, a group of writers, "liberals and radicals"; Jack London and Upton Sinclair were occasional visitors. Mark Twain, at the height of grizzled fame and influence, lived nearby, "and often came in to drawl out stories before our hearth through the smoke of his cigar."

From a Russian émigré—a Zinovy Peshkov, who was an "adopted son" of Gorky's, and of whom more later—Poole learned in advance of Gorky's coming. Quickly an American committee was formed, including Mark Twain, William Dean Howells, Jane Addams, Arthur Brisbane (Hearst's editorial genius, the wise old man of *Citizen Kane*), S. S. McClure, the magazine publisher, Robert Collier, owner of *Collier's*, Finley Peter Dunne (Mr. Dooley, over whose mordant political wit newspaper readers chuckled), and others. Twain agreed to be chairman. He and Howells were the keys to the committee's strength.

The Gorky movement was to be launched with a stag dinner at the A Club the night after his landing. Later that week a bigger dinner would be given by Gaylord Wilshire, owner-editor of the socialist *Wilshire's Magazine*, with H. G. Wells, Edwin Markham, Charles Beard, Franklin Giddings and John Spargo among the guests. Then there would be receptions and mass meetings all over the country, "for, in the ten years since his first success," Poole writes, "Gorki's novels, short stories and plays had sold well in translations all over our land, and to millions of Americans his name had become a symbol of the cause of Russian freedom then so popular over here."

It was even rumored that Gorky would be invited to the White House; his American friends dreamed of a million-dollar campaign for the Revolution.

The meeting of Twain and Gorky, of course, would be the dramatic center. It couldn't help being: the poet of nature of the American interior, creator of the spirit of American freedom in nature, so nostalgically loved, Huckleberry Finn; and the poet of nature of the Russian interior, creator of barefoot Russian Huck Finns, himself a Russian Huck Finn, bard of the coming Russian freedom, who reproduced vicariously for many

Americans the freedom in nature Huck stood for; the one-time apprentice pilot on a Mississippi paddle wheeler, and the one-time apprentice (really a mess boy) on a Volga paddle wheeler, bringing the two great rivers symbolically together. The old rebel, now an honored sage, and the young rebel who might be his spiritual son. A meeting loaded with implications of deepest emotion.

Then one of the welcoming committee got a telephone call, and with it a tingle of apprehension. It was from a friendly Russian banker in Washington. He had heard—the Tsarist embassy was frantically spreading the word—that Maria Feodorovna Andreyeva was with Gorky. "You know," he said—and the ear of the man at the other end of the call must suddenly have got very warm against the earphone—"that Gorky is coming with Mme. Andreyeva as his wife, whereas Gorky has a wife and a child in Russia. He is not divorced from his first wife, and in American terms his present wife is nothing but his mistress."

Awful word! "We saw at once what a blunder it was," writes Poole. "Puritanism was still going so strong that our dream of a million-dollar campaign might all come to nothing if the story should be played up the way the Russian embassy hoped."

As Gorky's ship entered the harbor, a band of his admirers seized a revenue cutter, raced to the ship at Quarantine, and hastily—through a Russian exile in the group—warned the bolshevik manager of Gorky's tour, Burenin. Burenin conveyed this to Gorky. His new American friends were urging that Maria Feodorovna, instead of going with Gorky to the hotel where Wilshire had reserved rooms, go at first to the home of John Martin, an English friend, on Staten Island. Gorky refused.

It seems that he and Andreyeva had been, indeed, dimly aware of a problem—or at least she was—and they had taken separate cabins on the crossing. But this was as far as Gorky would go. To treat a woman, *his* woman, so shoddily, and for *him* to stoop to hypcrisy—No. "In vain we declared our sense of outrage at the exposure being planned, but argued that the cause of Russian freedom was more important than any man's private affairs. Gorky remained adamant." All this, of course, was done by interpretation back and forth.

In desperation, one of the Americans took aside the newspapermen who had swarmed aboard. He explained the situation to them, pointing out that "the Greek Orthodox Church made divorce so difficult that thousands of Russians in good repute separated and remarried without a priest and yet were commonly regarded as man and wife," which, alas, was simply not so; and that Gorky's formal wife, Ekaterina Pavlovna Peshkova, had long been happily remarried, which, strictly speaking, was also untrue. The Gorky "campaign" would be big news for weeks, he pleaded; "why spoil it by springing this sensation at the start?"

The reporters were, overall, a broad-minded bunch. According to Upton Sinclair, who was among them, they "all agreed that the American public had no concern with the marriage customs of Russia, and that this story had nothing to do with Gorky's present mission."

There is hardly any doubt they already had the picture, thanks to the Russian embassy, and a juicy story before them. Besides, it must have been galling that Gorky had tied himself up to write exclusively for Hearst during his American visit. Still, at this point, amazingly, not a reporter peeped.

The triumph began. Front-page headlines, on April 10, 1906, described admiring crowds at the pier. Gorky was quoted as expressing delight at coming to this "inherently free land." Asked what he proposed for Russia, he said: "We will follow the road the United States has opened." Asked if he had a message from Russia's people to Americans, he bowed low and said: "To your nation." GORKY AMAZED AT NEW YORK'S GREATNESS, ran banner heads . . . GORKY IN TEARS AT GRANT'S TOMB.

The *World* carried an editorial cartoon: "Let there be Light!"—the Statue of Liberty graciously bending down to Gorky and giving a light from her torch to his, which bore the tag: "For my people." The next day its cartoon linked Twain with Gorky, showing the Connecticut Yankee giving the Romanov throne a shove, sending a startled Nicky into space.

All the newspapers, in homey fashion, referred frequently to the great writer's charming wife, who was with him.

But other events followed fast.

Gorky and Maria Feodorovna were staying in a suite at the Hotel Belleclaire, on Fifth Avenue, taken for them by Wilshire. She apparently tried to avert catastrophe, but could not override both her inability to communicate in English *and* her Gorky. Many years later—obviously still feeling it as if it all happened yesterday—she would explain as best she could in reply to a written query by Gorky's biographer, Alexander Kaun: "Alexey Maximovich paid for his rooms, and I paid for mine. A.M. went out, received callers, attended meetings, dinners, and so forth, while I, an absolutely private person, did not appear with him anywhere, being of the opinion that this would be awkward for myself and unnecessary for the purposes of A.M." But then Wilshire arranged a reception—in her room!

"Unfamiliar with American customs," she wrote Kaun, "we were bewildered and astonished, when for two or three hours utter strangers kept on coming in a line, shaking hands with us, and saying something or other. As I have said, I knew no English then, and my French, German, and Italian were of no help. I asked A.M.'s secretary: 'What is the matter? Why are these people passing in line?' He knew nothing about it either, and the reception arranged by Mr. Wilshire was a surprise to him. As it appeared later, among the visitors were many known and even celebrated men."

The band of American friends of Gorky was not without realists, who knew trouble when they saw it staring at them. "To make hay while the sun still shone we made the most of our dinner on April 11, the next night." Just before the dinner, the Japanese cook—probably still celebrating the victory of Tsushima Strait, or the taking of Port Arthur—struck for a raise, and got it, but he saw to it that the meal was bad. However, "our guests cared little about what they ate—for Gorki, lean and gigantic, dressed in blue blouse and black trousers tucked into high boots, held all of us spellbound by the stories which in his low, deep voice he told through Narodny (a Russian exile, their interpreter) to old Mark Twain."

An idyllic earthy scene, the young raconteur and the old one; we can imagine the looks that passed between them. Twain was "humorous and brilliant, as usual." He apparently had not been let in on the little problem. Himself originally a bitter critic of the conventions, he had long decided he couldn't lick 'em and had joined 'em. The straiter-laced Howells didn't know either; or maybe he did—for he wasn't there.

The great literary dinner to be given by Twain and Howells was announced, and also a big meeting planned in Faneuil Hall in Boston by Alice Stone Blackwell. Telegrams from Jane Addams and others were read. Flash bulbs went off, while Brisbane dictated to his secretary an editorial appeal for funds for the Russian revolution, to be run in Hearst papers across the country.

The second development was at the newspapers. It seems that a woman reporter from the *World* finally spilled the story to her city desk. At the same time, says Poole, it was learned that Gordon Bennett, publisher of the stanchly moral *Herald*—then living in Paris with a young Russian countess—had cabled his paper to run an exposure of Gorky's "mistress."

The third thing that happened was very blunt. The fact was that the Russian revolutionary movement was not the only socialist movement in the world. In America there was the I.W.W. (International Workers of the World—the "Wobblies"). Under the Wobbly leadership of William (Big Bill) Haywood and Charles Moyer, the United Miners had called a strike, there was violence, and these two men were now in jail in Idaho, on trial for their lives.

According to Upton Sinclair, Wilshire drafted a wire from Gorky to Moyer and Haywood, and passed it to Andreyeva, asking her to have Gorky sign it. This caused panic among the moderate wing of Gorky's supporters. Says Sinclair: "If Gorky supported Moyer and Haywood, he would get no money from the liberal millionaires of New York, the Schiffs and the Strausses and the Guggenheims and the rest, who might be persuaded to subsidize the Russian revolution, but who had no interest in industrial freedom for America! The matter was explained to Gorky, and he gave his decision: he was an international socialist, and he would protest against the railroading of the two radical labor leaders to the gallows." The wire was sent.

Greetings to you, my brother socialists. Courage! The day of justice and deliverance for the oppressed of all the world is at hand. Ever fraternally yours,

Maxim Gorky

Kaun writes that the wire was never cleared by Gorky, but that Wilshire read it to the afore-mentioned Zinovy Peshkov, who approved it as "expressing Gorky's sentiments." Says Kaun: "This circumstance clears Gorky of at least one gaucherie." This version Gorky himself must have told him.

Sinclair wrote: "So far as the marital part is concerned, I think he [Gorky] was guiltless, bescause he had no idea he was doing anything wrong."

The wire to the I.W.W. leaders probably did it; but it was "the marital part" that would be used on him, to the hilt. All was ready.

The next morning the *World* came out with front-page pictures of Gorky with Ekaterina Pavlovna and their Maximka, and of "the so-called Mme. Gorky who is not Mme. Gorky at all but a Russian actress, Andreyeva, with whom he has been living." The story itself, Poole says, was "on the surface not brutally unjust, but deadly in the effect it had on the puritanical New York of those times."

Within a few hours, Gorky and Maria Feodorovna were put out of Hotel Belleclaire. Wilshire pleaded with the manager, who said, "This is not Europe. I'm running a family hotel."

They moved to the Brevoort, and were put out early that evening. They moved on to the little Hotel Rhinelander, across the street. Then they went—by this time Maria Feodorovna probably gave up trying to be a "completely private person," and went with him out of self-protection—to a small socialist meeting. When they came back after midnight, their luggage was piled on the sidewalk, in the rain. "There they stood, a bewildered group, on the sidewalk of a foreign city, in the dead of night." Gorky managed to laugh, and said "if necessary he would sleep in the streets, as he had done before." Maria Feodorovna finally did go to Staten Island. Gorky slept in a spare room at the A Club.

The next morning "the full implications of the outrage came," writes Poole, "in brutal newspaper accounts of their plight and in messages from groups in New York and elsewhere cancelling meetings and dinners." Even the redoubtable Alice Stone Blackwell found she had to cancel the meeting at Faneuil Hall.

The metropolitan papers, except Hearst's *American*, followed the *World*. "The purity of our inns is threatened!" cried the *Sun*. Then came the magazines. Let the rest be imagined.

H. G. Wells had come from England to be one of the distinguished guests at the great dinner now never to be given. He was dazed by what happened, overnight, to Gorky. In the absence of "divorce facilities for men in the revolutionary camp," he saw Maria Feodorovna Andreyeva standing to Gorky as George Eliot stood to George Lewes, "and I suppose the two of them had almost forgotten the technical illegality of their tie, until it burst upon them and the American public in a monstrous storm of exposure... At one moment Gorky was in an immense sunshine, at the next he was being almost literally pelted through the streets... To me it was astonishing—it was terrifying. I wanted to talk to Gorky about it, to find out the hidden springs of this amazing change."

Wells came to the A Club and told Poole: "I've been hunting this whole city to find Maxim Gorky and tell him what I think of this outrage. I have heard that he is with you." Poole drew a deep breath and lied.

For the A Clubbers were still clinging to a hope. Maria Feodorovna was coming in regularly from Staten Island, "to soothe Gorky down. For Maxim the Bitter was surely a bitter man at this time!" Poole and others were pleading with him "to help us save for Russian Freedom what we could of his big mission here." It might be done; there was still Mark Twain.

Howells had already left by the nearest exit, but "if only old Clemens would remain as chairman and come out strong in a public appeal, we felt that his great reputation might even then turn back the tide." Twain told them he would think it over, on condition Gorky be kept quiet, and absolutely hidden. Poole managed to convey this, somehow, to Wells, who asked him to tell Gorky that when he came to England, Wells and his wife would like him and his wife to stay with them.

Then Wells, like the man from Mars, wandered on through the streets of an America screaming excoriations and lewd jokes at Maxim Gorky. "The writers of paragraphs racked their brains to invent new and smart ways of insulting Madame Andreyeva. The chaste entertainers of the music-halls of the Tenderloin district introduced allusions." He was told of someone asking a young reporter what Americans would have said if Benjamin Franklin had been treated so on his mission to Paris to win support for the American War of Independence. "Benjamin Franklin," said the reporter primly, "was a man of very different moral character than Gorky." Wells mused that Franklin's morals were indeed different from Gorky's, but not in the way the bright young reporter seemed to think.

Wells's friendship with Gorky was to stay through the years, in spite of the barrier of language. They were in touch to the end of Gorky's long, gruelling life; Wells was probably one of those who tried to make contact with Gorky just before Gorky died.


While the faithful, "detesting" their role, hid Gorky as if ashamed of him, waiting for Twain's crucial decision, the country's "moral outrage" swelled, and much of the sympathy among liberals for the Russian revolution changed into fear. A sudden connection had been made in many minds between the I.W.W. and the Russian revolutionary movement, through the medium of Gorky.

Ambrose Bierce (whose stories Gorky had forced Tolstoy to read) wrote a friend: "You are wrong about Gorky—he has none of the 'artist' in him. He is not only a peasant, but an anarchist and an advocate of assassination—by others . . . His 'career' in this country has been that of a yellow dog . . . I was myself a dupe in the matter . . ."

That a poignant new light on "revolution" had suddenly come through was shown in an editorial in *The Bookman*, an important magazine of the time. Gorky himself, "a product of the slums, for years a tramp," was not so ludicrous or unsavory, the magazine said, as the "amateur anarchists and pink-tea nihilists" of America, who, unable to realize the horrors that would go with a revolution in a brutish land like Russia, had welcomed Gorky not as a writer but as a revolutionist. "They were willing to applaud rape and rapine when rampant over the whole of a mighty empire, but the irregular domestic relations of one individual and the violence of a handful of striking miners, when these things occurred upon American soil, seemed to them unsavory and repellent."

This must have been what happened. To many thousands who had prepared to cheer Gorky wildly across the country, he had suddenly become repellent—a foul animal of some kind, a disease-bearing cockroach.

It was a minor trauma for America, a step toward slightly more awareness, even though the means for this bit of growing up was the crassest hypocrisy. But what a trauma for Gorky! Much had happened to him in life, but he had never had to be hidden from the eyes of men like a verminous immoral thing—this man whose whole life and art were fixed on the search for morality.

The next day Twain's answer came. He was quitting. Tom Sawyer had decided not to have anything to do with Huck Finn.

Twain's biographer, Albert Bigelow Paine, has described the old writer as staggered by the blow of the *World* story. He quotes him saying to Dan Beard: "Gorky has made an awful mistake, Dan. He might as well have come over here in his shirt-tail."

In a letter, Twain went further. "Gorky is a puzzle and a vexation to me. He came here in a distinctly diplomatic capacity—a function which demands (and necessitates) delicacy, tact, deference to people's prejudices ... He hits the public in the face with his hat and then holds it out for contributions. It is not ludicrous, it is pitiful."

Twain was far from being free of conscience about it. Huck had never quite died. And eventually Twain was judged by others.

H. L. Mencken wrote: "It seems to me that Clemens was eternally disgraced by his action in the matter."

Still struggling to justify himself, Twain wrote an allegory, "The Gorki Incident," which was not published until long after the death of both men. Its hero was a native of Tierra del Fuego, named York Minster, "a likeable young fellow, bright, animated, rather handsome, and of a particularly shapely figure," who was accustomed to go naked.

He was fitted out with Christian clothing, taught the rudiments of English speech, and taken to England. Invited to the Court of St. James, he thought he should resume his national costume for the occasion, "thinking no harm"—and appeared "in the midst of that gorgeous assemblage clad only in his awful innocence." He emptied the place in two minutes by the watch.

It was a fair joke, but to Twain himself it still must have tasted sour. He felt he had to add something, a dour ode to Custom: "Laws are sand, customs are rocks. Laws can be evaded and punishment escaped, but an openly transgressed custom brings sure punishment . . . Custom is custom: it is built of brass, boiler-iron, granite; facts, reasonings, arguments have no more effect upon it than the idle winds have upon Gibraltar."

He still didn't feel right, and added a kindly homily, for the benefit of York Minster: "After reflection, he put on his clothes again."

Of this allegorical fragment by Twain, Van Wyck Brooks wrote: "What would Emerson and Thoreau have said, fifty years before, of such an argument, such an assertion of the futility of the individual reason in the face of 'brass, boiler-iron, granite,' and mob emotion? It is perhaps the most pitifully abject confession ever written by a famous writer."

So Gorky, while naïvely causing his own downfall and agony, forced America—in the person of its loftiest artistic force, Mark Twain—to drop its fig leaf and show how little remained of an earlier homespun moral integrity.

Twain had tried to write about Gorky. Gorky, too, would try to write about Twain; and his fragment, entitled only "M.T.," likewise was not published until long after death. Twain had managed two pages; Gorky could not even do one. The scene: a dinner, where a famous old writer, now a charlatan jokester . . . and yet . . . his eyes cunning, but wise . . . very like an American Luka, in fact . . . once perhaps a holy wanderer . . . now a smug trickster . . . and yet . . . talks sneeringly about revolution . . . all very dim . . . the fragment trails off . . . Gorky was too hurt to go on, and buried it in his papers.

For there really was a kinship, and perhaps he—much younger, with that outgoing need and enthusiasm—had discovered it more surely and clearly than Twain ever let himself. This man, Twain, could have become his next idol. Gorky had moved on the road from Tolstoy to Lenin, but he really wanted a man far more humanistic, and aware of life's roundness, than Lenin could ever be. That was Twain. But it was not to be, just as Tom Sawyer and Huckleberry Finn, when they grew up, could not live together. Left was only the pain and, for Gorky, the awful mortification.

Although all was lost, the last-ditchers dragged Gorky to a press conference, where he "made strong appeals both for the woman he loved and for the great cause he had come here to aid. It did no good." He then went to join Maria Feodorovna on Staten Island.

There, Poole feels, a healing process did begin for Gorky, as he "realized, that despite all the puritanism on earth, the Russian revolution would grind inexorably on to fulfilment." He describes an evening spent by the faithful and Gorky on South Beach.

It was empty at that time of year, so we built a big driftwood fire and cooked our supper there. The clusters of lights by tens of thousands twinkling at us from the great harbor of New York made a spacious background for our guest. At that time only thirty-eight years old, gaunt and gigantic, he knelt on the sand, with an old slouch hat pulled down over his blunt Slav face and his eyes and, with his wife translating (of course, into French), told us stories of the Russia he knew. And then, toward the end of the evening, he recited a Russian translation of Poe's *Raven*. I can still hear his deep musical voice, so dramatic with all its quiet, sounding after each verse the fatal refrain—Nikogdá.

He and Andreyeva stayed with the Martins on Staten Island for some weeks—and for years afterward the Martins put up with insults from neighbors because of it. Then they went together to the Martins' cottage in the Adirondacks, for the summer. "In the evening," Kaun writes, "they would climb trees, and from his perch Gorky would teach them Russian phrases. One of these was: *Lyubitye drug druga*—love one another."

This is real evidence that a healing process had indeed taken place. It is even possible to trace its two stages, in writing—as in what he wrote Gorky is always to be traced—and he wrote furiously, on Staten Island and in the Adirondacks. The first stage is one of a purge, in rage and repudiation. The second stage is a final sentimental beatitude, in which revolution became religion—a novel which was to become a bible, literally, from which millions would draw ecstatic inspiration.

## CHAPTER 18

THE purge took the form of violent and bitter articles and stories
about America. Some were translated and printed (in *Harper's*,
*Scribner's*, *Appleton's*), further increasing America's righteous indigna-
tion.

New York became "The City of the Yellow Devil"—gold, Mammon.
It is guarded by a massive, bronze, blind statue—the statue of a woman.
(In his original manuscript, Gorky wrote "massive and vulgar," then
crossed "and vulgar" out; even in the depths of fury and hurt, his rever-
ence for words like "Liberty" and "Woman" had not quite forsaken him.)

In this dreadful city, "it seems as if everything—iron, stones, water,
wood, is full of protest against a life without sun, without songs and happiness, imprisoned in heavy toil."

From afar the city is an enormous jaw with uneven black teeth. It
breathes clouds of smoke, pants like a glutton. Entering it, one feels he
has "fallen into a stomach of stone and iron," which is masticating and
digesting millions. This "triumph of iron" is due to the power of Gold,
which "surrounds man with its web, deafens him, sucks his blood and
marrow, devours his muscles and nerves." The dirty leaves of trees hang
dead from their twigs. The bronze, dirt-blinded statues in the abject sooty
parks seem to ask: "Could I have wanted to create such a life?"

He describes the people working at their windows, or merely sitting,
heads resting on the sills, as the "El" clatters by between tenements. "No
hatred in their eyes at the supremacy of iron." A child hangs, screaming
and scratching, at the hungry blue breast of its mother, in a tenement
hallway.

This is not just the fury of a badly hurt man. Protest was basic to Gorky.
He breathed in protest, and saw it in everything around him. All he had
to do was change a few adjectives, add the specific emotions of his
humiliation, and the "bestial" Russian life he knew became the dead and
frantic "iron life" of America.

And there was truth in it, besides; curiously, the overwrought descriptions and impressions are literature, because they express truthfully—in emotionally heightened form—the reaction of a young being confronted for the first time with the frightening "soulless" quality of modern industrial society: New York was then its great outpost. The El is gone; but the scene was exact.

A "kingdom of loneliness," conveying the illusion of a kingdom of beauty. See Coney Island. When night arrives, from above the ocean suddenly rises "a transparent city, all of flame." There in the soft gloom, on the ocean's swelling breast, it seems, is "a big cradle made of flowers and stars—and on it, at night, rests the sun." (He never wrote a truer Russian folk image.)

But the rising sun "brings a man near to the truth of life." In the huge crowds there is no joy or happiness. These million fires seen at night only produce a mocking illumination. The soul is oppressed, desiring one real flame instead of these million tinsel ones. The people, like clouds of black flies, jam the boardwalks and beaches. "It is a hades of paper maché."

Nor is this untrue, either, to life, or to the America he found: the hypocritical temperance barker; the people thronging to see the "secrets of sin"; the omnipresent warnings: "Not Allowed" . . . "Not Permitted"; the monkeys teased cruelly in the zoo, and the people becoming uneasy, as if they themselves were being tortured. Only at times his sense of proportion, as his wounds burn, as the purge works, goes out of kilter, and he loses control: "Greedy and vicious, they show the disgusting nakedness of their lies and their naïve cunning, their hypocrisy and the unsatisfied strength of their greed."

Finally, Sunday comes, and he watches with real inward perception, and sees that "on many faces is noticeable a despondent irresolution, almost a worry"—there is no work to drive them frantically through their lives.

He even manages—healing was taking place—an ungainly humor. He goes to interview an American capitalist, expecting to meet a man with three paunches and one hundred and fifty teeth in his mouth, who annihilates the most costly food, geese, peacocks, suckling pigs, radishes with butter, puddings; by evening he is so tired of eating that a Negro servant must chew his food for him and then place it in his mouth; finally, covered with sweat, panting, he is carried to sleep by his Negroes. In the morning, at six, he again begins his tormented life.

In reality, he meets a long gaunt man, wrinkled hands folded over a normal-sized stomach. He explains to Gorky he only eats twice a day. "Then what do you do with your money?" "I make more money with it." "Why?" "To make more money." "Why?" The millionaire leans forward on his elbow and asks: "Are you crazy?"

So much for the economic side of capitalism.

It is in a short story, "Charley Mann," that the wounding experience of Gorky's meeting with America is portrayed most touchingly and, characteristically, in the form of allegory. Charley is the American version of "Man"—the object of Gorky's long admiration—and the story has a kind of Wild West setting.

Charley lives alone; he is solitary, vicious, indrawn, and morose. A dangerous bear is loose, which has been mauling women, and Charley is the best hunter in the region; but he refuses to hunt the bear because in this season bearskins don't bring good money. One day, however, he goes out and traps a young falcon hawk—a proud, free thing, roamer of the high skies. He ties the hawk to a stake, and tortures it. He tells himself he wants to tame it.

The bird fights proudly, refusing to let him approach. It refuses to eat; it would rather die then be craven. Charley, infuriated, beats it more cruelly, standing at a safe distance. Half beaten to death, the falcon turns to Charley Mann its tortured face—and suddenly, we are aware that the falcon is Gorky!—and that he himself, writing the story, is not aware how completely he has revealed his terrible pain: This is what they did to me—me, the Falcon!

At last, a vestige of conscience stirs in Mann; or maybe his sadism is sated. He cuts the rope, and the wounded bird staggers, tries its wings, manages to rise, gathers its strength, and flies to freedom.

This is how York Minster, the naked savage, saw himself in reality, and how it felt to be the object of the civilizing mission of Twain's America.

And after all that, Gorky was even able to remember again the promise in the America that had so tortured him, and to lecture it, the way incurable moralists do, about its vast possibilities.


And it seems to me that when America will turn her energy to the quest of liberty of the spirit, the world will witness the spectacle of a great conflagration, a conflagration which will cleanse this country from the dirt of gold, and from the dust of prejudice, and it will shine like a magnificent cut diamond, reflecting in its great heart all the thought of the world, all the beauty of life.

The whole process of purge and healing could hardly fail to end in a new affirmation of revolutionary faith. And this crossed with another process, more mysterious, the religious, which he had suppressed as much as he could through the stormy-petrel years. It was surely the American experience, straining all his powers of self-preservation as a man, which crystallized it. The upshot was a novel—final product of Staten Island and the Adirondacks—which became the world's best-loved work of proletarian literature—the *Uncle Tom's Cabin* of the twentieth century. It is not the least of the wonders America has wrought.

"Mother" became not only a book that hastened the Russian Revolution, but a stirrer of both revolutionary and generally idealistic social forces all over the world. It was to be translated into twenty-eight tongues, in hundreds of editions, and devoured by millions, including the Indians and Chinese.

By crossing the religious attitude with the idealized image of militant workers, drenching action with sentiment, "Mother" offered, to all those who wanted to believe in something, something to believe in, at a time of industrial stress and upheaval.

As writing, it may well be the worst thing Gorky ever wrote. Some claim that honor for the prose poem "Man," on the grounds that it is more concentrated; but others point out, rightly, that "Mother" is much longer. Gorky made clear, many years later, that he did not delude himself: " 'Mother' is a really bad book," he told a friend, "written in a state of resentment and irritation."

The story is of a widowed mother and her son. Her name is Pelagea Nilova, and Gorky's names always matter. This is the Pelagea of "Foma Gordeyev"—his idealized peasant woman, who originally was Old Isergil —but now lifted up beyond all sensuality; and her patronymic shows she is the daughter of Nil, that historic first proletarian hero, of *Meschanye*. Her son is Pavel (Paul).

They live in a shack on the edge of a town near Nizhni Novgorod, and Pavel works in the factory. The simplicity, the inner goodness of the mother, the undefined nobility of the son, move the heart, with a gentle saccharine motion. They are sainted figures. An excerpt will give their flavor. The son has suddenly told his mother he is bringing guests; she trembles and sobs, for she is afraid of strangers.

He bent down to her face and sternly—just like his father—said this:
"Through fear we are all lost. And those who command us make use of our fear and frighten us still farther."
The mother mournfully wailed.
"Don't be angry. How can I not be afraid? All my life I lived in fear. My whole soul is overgrown with fear."
Not loudly, and more gently, he said:
"You must forgive me—it cannot be otherwise."

The visitors from the big city are revolutionary organizers (what brand, Gorky leaves undefined, as always). The little mother is frightened of these learned folk, but soon begins to see they are sweet, fine people, both the men and the women, of whom one soon loves Pavel. And in a little while, we see the dear little woman stanchly learning to read, for she wants to know these deep thoughts her son is thinking. What she reads we are not told, but—knowing how Gorky felt at the precise time of the writing—it was probably a couple of books by Lenin.

There is a strike. Pavel harangues the workers. A procession, with banners. Pavel is jailed. Someone needs to distribute revolutionary leaflets. Our Nilova—Mother—volunteers! She hides the leaflets under her hot rolls, which she brings into the gate of the plant for the workers' lunch.

Pavel and his comrades are tried. He addresses the dishonest judge—and lo! it is not he and his but the judge and society who are judged:

And he, erect and tall, standing firmly and vigorously, stretched out his hand to them while he spoke distinctly:
"We are revolutionists, and will be such as long as private property exists...We take our stand against the society whose interests you are bidden to protect as your irreconcilable enemies, and reconciliation between us is impossible until we shall have been victorious..."

This speech, in history's light somewhat painful, caused vibrations in many a heart around the world. Pavel concluded: "You have torn man away from life and disintegrated him. Socialism will unite the world, rent asunder by you, into one huge whole. And this will be!"
To make sure they got it, he stopped a second and then repeated in a deeper tone, with greater emphasis, *"This will be."*
Pavel is sent to Siberia, and Mother sends his sweetheart after him with

her blessings. Some day she will dandle their children, her grandchildren. Meantime, we see her, leaflets crammed in her basket, boarding a train on a dangerous mission, being seized by the police (after managing to pass the bulk of the leaflets to eager waiting hands), being roughed up, crying out: "You will not drown the truth in seas of blood!"—being choked by the police, managing to say, with a rattle in her throat, "You poor, sorry creatures..."

This tearjerker, with its wooden people, loaded with clichés, once touched off the emotions of countless numbers, who were mutually creating in those years a new-old religion whose divine figures were "The Proletariat," the simple and downtrodden workers, the poorest of the poor.

And strangely—and this is true of much of Gorky, as if a latent life beats in even his dullest and most foolish creations—it is not dead. There are places where it not only moves the heart today, but where it has gained what it never had, the nature and dimensions of art.

As made into an opera in the Soviet Union, by the contemporary composer Khrennikov, with libretto by Faiko, given at the Bolshoi, "Mother" suddenly begins—after a slow start—to move and breathe. Massed effects take place that recall the dramatic paintings of Giotto and Mantegna, and for which there are few parallels on the modern stage. The fervor—that of a crusading religion—transmits to the audience; the wooden heroes, mother and son, become believable; the naïveté of valor, which Gorky's own novel failed miserably to bring to life, in this transformed version beats in reality. A scene of pure inspiration, which was never in the novel, lifts the play at the end to a moral statement meant for today, and binds this statement, with brilliant art, to the Communist cause.

A drunken young merchant (young Foma Gordeyev, transposed by honest right into a different work) sees the Mother at the train station, lugging her leaflets; he is touched by her character, and her faith, but cannot quite reach her inspiration; he falls into the arms of prostitutes, drunk, while the Mother marches on to a final revolutionary triumph, red banners cracking, riding the legendary catcher of that well-known revolutionary train—which comes, loaded with Red Guardsmen, on stage. It is wild but truly effective; and what Gorky wrote was a jumping-off point. That poor work of his, now, nearly sixty years after it was written, is a powerful warhorse in the rearguard action of the Party, trying desperately to preserve a frame of mind which for many has no reality today.

The Soviet critics have a genealogy for the characters of "Mother."
They are supposed to be patterned on Anna Zalamova and her son Peter,
of Nizhni Novgorod; and the court scene is supposed to be based on a
trial of leaders of the Russian Social Democratic Workers Party, in Nizhni
in 1902. Needless to say, there is little to this, for real people and real
events, though Gorky tried to use them, never had much to do with the
real substance of his work, good or bad. These are pious images, developed
by an inner process, as Gorky's subterranean emotions kept up their
incessant search for hero figures.

They had been forced to the surface by his shocking American experience, and were bathed in the sickly sweetness of a religious vision still
in the yolk. This vision would be formed within another year, and then
it would be no Party vehicle, but one of the rare and genuine devotional
books of the twentieth century.

It took the whole summer of 1906, with trees to climb and reams of
paper to assault, for him to get enough out of his system to permit a
quiet departure from America. With Maria Feodorovna, he landed in
France. The French government had extended to Tsarist Russia a vital
loan. Gorky informed La Belle France that he "spit blood and gall" into
her eyes. He called on French workers to give arms to the Russian revolutionaries. As Kaun points out, Gorky the diplomat was "as tactful as a
drunken muzhik."

This left few places of refuge, and he was a wanted criminal in Russia.
He got permission from the Italian government—which he had somehow
neglected to insult—to go to Capri, and there he and Maria Feodorovna
settled. On this island he would spend six years, momentous for both
literary achievement and self-discovery. But before really entering this
Capri period, he attended the Fifth Congress of the Russian Social-Democratic Party, in London. There Lenin was fighting for control of the
Russian revolutionary movement.


The Congress started in Brussels, in May of 1907, but the Tsarist government pressured the Belgian, and the revolutionaries had to leave. They
went to London. There were something like three hundred voting delegates, but nobody knew for sure; the figures kept changing as men came
and went and their "mandates" were challenged. There were plenty of
nonvoting delegates, too.

Gorky was probably a guest of honor, though some sources refer to him as a nonvoting delegate. He himself told Kaun categorically (in 1927) that he had never actually been a member of *any* party; and this is important for a clear view of the man. It is possible he was considered a kind of delegate—representing Gorky. He was something special, and the state of the revolutionary movement was still anarchic—except that Lenin was always determined to have a voting majority, regardless of means.

Lenin had not wasted time in his drive for a secret, "hard" party, dedicated to political overthrow, and opposed to the "softer" mensheviks and to the "economists," who stressed the need to educate the workers and help them, through trade union struggle, improve their economic conditions. He had declared that against these opponents he would *"always wage a war of destruction"* (he loved to underline); and he meant it. His two main opponents now were Plekhanov, founder of Russian Marxism, and Martov (Julius Tsederbaum), and he was out to destroy them. At stake was control of the "center" of the Social-Democratic Party.

The delegates were high on fighting spirits but low on money. The unforeseen expense of having to go first to Brussels and then to London had drained most of them. Many would either have to starve or find jobs and postpone indefinitely returning to Russia. They got desperate as the Congress dragged on, with much infighting over procedure and over which credentials were valid. By the end of the Congress they were £2,000 short of being able to pay for all facilities.

They tried to arrange with English businessmen for a loan. It was found that there were only two of them whose signatures carried any weight. They were Plekhanov and Gorky. Plekhanov refused to lend his name. The money was borrowed under Gorky's endorsement.

This is the story as Kaun got it from Gorky. He adds that the businessman who laid out the cash asked an odd price: he demanded the signatures of all the delegates—"perhaps as a souvenir." When the Party central committee eventually repaid him, it retrieved the list of signatures—Lenin's, Martov's, Trotsky's, Plekhanov's, everybody's—in alphabets ranging from Armenian and Georgian to Lettish and Yiddish.

There is a different, and perhaps more realistic, version of the same story, given by Leonard Schapiro, the foremost Western authority on the history of the Communist Party of the Soviet Union. It does not mention Gorky, but says the delegates were rescued by Plekhanov, who succeeded in borrowing the sum from an industrialist, Joseph Fels. It was supposed to be repaid by the end of the year, and the promise was signed by all the delegates. "The money was repaid, after repeated demands, but not until after the 1917 revolution."

If Schapiro's version is right, and not that given to Kaun twenty years after the event by Gorky, it may be the main thing shown is how Gorky felt about Plekhanov: a man who didn't trust his fellow revolutionaries enough to sign a piece of paper. (In view of the trouble Fels had collecting, this would only be evidence, however, of Plekhanov's unswerving Marxist realism.)

The fact is, Gorky didn't like Plekhanov. Plekhanov was of the intelligentsia, reserved, well-dressed, and unable to hide his arrogance. He must have put Gorky in mind of some of the well-dressed, proper Americans who had decided he was a savage—and of the Kazan intellectuals who considered him a museum specimen.

Plekhanov had the additional misfortune of believing one should be honest about literary opinions—well, within reason—and he didn't think much of the tedious plays Gorky had been hammering out under the influence of the bolsheviks, even though they were politically useful. The fact that he picked out one of these plays, "Enemies"—another product of the idyllic American visit—as pretty good probably only confirmed Gorky's belief he was a snob and a hypocrite; in his own heart Gorky knew all his works written for the Cause were mediocre.

"When I was led to Plekhanov," Gorky was to write, "he stood with arms folded across his chest and regarded me with an air of stern boredom, like a teacher, tired of his obligations, regarding a new pupil. He said to me, 'I am an admirer of your talent.' He added to this trite remark nothing that sticks in my memory. And throughout the Congress, I didn't feel any wish to have a heart to heart talk with him."

Oh how he needed that sense of being able to talk heart to heart. And then along came Lenin!

"He took me strongly by the hand, he looked piercingly into my eyes, and said, like an old friend, in a pleased voice: 'I'm glad you came here. It seems that you like scraps, isn't that right? Well, there's going to be a nice scrap here.'"

Just right. He had been Lenin's pretty much already—remember, "Ilyitch loves . . . Ilyitch awaits . . ." But now, with an assist from Plekhanov, he was surely sealed and delivered, for good, it would seem.

Lenin had read the manuscript of "Mother." He "spoke of the book's faults," but reassured Gorky: "You did well to hurry it, this book is useful. Many workers have taken part in the revolutionary movement without thinking about it, spontaneously. Now they'll get a lot out of reading 'Mother.' "

Here was a simple, downright man, who put on no airs, didn't pretend he was judging artistic merit but simply said, "The book is useful." And wasn't that the main thing?

And it was true that Gorky had always liked scraps. Lenin made it sound like a kid's game, happy and salutary, nothing deadly.

In fact, "he seemed to me to lack something. He was, so to speak, too simple. One did not feel the leader in him."

That was his great secret, as a politician. Gorky was to find it out later—and it would be an awakening experience. He had met a most complex and mysterious man, whose chief stock in trade was homey simplicity.

"This man, bald, pudgy, well-built, stroked with one hand his Socratic temple, and with the other pumped my hand."

How could a Gorky resist a Socratic temple, that homey, homely baldness of the shining mind? He was magnetized. He was taken.

With Trotsky, who was sitting out the scrap between Lenin and Martov and Plekhanov, Gorky found friendliness possible. Trotsky liked him at once as a man, though he had reservations about his work: "romantic." He gives an account of how he met Gorky. He was accosted by "a tall angular man with a round face and high cheekbones, who wore a round hat." Gorky said, "I am your admirer," and told of reading Trotsky's political pamphlets, written in jail. Trotsky said he was Gorky's admirer too. Apparently Gorky sensed no snobbery—it was not in Trotsky.

Gorky, Andreyeva and Trotsky went about London together. "When some beggar would shut the door of the cab behind us," wrote Trotsky in his memoirs, "Gorky would plead: 'We ought to give him some of these pence.' To which Andreyeva would answer: 'They have been given, Alyosha dear, they have been given.' "

At the Congress itself, Gorky was a Lenin cheerleader. He "could always be seen in the dark corner of the church, where the meetings took place, eagerly listening to the debates, and expressing his sentiments by applause or disapproving remarks. In the intermission he invariably conversed with groups of bolshevik workmen in the court of the church, pumping them for information about themselves and their shops, and telling them amusing stories."

Gorky himself makes clear that the views he loudly expressed, during and between meetings, were those of Lenin. Plekhanov's cold meticulous arrogance in debate repelled him; of course he had already been repelled. As for Martov, Gorky didn't want to listen. What Martov had to say was too moderate, too reasonable, and Gorky (still only a few months from his torture at the hands of Charley Mann) was not ready for it. He only describes Martov as a man torn by anguish, trying to reconcile where there can be no reconciliation—not realizing that in years to come he, Gorky, would also be just such a man.

Lenin could hardly fail to come out the victor. The bolsheviks had already built a machine, being better financed by far than the other factions—thanks largely to the death benefit of Savva Morozov's insurance policy, supplemented by "direct expropriations": train robberies and the dynamiting of banks, on Lenin's orders, with Stalin as direct chief, carried out by a lovable and devoted gangster named Kamo. Lenin himself scrupled at nothing in the political infighting. He could "veer, prevaricate, intrigue and sow confusion, seeking support from the devil himself if it offered, without for a moment imagining that his conduct might in itself be considered of any importance when judged in relation to its ultimate end." Martov, on the other hand, was "a prisoner of standards of behavior and of principles which he never thought of compromising." They were ill-matched, and Lenin would always win. As for Plekhanov, he had no magnetism, and he too was a gentleman.

The points won at the Fifth Congress were not dramatic, but with what Lenin won before, and after, they were a step toward the creation of the hard, effective, and—finally—tragic Party machine he was determined to have, and toward the monolithic state that would come from the bolshevik revolution.

Gorky was Lenin's man; and yet, strangely enough, the Congress had hardly ended, he had hardly returned to Capri, when something changed. It was as if the years of the Stormy Petrel, the agony of the American experience, the maudlin yet rousing book "Mother," his excited partisanship at the Congress, all had really been leading him toward something else . . . a need to look more closely at . . . something. And that something was not Lenin's.

# BOOK III

*Search*

## CHAPTER 19

IN a way, living in exile on Capri was being a holy hermit—one of Gorky's conflicting ideals. At the same time, he—and Maria Feodorovna, undoubtedly, more so—must have been impelled for a time (he would never be again) to live well, as befitted a famous writer and his beloved. The sense seems to come through that he felt a need to compensate her, the daughter of a general, for what she had sacrificed for him. Besides, he must have been showing the Americans who had mocked him: see how that Savage knows how to live! And finally, inner changes were taking place (also probably an aftermath of America)—a long-delayed effort to come to terms with himself, to find out what he really was. Clarification is what the holy hermit seeks, far from the usual haunts of men.

He and Andreyeva lived in a villa that had been converted from a monastery, atop a cliff, reached by a funicular. One wall was of glass, looking down on the Mediterranean, with Vesuvius smoking afar. A big dining room was filled with Russian visitors—writers, actors and others—in Italy as tourists, or simply staying with Gorky to rest after enforced Siberian vacations. One may visualize Maria Feodorovna determining that theirs would be a cultivated exile, a court of Russian arts and letters.

There was a garden; parakeets were imported from Brazil; there was even a chef. Snide accounts by visitors portray Maria Feodorovna as a rather giddy snob; there is probably a measure of truth here, but she was adept at making enemies, and many could not resist the urge to get back at her. Gorky, one account says, at the dinners he and Maria Feodorovna gave, revealed himself as a man without formal education by referring to "the celebrated German philosopher Immanuel Kant" (instead of simply saying "Kant"), and so forth. This seems a small crime.

The best piece of furniture, nevertheless, was his work desk. And at it, on Capri, Gorky began to face the disparity of his professed beliefs and the persistent intuition of other feelings in long unexplored depths. The psychological process, by which the man strove to find again his own nature and outlook, is clear in two novels of 1907, his first two major works done on Capri.

The first, "The Story of the Man Nobody Needed," originally called "The Spy," was about a poor uncouth orphan lout. Yevsey Klimkov would lurk in dark corners of the village church, hoping to find something "that would embrace him, caressingly press him to itself, and tell him things as, once, his mother used to do." To the kindly, simple smith who raised him he would put strange, foolish, childish questions. "Is it possible to live so as to go everywhere and see everything, only so nobody can see me?" And, "Does the Unclean Power come into the church at night?" And, suddenly, "And what about God?"

"What about him?" (asked the kindly smith.)
"Why does God let devils into the church?"
"What's it to him? God isn't the church watchman..."
"He doesn't live there?"
"God? What for? His place, orphan, is everywhere. Churches—are for people..."
"And what are people for?"
"People—they're...that is...for everything. You can't do without people...y-yes..."
"Are they—for God?"
The smith looked from under his brows at the orphan, and answered after a pause: "Of course."

Here are the old quandaries and inner travail again, so long obscured by the hectic service to the Cause. Gorky was retracing his steps, through Yevsey Klimkov, back to Alexey Peshkov, the hurt desperate orphan, preparing, like a man getting up the courage to try a frightening path, to abandon the false props provided for him by Lenin. He was not yet ready; but these bedrock questions—"What about God?"..."What are people for?"—were his preparation.

The harsh, painful, bleak story that develops is like a one-stringed instrument giving out a single wailing note. Yevsey's path leads downward, to a job in the secret police, as an agent-provocateur who trails and traps revolutionaries. First an unsuccessful inner struggle takes place; his intelligence is too weak to cope with the temptations of evil. The pages are lit weirdly with the sense of feeble light attempting to break the darkness. The descriptions of the fear-filled psychotic milieu of the secret police seem written in a sweat of psychic recollection. The intensity with which the writer's terror—at what he himself might have become—is expresssed is exceptional.

Gorky must have felt the flame of his faith, as he had known it, was dying out; and to sustain it, to exorcise the forces corroding it, he projected the most terrible alternative he could: the fate of Yevsey Klimkov, an orphan like himself, cast into darkness without a faith to sustain him. It is a demon-haunted novel.

At last, for Yevsey, the inevitable suicide—the man nobody needed.

The first chapters were published by Gorky's own cooperative firm, "Knowledge." The rest could not pass the Russian censor; an edition was run off but with the part about the secret police excised. He brought out the entire novel in Russian only in 1917 (after the March revolution, not that of October). This shows he believed in the book (he was right: next to "Foma Gordeyev" it is his best novel); and he wanted it on record, as evidence of an inner struggle whose nature he hardly knew.

It was the kind of inner struggle that precedes a confession.


Immediately after the novel about a creature of the secret police— and part of the same mysterious self-exploring process—came a novel about a man who seeks God.

"The Confession" is a rare original work. It is the only novel ever written which states clearly and frankly the religious reasoning at the heart of the modern communist movement. An allegory, like *Pilgrim's Progress*, it is really the story of Gorky's life up to that point, seen as a religious quest—from orphan childhood in childhood's folk Christianity, all the way to the very different, yet startlingly similar, faith he had come to by 1907. The orphan hero's name is Matvey; the previous novel's hero was Yevsey; both are Alexey—the orphan Peshkov boy to whom the ikon makers had presented a lovely ikon of Alexey, Man of God, on his name day. Gorky had rediscovered himself.

How allegory works, in Gorky's writing—a process only partly conscious—is illustrated by Matvey's first big experience when he has set off to be a wanderer to holy monasteries, seeking old and holy men as models. They all turned out to be charlatans, and the most bitter disappointment was with a seemingly wise, wonderful monk, Brother Anthony.

The relations here shown are complex: adoration, jealousy, rivalry . . . the feelings of a son; and indeed the foundling suddenly demands: "Aren't you my father?" Anthony, an extremely worldly, arrogant monk, who lives richly, tells coarse stories about women, laughs at Matvey: "Hardly! When were you born? Where? . . . No—at that time I was not in those parts."

When Tolstoy read "The Confession," he is said to have suddenly cried out: "Eesh-tih!" ("Wow!"—or, "You don't say!") He had insisted Gorky was religious; but surely had not expected to meet himself as Brother Anthony. The whole episode is Gorky's first, poetic effort to tell the story of his ambivalent, emotional friendship with Tolstoy.

Matvey next joins the throngs going on holy pilgrimages ("marches of the cross"). This movement of masses stirs him, "promises to open something to the soul . . ." And well it might: for these marches of the cross are not only the religious processions that thrilled the young Gorky when he wandered Old Russia; they are also Gorky's poetic symbol for the communist movement. This kind of doubled symbolism is typical of Gorky's writing, and especially of "The Confession."

But Matvey also sees the inner desperation that impels the marchers. The color and beauty of the processions rest on squalor . . . "The people crawling along like a huge gray worm . . . crying to one another: 'Pace! Step up the pace!' and over them, bending their heads to the ground, swims the yellow bird of the ikon . . ." while beside the road sit the sick, their sores running pus, armless, legless, blind . . . whining, their wounds burning in the sun . . .

"Not this!" Matvey cries.

Again the double symbol: This outcry against "Holy Russia," with its pathetic squalor and superstition, is at the same time an outcry against false political crusades, by the fanatics of life, undertaken so often only for "relief from their hurts." Two entirely different thoughts have been condensed in the "Not this!" into a single expression.

For the religious mystic, rejecting the usual answers, there must finally be something positive, usually by means of some decisive encounter. One night Matvey lies on the earth, on a lonely road, near a certain hill. The earth seems to nurse him, like a great mother . . . "You can hear her breathe, you want to guess what dream appears to her and what powers secretly ripen in her depths . . . You see yourself as unbreakably for ages belonging to earth, and gratefully think: 'My own.'"

And on that hill the coming day, he meets a truly wise man . . . a *good* man. His name is Yegudiil.

Now Yegudiil, long before he appeared to Matvey, was, in an old buried schismatic Testament somewhere (did Grandpa read it to the boy? or Grandma tell him?) none other than the one just judge, of the twelve assigned to judge Christ, who alone refused to condemn him. And long after that, about twenty years before this story, Yegudiil was the pen name that Alexey Peshkov, later Maxim Gorky, used on the Samara "Gazette." It is only right that it be Yegudiil who shows the God-seeking man his way.

First he tells Matvey that "In our present life there isn't now a real, lawful master; he hasn't come yet." "Who then is the master?" Matvey asks. "The Lord?"

Yegudiil smiles (Luka-like). "No, nearer to us." It would be best if Matvey himself would guess. Those who first believed in Christ were those who before meeting him awaited him with their hearts . . .

This sounds, at first, as if some one man is to be the new, lawful master—literally: "boss." In the heart of each revolutionary movement has been this ambiguity: a fork in the emotional road, one branch leading to the original ideal, the other to a master of life, and death: a Stalin.

The People, Yegudiil explains, had always in the past lifted individual men to power, who always betrayed and oppressed them. Only when they realized that *all* must rise to the heights, and when many men of good will wove together thoughts of justice and equality, "there emerged the living God, the gentle child of the People—Jesus Christ."

With this affirmation of the gentle Christ, Yegudiil (Matvey's inner self) sends Matvey off, to go work in a certain factory, where are Yegudiil's friends. And now comes a "going to the People" in its twentieth-century form—a "going to the Workers." This was the emotional path Gorky himself had taken. Many would take it. In America in the thirties, in the Left-Wing movement, going to work in a factory became literally a path to personal salvation. Faithfully, in naïve poetic symbol, Gorky identifies in this book—it has never been identified as clearly—the vision that moved the Left Wing—of the Workers as the Chosen People.

To the factory, "all roads seemed now to lead." And there, in workers' huts in the forest nearby, Matvey meets the *God-builders!* The main ones are Mikhail (Michael, surely the Archangel) and his uncle, Peter; between them, they have the keys. As for Yegudiil, it turns out that he, who in the wilderness shows men the true path, is better known to them as John.

It is Mikhail who helps Matvey "build God in himself," by continuing the revelation begun by Yegudiil. This human life, he tells Matvey, became so "ragged and unworthy of reason" the day the first human personality tore loose from "the wonder-working strength" of the People, its mother, and squeezed itself, in fright, into a helpless and evil clump of trifling desires—the "I." Each "I" hates and injures every other; yet, remembering its birth in the Whole, each "I" torn from the Whole keeps trying to bring together the Whole again in its early might.

Says Mikhail: "When the People splintered into slaves and rulers, into bits and pieces, when it tore asunder its thoughts and will—God perished." But when the People again flow together as one, an irresistible strength will rise in it, "and God will be resurrected. He it is whom you, Matvey, seek."

This is the theory of "God-building." It would become a scandal in the Russian revolutionary movement.

There was a man, in real life, to whom Gorky owed its structure. But it was Gorky who gave it true religious feeling, and poetic expression.

The forest beside the factory is actually a school, where Mikhail and Uncle Peter teach God-building to the workers. There are also secular subjects: the power of money; the degradation of the workers; and the need to end the division of the people into social classes.

The discussion method is used. Students speak up. Matvey, for one, argues that "First a man needs to find his spiritual homeland, only then will he see his place on earth, then he will find freedom." But Mikhail insists that first comes the need to find each other, combine into a "wonder-working unity," and turn it against "the cunning foe." God can only rise "in the flame of sweet recognition of the spiritual kinship of each with all."

Here, in this theological novel of Gorky's, was stated (by the Archangel Michael) the emotional Rubicon crossed by those who became the bolsheviks. First must come the instantaneous moral—really mystical—decision; all else followed. What they themselves did not realize was that from then on they would have to follow Lenin, who, in mystic moral anger, in "the flame of sweet recognition of the kinship of each with all," had already long made his decision. If they had too, only *action* remained: "Follow me!"

The brief clash between Matvey and Mikhail was crucial. Matvey (Gorky) was questioning the need to cross that Rubicon. He was asking the revolutionaries first to stop and try to understand themselves. Mikhail temporarily overpowered Matvey (as Lenin had overpowered the young, malleable Gorky). But Matvey had shown an insight which, once gained, can never be lost. Those years were a turning point; with this book, Gorky's emotional allegiance to bolshevism was ended. The allegiance to a dream of communal oneness and good remained; but it was his own.

When Matvey leaves the God-builders and takes to the road again, one senses that the climax—the mystic's long-sought vision—is approaching. New feelings tremble in him, as if from each person were emitted a sharp, thin ray, which touched his heart, "and ever more eagerly I accepted these secret rays." (These are clearly ikon rays, from the aureole of a Byzantine sacred figure.) He wanders, now preaching his still unborn gospel . . . calling men to a new service and life while still not knowing his new God.

At last: "In Kazan province I experienced the last blow to the heart, that blow which completes the building of the temple."

That phrase, "the last blow," will recur to Gorky once, probably his last words—like Goethe's "More light!"—pointing to the vision in this book as his ultimate, irreplaceable.

A column of marchers of the Cross came up a hill, carrying a wonder-working ikon of the Mother of God. A red pennant burned above them, sprinkling them with blue sparks; the image of the Mother of God calmly rocked above them, like a bird of fire. At the city's gates, in a cart, lay a paralyzed girl. Around her the hope-filled people had congregated. Matvey had been standing on a hill nearby. Suddenly he remembered Yegudiil's words: "The People is the God-builder!" He rushed down, crying: "Rejoice! . . . Give strength from all strengths!" He melted into the marchers. All proceeded—a single being—on the march of the Cross.

They encircled the paralyzed girl. "Prayer!" With all their strengths, expressed by the sign of the Cross, the people strove to uplift the girl, "tens of eyes pouring their rays" into her, many hands making the sign of the cross. Finally they seized her, lifted her up, and—

Quietly walks among us the healed one, trustingly presses her new life-filled body against the body of the people, smiles, all white, like a flower, and speaks: "Let me—I—can . . . alone."

Hundreds of rays of light (from the people) uphold her.

That night, sitting by an inland sea, Matvey felt everything he had learned forming a unified light in him, which he reflected back into the world. He saw the world like a fiery flood of strength, flowing toward its confluence in one strength, its goal, "unattainable for me." But in this very unattainability was the source of endless spiritual growth.

And in the morning the earth stood before Matvey in fall plumage, "a holy place of pilgrimage to a holiday of beauty and truth." And he saw her master—"the deathless People."

He prayed:

"You are my God and You create all the Gods ...
"This I believe and confess.
"And I return there where men are freeing the souls of those close to them from the imprisonment of darkness ... lighting before the People its secret face ... revealing to the People the unified and true path to common flowing together for a mighty work—the world-wide building of God!"

Gorky was in his fortieth year when he wrote "The Confession." It marked the mid-point of his career, and the crisis of his art. It also marked, and to an extent precipitated, a furious crisis in the entire communist movement.


# CHAPTER 20


THE story of "The Confession" did not begin or end with its writing. The God-builders did not remain creatures in a book. Thanks largely to Gorky, they—and their "God-builders' university" as well—became very real. The God-building Movement—so it was called— was strong enough, finally, to cause the last serious split among the bolshe- viks before the 1917 Revolution; it marked the last serious challenge to the supremacy of Lenin's will. Gorky led this movement—he and two others.

This strange story has remained nearly unknown, just as Gorky's book, so crucial in his development as a man and an artist, is almost unknown. It was a strange time, which Gorky's book reflected: a time of recoil, on the part of many, from the headlong revolutionary drive, an effort to examine, to regroup, to start again toward old ideals by new roads.

As Marxism's army was growing, sweeping up rebels, angry men and rejects, Lenin had formed within it his bolshevik faction, and given it a mold. A special stamp of orthodoxy was put on the faithful: unvarying answers, the assurance of unity and militancy. Lenin was the right man to impose gospel, keep it pure, and forge the rigid means of triumph. A whole program of life had been worked out, and an organization built to carry it into battle. And by now there existed in Russian cities a nucleus of workers prepared to accept the bolshevik faction of the Social-Democratic Party as their captain.

But all this time—while dogmas were jelling and cadres forming—new ideas were also ripening in silence, and finally began to stir. Wherever life stirs, an already set mold is in danger of being broken.

For science and thought had gone on, astonishing as this may have seemed, after the thunderclap of Marx.

By the century's turn, probability laws were being suggested (instead of causal laws) to describe the life of the universe; this itself was a blow to "final truths," on which Lenin's hold on the faithful depended. In 1900 Planck introduced the idea of quanta. Einstein extended it in 1905, and was already working toward a theory of relativity. Some parallel thinking had been done, even earlier, by Mach, who will be important in this story. Bohr and others were analyzing the structure of the atom. Americans had picked up the vital leads of Locke and Hume about the role of the senses; Europe was belatedly following. All this meant taking a closer look at the creature adored by Gorky: man. Freud had turned his surgical knife on the creature's psyche.

This revolution of the understanding was first cousin to that Revolution on whose barricades (1830, 1848, 1870, 1905) so many had fallen; and for whom the zealots of the bolshevik faction (in passion and with Leninist determination) were preparing new barricades. But it led to uncharted ground, new perspectives. It was a rival and a threat.

Outside the charmed circle, Marx's neat tri-level "law" of history was beginning to look more like teleology than science. Even within the Social-Democratic movement, the religious awe before *Das Kapital* had been pierced by Eduard Bernstein. The Book, Bernstein said (in his own book, "Evolutionary Socialism," with statistics to back him), was better as sociology and moral guidance than as economics, for Marx's theory of the increasing gap between the classes did not correspond to reality. All this while Lenin and his followers (like Snow-White's gnomes singing at their toil) were nailing Marx's and Engels' every sentence into a creed, the Last Word for all times and all men.

New insights, and the fanaticism of the revolutionary movement, had already driven away many—especially if society gave them a place again to grab hold. By the start of the century, as Marxism began to congeal into Leninism, there was a whole reservoir of ex-Marxists. One of them, Berdyaev, came to a mystical religious philosophy, which he himself called "Christian communism."

Because he had been exposed to the living religious enthusiasm of the Russian revolutionary movement, Berdyaev spoke from a modern hilltop; he is one of the acknowledged fathers of Christian existentialism. He declared that historical Christianity was coming to an end; a rebirth was to be looked for "only from a religion of the Holy Spirit"; Christians would have to learn much from atheism. "That which rises up in human consciousness against God in the name of man is also an uprising of the true God himself. Revolt against God can only be ... for the sake of a higher idea of God."

This—written by Berdyaev long after the 1917 Revolution, in Paris exile—could have been a review of "The Confession." He could not have failed to recognize Gorky's book as the guidon of that religious revolt which was the heart of the dream of Russian communism whose origins he described. And, long before he wrote "The Confession," Gorky—like his two chief comrades of the God-building movement—had read and been affected by Berdyaev's earlier works.

In those who, unlike Berdyaev, had not abandoned the revolutionary movement, the note of Christian socialism was muted, or silenced, as they strained forward in the name of "Science." But with the bloody failure of the Revolution of 1905, soul-searching on a mass scale set in—as always after a great failure. The callow turned to easier ideals: sex and the fast ruble. Some, more complicated, began a search for a mystic meeting of man and God, body and spirit; unfortunately, their noble quest usually ended in ultraconservatism and racial bigotry, the mark of spiritual failure.

The fate of others was worse. Andreyev, Gorky's friend, had seen the Revolution's dirty side and wanted no more of it. But he was stuck, not being a reactionary and with no strong vision of his own. While Gorky was endangering his integrity out of a need to hang on to the hope held out by bolshevism, Andreyev was destroying himself as an artist, for his revulsion (without replacement) left him a prey to his old weaknesses as a man and writer—inanity and false effects of style. He and Gorky broke, during the Capri period, over an anti-revolutionary play by Andreyev ... over their philosophies of life ... perhaps over something personal that Gorky refused to forgive; the story, as its blurred outline comes through in their letters, is emotionally tangled. The frail and rather precious friendship could not be brought to life again. This was fatal to Andreyev's career: he did not really fit with the Right, while Gorky had been his lifeline to the Left. He would die in exile, across the Finnish border, to the noise of guns attacking and defending Soviet Petersburg—a bitter story, a talent nearly altogether wasted. The time was full of such tragedies.

But disenchantment was also reflected, in that period of recoil, at the very core of the revolutionary movement, where Gorky then belonged. For a long time, socialism, the holy end, had made all means to it holy. Now, "many who had been sucked into the radical movement from their student days paused for the first time to examine its premises." Many suddenly doubted whether the monolithic party which Lenin wanted was their answer; many wondered if the ends really justified *any* means. "Where shall we find the Law?" one writer cried in despair. "In the Party program? In Marx? In Engels? In Kant?"

Like Gorky's early characters of fiction, most of the idealists of Revolution were men who had sought "a Law to live by"; their life story had been one of moving, in their loyalties, from Kant to Hegel to Marx; now it was all undone. Kant, for all his pedantry, had laid down a moral principle: to act at every moment so that if all acted likewise the universe would be morally perfect. To even consider this meant a vast detour on the revolutionary road.

Hegel's inevitable progress of history, with violins added by Marx, had been the music that formed their spirits—and Lenin's machine. Now the machine was endangered—Lenin sounded the tocsin—by this wave of "subjectivism," this new worry about the means to the ends.

Within the citadel of the bolshevik faction itself the centrifugal forces acted; and there, in fact, the most serious heresy began. Foremost of those who wanted to explore other paths to revolution was A. A. Malinovsky, whose Party name was Bogdanov—"Given by God." He had come to Lenin's rescue at a dark moment following Lenin's break with Plekhanov. Now Lenin and Bogdanov and Plekhanov were the Bolshevik Central Committee; and the first two, in alliance against Plekhanov, controlled both the committee and the new party paper, *Proletary*.

Even in the striking and fantastic gallery of the revolutionaries, Bogdanov was outstanding. The son of a priest, he was a trained physician, a student of physics, an economist, a philosophic thinker, and a poet. His poetry is lyrical and full of social feeling, revealing a man who, like

Gorky, was on familiar terms with God and accustomed to inveigh against
him:

> Answer me: what is the reason
> for the lies, rape, evil done to others?
> See below us spread this valley
> running with the blood of brothers.

Bogdanov's wide reading had taken him to the work of Ernst Mach,
the Czech mathematician, physicist and philosopher. Mach, inspired by
both Kant and Hume, had come to feel that all of existence as we know
it is created by the way all individuals, acting as a single complex, organize
the sum total of their sense experience. "All of humanity is like a bed of
coral." It participates in its entirety in the formation of every idea; and
every idea, once enunciated, is the common property of all. "The ideal
ethic which is based on this concept will be equally removed from asceticism, which cannot be supported biologically, and from the insolence of
the Nietzschean superman, which other men cannot endure and which,
let us hope, they will not endure."

Here are the leading ideas of "The Confession," without the ikons. To
one like Gorky, egalitarian, repelled by the ruthlessness of the overman,
desirous of communal warmth and security, Mach's thought, transmitted
by Bogdanov, must have struck a deep response.

Mach didn't think there were "final truths"; he accepted even time,
space and the atom only as "hypotheses," and from there moved on toward
the most modern insights. Einstein said he came close to anticipating, by
half a century, the general theory of relativity. For Mach, reality might
be either spiritual or material; in any case it too was not final; it was
constructed by humans as they went along. This is akin to pragmatism;
William James visited Mach respectfully. Today's child psychology and
educational psychology acknowledge him.

Bogdanov grasped at Mach's idea of the human coral bed—the total
social organization of experience. Perhaps to *reorganize* experience was
the real revolution that was needed; revolutionizing an external world was
of dubious use, unless something inside the human ego could also be
transformed.

To prepare a base, Bogdanov outlined a philosophy, using Marx's social
dialectic and Mach's coral bed, in tandem with Darwin and Kepler: There
is a positive selection which spreads veins of life's energy but also mul-
tiplies inner contradictions, using up more energy than is created; and

there is a negative selection, which culls away outlined forms, so that although it squeezes life it actually opens the way for new energy creation. Crises, like revolution, are such negative movements of the dialectic, doing the necessary simplifying and harmonizing of life, for a new expansion. Once men understood these laws, they could proceed, within their immutable limits, to reorganize the education of human impulses and thoughts, toward a far better society.

This interesting effort to give life to the rather heavy and static ideas of Marx, by fusing them with others, horrified Lenin, as did the idea of inner change. He hated that word "inner," just as he hated "subjective."

By 1907, when Gorky was finishing "The Man Nobody Needed" and feeling the seed of "The Confession" astir, Bogdanov was looking for a place to start on his program of social reorganization. This should properly be with the proletariat, the lowest class and with the longest future. Thus, "proletarian culture"; here the process of reconstructing humanity could begin.

Change could then assuredly take place in the most desirable direction. The workers would be ready with their own culture, based on true knowledge, to take over as the malorganized old system fell in ruins. But where would this have left Lenin, and those around him, whose whole emotional life now depended on overt revolution?

At the same time another man was searching for new answers, new paths: another ranking member of the bolshevik faction—Lunacharsky.

A more determined romantic than Gorky, Lunacharsky had moved from religion and religious art to socialism, without ever really giving up his first loves. While Gorky was writing "The Confession," he was working on *his* book, "Religion and Socialism." Poor Lenin was now beset on three sides by the religious heresy.

Lunacharsky's starting point was an early book by Berdyaev. Agreeing that socialism was a faith, he would not follow Berdyaev to mysticism and a personal God; but the essence of religion, he wrote, could outlive its various forms. God was a form of hope, a concept of necessary illusion. The prophet is one who demands a re-examination of the agreement with God, and this always becomes also a re-examination of social relations.

Tracing all the ancient and modern religions, Lunacharsky declared the positivists were too narrow: religion, stripped of dogma, means enthusiasm, "and without enthusiasm it is not given to people to create anything great." Christianity was an orphic Judaism; and in the Christ legend there was too much acceptance; but also in it was a creative democratic feeling which "forecasts the future." He finally offered Marxism as the religion of the future as well as a social program. This could usher in the Kingdom ("Tsardom") of Humanity; thus he describes the coming communist state.

## CHAPTER 21

THE cross-fertilization of love and science, aesthetic religion and coral beds, took place—where could it more properly?—on the Isle of Capri. There Gorky had his stronghold, and nearby Bogdanov and Lunacharsky (brothers-in-law: Lunacharsky's wife was Bogdanov's sister) came to rest from intra-Party battles. There the three of them must have paced the cliffs above the Mediterranean together: the man whose writing had always been a form of guerilla warfare with God, the man who had taken the Party name of "God-given," and the former Talmudic scholar.

From these sessions Gorky went back to his desk and completed "The Confession." Then, Gorky-like, he decided it wasn't enough to have a God-builders' university in his book; let a start be made in real life.

From this point, the story is a fabulous one: the Capri school for revolutionary Russian workers.

Though both Bogdanov and Gorky were steering toward a utopian academy, it took one more character, named Alexinsky, to help it become practical. Another bolshevik stalwart, he had represented the workers of Petersburg in the Second Duma.

When the Duma was dissolved by the Tsar, Lenin assigned Alexinsky to "oversee the doctrinal purity" of a Russian-language magazine put out by Armenian students in Geneva. The magazine folded, and Alexinsky turned his revolutionary concern to the fact that in Russia the battalions of future Social Democrats were being decimated; study circles could hardly meet even secretly, as the police struck with arrests and deportations. He had a bright thought: to create, abroad, an "advanced school for propagandists."

He came to Capri, and talked with Bogdanov, Lunacharsky and Gorky. Their ideas weren't exactly the same, but they could be dovetailed; and Alexinsky had fresh connections with the workers' centers in Russia. Gorky, Alexinsky writes, was thrilled; he was upset at being so removed from the Russian working-class movement; now the workers could be brought to him. He insisted the school be organized at once, on Capri, and even promised a "Maecenas" to put up money. Savva Morozov was dead; maybe he had another candidate; more likely Horace himself— Gorky—was the Maecenas.

First they needed students. The "organizing committee" sent a "delegation" to Russia, to recruit at the main workers' centers, and to propose that the local Social-Democratic Party organizations choose candidates for these scholarships. The organizations "responded with enthusiasm," and in a few weeks the scholarship students started to cross the border in secret. It could only have happened in Russia.

They wanted a broad faculty. So, while giving preference to bolsheviks among the distinguished professors to be invited, the committee also cordially offered chairs to ranking mensheviks like Martov and Dan; and to Plekhanov, Trotsky, and Karl Kautsky and Rosa Luxemburg of Germany. The school could have proved a feast of reunion for the shattered and warring socialist factions; this must have been Gorky's naïve hope: the first step to God-building.

The chief mensheviks, fearing a bolshevik trap, declined. Plekhanov, who scorned Bogdanov's idea that "proletarian culture" could come *before* instead of only *after* the revolution, didn't bother to answer Gorky. Trotsky apparently was intrigued, and told Gorky he would come, but then "couldn't." He was at that time a loner—with neither the bolsheviks, mensheviks nor Plekhanov—and he must have guessed the school might infuriate Lenin; he would wait and see. Kautsky, revered elder of all Social Democrats, replied that he worked better with pen than with mouth. Rosa Luxemburg also decided the water around Capri was too warm.

So the school would not represent the whole party; but this was only the start of its tribulations.

Lenin had been urgently invited. Gorky was no longer under his spell, but respected him as the party's dominant figure. But Lenin was just then preparing to break with Bogdanov and oust him from his place in the bolshevik leadership. He was furious at Bogdanov's "Machism," as a threat to dogma; more immediately galling was that some of Bogdanov's followers, on grounds of principle, insisted the bolsheviks should not take part in the next Tsarist duma—while Lenin was sure the best way to torpedo the autocracy, at this stage, was to work through parliamentary channels. Of course Lenin was also angry about "The Confession" and

"Religion and Socialism." He refused Gorky's repeated invitations to teach a course. And he was only getting warmed up.

Determined to wean Gorky away from Bogdanov and Lunacharsky, he wrote to Gorky that *their* ideas were "absurd, pernicious, philistine, wholly priestish, from beginning to end." He wrote: "I am not going to argue with men who have gone off to preach the fusion of scientific socialism with religion." He added a postscript: "Especial greetings to Maria Feodorovna; she is not, I hope, for God, eh?"

Gorky parried. Back came a wire, Capri to Paris, signed by both Gorky and Maria Feodorovna, with a final plea for Lenin to come and prevent a break. Lenin wired back refusal.

On second thought the astute politician must have realized things had gone rather far on Capri. He sent a follow-up letter, urging the mavericks not to let differences in philosophy get in the way of political work, that Lunacharsky accordingly continue to support the bolshevik newspaper, *Proletary*, and that Bogdanov raise more money for the bolshevik organizations.

But the stakes were too big: the fate of the heresy would decide what ideas and whose mentality were to lead the revolutionary movement. A split in the bolshevik faction was in the making. Lenin was already in action, while Bogdanov was meditating on proletarian culture, Lunacharsky preparing his lectures on religious art, and Gorky writing letters everywhere trying to make everyone happy.

Meanwhile, twenty Russian scholarship students were stealthily crossing the Alps.

They were led by one Mikhail Vilonov, a worker who had become a bolshevik, been in prison several times, escaped, been caught, beaten, contracted tuberculosis. The Party had helped him escape abroad, and he had gotten to Capri—to be embraced by Gorky, Lunacharsky and Bogdanov. So delighted was he with the climate and new exciting friends that he resolved other workers must "taste of paradise." He sneaked back into Russia—this is the account Gorky gave later, and it probably explains the "delegation" referred to by Alexinsky—and it was he who got the Party to agree to send groups of intelligent factory workers to Capri.

They must have started some time in 1908—the Russian sense of time, in those days, was fairly Biblical; nobody looked for another revolutionary effort in the near future, and a year or so either way did not seem to matter. The Tsarist authorities, however, were right up to date on the project, and arrest orders were sent out. The scholars used part of the money the Party had given them to buy their way across the Russian border; tuition would be free.

At one border town they had been instructed to go to the house of a socialist midwife. Their password was: "My wife has given birth to triplets." One at a time they approached this stop on the underground railroad, and so twenty times that night the maid answered the door, each time to be greeted by a man who explained to her that his wife had just given birth to triplets.

So as not to neglect their education on the way, they paused at various capitals. In Vienna, Trotsky, still a prospective member of the Capri faculty, met them and took them through the city's museums.

Also, there were letters for them, to be picked up en route, and after they got to Capri, from Vladimir Ilyitch Lenin.

Before starting out, the students had learned of Lenin's refusal to join the faculty. Puzzled and hurt, they sent Lenin a formal summons, in the name of the Moscow Committee of the Social-Democratic Party, to appear at Capri. In case of refusal they would bring charges of breach of discipline.

This gave Lenin a chance to enter into a long and friendly correspondence, which he never let lapse. He told them they were "fine lads," but "not experienced in political struggle." He would be happy to teach them— if they would come to Paris. In the suburb of Longjumeau he himself, as it happened, was starting a workers' school; and it was not a rump school like the one on Capri, but fully accredited, including not only bolsheviks— himself, Kamenev and Zinoviev—but also the chief mensheviks—Martov and Dan—on the faculty.

So while the scholarship students strolled on, dodging the police at various frontiers, finally descending Italy toward the Isle of Capri, they were already enjoying the prospect of an extension of their *Wanderjahr*. Five months on Capri, then on to Paris; why not?

All this time, within the Party, Lenin's attack on Bogdanov's heresy was mounting. He was aided by Plekhanov, temporarily again his ally, who fired volleys of intellectual disdain at Gorky and "The Confession": "Gorky preaches what Lunacharsky does. But he knows less (by this I do not mean to say that Lunacharsky knows much); he is more naïve (by this I do not mean to suggest that Lunacharsky is devoid of naïveté); he is less versed in the contemporary theory of socialism (which does not in the least imply that Lunacharsky is well versed in it). For this reason his effort at clothing socialism in the robe of religiosity proves even a greater failure."

This was in the *Proletary*, whose expanded editorial board had by now "excluded" Bogdanov. Bogdanov, Lunacharsky and their supporters formed their own magazine, *Vperyod* ("Forward!"). Gorky kept writing Lenin to try to heal the split, and did not formally join the *Vperyod* group. Lenin urged him by mail to abandon his aberrant notions— "whether about God or Godlings." He was gentle, understanding, and scolded Gorky like a father. Meanwhile in continued adroit maneuvers he got the Bolshevik Center in Paris (in June 1909) to denounce Bogdanov and Lunacharsky for "preaching faith and God-building," and thus in effect read them out of the bolshevik faction of the party.

At about this point, also in the summer of 1909, the wandering scholars arrived.

We may imagine the Russian greetings—bear hugs, and the traditional kisses on both cheeks—one, two!—one, two!—and the repeated toasts, before classes began.

The school on Capri, as Gorky later described it to his biographer Kaun, was lively, "pupils refusing to swallow the wisdom of the lecturers whole, but engaging in heated arguments and discussion." As it comes through from what he told Kaun later, and from Alexinsky's memories, it really was something like the God-builders' school in "The Confession" —a dream come true, and with Gorky as the head God-builder, like (the Archangel) Mikhail!

Bogdanov taught political economy; it was there he must have evolved his "Question and Answer" catechism, which became standard for left-wing "workers' schools" internationally. Pokrovsky taught history; after the Bolshevik Revolution he would be the dean of Moscow University.

Alexinsky taught syndicalism, and finance; Lunacharsky, the history of the labor movement and of revolutions—and, oh yes, the history of art, which proved the most popular thing in the curriculum. Gorky taught Russian literature; we know he included lectures on Gogol, Leskov, and Pushkin.

Often mock debates were held. The faculty and students took the roles of various Russian political parties. Gorky, according to Alexinsky, always took the role of the extreme reactionary, one of the native-fascist "Black Hundreds," and thoroughly enjoyed himself, also delighting the students. We have seen repeatedly how in his writings his real heart often ached to be with the villains, while his moral sense forbade it. Acting is a great release.

Lunacharsky, as part of his course on art history, took the students on a tour of the churches and museums of Rome; and they also had the benefit of contact with men in the arts and professions "who constantly flocked to Gorky's villa and readily displayed their talents." Gorky wrote to a friend "rhapsodically, about the superb lads whose companionship he cherished beyond words." This period was probably among the happier ones in his whole life. It was brief.

Lenin kept up a chummy correspondence with the students, urging them to abandon the outlawed school and come to his. He got five of the workers to quit suddenly in mid-semester, and go to Paris; among them was the redoubtable Vilonov. The others stuck it out for the length of the courses, then went on to Paris, too.

"Alas," wrote Kaun, "essentially non-political, Gorky was forcibly involved in party wrangle and squabble, which poisoned the joyous atmosphere of the school, and eventually destroyed it. Lenin was responsible for this turn of affairs; he was always ingenious, and nearly always successful, in his methods of attack against his enemies, and as such he regarded the Capri school."

Gorky was chagrined and upset; but Lenin had managed to drive a wedge between him and Bogdanov, and also then managed, through the intermediacy of Vilonov, to preserve his relation with Gorky. He was able to write Gorky, as the good politician is always able to make a nice gesture after winning the game, "I grasp your hand and the hand of Maria Feodorovna, for now I am enabled to hope that you and I shall yet meet not as enemies."

The school was destroyed, Lenin concentrated artillery on the "Forward" group, and Bogdanov was finished politically. Some of those who had stood with him came back to Lenin and therefore to the possibility of influencing the revolutionary movement; these God-builders who ate humble pie included a number of the better thinkers and more cultivated men among the bolsheviks.

Lunacharsky justified Lenin's confidence that "he will come back to the Party." He took part in the October Revolution, and became the Soviet's first commissar of culture and education, and one of the humanistic influences in the first, often inhuman years. He was even able to defend Gorky, in the thirties, when Gorky incurred the wrath of the fanatics in power.

Alexinsky trotted back to Lenin at once, but later broke with bolshevism (over the issue of supporting World War I), and ended his life
in Paris a stanch antibolshevik.

Bogdanov was never reconciled to Lenin, and never surrendered; and
this Lenin never forgave him, nor did others. Lenin's one, revealingly
empty, effort at a statement of a philosophy about life, his book "Materialism and Empirio-Criticism," was written by him in an effort to dispose
of Bogdanov's ideas.

Bogdanov took no part in the October Revolution, but immediately
afterward he came back to his country and, things still being rather
chaotic, was able to set up his organization for "proletarian culture,"
which among other things encouraged young writers of proletarian origin; it was a factor in the emergence of some of the early Soviet poetry
in the "renaissance" of the twenties. The Party's fanatics finally destroyed
his organization, and drove him out of government. He went back to
medicine, becoming director of the Institute for Experimental Research
in Moscow. In 1928, working on a new type of blood transfusion, he
performed it on himself rather than try it on anyone else, and died.

So implacable were his politically successful foes that, though his influence lives, his views and his poetry and even his name are buried.

With the disruption of the Capri school and the fall of Bogdanov,
Gorky had to move away, whether or not he wanted to, from these
influences which had culminated in "The Confession" and the God-
building school. Maria Feodorovna helped. Lunacharsky's baby daughter
died, and at the funeral the bereaved father read an improvised sermon.
Maria Feodorovna couldn't help laughing. This brought on a split between the families. Gorky backed out of an ambitious project he and
Bogdanov had been planning—an encyclopedia of science, written for
"the common reader." By 1910, the "Machist heresy" was done for, and
Lenin could visit Gorky on Capri; Bogdanov and his associates were gone.

The two men went fishing together. The Italian fishermen explained
to Lenin how to pull in the line when he got a nibble. "Così—drin-drin.
Capisce?" Lenin: "Aha! Drin-drin?" Long after, the fishermen kept asking
Gorky: "How is Signor Drin-Drin? The Tsar won't catch him, will he?"

The fires of folk religion would never break out again in Gorky; but
the experience, with its degree of self-awareness, had matured him. He
never again would have a crush on Lenin. His correspondence with Lenin
contains reluctant admissions that he had gone off the straight path; but
he never really repudiated "The Confession," no matter how hard Lenin

tried to make him. His stand at the time of the Revolution, now soon to come, showed he had stored up memories, and had learned much from this drastic experience and insight into Lenin, gained in defeat. The work, too, that he produced from then on shows, overall, a greater degree of self-assurance. It would seem that "The Confession," by pulling him to the inmost limit of his true beliefs, also made possible the controlled and artistic self-revelation of the great autobiographical books.

As for Lenin, one of his many talents was his ability to constantly keep a hand on Gorky. But besides, there is evidence that he genuinely liked the man. He clucked over him; and this clucking—like the old scrunched-up shoes he wore—was one of the traits with which he won hearts and disarmed adversaries.

Gorky wrote to Lenin that, as he sat working in his villa, his hands were shivering with cold.

"What do you mean, my dear man," clucked Lenin, "by behaving so abominably? Overworked, tired, nervous! That's rank disorderliness. At least on Capri, especially in the winter when you probably have few invaders, you ought to lead a regular life. Is there no one to look after you, and is that why you're going to pieces? For God's sake, that's bad! Get yourself in hand and follow a strict routine, please do! It is quite inadmissible to be sick at this day and age. Have you, by any chance, begun to work nights? When I visited Capri you kept saying that it was only I who introduced disorder, and that before I arrived you used to go to bed early. So! Get rested and establish a proper routine, without fail!"

## CHAPTER 22

FOR close to five years, Gorky had felt duty-bound to serve Lenin's creed, which he believed had saved him from inner desperation. Trying to transform the creed into a living faith, in "The Confession," had meant a near break with Lenin, and the end of the crush. But if the emotional thralldom was over, there remained both a sense of defeat and a somewhat awed awareness of the power of a scruple-free man, who by skill at manipulating men, and determination, can shatter any coalition of idealists.

In these psychological circumstances, there had to be a period of partial retreat for Gorky, a psychic pause, just as there had been—though hectic outer activity went on—after the wild, blind protest of "Foma Gordeyev's" ending, before Gorky found Lenin's salvation army.

He had freedom and solitude on Capri, and worked hard, as always; but his villa was constantly full of social and literary visitors, and even hangers-on. The need to be bountiful, to provide a "center" for others, is a quality in itself that can rarely stand examination.

The inward discouragement and the psychological retreat are shown in the return by Gorky to "social realism"—his usual device when beset by inner perplexities—in two novels that mark the next, his middle, period on Capri. The books are stamped by a fatalistic feeling that someone Lenin-like is the only likely savior, or master, of Russia.

The better novel by far is "Little Town of Okurov" (bitter negative echo of "Little Town of Bethlehem"). It is a lethargic mean little town, in a lethargic, besotted land. The time is the eve of the 1905 Revolution. "The sky covered the town like a gray, heavy hat, clouded the distance, and flung down on it, as if seeding, a fine dampness of light-ash color."

One "hero" is a drunken roisterer and police-hired thug, who is also a man of natural warmth and desires. His name, Burmistrov, contains the first syllable of *burya*—the Storm. He is the elemental man of the mob. Ths other "hero" is Simeon, a timid yearning yokel, a poet, too weak to live or love successfully. Here again, are Gorky's old contradictions: The good is no good for anything; the bad is strong and warm, and strength and warmth are good.

The action centers on Madam Felitsata's Little Paradise, the town brothel, done with reality and charm. One of the girls, Glafira, the same statuesque, vivid brunette who has been met before in Gorky's work, is Burmistrov's loved one. Simeon also yearns for her, and tries on her his faltering, bitter, sad poems, each of which he wants to be "like a prayer."

> In the dark streets the pitiful children
> Perish of cold and hunger ...
> Rarely does the caress of father-mother
> Caress them, only when dead
> Are they loved—on the way to the cemetery.

This may be taken, if one likes, as the belated lament for Alexey's little brother, Maxim, who died on that Volga boat, and was carried ashore in a little box for hasty burial.

Father Isaiah Kudriavsky (a parody of Bishop Khrisanph) encourages Simeon to go on writing poetry: "Praiseworthy, Simeon, praiseworthy! Both the direction of the thought and the simplicity of style—strongly touch the soul. Work, young one, don't bury in the ground the talent given by God, and with the help of Simeon, the host of God—your patron saint—you will rise, from gloom to the heights!"

This was how Gorky really felt his poetry should be praised, and on these high grounds. He buried it in his novels, and sneered at it himself by attributing it to weak or deficient characters, like Simeon. This was the distressing fate of most of his poetry.

A spokesman for the town at large says: "We live rottenly. In youth we rob the earth. When old we try to climb the sky, staggering into monasteries, into prayer . . ." This was the bitter comment of Gorky, the moral idealist, on what he considered the spiritual bankruptcy of Russian life: the idea that one can live badly, and do anything, and then wash it out by prayer at the end. (Years later, he himself would be impelled to believe that it was impossible to live without sinning; life would not permit him to be so morally righteous.)

All the time, in the distance, in the suburbs of Okurov, coopers are heard hammering the staves that will bind great barrels of the future: TOOM—TOOM—TOOM.

Glafira grows sorry for Simeon, and lets him come to her. Burmistrov, in a drunken rage, murders the poor scarecrow of a poet. Glafira runs away, and gives herself to the lecherous old police inspector, for protection. He tells her, before throwing her out in the morning: "I keep thinking: How cheap a man is in Russia. And how unnecessary to anyone, honest to God."

"Revolution" has started—something chaotic, incomprehensible; the town's bells ring wildly. Burmistrov, who was jailed for the murder, gets out and nobody cares. "What's it to me—freedom?" he shouts. "I killed, and I'm free! I stole, and I'm free!" Life is lawless again; Gorky has returned to the despairing negative outcry of the early novels.

Burmistrov feels a need to confess, but then comes a brilliant thought: he really killed the poet for his sacrilegious verses, and God gave him the strength to do it! The mob acclaims him. His conscience tearing at him, making him more brutal, he leads a charge of the know-nothings into the town square. The book ends with all the miserable, vicious citizens of Okurov fighting blindly and savagely in the now thickly falling snow, which will soon obliterate the town.

"And ever the tireless man worked on—somewhere on Cockcrow Hill. He seems to be hammering out a strong hoop for the whole city, stubbornly and confidently beating it out: TOOM—TOOM—TOOM ... TOOM—TOOM ...

Who is this cooper so confidently and stubbornly on Cockcrow Hill (where the cocks crow in Holy Russia, announcing dawn) beating out the hoops of a New Law, that will confine this sprawling, bestial lawless Russian life and people? In the context, it can only be Lenin.

The retreat continued in another, longer and inferior, novel of 1909–1910, "Matvey Kozhemaykin." Self-hatred, carping, tedium permeate this life story of a man of Okurov. In the end there is no coherent view, only a dull anger at life, a passive yearning to live better, that fall short of meaning. An unparalleled paean to Mother Volga, and other fine moments, are lost in the shapeless failure.

It seemed that the stormy petrel was slowing, weakened by years of careening, the last wild flight ("The Confession") having ended in disappointment, which had passed into a perhaps premature autumnal maturity; now he would circle predictably about old themes, taking out his inner conflict in tedium and spleen.

But in the year 1911 a memorable new, unexpected note is heard, sudden and clear, out of the conflict of instruments which was Gorky's usual inner state. It rises clear of tortured quandaries and allegories, of hysterical police spies and even of God-seekers and God-builders, clear of unanalyzed yearnings and anger. A man is talking.

He is talking about another man, much older, whom he met years ago, and whom he observed closely. He seems to have touched and probed the other man, with hands as well as eyes, with intellectual feelers, and feelers of sensitivity. He portrays him at near distance, with warmth, curiosity, admiration, but not uncritically. It is like a portrait by Holbein, or Vermeer, or Rembrandt. Byzantium's ikons have been left behind.

This is an essay about the Russian Populist writer and intellectual Karonin-Petropavlovsky, written for a magazine ("The Contemporary," a publication against which Lenin had warned Gorky, for its "doubtful tendencies").

He had met Karonin twenty-two years earlier, when he was twenty-one. The cud must have been worked over, through the years, brought up and chewed again ... to be at last digested.

The essay starts on a note of self-deprecation. "Leaving Tsaritsin, I hated the whole world and stubbornly thought of suicide ... I wrote poisonously satirical verse, cursing everything that existed, and dreamed of helping start an agricultural colony."

A few more mock-heroic (but revealing) flourishes, then the notes glide more truly, and within two paragraphs the transition into the true cadence is made.

... I had read much, and my notion of a Russian writer had jelled into a beautiful storytale image; he was a stern truth-crier, alone among people, loved by none, wielding an invincible power of resisting the enemies of justice, and, even though the enemies are determined to freeze out his soul, it flames without waning and, in spite of all, strikes light in the darkness.

N. E. Karonin was in accord with this notion. I had read nearly everything written by him, and just recently had become acquainted with the story "My World," where there are words that struck me in the heart:

"In the world there is nothing more precious than thought. It is the beginning and end of all existence, the cause and the result, the moving strength and the final goal. Who can force me to give it up? People are splendid only in the measure that this world-strength is in them. If the world is still enveloped in darkness, it is only because thought has not lighted it; if among people a large part are vile, it is only because thought has not yet freed them from madness."

This, the old belief of the Enlightenment, and of nineteenth-century Russia's moderate radicals and liberals, was really Gorky's ideal, though he quoted it, in his shy, sly way, from another man. This image of "the Russian writer" always had been his clearest image of himself; and from now on he would be less ashamed of it.

Then follows a rare scene, a dramatization, simple and sincere, of an encounter that makes a difference to a young man:

Karonin met the young tramp, Peshkov, at his door. He wore an old reddish jacket, over a shirt "no better than mine"—a button on its collar missing; crumpled pants, "also no better than mine"; his long hair was tousled, his eyes kind, tired, and a bit protruding. "In answer to his questions I silently nod my head, say 'yes' and 'no,' but all the time I am pleased to be looking at him."

Karonin took him into his study, sat him down, and talked to him. It is hard to transmit the atmosphere of his words. They are business-like, everyday; but the man comes through beautifully.

"Do you know—why do you need an agricultural colony? You don't need it. You're seeking idealism, aren't you? Well—"

And he explained that there was nothing idealistic in burying one's soul in the earth, surrounding oneself with trivialities. One should struggle against trivialities, not convert them into duties.

He drew a long line in the air with his hand, and chopped it off in the middle with a decisive gesture, and then wrinkled his face, sighed:
"A c-colony-ekh? D-do you really need it?"

And perhaps more telling than Karonin's words, his slight stutter, his gesture—and important for an understanding of Alexey Peshkov—Maxim Gorky—was the reaction of the young man:

More than a thousand versts I had carried the revery of an independent life with people who were friends, of land which I myself would plow, now, and with my own hands gather its fruit, of a life without anyone commanding me, without a boss, without degradation . . . And a quiet, soft man gave his hand a wave, and it was as if he had cut off the head of my revery. This happened suddenly to me . . .

And only now, by means of this passage, throwing its light more on creator than on created portrait, one can see with some precision the psychological path taken by young Peshkov (a path he obscured while telling about it, truthfully, in his autobiography):

In 1887, in Kazan, young Peshkov had tried to kill himself. In 1888 he picked up for a last time an intermittent dream—to go live on the land in a Tolstoyan colony, without a boss, without degredation. In 1889 he gave up this revery ("its head was cut off"). It was after that, perhaps immediately after, that he really began to be involved in the revolutionary movement. His first arrest was in 1889.

Men like Karonin and Korolenko influenced him more than he ever could admit, except in this shy, indirect way; probably more than men like Smoury. Walking in the fields, Karonin told him:

The Russian writer always wants to write something of a gospel, a book for the whole world ... This is a general striving among large and small writers, and, do you know, often the small ones somehow feel the eternal truth more truly, more deeply than do the geniuses—that's what you shouldn't forget, that's very important! Russian literature— is something special—it's, so to speak, a form of holy writing, and one has to read it very attentively, very!

The attentive reader of the essay, in turn, comes to feel, subtly, as if a straight line has been drawn through Karonin, the writer, and himself ... so that he is linked to Karonin and the essay organically and naturally, learning things worth learning about a man, of men, a nation, a people, a bit about life ... and hardly aware, any longer, of the young man who is the intermediary, the middle point on the line.

That young man has nearly effaced himself—after the opening remarks about his agricultural colony dream—effaced himself gracefully, with a grace beyond his years ... but he is the liquid medium of transmission, for that kindly, thoughtful, rather original man Karonin—who clearly suffered much himself, but refused to transmit his suffering, insisting rather on transmitting his ideals to generations unborn, without knowing it, by the transparent medium of that strange youth, Peshkov.

He lived in a constant anxiety over the fate of people, in continuous striving to earn his bread, and this tense nervous life greatly helped ill- ness to destroy his body, tortured by prison, convict-marches, exile. Ever more feverishly burned his eyes, more dryly sounded his cough.
He left Nizhni and died.
Someone told me that on the day of his death Karonin admitted sadly: "It turns out that it's much simpler to die than to live."

This portrait of an old Populist was not just an achievement but a breakthrough, to a new vein, deep, fresh, and authentic, such as an artist is seldom granted. It opened a new flowering period for Gorky.

One more psychological step was needed to clear the road for the autobiographical books. It was made the next year, 1912, in the form of a short story of no appreciable artistic merit; its merit in helping to understand Gorky is great.

"An Incident in the Life of Makar" is the reasonably unglossed story of his suicide attempt.

It is a revelation of desperation, of anger at the world, of the amazing depth of the rejection by his society that Alexey Peshkov had felt, the impossible gap between whatever he wanted to attain and his possibilities of attaining it in the society as it was then; and of the degree of his own stubbornness.

This young man went out and bought an old pistol, unravelled the belt-roll of rusty bullets he bought with it, loaded it, left a note saying, "If this incident disturbs you, please forgive me—M." (Here the story was not quite truthful. The note actually blamed "the German poet Heine, who thought up toothache of the heart"; the young man also wanted his body to be opened and examined, to see what devil had settled in it. This was just too foolish to remember.) Then he went to the top of the hillock above the city dump; en route, he passed the old Tartar night watchman, who had found an abandoned kitten, freezing, and advised the old man to warm the kitten inside his shirt. Above the dump, he put the pistol to his heart—the place of which he had ascertained (incorrectly) by careful study of an anatomy text—and pulled the trigger. The pistol failed. He examined it, and while he was doing so, pressed its trigger and it fired past him, singeing his hair. He quickly put it to the chosen spot and fired again, into his lung. When he realized he had not quite killed himself, and had failed to roll down into the dump, to be buried under snow for the winter, he was furious.

He was found by the Tartar watchman—carrying the kitten inside his shirt—who trundled him in a barrow all around town a couple of hours till he found the hospital. Peshkov was still angry about his failure, and planned to kill himself as soon as he came out. Only finally the kind solicitude of one of the girls who worked in a store near his room, and then of his fellow bakers (these are the Twenty-Six; she, possibly, the One), brought him back to the sun of life.

The autobiography he was now preparing to write would not invert the incident; but it would screen out the most striking elements of the pathological. The transformation from raw life to art is subtle and tasteful. The true story remains a document for understanding Maxim Gorky, or Makar—this being also the name of the rebel without a Cause who had been the hero of Gorky's first published story, "Makar Chudra." It also helps understand the depths of rejection and determination which make up the psychology of revolution.

Once he had managed to tell the story of his suicide try, he was ready to begin "Childhood," his first great autobiographical book, whose pages were the base for the opening chapters of this study.

## CHAPTER 23

"CHILDHOOD," is a seemingly artless affair. It tells the simple story of a childhood in the 1870's in Old Holy Russia. Yet so much of life is in it, it states the variety and complexity of things so clearly and fully, that it puts the great majority of "grown-up" books to shame.

There is every reason for recollections of childhood to be scattered, mannered, falsely gilded; most avoid them. Some hate themselves too much, some hate others too much; some are too hurt by defeats, others too proud of how far they have risen. The poses of manhood and womanhood descend, in retrospect, on the child. But this book of Gorky's—the story of the childhood and growth of Alexey Peshkov—is like the past quarried suddenly out of the dead ground, completely alive, and full of new adult meaning.

It is highly poetic. The world of things and the world of animals and the world of people all live, and all with equal poetry. "Unnoticed, the sun swims above the Volga." "A gold leaf of autumn floats on the water." "The houses press together, like beggars on a stoop." The bullfinches, proud of their beauty, sit on their thickets "swaying like living flowers," and "sprinkling the snow with blue sparks."

The description of the down-to-earth, of lower middle class urban life, in that time, in that land, is so clear and unstrained as to confer on these things a kind of eternity: the red and gold flame in the stove, the milky clouds of smoke over the dye vats in the yard, which settle, dove-colored, on the slanted roof through whose cracks show dark-blue sky ribbons... "The wind grew quieter, somewhere the sun is shining, the whole yard seems to be sprinkled with glass dust, on the street a sleigh scrapes as it crawls along, blue smoke curls up from the chimneys of houses, light shadows slide along the snow, telling a story (*skaz*) of some kind."

Life is a skaz—a story immemorial, a tale, both beautiful and painful, bright and mysterious, gay and terrible.

Here, one feels sharply, is the authentic world of childhood, none of its feelers broken, none of its poetry lost, while, stronger and stronger, the shadows of ugliness, poverty, viciousness, violence and violent death, throng up into the skaz. There is, finally, the sense of a double-winged movement, of Grandma's white pigeons (the angels) flying back and forth between the world and God, and of the deeds and cries and unfair suffering of the little boy and those all around him, like black pigeons circling and lamenting low over the ground, until finally white and black are mingled in a skaz both fearful and beautiful.

Here is the whole range of humans as they are, all in the little city of Nizhni, all in the slatternly, sinking circle around the home of the Kashirins; the artisan-shabby, the shopkeeper-poor. Here they are, the good who are bad and the bad who are good, the vicious and poetical who are both, pressed each to each, working against one another and themselves, as it is in life, consoling and hurting one another. None could rise higher, spiritually, or fall lower. It is an egalitarian book, documented from life.

The story conveys some things—as the most simple and artless stories sometimes do—far better than hundreds of learned tomes and complex works of art. One thing it conveys is the sense of brutality in which a part of the Russian population lived, the sense that *nobody cared about anybody.*

Grandma questions Grandpa, for Alexey's benefit (the boy sits, as often, beside one of them), about how the peasants were hunted down when they ran away (before the Emancipation); how they were beaten, their nostrils torn open, how they were marked on the forehead with knives.

Alexey: "For what?"

Grandpa: "For leaving. It's hard to say, who was to blame: the one who ran away or the one who hunted him down—it wasn't for us to understand ..."

They go on talking, forgetting Alexey. Their voices sound in harmony, it seems to the boy they are singing a sad song, "of sicknesses, fires, people being beaten, accidental deaths and nimble knavery, of beggars for the sake of Christ, of stern masters ..."

There emerged, as the boy grew, a sense of "the crowded stifling circle of horrible impressions in which, to this day, the simple Russian lives."

And here is the way he saw himself:

In childhood I envisioned myself as a hive, to which various simple gray people brought, like bees, the honey of their knowledge and their thoughts about life, preciously endowing my soul, each as he could. Often the honey was dirty and bitter, but all knowledge is still—honey.

This in itself is enough to disprove the fanciful theory of some Soviet critics that a key to Gorky was his "hatred of grayness," which would make him a counterpart, in literature, of the arrogant aristocrat Lenin. It was that very "grayness" (moderation, the compromise at the heart of life, the rejection of fanatical extremes), the mark of the common human, which was his first love. He also reacted against it, cried out against grayness—he was crying out at the hurt and stifling of his childhood and early youth. But this same quality, that of the commoner, the siskin, the hero of "The Confession," is his connection with the whole living world. To try to make of him a lover of black and white, a hater of the gray common denominator, is to falsify the man at his root.

The autobiography makes clear that much of what he had written till then was only an effort to use selected parts of a life already totally assembled inside him: magnifying, transposing, abstracting... what most writers do. The profession of being a writer makes it easy to forget that the whole loses its life, or a good part of it, when dismembered. Nearly all of Gorky's inferior and mediocre work, the ambiguous incomplete characters, the unresolved themes—one now sees, meeting their originals—were only efforts to abstract from that rich hive.

The germ of his social view comes clear, in his account of the descent of the Kashirins, as Mike and Jake are not up to expanding the business and the line. In business, like poker, it was raise or call, and the Kashirins could not raise; they fell.

This Kashirin business is the only prototype of all the businesses in Gorky's grown work, from the business of Foma's family through the business of the family of the Bessemenovs, the Artamanov business, the Zikovs, the Bulichevs. It was the only one he ever knew. His entire social theme consists of a hurt, angry, deeply felt statement, often repeated, about the seemingly inevitable decline, decay, ruin, of the small provincial businessman of Tsarist Russia; he knew it on his own back, in the heartbreak of his childhood and early youth.

From this insight he went on to develop a theory, as men do from bitter personal experiences: that the strong from the lower classes rise (as Grandpa had risen), build families and businesses, and then the children tend to be smaller, unable to carry on; in two generations—later, he allowed for three—there is rise and fall, either by a law of quickly diminishing biological quality, or in divine recompense for sins committed on the way up, or simply by the inexorable force of crude economic competition.

"Our children didn't come out well," Grandpa says. "Where did our strength and our sap go?" And, "Didn't we work for them? Didn't we sin for them?" he cries. These outcries are, invariably, the whole heart and substance of Gorky's "social" plays and novels.

However Gorky puzzled over the possible reasons for what took place, the upshot of all the reasons finally seemed to him "unworthiness." The children, decadent, lose their heritage, and fall; in later images, they are "swept aside."

Just as the fall of the Kashirin business is his one social theme, so this is his one social theory. He expressed it in the strength of youth in "Foma Gordeyev," then again and again, often transposing the clef to portray different classes, a transparent device. Only in "Childhood" could he bring to bear also his knowledge of their inner human splendor, so that in the conflict between this and their mean, brutal circumstance there is real depth.

From this breaking world of the lower meschanye he had been pushed, or ran away, into the world of the *bezprizornie*—the homeless boys—and from there it had been a quick step to the barefoot bums; and from there he had risen, by his own strength, into the world of art and of social action.

This helps understand the whole man. He felt he had no past, he had been deprived of it; he was self-born. He had to create his own past, in the form of an epic; then try to translate it into art—which could help provide a past for others like himself.

There are many things which, fogged in anger or ambivalence in his other work, "Childhood" makes come clear. This is right, for the child is father of the man.

It was after having been whipped unconscious by Grandpa (who had grown vicious with failure and the shattering of hope), during his recovery, that Alexei felt he grew. "From that day there appeared in me a troubled concern for people, and, just as if skin had been torn from my heart, it became unbearably sensitive to every injury and pain, its own and others."

Finding parallels for this sweet-and-sour, dark-and-light epic may help find a place—a "geography"—for Gorky the Stormy Petrel, with his deceptive blend of simple and complex.

For comparison, three authors who wrote autobiographical works in

English come to mind: O'Casey, with his many-hued poetry of the Dublin poor; Farrell, with his harsh but poetic novels of the Irish lower middle class of Chicago; and the Joyce of the early Dublin stories. The link provokes thoughts: that in each case the artist's emotional life rose from the matrix of a gaudy, idolatrous religion, much like that of Old Russia; that differences of place and speech may be less important than is believed; that colonial status may be less a formal thing than a grievance of the heart; that the beauty of the common, seen from *within*, is international—a placeless, timeless love and compassion for the gray bulk of the tragic majority: one's own.

In this respect, and maybe in this alone (but it is important), the humanism of Tolstoy is synthetic, Gorky's real; it could not be otherwise. On the one hand—and this is the cross of the artist who does not come from "children of the sun"—the vision is likely to be permanently limited, by tenement walls (or, as in Gorky's case, walls of anger and hurt) around childhood's streets. On the other, there is somehow this deeper grasp of the common roots of humanity.

It seems almost as if the less fortunate, forming a gray dogged army, try to offer their loved ones, who may become their champions, a deep-down beauty that can match the beauty acquired, through education, cultured society, freedom to meditate, by the intellectual, the *barin*, the scion of the fortunate few.

Vast and poignant is the gap of "where one stands in life." Between this "Childhood" and that depicted, with art and sincerity, by other Russians—Herzen, Aksakov, Tolstoy—there is hardly a similarity, though they clearly described the same Russia. But between Gorky's story—that of the first Russian of a common class who *dared* and was artistically able to write in depth of his childhood—and those of the Irish and American commoners, there is an immediate likeness. The figures, their pains and joys and problems, are the same. It is an internationally recognizable land.

Where Gorky is set apart, from these too, is by his long attachment to a traditional and unsophisticated religious view. Most of his works until "Childhood" had been transposition of religious themes: devotional stories, of beggars, hermits, or, often, confused religious rebels. His sublimated religious fervor passed into much of the so-called proletarian literature.

Here lies perhaps the greatest importance, for him, of "The Confes-

sion." Once he stated his religious view directly, free of romantic or bolshevik sublimations, he was next able to trace its origin to Grandma and
Grandpa; the process of clarifying took the form of "Childhood." The
unveiling of these influences, in the course of the book, is one of its
driving powers and one of the reasons it strikes with such careful clarity.
Once a thing is examined, it no longer has its old power over a person.
He still *wanted*, after "Childhood," to see a God (the divine human)
born in the people, but this was now a metaphor whose human meaning
he knew. He was no longer a religious writer in the former sense, of
one who is impelled by emotions he does not understand and which
shape everything he does to a preformed otherworldly model.

The freedom from the bondage of emotion is what gives this book
such a new-born look, like that of a man seeing for the first time with
clear eyes.

And still the religious sheen is there. Life with all its harshness and
cruelty is still depicted as if "sprinkled with gold dust"; but this gold-
dusting is now less a compulsion than a technique, in the manner of
Rembrandt. The emotion is all there, but the vision is from outside,
steady. It is his first masterwork.

Many rays spread from the book of "Childhood," showing what has
become clarified, for Alexey Peshkov, by the harsh maturing of life, and
what remains in perplexity.

For example, Alexey's Uncle Jake, the brawling fool, is portrayed as
he strums a guitar and sings, evenings: "His music demanded a tense
silence; in a hurried stream it ran somewhere far ... Beneath this music
one became unhappy for all and himself, big people seemed small, and
all sat motionless, immersed in thoughtful silence."

Repeatedly, in his early work, Gorky had tried to state, by allegorical
figures and romantic figures of fiction, his conviction of the redeeming
power of music: that it is a dying away of earthly standards; the struggle
of souls to climb up and away ... a quick sly dancing step out of the
rational into the insentient ... an equation cutting across the equations;
perhaps, the reservoir of any final hope. In "Childhood" he was able for
the first time to embody fully this idea—part of his great theme of the
divine in the human, the theme of "The Confession" and of his entire
life—not in symbolism but in living, natural creatures, as close to him
as his Uncle Jake. Religion has become humanity; here are earth's natural
creatures, but they are instruments of immortal music and shot with gold.

His philosophy of government is here too, as it was stated to him by Grandpa, and he never revised it. The people, like children starting a game, work out rules, as to how to live together: these are the Laws. As for the official, he is an ozornik, who comes to break the Laws. This was Gorky's stand. From there he moved to the galling question of where a New Law could be found, and who would bring it. To this, he never found a good answer.

Finally, Good and Evil: who is good, who wicked—another question he never really resolved. In Grandma's ballads and tales not only the hermits and holy wanderers were glorified, but the warlords and robbers too, their necessary counterweight, equally legitimate. The hypnotic sway of this certainty was never overcome. It would always drag at him, urging him still to admire that robber-knight Lenin, who did his deeds not for himself but for his only son: the people of Russia, and international humanity.

Against active, determined masters of life, who could truthfully give "quiet truth" better than a draw?

Grandma sits atop the big stove in the kitchen; the family and lodgers, for the Kashirins now rent rooms, sit around her. Alexey is on the step of the stove, seated between her knees. She chants her magic tale, of the battle of worldly power against quiet truth, of the wicked warlord Gordion, who commands brave Ivanushka-Warrior to go kill the Ancient Miron, the hermit, "quiet truth's defender," and bring him his head; and Ivanushka goes.

The Ancient knows why he has come. The warrior, ashamed, prepares to carry out his mission. He orders Miron first to kneel and pray "for the whole race of people." The Ancient kneels, beneath a young oak, but warns him: "You'll wait a long time. Mighty must prayer be for the whole race of people. It would be better to kill me at once, so as not to hang around needlessly." "No," boasts Ivan-Warrior. "Once said is said! You just pray, I'll wait even an age for you."

> Prays the hermit until evening,
> From evening he prays until the morning's dawn,
> From morning's dawn straight through till night,
> From summer he prays to the next spring.
> Prays Miron year after year,
> The oak that was young reaches to the clouds,
> From its acorns grows a thick forest,
> But to the prayer of the holy one there is no end!

And so they stay until this day, the ballad continues, the Ancient quietly praying to God and the blessed Mother of God, for all people; Ivan-Warrior standing beside him, his sword long become dust, his wrought armor rust, winter and summer, charmed in the spell, untouched by wolves and bears, spared by gale and frost, unable to move or utter a word. This is Ivan's punishment, for:

> He shouldn't have obeyed the order,
> He shouldn't have hidden behind someone else's conscience!

> And the Ancient's prayer for us, sinners,
> Even to this kind hour flows to the Lord,
> Like a bright river into the ocean-sea!

The skaz done, one of the lodgers suddenly leaped up, and cried: "That's true, that's true! One cannot live by someone else's conscience!"

That was the point of Grandma's fairy skaz, and Alexey learned it.

Many never did; all history is the witness. This refers not only to Black Hundreds, or Southern lynchers, or Nazi brownshirts, but to "idealists," "thinkers": Dzerdzinski, killing by the thousands, hid behind Lenin's conscience; Lenin, approving, behind Marx. Marx, strong thinker but angry dreamer, hid his conscience behind Hegel, history, economics—which last he despised, and rattled off like a man brushing away flies.

But Gorky knew what they never could, from Grandma's ballad. And once a man knows, he is even more liable; there has to be, then, an indication that he did not pretend *not* to know, for the sake of wealth, or praise, or women, or anything else—short, perhaps, of life. The rest of this story will be an effort to see if it is fair to say that he did try to live true to the ballad; that where he strayed it was because he fooled himself; and that where he fooled himself, and others, it was in trying for that—draw, on behalf of quiet truth; that his weakness was not servility; and that the moral issue was not forgotten.

For now, what is even more useful is that the skaz, remembered word for word nearly forty years after it was spoken, also provides a missing key. "The Confession" flowed, by way of "The Lower Depths," from the Siskin and Danko, the twin allegories. One may guess that to get closer to the root of the man's vision it is necessary to go back behind these two, which are already elaborate constructions, daydream built on early material and recalled in his twenties. As in any artist's case, the thing is to go back to the earliest poetry. But this poetry is lost, destroyed by the young man after Korolenko disdained it. Still, one fact remains, that the chief poem was a "Song of the Old Oak." This bring us, in one bound, back to the ballad, to the young oak which bows before the praying hermit, and finally grows old as he prays on, and reaches to the clouds, and creates a great forest.

We are near the source, then. And it comes from way down, in the mythic awareness of a people of moral truths, and of the conflict of power and truth.

"Childhood" must have been written in late 1912 and the early part of 1913, on Capri. It was printed serially in an independent Russian literary newspaper, starting in August of 1913. This was just prior to his return to Russia. The constant effort of the bolsheviks to "keep a line open" to Gorky, and probably his willingness, are shown by the fact that the first chapter was also published in a bolshevik magazine, in September; though not the remainder. (He was no longer their baby; and the book was not especially *useful* to Lenin.) As a hardcover book, "Childhood" was brought out by his Berlin publishers.

"Among People," the next biographical book, was begun in Russia, in 1914, and appeared in "The Russian Word" late in 1915. By then many things dragged at him, including the war, but the quality of the work is undiminished. The early part of this study sketched the story he tells in "Among People"—the glistening, sad, sound-filled unfolding epic of the eager growing boy and youth, thrown out on the mercy of a sprawling, poetic, bestial country.

In it, the concept of himself as the hive to whom all the gray and multi-colored humans brought their honey, bitter and bittersweet, proliferates into an active searching out of the honey. He becomes a rummager among interiors, a spy, a ferret of human souls. When he meets Jake the Stoker, his fellow toiler on the Volga paddle wheeler, he begins a relentless pursuit: "For me he was a locked chest, secreting something I had to get at, and I stubbornly kept at him for the key."

This he will do with endless common Russian folk: the ikon makers, stevedores, tramps, peasants, tavern singers; with old Populists, heroes fallen in battle for the people; finally with Chekhov, Blok, Tolstoy. None were sacred; yet all were equally sacred.

Are these splendid works an "imitation of life"? The very idea of art is an imposition of form on life, which everywhere seems to have a fierce, sullen habit of being senseless and chaotic. The Russia from which he grew and into whose dirty depths he was thrown was the most formless, chaotic of lands. He finally imposed on it, and thereby on his life as well, a form. He did this by means of redeeming emotion, dogged thought, insatiable reading; finally, by overall judgments of value, the conclusions drawn from overwhelming experience, which the matured man, gentle but tough and resilient, was then able to graft on the body of the sights, smells, sounds and music of childhood and youth. In this sense, the autobiographical books are more than an imitation of life, or a re-creation.

The stream flows on, the source seems endless.

# BOOK IV

## *Storm*

## CHAPTER 24

SOME think that autocratic Russia, in its own ponderous, cruel
way, was on the road to progress just before World War I. The
zemstvos were encouraging secondary education. There were high
achievements in literature and music, science and the humanities, in this
late Byzantine "silver age," although much of the achievement now seems,
in retrospect, a dying gleam. The Duma was a parliament of sorts, some
land reform had taken place, a class of better-off peasants had come into
being—possible independent small farmers of the future. The number of
industrial strikes—a gauge of "worker awareness"—had risen rapidly
through 1913. Populism, Social Democracy, liberalism—there is nothing
but leaves a mark; there was a new outlook.

The war, into which the moronic dynasty threw a country unable to
wage modern war, must have killed any chance of a normal transition.
The inevitable rout would fire violent protest and make gradual change
impossible. But nobody knew it, least of all the revolutionaries, when the
hour of revolution arrived.

A prophetic event, in 1912, was the shooting down of two hundred
striking workers in the gold fields of Lena, in Siberia. Gorky wrote a
denunciation for the bolsheviks. But he was also contributing to moderate
reviews. All the evidence is that he had decided to find his own answers,
as a Russian patriot and humanist, not necessarily committed to revolution. The writing of "Childhood," with its clear gaze, must have furthered
the emotional freeing of himself for moderation.

The slipping of Lenin's fatherly hold was signalled by a one-way clash
over the idea of God. Gorky sent a Moscow daily a protest against the
presentation by the Moscow Art Theatre of Dostoyevsky's "Possessed."
He had always felt Dostoyevsky's keen but sickly talent hurt Russia, by

inspiring it with the ideal of "Karamazovism" (the way gangster movies on TV injure American children). Then, facing the question of whether better ideals were indeed possible, he said: "As to God-building, it is better to let it go for a while—it is a useless occupation: why seek what isn't? Not having sown, you cannot reap. You have no God, you have not yet created one. One does not seek Gods, one creates them . . ."

Lenin sent a furious letter—if still fatherly, that of a furious father. "It follows that you are against God-building only for a while!! . . . God is (historically and actually) first of all a complex of ideas that rise from the oppression of man both by external nature and by class tyranny, ideas that perpetuate this oppression and *lull to sleep* the class struggle . . ." And so on, at length, until at last signed "Your V. Ulyanov," instead of, as always before, "Your Lenin." (The next day, V. Ulyanov hastily sent a somewhat apologetic letter, and did sign it "Your Lenin.")

There was no reply.

In fact, throughout Gorky's last year on Capri, there was a drumfire of chummy letters from Lenin, determined to hang on, with hardly a reply from Gorky. From early 1913 until a year after the October Revolution— late 1918—he kept away from Lenin, personally and in correspondence. To Lenin's coming to power Gorky, as will be seen, would offer determined resistance. That letter about God must have confirmed what he had already come to see: he was dealing with a man whose mind was *fixed*.

In 1913 the Romanovs celebrated the three hundredth anniversary of their reign, and an amnesty was declared for certain kinds of political exiles, including writers. Gorky was worried about returning. He was not just a writer; he had been one of the chief organizers of the march of the workers on Red Sunday. Bills had been posted: "Wanted: the Nizhni-Novgorod member of the dyers guild, Alexey Maximovich Peshkov (Maxim Gorky), indicted under articles 1 and 4 of statutes 129, 73, and 132 of the Criminal Code." But by now he was desperately lonely; and the breakthrough to self-discovery having been made, he no longer needed Capri as a monastery of self-discovery and spiritual refuge. Chaliapin had taken the amnesty, knelt before the Tsar (causing an uproar in which some Social Democrats quit the movement), and he reassured Gorky. Gorky crossed the border into Russia, in December of 1913, without passport or visa.

He stayed in Finland, but visited Moscow and Petersburg. The police let him alone; he stopped ardent revolutionaries from staging demonstrations for him.

In August of 1914 the war that would be fatal to so much, that would open the modern age, began. Gorky made a trip to Kiev, where Andreyeva was acting—she had left Capri long before he did. The Kiev police reported that Gorky had been visited by representatives of the local tailors union—Social Democrats. "When they asked him how he regarded the war, he answered that he was 'tangled up' on the question himself."

But when his views got untangled, they were against the war—against War, period. He was in the minority. A big part of the intelligentsia, including radicals, answered the trumpet call.

World War I, in fact, split wide, and permanently, the Social-Democratic movement. Most German Marxists, when Germany struck into Belgium, suddenly discovered they were patriots. "The menace of Tsarist autocracy" helped many, including Kautsky, accept the war. Only the little crippled Rosa Luxemburg, with her Spartacists, balked, crying from underground: "Everything that we have preached to the people for 50 years... has suddenly become empty talk... Never has a proud ideal been betrayed so shamefully." The Social Democrats of France and Italy supported the war, too, against German militarism.

In Russia alone a part of the Social Democrats stuck by internationalism. For one thing, they still took their theory straight; besides, the German and French Marxists could offset theory with dreams of victory, but the Russians knew their own country too well. Lenin, from Geneva, shouted that it was the duty of socialists to transform the nature of the war: "Raise high the banner of civil war!" This was not what Gorky meant by internationalism.

The graft and mismanagement in the Tsarist war effort dazed even blasé Western observers in Petrograd. Russian infantry marched through the city toward the front with only the front ranks carrying rifles; the boys behind them would grab the rifles when they were killed. While in cafés in the West toasts were drunk to the "Russian steam-roller," the peasant youths were led, or misled, out to be slaughtered, without artillery, shells, shoes, transport, or food.

Gorky became the center of a group of varied Left intelligentsia. He founded two magazines, *Letopis* ("The Chronicle") and *Parus* ("The Sail"), then a daily newspaper, *Novaya Zhizn* ("New Life"). This last became the most widely read sheet among the Russian intelligentsia. Everybody cursed it.

The chief of the Petrograd secret police, reporting on "The Chronicle," said it was "bolshevik and defeatist in tendency," but that editors and contributors kept apart from party organizations, "being more cultivated and materially better off than the workmen who fill the rank and file of the Social-Democratic Party." Besides, "Gorky has become 'bourgeois,' as they say in party circles, his glamor as a Social Democrat has grown dim, and he has altogether discontinued his active work."

Lenin kept an eye on him. His sister Yelizarova (a "pure" and dedicated type of person, who served on occasion as his spy) wrote him (in invisible ink) of her interview with Gorky. Gorky had promised her to publish some of the bolshevik literature, but when they submitted an article by Zinoviev he returned it. She explained to her brother ("James," in the secret code) that Gorky's trouble was he "can be easily bent one way or another, and has a forgiving soul."

To Kaun, Gorky denied ever having been a defeatist, and "no one who knows his warm, unreasoning love for Russia may doubt his denial." His own articles, in "The Chronicle" and then in a column in the "New Life," at this time rarely dealt with politics. The cultural backwardness of the people, the urgency of a war "against the inner enemy" ("Asianism")— these were his themes.

His main collaborators were Bazarov, a gentle creature who had been Bogdanov's ally in the battle for God-building, who had tried to reorient Russian Marxism in line with contemporary philosophy and physics, and whom Lenin attacked violently as a "Machist"; and Sukhanov, a nonparty man but an admirer of Martov, the leader of left menshevism. Sukhanov's memoirs of the coming revolution would be its historical classic. He was Gorky's chief editor. Articles were contributed by Lunacharsky, another old God-builder, now back in the bolshevik stream but still the man of emotion, lover of culture (he would burst into tears when the news came that the Winter Palace was being shelled by the *Aurora*).

As long as his paper ran, Gorky took full responsibility and gave his editors full freedom. Sukhanov stated that Gorky never once asked to have a change made in articles or editorials, though often their views were not his, and he took the rap for them. His own views he stated in his column and an occasional lead article.

His creative work of this period—from the last years on Capri to the gale of Revolution—confirm the impression of a man who has moved toward clarity and moderation.

Along with youth and the religious compulsion, the need to sentimentalize is gone, and romanticism with it, except in the stage-settings—the

Russian scenery he still loved, and that "unreasoning love" for people, especially Russian. Coupled ironically with this, a theme that occurs several times is the irrational beastliness, the desire to hurt and spoil, that rise in so many of these common Russian folk, usually so lovable. He is still the rationalist, and cannot swallow the irrational.

The yearning for the natural is still there: one sketch describes a big fellow sitting on a Volga ferryboat, his horny hands, like big dark curled talons, spread on the bare breasts of his sweetheart, who lies across his knees. He is proud of her breasts and his possession of them, she is proud too, and proud of his pride; and they refuse to be moved by envious efforts to shame them.

Another sketch, called "How the Song was Put Together," is Chaucerian in clarity, but embodies things of which Chaucer never dreamed.

Here, now, is how two women put together a song, to the melancholy sound of bells, on a summer day.

One woman is a cook, the other a chambermaid. They pass the time of day, in their summer-drowsing town, on a stoop, gossiping; then one suggests they make up a song; and they do. The older woman sings out the first lines:

> Ekh, on a white day, in the clear little sun,
> Of a bright little night, in sight of the moon-month...

The younger, in a soft voice, improvises the third line, and the first woman completes the stanza; and so on, till the song is done, and they part to resume work. Stripped of the witching oral lament of Russian folk song, the verse is banal. But the real melody is in the idea: This is the way, if people were quite free, *all* would be done—happily, cooperatively.

This story appeared in his "Chronicle," late in 1915, along with his editorials critical of war, his defense of the civil rights of Jews, his polemics against "Asianism" in Russian life.

There is a sketch, too, of the young Peshkov visiting a well-to-do merchant family for dinner and more than dinner. "Respected sir," reads the invitation, "I beg you earnestly to sacrifice tomorrow to us, for third-floor pleasure." The young man arrives, change of clothing in a sack in his hand. Clearly he is a liked and oft-invited guest. There are many loving touches here: the ritual of the steam bath, in which the men partake; the guzzling of good food, the vodka, the off-color jokes, in which the wives of the two merchants take part; young Peshkov, as always, is a silent instrument, a mass of stringed sensitivities, eyes, ears, through which all this music flows.

The two merchants—the host and his best friend—end the festivities, in accord with ritual, by performing parlor magic: the one dutifully, the other with the joy and the intensity of a child. Only afterward, loneliness and despair close in on the merchant who is a child. Life is a bitter emptiness he tries to fill with parlor magic, with the innocent ritual of third-floor pleasure. But then, this is after a lot of vodka; and we still feel warm because we have met a good man. And young Peshkov—now the middle-aged Gorky—is capable of giving him his due.

This was published in 1916.

All is seen from a different slant. There has been much reconciliation. There is a thoughtful regard, an effort to see in the round, to recognize much that once, because of inner desperation, was suppressed.

Only one story—curiously, the last before the Revolution's gale—is a step back, toward a romantic and sentimental use of the emotions. And it is a success: a small, tearful gem.

In the muddy city street, young Alexey Peshkov, who sells kvass for a living, comes on a squat, bedraggled woman, jumping up and down in a huge mud puddle, screaming drunken defiance at the world. He carries her out of the puddle, and takes her to her ill-smelling cellar, where her son, who was born with both legs paralyzed, awaits her.

His little face was serious, sharp-nosed, with full lips, like a girl's—a face drawn with a thin brush, strikingly out of place here in this dark, damp hole.

While the mother falls down in drunken sleep, the boy keeps asking Alexey whether he should put out the oil lamp.

"Why?" I asked stupidly.
"You know yourself," he said, terribly simply, and stretching himself, he added:
"They all lie with her."

Alexey reassures the boy, and their brief friendship begins. L'ion'ka shows his new friend his "zoo"—a poor, battered collection of cardboard boxes, in each of which scrambles or buzzes an insect . . . each named after one of the men who have come to "use" his mother. They are his poor, sardonic world.

"She's good," he assures Alexey, confidentially, "only she's a drunkard. Well—on our street—all are drunkards."

He smiled charmingly, with such an enchanting smile that I wanted to bawl, to shout out to the whole city my unbearable, burning pity for him. His pretty head shook on its thin neck, just like some kind of strange flower.

L'ion'ka is doomed to die soon—he talks about it calmly. The most terrible thing in the story is the realization that nothing can be done. His bed is a drawer-chest, in this cellar of dirt, filthy rags, spiderwebs. He loves terrible dreams, which keep coming: a tree growing downwards, roots stretching into the sky; his mother lying naked, a dog eating her stomach . . .

"Listen!" he demands. "If I feed a roach, and feed him, will he grow up to the size of a horse?"

Alexey is moved by love and pity.

It was clear that he believed in this; I answered: "If you feed him well— he will."

"You see!" he cried joyfully. "And Mama, the fool, laughs at me! . . . A cat too, if I could feed him, would grow—fast—to the size of a horse— right?"

And Alexey continues the Beautiful Lie.

"Why not? He could."

This—with its L'ion'ka, pretty, doomed, flower-like head swaying on stemlike thin neck—may be called the last flower, in Gorky's creative work, of sentimentality, and of romanticism too; a moment's regression.

Of all Gorky's works, this story Lenin (according to Krupskaya, his wife) loved best; and yet it was not a story that could be *directly useful*. One has the right to guess that this man of expediency really was hit by it, where he lived. And this casts, in turn, a flicker of light on Lenin's mysterious, guarded, essentially withdrawn personality: at base, wild romanticism, sweet sentimentality.

The flaw in this whole story is that pity is a treacherous emotion, psychologically akin to disdain.

In Gorky's case, the pity was a great hurt at suffering and ruined lives. But even the pure emotion, when so sentimentally used, cannot help being translated into an unreal downward look, which does not really help, or help men understand, but only clouds them up with clotted emotions.

This was a weakness in Gorky; and in all Russian idealism.

The boy sleeps. His mother and Alexey talk, like old friends. As Alexey is leaving (this is the last time), the boy screams in his sleep. Walking away through the dank yard, Alexey hears the mother singing a "cradle song."

> Will come the Ugly-muggers
> And bring the Fall-uponers;
> They'll bring the Fall-uponers,
> And tear my heart apart!
> Oh woe, oh woe, oh where
> Is there to hide, where?

And the story is called *Strasti-Mordasti*—the "Ugly-muggers."

It appeared in Gorky's own paper, "The Chronicle," in January of 1917.

# CHAPTER 25

FEBRUARY of 1917 came—with its revolution unbelievable, unstaged. Its story has been told often—most stirringly by Sukhanov and by Trotsky. The slaughtered Russian armies reeling back on Riga ... mass desertions ... the peasantry starving and mutinous ... the proletariat of Moscow and Petrograd come to boil ... street fighting ... the revolutionaries dazed and unprepared when demonstrations started ... the refusal of the Cossacks to shoot ... the uneasy surges of bodies, like a wavering pendulum of history, driven off its beat and not yet sure of its new beat ... the coming over of the key regiments, the Preobrazhensky, the Semeonovsky ... the Lettish Rifles ...

The brief government of Lvov and Miliukov, then of Kerensky—the road to power was open, but the revolutionaries decided to shield themselves behind the middle class. Common sense warned them the web of society could not be broken with impunity, and the writings of Marx and Engels seemed to say "a bourgeois revolution *must* precede a proletarian one."

Gorky met the Revolution not exactly like a bride: deeply glad at the fall of the corrupt, stupid old order, but with deep doubt about the already brutalized people's ability, in the terrible conditions of war and revolution, to stay human.

This was how he stated this anxious theme:

The Russian people have been wedded to liberty. Let us trust that out of this union new strong men will be born in our land which is exhausted both physically and spiritually. Let us firmly believe that in the Russian man will flare up in a bright flame the forces of his reason and will, forces that have been extinguished and crushed by the age-long yoke of a police regime.

The old order's legacies of "filth, ignorance, barbarism, stupidity, vileness," were a living danger. The old order had been overthrown because it was so corrupted, and many had been corrupted by it. Man (capital letter) must be armed, now, with reason, knowledge, culture. Simply overthrowing the monarchy might mean that the revolution "had merely driven the old disease inside the body." The war slogan, "Citizens, the motherland is in danger!" must be replaced by "Citizens, culture is in danger!"

To start doing something about it, he organized a Free Association for the Development and Spread of the Positive Sciences (shades of Franklin's Philosophical Society); and a society of Culture and Liberty. These efforts to unify Russian intellectuals were, to Lenin the great differentiator, a dangerous thing.

In the tangled, tumultuous crisscross of politics and events between the February Revolution and the bolshevik one of October, Gorky and his editors of "New Life" picked their way, staggering. The jingo press screamed "New Life" was bolshevik and pro-German. Lenin's paper stormed: "New Life" represented the obnoxious danger—false unification. After April, when Lenin's program for immediate seizure of power was clear, "New Life" went into strong opposition.

Trotsky, back from exile in the United States, came to "New Life's" editorial room and met with Gorky and his staff. Trotsky was looking for a base of operations; but he was already moving toward Lenin, while Gorky's editors (not Gorky himself; he was committed to nobody) favored Martov's little bunch of Internationalists. Trotsky may have wanted to capture Gorky's paper for Lenin; he later denied this, saying he was really just scouting the terrain, and decided these men were talkers, not doers; he now called Gorky "culture's psalm-singer." He himself was to become, in a few weeks, the foremost of doers—the man who made the Red Army, won Lenin's revolution.

Gorky hated the factional strife, the politics; he said he felt for politics "an organic disgust." His theme of culture was just tolerated, in respect for his revolutionary past. He wrote a manifesto "To the Nations of the World," calling for peace without annexations or indemnities (which Lenin would later propose, as a brilliant political stroke); the Petrograd Soviet rejected it as "inopportune." Sukhanov didn't like it either: "It contained not a gram of politics."

The only time Gorky actually spoke before the Soviet, he urged that the victims of the February Revolution, without specifying sides, be buried with honor in one of the city's main squares; his proposal was rejected.

The Soviet did adopt, and circulate, his appeal for preserving national monuments:

Citizens, the old masters are gone, leaving behind them an enormous heritage. It now belongs to the whole nation.

Citizens, guard this inheritance, guard the palaces, they will become palaces of your national art, guard the pictures, statues, buildings—these are the embodiments of the fine things which gifted men have created even under the oppression of despotism, and which testify to the power and beauty of the human mind.

Citizens, do not touch a single stone, guard your monuments, buildings, old objects, documents—all these are your history, your pride. Remember that this is the soil from which your new national art will grow.

The Executive Committee of the Soviet
of Workers Deputies.

This vision of a nation made habitable for cleaner, better humans was his real desire for the Revolution. To whatever extent his hope has come true, he is one of those for the land to thank; to the extent it failed, the tragedy marked the rest of his life, and the final phases of his art.

Time flowed toward October. The ruined country was sick of war, and no government that insisted on keeping it in the war could hope to stay in power. It should have become clear to the intelligentsia that the "bourgeois revolution" of February would move to something far more drastic unless the country was given the promise of quick peace, and of far-reaching reforms. But they felt bound by obligations of honor; besides, they feared the economic vengeance of the Allies as much as German occupation. Kerensky called for "glorious" attacks, while the army melted; there was even a try at a rightist coup by the Cossack general Kolchak. All the while the workers of Petrograd and Moscow were gravitating to the bolsheviks; the rioting peasantry followed. The bolsheviks promised land and peace.

Gorky did not want the war, but he did not want the bolsheviks to take power either; this became startlingly clear as the moment for seizure of power neared.

The famous "July days" saw a self-aborted bolshevik putsch. The sailors came from Kronstadt (led by Lunacharsky, of all people!), the bolshevik-oriented regiments were ready; but Lenin drew back at the last moment, deciding the apple of time was not quite ripe.

At once Kerensky decreed the arrest of the bolshevik leaders. Lenin, with Kamenev and Zinoviev, went into hiding, and the three sent an appeal to Gorky, asking for "hospitality" for their articles in "New Life." He gave hospitality, and also printed Trotsky's open letter saying he shared Lenin's views and demanding to be arrested (his wish was granted); and Gorky also printed a series by Martov, declaring that the bolsheviks were defeating the aims of the Revolution. In August, "New Life" appealed to voters to reject the bolshevik candidates for the coming Constituent Assembly.

All this while, the Right raged at "Gorky's circus riders and cannibals, who are more harmful than the bolsheviks, because the latter reveal their intentions openly, whereas the New Life chaps hide under the mask of culture." Finally, in defense, Gorky stated what was more than just his political credo:

For seventeen years I have considered myself a Social Democrat, and have served as much as I could the great purposes of that party. At the same time I did not deny my services to other parties, unwilling to spurn any vital cause. I have never sympathized with people who become fossilized and petrified under the pressure of the faith they possess . . .

I shall say more: in every group and party I regard myself as a heretic. In my political views there are, most likely, a number of contradictions, which I cannot and do not want to reconcile. I feel that for the sake of my inner harmony, for the sake of my mental peace and comfort, I would have to kill utterly that part of my soul which loves most passionately and achingly the live, sinful, and—by your leave—wretchedly pitiful Russian man.

The Bulgarian minister to Germany wrote to Gorky, asking him to act as mediator for a general armistice. Gorky printed his letter, but in the prevailing war hysteria he felt he had to preface it with a paragraph calling it "infamous and silly." This did not keep him from being called a German agent, a traitor to the motherland. To his attacker Gorky replied: "Motherland means one's people. I have been serving my people for a quarter of a century, and it is not for you, miserable man, to judge and accuse me."

Against a background of military catastrophe, peasant riots, and the methodical organization and propagandizing of workers and soldiers by the bolsheviks, Kerensky's government held less and less real power. The bolshevik star became recognizable; the more moderate revolutionary groups sat stupefied, thumbing Marxist texts. While Lenin led the bolshevik campaign from hiding, and Trotsky's military-revolutionary committee took over all posts of real power, Martov issued a poor chirp, calling on the soldiers and sailors to refuse to take part in any bolshevik demonstration.

At the last minute, it was in "New Life" that Kamenev's much-quoted letter was printed, saying that "I and Zinoviev and other expert comrades" —some insist that Stalin was among them—opposed a rising, as "undesirable and fatal for the proletariat and the revolution . . . an act of despair."

And Gorky's own lead editorial read:

Ever more persistent rumors are spreading to the effect that on Nov. 2 [new calendar; Oct. 21 in the old] a "bolshevik rising" will take place. [Gorky's information was accurate; the coup was postponed by Lenin for five days.] In other words, that the hideous scenes of July 16–18 will be repeated. That means that once more there will appear motor-lorries overfilled with men with rifles and revolvers in their trembling hands, and these rifles will shoot at shop windows, at people, at random . . . All dark instincts of the crowd irritated by disorder, by the falsehood and filth of politics, will flare up . . . People will be killing one another, in their inability to destroy their own bestial stupidity.

The unorganized crowd will creep out into the streets, hardly understanding what it wants, while under its cover adventurers, thieves, professional assassins will set out to "create the history of the Russian revolution."

In brief, there will be repeated that bloody, senseless slaughter, which we have already witnessed, and which has undermined through our whole land the moral importance of the revolution, and has shaken its cultural meaning.

He called on the Bolshevik Central Committee to refute the rumors of a rising, "if indeed it is a strong and freely functioning political organ capable of directing the masses, and not a willing toy in the hands of the bestialized mob, if it is not a tool in the hands of shameless adventurers or demented fanatics."

This was clearly his view, at the moment of the Revolution, of the man who had meant a good deal to him, and whom he would yet help enshrine in glory and myth: for it was clear, from the records of that struggle, that it was this one "demented fanatic," Lenin, against a majority in his own central committee, who was determined that a rising should take place, and saw to it that it did.

The rising took place that would change everything in our world: a highly organized military coup, managed by the bolsheviks, but carried out by soldiers, sailors, and workers.

Kerensky called for troops. Some teen-age cadets and the Women's Battalion responded. The military-revolutionary committee issued Trotsky's orders: "No hesitation or doubt. Firmness, steadiness, perseverance, determination. Long live the Revolution!" Kerensky appealed to the Cossack regiments: they refused. The cruiser *Aurora* anchored in the Neva. Sailors led the clumsy storming of the Winter Palace. On the morning of November 7 the provisional government was declared overthrown. That evening Lenin came out of hiding and announced to the Soviets at Smolny: "Comrades, the workers' and peasants' revolution ... has been accomplished ... In Russia we must at once engage in building up a proletarian socialist state. Long live the world socialist revolution!" Privately, accounts agree, most of the bolshevik leaders did not expect to outlive the few days of the Paris Commune.

Sukhanov describes pathetically how he and a few others would have liked so much to stay with them, to keep the revolution and the government from being purely bolshevik, to exercise an influence of moderation, and not to be "thrown aside" by history. But, by the book, a bourgeois revolution had to precede the proletarian one. Sadly he watched Lenin and the rest of the conquerors, on stage, link hands and chant the "Internationale" in a religious flame.

Gorky was not with them on stage in flesh or in spirit. But he did not feel forced to walk out, because the sacred Marxist writings were not his bible. He could, like the Old Oak of that early poem, stand alone. And he did.

One observer would later say: "He was in 1918–21 practically the only independent public force outside the government in the whole of Soviet Russia."

Gorky had once sung ecstatically of the coming storm. Maturity had brought common sense and moderation; he now realized how destructive and senseless such a storm was, and wanted more than anything else in the world to avoid it. But life's irony is constant: by this time, circumstance had combined with the wild vengeful emotions he had once helped unleash. The storm came.

The bolsheviks had taken power; but keeping it was something else. The new regime was despised and mistrusted by all who till then had been in charge of the vital facets of national life: commerce, industry, transport, the civil service, the army. At what point might passive resistance pass into sabotage, sabotage into counterrevolution?

There was passive resistance, and sabotage, and there were plans for counterrevolution. But having lived by plotting, the bolsheviks saw plots even where there were none, saw in reluctance sabotage, in disagreement mortal enmity, in a gentle upbringing the certainty of counterrevolutionary intent. This was one of their psychological misfortunes, and the nation's.

In this situation, and frightened by their own isolation, they "safeguarded the revolution": repression, terror, the birth of the dreaded Cheka—"the Extraordinary Commission."

Gorky's paper had attacked "from the moment of the insurrection." Its editorials were entitled "The Breath of Death," "Demagogy and Impotence," "Madness." It kept calling for a "united revolutionary front," instead of bolshevik rule alone.

"He was outraged by the fact that as soon as they came to power they adopted against their opponents the same repressive measures from which they had so recently suffered themselves."

The rest of the opposition press was shut down; because of Gorky, "New Life" was not molested—for some time.

He stood against the new regime, but was hated by its foes. Andreyev, once perhaps his closest friend, considered him a traitor. The extreme Right of the intelligentsia called him, behind his back, "a Negro in a silk hat"—the worst term of scorn they could imagine; later, "the Smerdyakov of the Russian Revolution." He was close to the bolsheviks, he had helped betray Russia.

But precisely because he was close to the bolsheviks, the intelligentsia— including those who despised him—clustered around him, beseeching help. He was the only one who could intercede for those the bolsheviks were throwing into prison. If a life could be saved, it was only he who would even try to save it.

He took their insults and hatred, and helped them when he could. Strange, painful emotions must have been at work in him.

The diary of one of them, a lady poet, sensitive and virulent and bigoted, describes the visit of Gorky to the apartment of a mutual friend, where he was asked to intercede for one of Kerensky's jailed ministers. Gorky, according to the diary, looked "dark, black . . . He talks as if he were barking." He said, according to the diary, "I am . . . organically . . . unable . . . to talk to these . . . scoundrels. To Lenin and Trotsky." He said he had just written an article for "New Life," denouncing the arrests. "To hell with articles!" cried the lady. Then she pounced on Gorky.

"None of your articles," I told him, "will place you apart from the bolsheviks, the 'scoundrels,' as you call them; you must get away from their company. Aside from the 'shadow' which falls on you because of your nearness to the bolsheviks, what of your own self?" I asked. "What does your own conscience say?"

He got up, barked something huskily: "If I should . . . get away . . . to whom shall I go?"

Many of these people were haters of much that was dear to him, bigots, the very ones to whom he was a low-born oaf, "a Negro in a silk hat." But they were still intelligentsia, "the bearers of culture"; they loved and wrote books and poetry. In protecting them and their friends he must have felt he was acting for the culture and humanism of Russia . . . And his tortured question—"to whom shall I go?"—sounds real. This was the quandary of his life, in which he would finally die.

The article he had tried to tell her about indicted Lenin and Trotsky for leaving the ministers of the deposed Provisional Government in prison, "in the hands of people who have not the slightest conception of personal freedom, of the rights of man." Then it went on:

Lenin, Trotsky, and those with them, have already been poisoned by the rotten poison of power, which is evident from their disgraceful treatment of freedom of speech and person, and of all those rights for whose triumph democracy has struggled ...

The workmen cannot fail to understand that it is on their skins, on their blood, that Lenin is performing a certain experiment ... The workers must not permit adventurers and madmen to heap on the heads of the proletariat shameful, senseless and bloody crimes, for which not Lenin will pay, but the proletariat alone.

He underestimated Lenin's staying power; and feared a coming White vengeance.

This theme, of Lenin the mad chemist, the ozornik, was developed by Gorky further in a sharp portrayal, far less famous than his essay about the man seven years later, upon Lenin's death—and far different.

Lenin himself is, of course, a man of exceptional force. For twenty-five years he has stood in the front ranks of the fighters for the victory of socialism, he is one of the biggest and brightest figures in international Social Democracy. A man of parts, he possesses all the qualities of the "leader," not excluding the indispensable absence of morality and a purely aristocratic merciless attitude toward the lives of the common masses.

Lenin as a "leader" and Russian aristocrat (certain mental traits of this defunct class are not alien to him) deems himself in the right to perform over the Russian people a cruel experiment, doomed to failure in advance.

Exhausted and ruined by war, the people have already paid for that experiment with thousands of lives, and now will be made to pay with tens of thousands more ...

This inevitable tragedy does not embarrass Lenin, slave of his dogma, nor his sycophants—his slaves. Life, in all its complexity, is unknown to Lenin. He does not know the mass of the people, for he has not lived with them; only from books has he learned ... how one can most easily infuriate their instincts. The working class is for Lenin what ore is to the metallist. Is it possible, under the existing conditions, to cast a socialistic state out of this ore? Apparently, it is not possible; yet—why not try? ...

He is working as a chemist does in his laboratory, with the difference that the chemist employs dead matter with results valuable for life, whereas Lenin works on living material and leads the revolution to perdition.

In the reasoned judgment of Alexander Kaun, twelve years later, "essentially Gorky has not changed his estimate of Lenin, except that at one time he extolled the very traits which at another time he condemned."

In this remark, which seems just, lies one of the interesting things about the human situation: The amoral usually triumphs, and because it is so strong the moral admires it; finally, because this is too upsetting, the moral goes to work and transforms the amoral into a moral image. Gorky was very human, and could not help going through this process to some extent; although not as much as most people do—he fought hard and consciously against it.

But this was for the future. In 1918, Gorky's words stung the bolsheviks, though Lenin himself only commented that Gorky "was always arch-characterless in politics." He was attacked as one who had at last "taken off his mask." He was attacked as "nonproletarian": of course this was true—he was of the lower middle class, the meschanye. He replied he had always considered it as wrong for a proletarian as for a nobleman to boast of his class.

The *Pravda:* "When at the future bright festival of nations former involuntary enemies will merge in one brotherly people, will that peace banquet welcome Gorky, who has so hurriedly deserted the ranks of genuine revolutionary democracy?"

Gorky: "It goes without saying that neither the author of that article nor I shall live to see the "bright festival"—it is too remote, and many decades of stubborn workaday cultural labor will be required for the creation of such a festival. As to a festival at which the despotism of half-literate masses will celebrate its easy victory, while the human individual will remain oppressed as before, as ever—at such a 'festival' I have nothing to do, and it is no festival to me."

The trouble, he insisted, was at the root: the brutality of Russian life. And to cure it by brutality would only embed it deeper. Could the Russian people, "slaves of yesterday," rule without "unbridled despotism"? He doubted it.

"New Life" kept up its barrage. Gorky's coeditors would—years later —pay for their opposition with their lives; the motive of vengeance was to be part of the triumphant Party's psychology.

The elections to the long-promised Constituent Assembly gave a majority to the SR's. At Lenin's insistence, the Constituent Assembly was promptly abolished. An attempted demonstration was suppressed by arms. Gorky wrote comparing this "massacre" of January 1918 with that of Red Sunday by the Tsar.

The Brest-Litovsk treaty, taking Russia out of the war, gave Germany access to the Ukraine's granary, freed its divisions for the Western front, and tore from Russia the Baltic provinces. Lenin and Trotsky had begged

vainly for Allied military help. They tried to stall the Brest-Litovsk negotiations, hoping for a German revolution; instead, the German army
started its long-deferred invasion of Russia. Lenin finally out-argued the
majority of the Bolshevik Central Committee, who still dreamed of con-
verting the war into a world proletarian revolution; Trotsky and Joffe
went back and signed the treaty "without looking at it"—there was no
way out. It was the key to the preservation of the bolshevik government;
but also, probably, it helped preserve Russia.

The intelligentsia's outcry against Brest-Litovsk was focused in "New
Life," the only organ of protest. "We are facing a band of adventurers,"
said an unsigned editorial, "who, for the sake of prolonging, if only for
a few weeks, the agony of their perishing autocracy, are ready for anything." A signed article by Sukhanov called the treaty "a disgraceful
suicide of the Russian revolution and a betrayal of the cause of the international proletariat." It does not seem that Gorky and his friends were,
here, as realistic as Lenin.

"New Life" was suspended. Gorky and his editors were asked to print
a retraction. They refused. The paper was permitted to resume. "While
Lenin was alive," Kaun comments, "he suffered opposition 'within the
family,' extending this term far enough to include even 'New Life.' "

But its days were numbered. Only Gorky's revolutionary past and his
popularity "with the masses" saved it, for a while longer, from the fate
of the other nonbolshevik publications.

And Gorky did make a dire enemy of one of the new masters: Zinoviev,
commissar for Petrograd and the northern oblast. He considered Zinoviev a demogogue, and one of those responsible for the terror. It was
Zinoviev who would later proudly say: "The bourgeoisie kill separate
individuals; but we kill whole classes."

Zinoviev challenged Gorky to a public debate. Gorky knew this would
be before a stacked house and refused. He started to get threatening letters, from workers and sailors, to "lay off." The typesetters refused to
print articles against the government, and several times the paper either
could not come out or came out in a limited edition or with pages missing.

*Pravda* insinuated about the source of "New Life's" funds. Gorky
named a private individual who had loaned him 275,000 rubles (the ruble
had long been greatly inflated), and added that he himself had also put
into the paper part of the money from a recent edition of his collected
works. Then he told *Pravda:*

During the years 1901–1917, hundreds of thousands of rubles passed through my hands for the cause of the Social-Democratic Party. My own share amounted to tens of thousands of rubles, but the greater part came from the pockets of the "bourgeoisie." Iskra was published with the money of Savva Morozov, who naturally gave the money not as a loan but as a donation. Your calumnious and filthy sallies against New Life disgrace not my paper, but yourselves.

By late 1918, in Kaun's words, "abandoned and opposed by every party and faction, the bolsheviks faced complete isolation, at home and abroad, and they decided to meet the issue squarely. The issue amounted to war against all and everything ... The country was set on a war basis, with the screws of dictatorship tightened to the last degree. The vestiges of democratic privileges were wiped out, and chief among them was freedom of opinion ... Under these circumstances, coupled with shortage of paper and electric power and the frequent sabotage of the typesetters, *Novaya Zhizn* finally gave up the ghost."

Kaun surmises Gorky must have felt relieved that the "protracted agony" was over. "Chivalry" had kept him at "New Life's" helm. Sole owner and publisher, he could long ago have washed his hands of it, and without his name over it, it would have gone down at once—under Kerensky, or under Lenin. His editors had involved him in politics far beyond his wishes, and he had backed them to the hilt.

Now, with "New Life" done for, he made a sharp personal turn. The country lay in chaos and suffering. It was near the beginning of winter. There were no food, no light, no heat. The bolshevik government stood with its back to the wall, using terror, while five White armies and British and French forces of intervention prepared for invasion. Capable foreign observers have said that the intervention, with the false hopes it aroused among those opposed to the bolsheviks, greatly intensified the Red Terror. There would be White Terror too, heartless and vicious.

It was at this time of deepest chaos and lowest ebb, that Gorky turned from knightly opposition and took on another role, which made him unforgettable: "rescuing, preserving and fostering whatever cultural values Russia possessed." This meant—reconciliation with Lenin.

It was September of 1918. Lenin was in an armchair; he had been wounded slightly, in the neck, by Dora Kaplan's bullet, fired when the Left Socialist Revolutionaries, made frantic by bolshevik repression, had turned to terror. At his insistence, her life was not taken; whether he could have stopped the reprisals that killed hundreds of other SR's is doubtful.

"We have gained one of our greatest victories! We have won over Maxim Gorky!" the bolsheviks wrote.

Others never forgave him.

For in this new role he could not help influencing men of culture to reconcile themselves to the Bolshevik Revolution.

# CHAPTER 26

IT is tempting to credit Gorky's decision to the pull of Lenin's personality, on Gorky's old need for a "father." There is some evidence, it is true, that the emotions toward Lenin, long laid to conscious rest, lived on in the depths, but no evidence that they commanded Gorky. One is compelled to feel that, while old ghosts must have stirred, that decision in 1918 was largely practical—in Gorky's typically idealistic, impractical way—and patriotic.

Here was Gorky's account, six years later, in his essay on Lenin, of his reconciliation with the man he had described as a mad chemist who experimented with humans:

Our meeting was friendly, but of course the all-seeing little eyes of Ilyitch looked at me, the sheep "gone astray," with evident regret. A very familiar look for me—for some thirty years I have been looked at in this way. I expect with certainty that I shall be accompanied into my grave with the same look...

"The union of workmen and the intelligentsia, what? [Lenin said, apparently responding to an idea of Gorky's.] That is not bad, not at all. Tell the intelligentsia to come to us. According to you, they sincerely serve the interests of justice, don't they? Then why do they keep away? Come over to us: it is we who have undertaken the colossal task of raising the people to their feet, of telling the world the whole truth about life; it is we who point out to nations the direct path to a humane life, the road out of slavery, penury, humiliation."

This was close to Gorky's old dream of the siskin, and of Danko. A tougher bird had made it become a possible reality; but Gorky—the siskin —was needed to form the union of workmen and intelligentsia, so all could reach that lovely meadow. As he turned from that meeting with Lenin and plunged into his new role, he might be imagined thinking: in the real world, this is what Danko would have done.

A more cunning, Luka-like explanation—but not really contradictory— of his motives is given by one who was then close to him: "The Social Democracy," he is supposed to have said, "must enter the ranks of the bolsheviks and, unnoticed, surround them. We must try to influence them, or else they will perform irrevocable stupidities!"

He had long seen lack of culture as Russia's great misfortune. Now, while the intelligentsia, "the resplendent veneer of Russia, receded into the background . . . perforce or through voluntary boycott and sabotage," the prevailingly backward, indolent, illiterate masses, "for the first time commanding the concern of the ruling classs," moved to the fore. "The thirst for knowledge among adults became so prodigious after the revolution that it taxed all the available cultivated men and women, in trying to supply the demand." Gorky became the prime organizer of adult education.

At the same time the masses hated whatever reminded them of the former ruling classes. Gorky pleaded again for preserving monuments and art treasures. The bolsheviks decreed confiscation and nationalization of art collections; he organized the supervision of such actions against vandalism and theft. Kaun recalls, rightly, that Bakunin, the aristocrat, idealized the people's "lust for destruction"; Gorky hated and feared it.

Indignantly Gorky would describe how, when several thousand peasants arrived in Petrograd in 1919 for a "conference of poor villagers," and were housed in the Winter Palace, they polluted not only bathtubs but also enormous numbers of precious vases—Sèvres, Saxony, and Oriental porcelain—using them as chamber pots. "That was not done from necessity—the palace lavatories proved to be in good order and the plumbing functioned properly. No, this hooliganism was the expression of a desire to spoil, to sully beautiful things. During the two revolutions and the war I have observed hundreds of times this dark, vindictive yearning of people to break, mutilate, mock and vilify the beautiful."

The bolsheviks generally accepted, even applauded, him in this role. But another side of it was harder for them to take: salvaging not books or cathedrals or paintings, but living men who were not bolsheviks—

scientists, poets, playwrights, novelists, artists, intellectuals of all sorts—from the revolution's often indiscriminate, often merely vengeful, "justice."

"The intelligentsia," Kaun writes, "in the early years of the bolshevik regime, were a stench in the nostrils of the masses, both because for a long time a considerable portion of the intellectuals practised sabotage ... and also because they filled the ranks of the interventionists [the White armies which invaded the land from all sides, with foreign backing]." They were blamed for everything, including the ghastly "cordon sanitaire" drawn by the Allies—led by France, which had substantial Russian investments—around Russia, which did not even permit medicine to enter the ravaged country; women and children had to be operated on without anesthetics or drugs.

The terrible Civil War pitted not only class against class but often, in the dire confusion of minds and emotions, father against son, brother against brother. There was no mercy. The land was steeped in blood. Cruelties were thought up, bizarre ways of torturing men as they died, that would have made the pious Middle Ages glow with envy. The horror and tragedy exceeded description.

The land suffered, and, partly in revenge, the gently raised intelligentsia suffered in high proportion. Reports of the Academy—to which Gorky had been elected as long ago as 1901, then excluded by command of the Tsar—listed, over and over, deaths "from lack of nourishment," "from physical overexertion." Part of the "people's vengeance," exercised on their behalf by the regime, was to see that the "idle" intelligentsia did their share of work—standing night guard in public buildings, collecting wood, digging trenches and ditches—whether or not the work was necessary.

Gorky pleaded with the government and the people:

The basic wealth of a country consists of the amount of brains, the number of intellectual forces nurtured and accumulated by the nation ... If we compel a skilful metal engraver to clean cesspools, if a goldsmith is made to forge anchors, and a chemist is driven to dig trenches, we are guilty not only of stupidity but also of a crime ... One must realize that the labor of a scholar is the possession of all humanity ... The premature invalidation or death of a scholar is an enormous loss for the country ... Herein is published the list of scholars who died within the last few months; you will note how great is the loss of scientific energy in our land ...

There was little food, no electricity, not even firewood for heat. There was no paper. Poets wrote poems on scraps of wrapping paper, toilet paper (until that gave out), paper for rolling cigarets; they read them aloud to their friends in unlit cold rooms or cafés—there was no hope of publication. At open improvised markets, people sold prized possessions for food—a coat for a herring—then shivered in their apartments in whatever clothing was left. Inflation ran wild: many families still possess 500,000 ruble notes from that day (value: a morsel of fish, or a loaf of straw-filled bread). The huge country's economy had broken down.

For the young, if they accepted the Revolution, and especially for those whom the Revolution dragged up from below, it was a period of fervid unleashing of energies ("a new world's a-bornin'!"), sometimes even surmounting the terrible conditions. It was a time of "freezing cold, rusty herring, torn rags, spotted typhus, arrests, breadlines." In the unheated theaters Red Army men sat, rifles in hand, "the cracking of sunflower seeds drowning out Beethoven's symphony." Nightly, men were dragged out of their homes "to render account in the cellars of the Cheka." Russia had become the mecca of all visionaries: Isadora Duncan danced by the light of lanterns brought out on stage, to the singing of "Boldly, comrade, foot it!" by thousands of voices hoarse with cold.

For the older, and for all not free of the middle-class taint, or who could not "accept," the terribleness and hopelessness were paramount. If ever there was a time of apocalypse, this was it.

When H. G. Wells came to Russia, the composer Glazunov begged him for help: to send him paper, so he could write his compositions down. The psychologist Pavlov worked in a room without heat or electricity, huddled in fur coat, cap, and gloves. He tended a patch of potatoes—his nourishment. Part of his time had to go to enforced janitor duty: he too was one of the suspect intelligentsia.

Gorky was now able to bring to bear his reputation, his friendships among individual bolsheviks, such as Lunacharsky, and finally his reestablished relation with Lenin, with the immunity which, as we shall see, it conferred; and his own sly cunning, and capacity for work.

He created, first, a Commission for the Protection of Monuments of Antiquity. This gave people jobs, and the right to food rations and lodging, besides saving heritages of art.

He formed in Petrograd a "Theatre of Tragedy," in which Andreyeva took part. There was an ambitious plan for producing classic tragedy, and for a new epic tragedy reflecting the heroic and tragic times. *Oedipus*

*Rex* was among the first productions. Employment of actors and play-wrights, of course, was one of the theater's chief functions: it enabled them to live, legitimately.

He had already in 1917 formed a Committee for Freedom and Culture. Now a contact committtee was named, with Gorky the key member, between this group (which included, informally, whoever needed a room, a job, or rations, and who was willing to give lectures to workers) and Lunacharsky, the Commissar of Education.

As part of the strategy of integrating intellectuals into the new structure so that they would be safe from terror and useful, he had Lunacharsky come to his apartment to meet the active members of the Free Association for the Development and Spread of the Positive Sciences (one of his first projects), and also to meet the representatives of "workers in the arts."

He organized cooperative lodgings and eating places—where intermin-able Russian conversations could also take place—for scientists, writers, artists, regardless of their sympathies. There was a Home of Scholars, a Home of Writers, a Home of Artists, and the definitions were flexible enough, being Gorky's, so that almost anyone who managed to get to him had a chance for a bed and food, if there was any. And he saw to it that there was.

He had done the same kind of thing, on a smaller scale, when he set up in Nizhni Novgorod a lodging for the barefoot bums. Now all the sensitive, cultured stratum of Russia was one big barefoot bum.

He organized—and this was one of his most stunning inspirations—an Institute of World Literature, with offices in both Petrograd and Moscow, whose task was the translation of world classics into Russian. This "writ-ers' project" made available to the masses treasures of the world's thought, starting with Goethe's *Faust*—how he scrounged the needed paper is a story in itself—and made legitimate work, and the right to lodging and food that went with it, available to intellectuals who otherwise would have starved or frozen to death, or been thrown into jail on suspicion.

Writing in London years later, as an émigré exile, Prince Dmitri Mirsky, the literary critic, said of Gorky:

... His activity in those dreadful years was extraordinarily useful and salutary. He played the part to which he pretended, of defender of cul-ture and civilization, as well as he could have done. The debt of Russian culture to him is very great. Everything that was done between 1918 and 1921 to save the writers and other higher intellectuals from starvation was due to Gorky. This was chiefly arrived at by a whole system of centralized literary establishments where poets and novelists were set to work at translations. The contrivance was by no means a perfect one, but under the circumstances it was probably the only one possible.

The writer Vladislav Khodasevich, then living with Gorky, has given an eyewitness account of Gorky's role and his fantastic Petrograd apartment.

Intellectuals sat around Gorky's table, late at night, reading and talking by the light of his kerosene lamp (a rarity in Petrograd in those days). In a back room lay a sick member of the royal family—one of the grand dukes, as a matter of fact—whom Gorky was sheltering from execution, guarded by a bulldog kept wrapped in a blanket so that he would not bite proletarian visitors, while his wife mingled with the guests in the front room. Interspersed with writers and artists were workers and sailors, come to Gorky to ask protection against the Cheka and Zinoviev.

"They came asking intervention for those arrested, through him they managed to get rations, rooms, clothes, medicine, fatty foods, railroad tickets, jobs, tobacco, writing paper, ink, false teeth for old men and milk for newborn infants—in a word, everything that could not be obtained without protection. Gorky heard everyone out and wrote innumerable letters of recommendation."

Just such intervention by Gorky had saved Khodasevich from immediate front-line duty, almost, as things were going, a sentence to death. He had been appointed head of the Moscow section of World Literature. When suddenly drafted, he turned to Gorky. Gorky sat him down to write a letter to Lenin; then Gorky himself hustled with it to the Kremlin. Khodasevich was deferred, and Gorky urged him to live in Petrograd instead of Moscow. Khodasevich ended up living in Gorky's flat, along with just about everybody else.

He came to know Gorky, as well as a man could, over a seven-year span. Their views of life were vastly different: to the younger man, of good family, the communist ideal, that had meant so much to Gorky and still tore him in half, was essentially sad, barbarian tomfoolery. But he was honest, sensitive, and discerning, and his long look at Gorky is invaluable.

His recollections at this point are supplemented by those of Chukovsky, one of the best Soviet critics, translator of Whitman:

He [Gorky] was the head of World Literature, Home of the Arts, Section of Historical Paintings, Union of Workers of the Verbal Arts, and so on, and so on, and so on. He not only presided at all our "commissions," but had taken upon his shoulders all our troubles and needs, so that if one of us had a baby born, Gorky obtained a nipple, if one fell sick with typhus, he interceded for getting for him a place in a hospital, and if one wished to go to the country for a while, he wrote letters to various institutions for permits to use the Sestroretsk resort.

I think if one should collect all the letters written by Gorky . . . in behalf of Russian writers, there would accrue a goodly five or six volumes: in those days Gorky wrote no novels or stories—only those endless letters . . .

Once a woman poet called on him, and after she had left he was told that she had only a few days ago given birth to a child. Gorky got busy, and she received a permit: Milkwoman so and so is hereby authorized to deliver milk to the wife of Maxim Gorky—and the poet's name was given.

Another time, Chukovsky informed him that a considerable food ration was coming to him for a lecture he had given at the Murmansk Railroad Club. Gorky asked if it could not be transferred to a certain woman translator, who was in great need. "How shall I designate her relation to you?" "Put her down as my sister."

Thus he accumulated "wives" and "sisters," as he had already accumulated "sons." One of the "sons," Yakov Sverdlov, by now had become the first president of the Russian Republic: he was to die soon, of typhus, and therefore is still one of the heroes, the only Jew whose statue stands among those of the greatest founders, in the Kremlin burial ground. Sverdlov's twin brother, also a "son" of Gorky, Zinovy Peshkov, whom the reader met once before, in America, was by now a dashing major in the French foreign legion, and would become a general and a confidant of de Gaulle.

"If we survived those breadless, typhoidal years," says Chukovsky, "we owe it in a large measure to our 'kinship' with Maxim Gorky, to whom all of us, great and small, became in those days a kindred family. I often chanced to see Gorky intercede for authors who had viciously baited him before the Revolution."

Kaun points out that many of these men "proceeded even more viciously to sling mud at Gorky as soon as they crossed the border of Soviet Russia." His role, they cried, was "the role at one and the same time of Cain, Judas, and Pilate toward his own people."

To exaggerate what he managed to do would be unrealistic. He himself said, with a disgusted wave of his hand, when someone spoke of those he had saved from the Terror: "It's nothing. For every one or two I get off, they manage to kill two or three hundred."

He appealed repeatedly to Lenin, by long distance phone, on behalf of the four grand dukes condemned to death by the Petrograd Cheka. Lenin promised to release them on Gorky's pledge. Gorky, rushing back from Moscow with Lenin's signed order, got the news at the station that the grand dukes had been shot during the night by order of Zinoviev. Gorky told Kaun that Lenin "had a veritable fit, rolled on the floor and howled," when he learned about it. As for Gorky, he went to bed, sick.

I troubled Lenin very often with all sorts of requests [Gorky wrote later], and at times I felt that my pleas for people aroused in him a certain pity for me, almost a contempt. He would ask me:

"Does it not occur to you that you are busying yourself with nonsense, with trifles?"

... And yet I do not recall an instant when Ilyich refused a request of mine. If it happened, indeed, that my pleas were not complied with, it was not because of his fault, but because of those damnable "mechanical shortcomings," from which the clumsy machine of Russia's state has always suffered abundantly. One may also allow for someone's malicious unwillingness to alleviate the fate of human beings, or save their lives. Vengeance and malice may often act also by inertia. And then, there are, of course, small, psychically unhealthy people with a morbid thirst for the enjoyment of suffering on the part of their fellow-men.

An unpublished memory, by one now far from Russia but then immediately close to the scene, may give us a closer look at a conversation between Gorky and Lenin—possibly this very one—throwing light on the nature of "trifles" and the relation of the mentalities of the two men.

Prior to the Revolution, an informal committee had been formed to help the plight of political prisoners. Gorky's wife, Ekaterina Pavlovna Peshkova, was on it. The committee negotiated with the authorities to be allowed to bring prisoners food, books, change of clothing, to transmit letters from relatives. It inquired about conditions. At the moment of revolution, one of the committee entered Peter-and-Paul prison and breathlessly announced to Dzerdzinski his release, "in the Revolution's name!" Soon the committee members were again bustling to and from the prisons, trying to do the same things for those imprisoned by Dzerdzinski and his Cheka.

One of them was visiting in prison when in the next cell she heard a youth—soldier? sailor?—talking to his mother. He was to be shot. "Mother,

I didn't do anything! I swear!" Son and mother cried. Our narrator went
to Peshkova, who went to Gorky, who went to Lenin. Gorky refused
to say anything afterward, but the story of their conference sifted back,
through one present at it. Lenin had put his head in his hands and said, in
irritated protest (here the narrator paraphrased, from memory): "Alexey
Maximovich, for God's sake—don't come to me with all these trifles. Don't
you understand—this is *one boy*. There's a revolution going on. Please
try to understand."

But many times Lenin let Gorky bother him. Two telegrams give a
rather dramatic illustration. The first is from Lenin to the Red regimental
command of Orel province, with a copy to the command at Malo-
Archangelsk.

12.IV.1919
The writer Ivan Volny has been arrested. Gorky, his comrade, asks
earnestly for the greatest care and objectivity in investigating him. Can
he not be freed under close observation? Wire.
                          President of the Soviet of People's Commissars Lenin

The second is two days later, addressed to Gorky:

14.IV.1919
The chairman of the Orlov investigation commission Chuzhinev wires
me that Ivan Volny has been temporarily freed until the case is clarified.
                                                                              Lenin

And there is a famous notation, scrawled by Lenin on somebody else's
letter to Gorky containing a request for help. It is addressed to all Soviet
officials, for Gorky's use whenever he needed it:

Comrades! I beg you earnestly, in all cases when Comrade Gorky will
turn to you with similar requests, to give him *every* cooperation, and if
there are any obstacles, hindrances or objections of one sort or another,
not to fail to inform me of what they consist.
                                                          V. Ulyanov (Lenin)

## CHAPTER 27

BLOK, the "poet of the Revolution," who tried so hard to accept it, was a desperately sick man. Gorky had gotten him a job on World Literature; then, for months, clamored for a permit for Blok to go abroad to recuperate. He managed to get it, on the morning after the night in which Blok died.

During the long negotiations for Blok, Gorky had also put in for Sologub, a poet and storyteller, morbid and refined, whose work Gorky had always hated as decadent. He fought for the two poets equally. Lunacharsky finally managed to put Gorky's request on behalf of the two sick writers before the Politburo. The ruling came back: Sologub may leave, Blok may not. Thereupon Lunacharsky made a stirring plea, of which he sent a copy to Gorky: This ruling was injustice to Blok; Blok was the poet of the Revolution, while Sologub was "our enemy," hated by the proletariat, had done counterrevolutionary pamphlets. The result was that Sologub's permit was revoked.

Khodasevich relates that Gorky called him into his study, showed him Lunacharsky's proud report on his efforts, and asked: "How do you like it?" Khodasevich said, "He's a fool." "A son of a bitch!" cried Gorky, then apologized; he seldom swore, Khodasevich recalls, and was upset when others used vulgar language.

But sometimes Lunacharsky did not gum things up, and was of real help. He was one of the forces of humanism on whom Gorky could rely.

Gorky tried to save the poet Gumilev, whose work had been admired by the royal family, and who was imprisoned on charges of being involved in a White plot. (He probably was; it was hard not to get involved, if one was young and sympathized with the White cause.) Even émigrés who hated Gorky apparently agree that he prevailed on Lenin to send a last-minute telegram. It either came too late or was ignored: Gumilev, with the others taken in the plot, was shot.

Each killing—based on fear, vengeance, theory—was to bear its fruit of unforgiving hatred. And even if someone wants to forgive the killing of those dear to him, those who did the killing cannot believe him. These are psychological matters—and the bolsheviks were weakest in psychology.

The writer Vsevelod-Ivanov was one of the poor but eager young men who came to Moscow with the revolutionary tide. He had manuscripts but no boots, and no place to sleep. Diffidently, he asked to see the great Gorky. Gorky read everything he showed him, wrote comments all over it, urged him to go on writing (and later, when he had scrounged enough paper, helped him get it published); then he arranged for a room for him in the Home of Writers; then wrote out an order for boots—he was one of the few who could. Vsevelod-Ivanov got the boots, but Gorky forgot and ordered more boots. The young writer ended up with three pairs, before he could get Gorky to stop.

The news that there was a man who could help must have spread far beyond the intelligentsia of science and letters. A stranger wired Gorky that at a railroad station in the provinces he had been robbed of two pairs of pants and money; what was Gorky going to do about it? A lady came to Gorky, "bearing on her body," as Gorky recalled it, about four pounds of silver and two of gold, to ask him to free her two husbands, who had been jailed by mistake. Gorky promised to make inquiries—he never refused, and nearly always did. The lady wanted to know how much he would charge her.

By 1921, however, his ability to rescue and help had become sharply curtailed by his feud with Zinoviev. Gorky abhorred what he felt was Zinoviev's motive for repression: vengeance. Zinoviev was supported by Kamenev. The feud was enhanced by bad blood between Gorky's Andreyeva and Kamenev's wife (Trotsky's sister), who had been put in charge of the department controlling the theater, a job Andreyeva thought should be hers. Meyerhold, the great director, got into the mess, supporting Madam Kamenev. Khodasevich composed a mock ballad, in the style of the old Russian heroic ballads, depicting this struggle; and Gorky loved to have him declaim it. But it was now hard to intervene for people singled out by Zinoviev; if he did, it could be worse for them. He could then only turn to Lenin. And for Lenin, Khodasevich wrote, Zinoviev was more important than Gorky.

Two stories are told by Khodasevich to support his view that it was the worsening of Gorky's position in Soviet Russia, a growing sense of disillusionment and helplessness, that finally made him leave in 1921, *not* his health.

One is the story of Moura Budberg, the last of the women important in Gorky's life. Khodasevich, who did not like this talented woman, insisted her main talent was "to attain whatever goal she set for herself." A baroness, whose husband had been killed by revolting peasants on his Esthonian estate, she moved in high society in Berlin, then in Moscow, with friends in both German and English circles. She became close friends with the British diplomat Lockhart, who was in Russia on an important secret mission. "A Russian of the Russians," he worshipfully described her, "she had a lofty disregard for all the pettiness of life and a courage which was proof against all cowardice."

Lockhart admired the revolutionaries in many ways, considering them idealists like the Puritans and early Jesuits. He opposed intervention by England, but when it came "I lacked the moral courage to resign." Tangled in a web of politics, he was imprisoned by the bolsheviks, then allowed to leave Russia. Thereupon Moura Budberg got a job, like everybody else, on World Literature. She tried to flee Russia, Khodasevich says, was caught and put in jail. She was one of the many Gorky managed to get free, and thence arose their friendship. But Zinoviev was now on her trail.

The climax of this story is connected by Khodasevich with another, fully in line with Gorky's character and with the facts of his fight with Zinoviev. It involves one of the history-making and shocking events of the time, which split a large part of world liberal opinion from the bolsheviks: the suppression of the Kronstadt uprising.

The Kronstadt sailors were the most romantic figures of the Revolution. Their adherence to the Soviets had been decisive. The flame from the guns of the cruiser *Aurora* became the Revolution's dream symbol. In Bill-Belotserkovsky's naïve and stirring play, "Storm," epitome of the Revolution's early spirit, it is a Kronstadt sailor who stands behind the commissar, like the genius of all that is great, simple and good, assuring the People's triumph.

In the spring of 1921, amid hunger, forced grain collections, and strikes by the industrial workers, the peasants around the naval base of Kronstadt mutinied, and the sailors, with some menshevik leadership, supported them. Trotsky himself, who had won their allegiance to the Revolution, now commanded the Red Army to move against them. Young bolshevik deputies from the Tenth Party Congress, called to volunteer because the army and workers were reluctant to cut down the sailors, charged across the ice. Kronstadt was taken, and then came the executions.

Trotsky explained, years later, that these were not the same sailors. Neither he, nor Lenin, nor the Revolution, ever quite regained their pristine charm for those who learned the muffled story. Khodasevich says he himself saw groups of sailors being led away to their doom, shaking their fists at workers they met in the streets, crying: "Traitors! Bastards!"

To Gorky, with whom Khodasevich was living, came sailors who had managed to escape the net, and told him about how it happened, and how Zinoviev was having their comrades shot. Gorky, says Khodasevich, finally accumulated documents purporting to show not only that Zinoviev was conducting merciless executions without trial, but also that he had, in fact, helped provoke the uprising. With these Gorky went to Moscow, where in the apartment of his wife, Ekaterina Pavlovna, a meeting was taking place, including Lenin, Dzerdzinski, and Trotsky; beside Dzerdzinski sat an armed guard of the Cheka; just prior to Trotsky's arrival, a squad of the Red Army had surrounded the apartment.

Gorky made his statement. They decided to call in Zinoviev, and hear his side. At the first meeting, Zinoviev had a heart attack; Gorky told Khodasevich he thought Zinoviev was faking—though he really did have a bad heart. The only result was that Zinoviev got a bawling out; and now he really had it in for Gorky.

At this point Gorky demanded an immediate passport for Moura Budberg, and got it; she left for Esthonia.

And Gorky's days in the Soviet Union, too, were drawing to a close. Khodasevich says that in his presence Gorky read a letter from Lenin urging him to leave, because of his lungs, and reacted violently to the cover-up; Lenin wanted him out of there. For Lenin it may be said he also didn't want to see Gorky killed; he could still be useful later—and besides, strangely, Lenin had always really liked the man.

This seems a close and plausible account of the events and motives that caused Gorky to leave Russia. If he really once had a plan for "cultural encirclement," that would take Russia's fate out of the hands of fanatics, it had certainly failed, as it had to; he was himself "encircled." When he told Kaun, in 1926, that he had left, on Lenin's warm urging, because his life was endangered by illness, this was expedient, in what he felt were his and Russia's best interests; and Kaun was surely aware of this. To have been frank about his relations with Lenin and his attitude to the bolsheviks would have ruined any chance to influence the Russian future.

This was Lenin's fatherly letter:

A.M.

...I am so tired that I cannot do a thing to save my life. But you, you spit blood, yet you don't go. Upon my word, that is both unfair and extravagant. In Europe, in a good sanatorium, you will be treated properly, and you will be able to accomplish thrice as much work. Upon my word. Whereas with us here you get neither treatment nor any work done, nothing but fuss and vanity, futile vanity. Go away from here, get well. Don't be stubborn, I beg of you!

Your Lenin

But a closer look has already been gained, which seems very authentic, at the months preceding that letter. Besides, it is all there in the letter itself —it just isn't spelled out. "Don't be stubborn."

He was still needed, for one more job, by the bolsheviks.

He may be imagined undertaking it, not with vainglory, but rather with a grateful awareness that he was needed...and perhaps a growing sense that his biography had become inseparable from Russia's. This sense of identity, and therefore of fitness as something to preserve in his actions, may have grown; it could hardly be avoided. It would determine his last years; probably, his end.

The job was—to appeal to America. The bolsheviks could not bring themselves directly—certainly not Lenin!—to beg manna from hated capitalist hands. For Gorky there was no problem: mutual charity is what humans are made for, Matvey the God-seeker would have said.

Hunger had become menacing reality as early as 1916. By 1918, a foreign observer in the provinces could describe "grim ghastly tragedy that clutched and strangled every impulse but the most primitive." In 1919, Herbert Hoover offered the Hoover Plan of a neutral commission to feed the hungry of Russia, as war-devastated Europe was being fed. Furious protest by the White generals and organizations, and welching by the French government, blocked it: bolshevism was a plague, to be combatted even by starvation.

The Polish attack on the Soviets brought more mutual devastation. The American Relief Administration began to operate in Poland. Relief was also offered to the Soviets, but it then looked as if the Red Army might take Warsaw, and dreams of world revolution were again afloat. The bolsheviks set unreal terms, and the plan again fell through.

The tide of revolution soon receded in Europe, but for Russia scorching Civil War continued, then drought bringing famine—a great famine, like the famines of old. The world for some time did not know, because of the wall of suspicion and hate between it and Russia. By the time America knew, "Red scares" and the Palmer raids were on, and it would not be easy to get approval of American aid, even if the Soviets appealed.

And they had to appeal. By the early summer of 1921 the famine was dreadful and insupportable, and across the Volga with it rolled the typhus plague. Desperate peasants and their children, having eaten the exhumed bodies of cats and dogs, tree bark, poisonous concoctions of clay and manure, and having begun to die from this nourishment, fled their villages for the cities. There were no trains, and people died waiting at the stations.

Imagine a compact mass of sordid rags, among which are visible, here and there, lean naked arms, faces already stamped with the seal of death . . . The waiting room, the corridor, every foot thickly covered with people, sprawling, seated, crouched in every imaginable position. If one looks closely he sees that these filthy rags are swarming with vermin. The typhus-stricken grovel and shiver in their fever, their babies with them. Nursing babies have lost their voices and are no longer able to cry. Every day more than 20 dead are carried away, but it is not possible to remove all of them. Sometimes corpses remain among the living for more than five days . . .

At last the appeal.

American relief officials guessed that it followed an internal Party struggle, between "Die-Hards, who refused to give up their principles, even if the peasants would die for them, and the more flexible and humane opportunists, who could see no advantage to the survival of Communism if Russia was ruined." The compromise was in the manner of the appeal. "The Soviet government itself did not at first ask for help: it allowed the Patriarch Tikhon and Maxim Gorky to do it."

Gorky's message, "To All Honest People," appeared in American papers on July 23rd:

The corn-growing steppes are smitten by crop failure . . . Think of the Russian people's exhaustion by the war and revolution . . . Gloomy days have come for the country of Tolstoy, Dostoyevsky, Mendeleyev, Pavlov, Moussorgsky, Glinka and other world-prized men . . . If humanitarian ideas and feelings—faith in whose social import was so shaken by the

damnable war and its victors' unmercifulness towards the vanquished—
if faith in the creative force of these ideas and feelings, I say, must and
can be restored, Russia's misfortune offers humanitarians a splendid opportunity to demonstrate the vitality of humanitarianism ... I ask all honest
European and American people for prompt aid to the Russian people.
Give bread and medicine. Maxim Gorky.

He was accustomed, when reading the manuscripts of others or his own,
to shed tears. How he must have bawled over that one!

Hoover's reply came by wire: "I have read with great feeling your
appeal to America for charitable assistance to the starving and sick people
of Russia, more particularly the children." (It was for the sake of the
children that Hoover's proposal was able to get through Congress.)

He spelled out the conditions, including the need for a formal Soviet
request, and noninterference with distribution. The A.R.A. would pledge
to supply all children and invalids without regard to race, creed, or social
status; its representatives would not engage in politics.

Gorky answered that the Soviet government would accept; then transmitted the formal Soviet request for help, signed by Kamenev, not Lenin.
In Riga, Litvinov and Lyman Brown (for the A.R.A.) signed the agreement. This began a tremendous movement of American supplies (800,000
tons of food and medicine) saving millions of lives, in spite of charges by
Zinoviev and other die-hards that this food was a "weapon," and over-
coming strong American opposition in Congress and press. By separate
agreement, many thousands of American families sent food parcels to unknown families in Russia. Of 160,000 children in Petrograd between three
and fifteen, 150,000 were fed regularly by the American kitchens.

When famine and plague were overcome, the Soviets thanked the Americans. But the A.R.A. staff valued more a letter from Gorky, by then in
exile, to Hoover.

... In the history of practical humanitarianism I know of no achievement which in terms of magnitude and generosity can be compared to
the relief that you have actually accomplished ...

The generosity of the American people resuscitates the dream of fraternity among people at a time when humanity greatly needs charity and
compassion.

Within a month after his appeal to America, Gorky had left Russia.
The timing, the circumstances described, the evidence of his good health
immediately afterward, exclude any explanation but profound discourage-

ment with what was happening in Russia, chagrin, the desire to escape to a monastery of refuge. He lived briefly in Germany, before going on to Sorrento in Italy. The writing he at once began projected, as always, his state of mind. Like many another poet, his first impulse was to turn to history and use it as a cloak for the retelling of his profound and agitating experience.

# BOOK V

## *Songs of Experience*

## CHAPTER 28

THE first major work Gorky completed after leaving Lenin and
Soviet Russia was a grim scenario for a movie (never made) about
the seventeenth-century Cossack rising led by Stepan Razin: idealistic at
least at the start, degenerating in blood and terror, unable to be damned,
impossible not to disavow.

Nothing was truer to Russia's harsh, thrilling history than Stenka Razin's
rising. Gorky's source was a splendid essay by the old historian Kostomarov. There Razin was described as a man of unflinching will; inflexible;
ruthless. "He was a product of an unfortunate layer of society; revenge
and hatred against this society were impregnated in his being."

In Gorky's script, however, the character and drama of Razin were
merged with those of a mysterious figure much closer to him—Lenin. The
script became his one real effort to grapple, by literary art, with the
nature and meaning of Lenin, to pass a moral judgment, if he could, on
this greatest of the amoral men he had known, who had so drastically
altered countless lives, and who had imposed his own will on Gorky's life
so mercilessly.

And to confront this figure of Razin-Lenin—

...Comes a young handsome fellow, on his back a bundle of wooden
pipes and reeds; to the belt of his kaftan [cloak] is fastened a staff—a stick
with a bent head. To this staff clings an old blind man, with a gusli hung
on his breast. He also holds a stick in his hand, and to it clings a second
blind man, and so, in a chain, holding onto the sticks, go four blind men.

This young piper, Boris, is of course Gorky himself, whose father had
actually led the blind to markets. The poor blind beggars are not only
Gregory, Grandpa's foreman, but all the poor blind beggars of life, whose

seer and champion the piper is. The gusli, the ancient knee-held harp of southern Russia, is the one Skitalets played, to which Gorky sang, on those "Wednesdays" in Moscow at the century's turn. The image, clear and bright, is that of the young idealist Gorky, the brave romantic, ready for a Cause.

Nowhere else in his creative work does this image appear. It must have taken a great effort to break through the shell of his reticence about what he was, and what moved him, in those years when he was pulled into the magnetic field of Lenin, from that of Tolstoy.

Razin rescues Boris from the local war lord. As they gallop into the free steppe, he talks with the youth, "caressingly laughing." This first sight of him is of a man active but kind, who can win a young heart; a man who has saved Boris from a mean life of vagabondage or servitude, for a noble, exciting Cause. This was how Gorky first looked, in gratitude, at Lenin. Boris will be the bard of the rebels, cheer them with song. This was how Gorky had once, for a few fateful years, seen himself in Lenin's movement.

The script is swift, lyric, with the gray-grained feel of early epic. Its heart is the relation between the idealistic Boris and the amoral Stenka Razin. The issue that divides them is the shedding of blood, to achieve a goal. Morality and the shedding of blood were what separated Gorky and Lenin.

When slaughter and pillage mar the cause, Boris looks at Razin more thoughtfully. "You don't care about people," he says. Razin frowns: "No, I care about people. For people, maybe, I would lay down my soul... You don't understand, bird." To the grim, determined leader, Boris the sweet singer is his other self, the being he was not—the "bird." (This was probably the key to Lenin's liking for Gorky.) When Boris protests again, Razin says (again it is clearly the intellectual, Lenin, not the peasant, Razin): "If you don't give people a shove, they'll never go anywhere—but once they go, it's hard to stop them."

It is Razin's mother who goads him, for she cannot forgive: "Moscow killed my son... my oldest." So must Lenin's mother have grieved, when her oldest was killed by Moscow; and her grief must have worked on Lenin. The execution of a beloved brother by the hated authorities was a coincidence of Lenin's life and Razin's. It was for vengeance, said Kostomarov, that Razin began his revolt.

The Razin Gorky created was not simply Lenin. Gorky was drawn to model the one on the other, by the parallel of sacred mission and ruthlessness. But Razin was also the spirit of elemental, merciless revolt—the spirit called up by Lenin from a slumbering deep, the long-repressed, largely irrational will of those below to break through into life ... a desire that demands compassion and sympathy.

It was hard for Boris to break from this compassionate spell. But at last there was too much killing. He is shown crying, breaking his pipe across his knees. "Let me go!" he cries to Razin. "I don't want to live with you!" He tries to throw himself overboard from Razin's barge on the Volga, but Razin clutches him by the shoulder, leads him away with a fatherly hand.

Having ravaged a Persian city on the Caspian coast, Razin heads back up the Volga, pursued by both Moscow and Persia. In the traditional folk song, "The Lay of Stenka Razin," the outlaw, feeling his fortunes ebb, throws his captured Persian princess into the Volga, to appease the river. "Volga-mother, accept my gift." His real motive, Kostomarov had explained, was to show his men he did not allow himself what he forbade them.

Gorky's treatment of this dramatic highlight is abrupt, almost furtive. He must have been shocked into sudden subconscious awareness that Lenin, the unacknowledged model for Razin, would not have abducted any girl, not even a princess. Lenin was even more chaste than Gorky. And to portray him killing a woman was too painful. Gorky could no more than glance at that scene, and moved the spotlight hurriedly to the moral relation of the two men, Boris (who slept through the killing) and Razin: Gorky and Lenin.

Razin regards Boris. "You want to go from me? I'm sorry for you, clean soul. You sing well. All right, go. Your path's not with me." In effect, this was what Lenin had decided about Gorky.

Put ashore, Boris is shown standing on the bank, weeping, waving his hat after Razin's barge. He has broken away from a leader, and a cause, too bloody; but he weeps!

Razin's revolt was doomed by its cruelty. Deserted by many Russians who had flocked to him but now have grown appalled, he has rallied the oppressed nationalities—the Mordvin, the Chuvash, the Cheremiss. Against them moves Boryatinsky's army of Moscow, Europe-trained. This will no longer be guerilla warfare.

Before the final conflict, Razin enters a hermit's hut and, agitated, justifies himself:

"Maybe I butchered many people for nothing, but still: my sin is not the Tsar's sin—not against everyone."

(This was the last justification, as Gorky saw it, for 1666–68, and for 1917–21.)

Razin gets up, covers his head, then adds: "If there's a God—tell him: on earth there's no way to do a righteous deed without sinning." (This was Gorky's own, bitter, self-destructive conclusion.)

The old hermit majestically tells Razin to get down on his knees and ask forgiveness. Razin refuses, and says: "Thank me for not chopping off your head."

Razin's forces are routed, and many captured. Saber-slashed, Razin himself is carried off the field by four Cossacks. (Throughout his script, Gorky tried to preserve Razin's image: in actual history, Razin took the remnants of his Cossacks and fled by night, leaving his Mordvin and Chuvash allies to be slaughtered.) The prisoners are lined up before Boryatinsky. Some are drowned, others thrown on hot coals. Rafts with gallows on them, carrying ghastly cargoes, float down the Volga.

Betrayed at last by the Cossacks themselves, Stepan Razin is brought into Moscow in a horse-drawn wagon, his younger brother Frolka trembling beside him. The most dreadful tortures fail to break Razin. Frolka, under torture, begs forgiveness. "Shut up, old woman," Razin tells him. "It doesn't hurt. You knew the happiness of a free life—now be able to bear unhappiness too." After more torture, Razin is quartered on Red Square. He laughs at his victorious foes as long as he is conscious.

In Kostomarov's essay, Razin said to his brother: "Recall our former life: we lived with fame, commanded thousands; now we have to be able to endure misfortune bravely." This is a man of will to power. Gorky's man, at the end, is closer to the romantic rebel, Gorky the stormy petrel of 1900, who wanted that great, vague, all-embracing "free life," that "happiness." Gorky wrote Razin's last speech from within: that was neither Lenin nor the historical Razin.

And who can be sure the real Razin, the gloomy stoical peasant, did not speak of human freedom at the end? In this doubt lies the compelling appeal of revolutionary idealism.

Years pass. In a forest clearing a group of bandits listen to an old man with a gusli, who sings:

> There lived and was a righteous Cossack,
> Lived Stepan Razin, Timothy's son.
> He punished the boyars, loved the poor...

The Sherwood-foresters thank him, give him money, and ask, "How do they call you, granddad?"

"Boris."

And again, this time in a hut "packed with grown-ups and children," Boris sits playing his gusli, and sings:

> Who served the people, he served God too,
> And his heavy sins—are not ours to judge.
> And here ends the story of Razin,
> Of the daring Stepan, son of Timothy.

Gorky clearly wrote this scenario driven by contrary needs: to tell the truth about Lenin and the Revolution, and to defend them.

To the French producer who planned to make the movie he wrote: "I have done everything I possibly could ... Wherever I could, without violating the truth, I softened the character of Razin ..." The sign of an inner weariness, after an exhausting inner struggle, is in this whole letter.

That inner split was mirrored in Boris the bard. He rejected Razin's cruel deeds and left him; then sang his glory at the end (the "glory-sing" is the literal word for this type of ballad, and this is what Gorky himself called it).

But artists have always sung bloody deeds to glory, covering up the fact that the positives of life often come from violence, "good" ends from bad or dubious means. Gorky was only far more honest than others. Boris' ballad shows the very process by which art starts its immoral glamorizing of the past.

And this scenario—one of his best works, untranslated, never filmed, unknown—lights up Gorky in his dilemma, caught between his moral nature and the things that were. In this light it is suddenly clear that he will return, at the end, to the Soviet Union. It is all determined, though nearly ten years of exile and indecision lie ahead.

The light is cast by the presence of the bard. Since Boris was how Gorky saw himself, all becomes understandable.

The tradition of the bard was to celebrate in song the lives and deeds— usually amoral—of men of action. In Gorky the barefoot bums found their bard, but the social critic and thinker in him made this role senseless. For a brief time in history, between barefoot tramps and bolsheviks, he was the bard of "the revolution entire," when idealists, rebels, most of the avant-garde thinkers, danced to the stormy petrel; but this did not last.

Next, the bolsheviks needed a bard to sit at the feet of Lenin, and this, in the fateful years of "salvation," Gorky became.

By 1917, he had long moved from the need for Lenin's salvation; and when the cruelty of the Revolution became clear, he left Russia.

And still, regret would recur. He still wanted to be the bard of Russia, in the sense that the "Homer" of the Iliad was the bard of the Greeks.

But Russia had become the Revolution, just as Greece had become the Trojan War. The bard's song could only center on the bolshevik rising and its central figure, Lenin. Nor could he reject the final heroism of either, any more than Homer could reject the whole bloody war, Agamemnon and Achilles, and still be the bard. He had no choice but to compose the glory-sing after all.

# CHAPTER 29

THE Revolution, which shattered so many lives, also had a shattering effect on Gorky. The works that followed "Stepan Razin"—and they represent the maturity of his art—have the character of fragments. Only if the fragments, like pieces of a mosaic, are put together, does one see a continuing unity in this man now so disillusioned and bewildered.

Some of the fragments took the form of essays—rather wonderful essays—about men and ideas he had known. It was a form of calling up reinforcements from the past. First came the great "Reminiscences of Tolstoy."

The portrait of Tolstoy was actually begun during the hurly-burly of Revolution. Gorky completed it in exile in the early twenties, while, sick at heart, he wandered central Europe, finally settling, like a flight-bedraggled bird settling somewhere just to be warm, in Sorrento on the Bay of Naples.

He prefaced it with a letter he had written to Korolenko in 1910, upon news of the death of Tolstoy. The letter itself is a moving work of art, like the lyric opening movement of the essay on Tolstoy.

When he heard of Tolstoy's death, Gorky had written Korolenko, he felt "as though I had been gripped by the throat and nearly strangled."

No man was more worthy of the name of genius: "great in everything—yes, in everything." Gorky had wanted to cry aloud, to all: "Look what a wonderful man is living on earth!" But at the same time he had always been repelled by the man's "stubborn despotic inclination to turn the life of Count Lev Nikolayevich into 'the saintly life of our blessed father, boyar Leo.'"

And so he promptly derailed, by the clarity of his testimony, the legend of "St. Leo," and preserved for us instead the indelible godlike pagan, the magnificent, iconoclastic, complicated, egotistical, human Lev Tolstoy. At the same time, he recorded the struggle of two irreconcilable, though somewhat similar, spirits, his own and Tolstoy's.

Gorky saw the real Tolstoy, "the crown of our ancient history," trying to stretch himself like a vast mountain across Russia's path to Europe, barring Russia from "the active life which sternly demands of men the supreme effort of their spiritual forces." He tilts against rationalism, preaching the ancient Russian view "that holiness is attained by flirting with sin." He tries to persuade people that earthly life is nonsense. This is harmful to Russians, for being so persuaded, and being naturally lazy, they stop trying.

His "overgrown egotism," furthermore, is monstrous—like that of one of those wild and selfish legendary Russian warrior-heroes: a Vasska Buslayev. Yet—"yes, he *is* great."

The letter's eloquence is headlong. Gorky had loved and hated the man, seen through him and recognized the glory in him. The thoughts strike out boldly, because the man writing them is confident of their ultimate sincerity.

Boldly he insists on the absence of any "religious faith" in Tolstoy, the religious preacher. Instead of a meek praying hermit under his oak, there sat under his cypress a great, weary, godlike old writer. The light the paragraphs cast moves back and forth, confirming, for instance, the identity of that enigmatic, quasi-holy man of "The Lower Depths," Luka.

All Russian preachers, with the exception of Avvakum and perhaps Tikhon Zadonsky, are cold men, for they do not possess an active and living faith. When I was writing Luka in The Lower Depths, I wanted to describe an old man like that: he is interested in "every solution" but not in people; coming inevitably in contact with them, he consoles them, but only in order that they may leave him in peace. And all the philosophy, all the preaching of such men is alms bestowed by them with a veiled aversion, and there sounds, behind their preaching, words which are beggarly and melancholy: "Get out! Love God or your neighbor, but get out! Curse God, love the stranger, but leave me alone! Leave me alone, for I am a man and I am doomed to death."

So Tolstoy really was the model for Luka, or at least Gorky thought he was. And this helps explain why Tolstoy (when Gorky read the play to him) disliked it at once, and asked Gorky why he wrote it.

But the light from that paragraph falls on more than one object. It has been seen how utterly pessimistic was Gorky's own view, his gaze dissecting life and showing—nothingness. (In a little while will come his exchange, on the subjects of reality and immortality, with Blok.) And still, from youth on, he had been spurring men to noble visions, having Danko wave his flaming heart before men leading them to lovely meadows, lying to a poor dying crippled boy who wanted to believe cockroaches could grow to the size of horses—anything, anything, so that people would be happy. "Be happy, damn you—and leave me alone! Leave me alone for I am a man and doomed to die and I want to contemplate the emptiness of eternity!" The masking of utter pessimism by inspiring vision—that came close to being his own desperate solution.

Then was Gorky simply projecting himself into Tolstoy? Hardly; the portrait is too clear, and too many things fit with the evidence in Tolstoy's own work. Gorky could not be devious; and the traits one picks out the most unerringly in another are usually those which reproduce traits of one's own. The most likely thing is that the two men were very similar in this respect: both desperately wanted happiness for everyone, but found it hard to believe in any themselves.

So Luka, that mysterious holy wanderer, was some part the real Tolstoy, some part Gorky's Tolstoy, and a good part (as the "Wednesdays" had guessed, and as Khodasevich concluded after living close to Gorky twenty years later) Gorky himself; altogether a complex, stirring, pathetic figure, a charlatan out of love for humanity, just as Meyerhold saw him and staged him, against Gorky's bitter protest.

It is interesting too that one of the last times the dying Lenin (another master of illusion) went out, he went to see "The Lower Depths"; somehow he wasn't happy about it, and couldn't stay to the end.

Yes, Gorky was very angry at his Tolstoy-Luka, preaching blessedness so as to get rid of people about whom he cared not a damn, being all wrapped up in himself. And still, when the telegram came: "LEO TOLSTOY IS DEAD"—

...It struck me to the heart: I cried with pain and anger, and now, half crazy, I imagine him as I knew and saw him. I imagine him in his coffin; he lies like a smooth stone at the bottom of the stream, and in his gray beard, I am sure, is quietly hidden that aloof mysterious little smile. At last his hands are folded peacefully; they have finished their hard task.

This is the grief for a father. And so that none can fail to recognize it, it is spelled out, at once, in that letter, in one of the great passages of literature.

As Gorky came walking along the Crimean coast, he saw Tolstoy, sitting on the shore among the stones, head in his hands, "the wind blowing the silvery hairs of his beard through his fingers: he was looking into the distance out to sea, and the little greenish waves rolled up obediently to his feet and fondled them as if they were telling something about themselves to the old magician." It was a day of sun and cloud; over the stones, cloud shadows glided. "He too seemed to me like an old stone come to life, who knows all the beginnings and ends of things, who considers when and what will be the end of the stone, of the grasses of the earth, of the waters of the sea, and of the whole universe from the pebble to the sun. And the sea too is part of his soul, and everything around him comes from him, out of him." Something in him stretched down into the darkness and up like a searchlight into the blue emptiness above. By his concentrated will he seemed to draw the waves and repel them, rule the movements of cloud and shadow. It seemed possible that he might suddenly get up, wave his hand, and the sea would become solid and glassy, and the stones would each acquire a voice and speak.

In my soul there was joy and fear, and then everything blended in one happy thought: "I am not an orphan on this earth so long as this man lives on it."

As usual in the case of a son's adoration, the words could not be wrung out until just after the father's death.

That whole letter is a long love-and-hate poem, by a youth who got a telegram telling of the death of his father—a father he had acknowledged, rebelliously come to hate...still loved...then rejected for another... castigated in memory...and now, "Dead—Dead—Dead"—felt a need to *tell the truth about.*

It is one of the great elegies.

The actual "Reminiscences," begun nearly a decade later, is calmer, as might be expected. It is a continuation of the letter—a ten-year break, between the first movement of this kind of sonata and the rest, in the eye of time, is nothing; the themes and images intercross. But the man is now seen a shade more gently, with a loving humor—as a son sees a father grown old, while the son has himself grown up—and his awe can be withstood, nor is his thunder so fearful.

This mood is in keeping; the focal description of Tolstoy is of a man who has just passed (1900) through a serious illness: "His illness dried him out, burnt something out in him, he became as if internally lighter, transparent, reconciled to life ... He listens attentively, as if remembering what had been forgotten or confidently awaiting something new, still unseen." Formerly, Gorky adds, he had seemed "a man to whom all is well known," who had resolved all the questions.

All this is so delicate. How much was the new Tolstoy, who now knew that even he was not immortal, and how much the more confident Gorky, his works starting to bring acclaim, and himself more sure in the presence of the once simply overwhelming man? Both things are conveyed.

The letter's lyricism had been borne on passionate sincerity flushed with recollections of romanticism, as things written by Gorky around 1910 still were; here, in the "Reminiscences" themselves, the lyricism is more classic. It subsists, rather, in the delicate, sure handling of each incident, each idea, the strict awareness of what he is doing: building a mosaic, using the technique of impressionism—short sections, some of a few sentences, some running to a few paragraphs, roman-numeraled.

The very device of the roman numeral was for Gorky a real find: in the whirling colored chaos of his life's experience, and with his high intelligence too capable of grasping simultaneously diverse things, he had always been hard put to find a form, to divide one image or action from another; the roman numerals offered a natural form, especially suited to him. It forced him to be strict, to distill his impressionism, strip away inessentials; and, as in the case of the script of Stenka Razin, it conveys swiftness, lightness, dramatic development ... until the reader of this essay realizes he is reading a short lyric novel!

The main thing about a novel is not that it is fictional—many novels have not a single imaginary thing in them—but that it usually explores a relation, both emotional and intellectual, among several characters. The letter to Korolenko had been a concentrated outcry of the emotional relation of Gorky with Tolstoy; that is why it is more like a poem. With the "Reminiscences" proper, there enters, with the entrance of other figures,

an interplay of thoughts and passions and beliefs that comprise the char-
acters and relations of several men, mainly Tolstoy, Gorky, Chekhov, and
Sulerzhitzky ("Suler," a romantic, sweet, rather feminine figure, drawn by
Gorky with quick strokes, most convincingly).

One further condition needs to be understood, in reading the work as a
novel: not the entire plot, the development of the men and their relation,
is overtly in it. Some is also in the letter; while some is in Gorky's reminiscences of Chekhov. This is in the spirit of the mosaic, of the unity of
the "Reminiscences," the unity of Gorky. They must be read together.

Only then the story he is telling, the images he is creating, all come
clear: the beauty and grandeur of the one man, the austere autumnal
poetry of the other, the young Gorky's role between them, that whole
vista of the noble and difficult and charming coming together, the pre-
carious friendship of sensitive outstanding men, in the Crimea, at the
century's turn.

The descriptive words that have been used—impressionism, lyrical quality, delicate and sure handling, strictness—suggest now, in music, first Bach
but even more Chopin, an evocation not at all strange in connection with
the work of Gorky. And, to confirm, it is Chopin's music that appears
early, as if ushering in the play of minds on the peaks of high things, led
by the mind and wizard-like, puckish spirit of that Jehovah Sabaoth, the
great pagan divinity, Tolstoy.

Goldenweiser played Chopin, which called forth from Lev Nikolayevich these thoughts:

"Some little German kingling or other said: 'There where you want
to have slaves, you must compose as much music as possible.' That's a true
thought, a true observation—music deadens the mind. Best of all the Cath-
olics understand this; our priests, of course, would not reconcile themselves
to Mendelssohn in church. One priest, in Tula, assured me that even Christ
was not a Jew, though the son of the Jewish God and his mother a Jewess
—he admitted that much, but still said: 'It couldn't be.' I asked: 'But how
then?' He shrugged his shoulders and said: 'For me, that's the mystery.'"

But almost at once—as if with the dying away of Chopin's music—
between roman numerals IV and VI—a clash is announced, subtle but
strong, between Jehovah, Lord God of Sabaoth, already a heretic version
of the great God, and his even more heretical lower-class disciple:

"The minority feel the need of God because they have got everything
else, the majority because they have nothing." That was how Tolstoy put

it; I would put it differently. The majority believe in God from cowardice, only the few believe in him from fullness of soul.

Tolstoy's statement, besides being disillusioned and realistic, was completely secular, dividing the motives of men, in their need for a God, in accord with their social condition. It was of the Enlightenment; it could have been made by Voltaire. Lenin, or Stalin, would have endorsed it. Gorky's riposte is absolutely classless, individual, in the spirit of primitive Christianity, the statement of a believer. Life, struggle, the horrors of war and revolution, disenchantment—nothing could shake him.

Tolstoy advised Gorky to read Buddhistic scripture.

Of Buddhism and Christ he always speaks sentimentally. When he speaks about Christ, it is always peculiarly poor—no enthusiasm, no feeling in his words, and no spark of real fire. I think he regards Christ as simple and deserving of pity; and, although at times he admires him, he hardly loves him. It is as though he were uneasy; if Christ came to a Russian village, the girls might laugh at him.

"The Confession" had shown how strongly Gorky felt about Christ. And his private views—which he would reticently reveal in the course of the "Reminiscences of Blok"—were also closer to the ideas of Buddhism, where these fork with those of early, and today's existential, Christianity, than to the this-worldly, practical Christianity of Tolstoy, or the views of Lenin and his crew.

Soon after occurs that wonderful passage in which Gorky and Tolstoy discuss the passions and jealousies of birds (about whom Gorky was an expert) and women (whom Tolstoy believed he knew thoroughly). The introductory paragraph pictures Tolstoy thus:

He sat on the stone bench in the shade of the cypresses, looking very lean, small, and gray, and yet resembling Jehovah Sabaoth who is a little tired and is amusing himself by trying to whistle in tune with a chaffinch.

Here in the fullness of his humanity is Grandma's God, whom she loved and hobnobbed with, but also a touch of the tougher, saltier God of Grandpa—in fact, he *is* a bit—just a bit—Grandpa! Grandpa in his karma as a *barin*.

Salty he was, this God of nature, this Jehovah Sabaoth. "It's not the woman who holds a man by his . . . . . but the one who holds him by his soul who is dangerous," he told the startled youth Gorky, who couldn't even bring himself to write that word. But he was now consciously taking notes.

For, as the story moves, the rivalry of Gorky and Suler for Tolstoy's affection has become clear; and takes the curious form of "who will write down the words of the godlike master," for later humanity.

It was Chekhov who had said to Gorky (quietly, dryly, one can see him): "Goethe's words are all recorded, but Tolstoy's thoughts are being lost in the air. That, my dear fellow, is intolerably Russian. After his death they will all bestir themselves, will begin to write reminiscences, and will lie." One can see Gorky silently determining *he* would assume this duty to Russian culture, though Suler was probably the one Tolstoy really nominated.

But there were also more deeply personal reasons for Gorky's watchfulness:

"I watched Tolstoy very attentively, because I was looking for—I am still looking for and will until my death—a man with an active and a living faith."

In that sentence is so much that goes to the depths of Gorky, explains so much of the chapters already written, and prepares for the final chapters.

Tolstoy, great and wonderful, still did not prove the man he sought; in his case, or at least as Gorky saw him, that active and living faith was no faith at all, except as an indefinable inner grandeur. The quest went on. He found Lenin. Ah! A man with an active and living faith. But it proved narrow and bloody, not really "living," though terribly active. In both cases he was repelled by the effort of a man convinced of his truth to force his belief on another. There would be one more, brief, tragic line cast to find such a man: Stalin. And that cast, in life's winter, could only lead to bitter disenchantment, and—death.

But at this moment the young man, Gorky, is still observing the old one, Tolstoy, who has rescued him (perhaps) from being an orphan. The main thing to find out about a man, he had decided in his childhood, is: what are his relations with God?

His conclusion about Tolstoy:

With God he is on very indefinite terms; sometimes they remind me of "two bears in one den."

The suspicious relations of Tolstoy and his God, walking around one another, sniffing, trying to work out a deal for lebensraum, are watched

by Gorky with the same intensity as that with which the boy Alexey
had watched the bargaining of Grandpa, at prayer, with his hard-bitten
God. Tolstoy was conscious of being spied upon, and he hit back, hard.

It was Chekhov who brought the message. This is in the "Reminiscences
of Chekhov," showing again the constant flow and circulation of blood
in the different essays; and also showing how Gorky was impelled to
the fragmentary, the mosaic, method.

Do you know why Tolstoy's attitude toward you is so changeable?
[Chekhov said.] He is jealous, he thinks Sulerzhitzky likes you better than
he does him. Yes, it is so. He said to me yesterday: "I cannot treat Gorky
with sincerity—I do not know why it is so—but I cannot . . . Gorky is an
unkind man. He reminds me of a theological student who has been forced
against his will to take the hood and has thereby become embittered toward everybody. He has the soul of a spy, he has come into the land of
Canaan, where he feels himself a stranger, watches everything that goes
on around him, notices everybody and reports to a God of his own. And
his God is a monster, something like a satyr or a water-sprite such as you
find in the tales of peasant women."

It is important that for Tolstoy the first question was still: "Whom does
he pray to?" while for Gorky it was: "How, and why, does he pray?"
In this is the change of the centuries (they stood at the breaking line),
the passage to the new from the old.

One thing that united them, however, was a belief that life was important, that if beings lived at all they should support not disintegration
but health. "Dostoyevsky," said Tolstoy, "described one of his mad characters as living and taking vengeance on himself and others because he
had served a cause in which he did not believe. He wrote that about himself; that is, he could have said the same for himself." And, "He [Dos-
toyevsky] felt a great deal, but he thought poorly." (Here the old man
hit the nail on the head.) And again, "He [Dostoyevsky] was convinced
that since he was sick the whole world must be sick."

He loved Chekhov and when he looked at him his eyes were tender
and seemed almost to stroke Anton Pavlovich's face. Once, when Anton
Pavlovich was walking on the lawn with Alexandra Lvovna, Tolstoy,
who at the time was still ill and was sitting in a chair on the terrace,
seemed to stretch toward them, saying in a whisper: "Ah, what a beautiful, magnificent man; modest and quiet like a girl. And he walks like a
girl. He's simply wonderful."

The theme of music recurs. Suler, the foil, asks Tolstoy why he called music, while discussing the poetry of Fet, "the mute prayer of the soul." Why mute?

"Because it's—without words. In sound is more soul than in thought. Thought is—a purse, there's nickels in it, but sound isn't filthied by anything, it's clean inside."

Then, after a while (laughing in his beard slyly), he added softly, as if with a caress: "All musicians are stupid people, and the more talented the musician the more limited. Strange, they are nearly all religious."

In this delicate way Gorky showed what Tolstoy wanted to believe, and how he went about it.

And maybe Tolstoy influenced him; or maybe this was another way in which these men were alike. Gorky, in his turn, would not close the door on the possibility that music might be the "mute" gate of the soul to the unheard "reality."

Tolstoy must have liked shocking both Gorky and Chekhov (the man he so loved, for being "modest as a girl").

"Did you whore around as a youth?" Tolstoy suddenly asked Chekhov.

Chekhov gave an embarrassed laugh, twisted his beard and muttered something that could not be understood. Tolstoy, looking dreamily out at the sea, remarked, "I was an inveterate . . . . . ." Again Gorky left blanks to represent this "salty peasant word."

The salty words he became reconciled to, but not Tolstoy's salty attitude toward women. He finally declared, as if hitting back, that it was "the hostility of the male who has not succeeded in getting all the pleasures he could"; then, more charitably, he decided it might be the hostility of the spirit against "the degrading impulses of the flesh."

This Victorianism—or asceticism—of Gorky's was the Siamese twin of his social idealism. It would be absorbed into the idealism of the Soviet revolutionary mentality. In fact, as he was completing the essay on Tolstoy, the first generation nurtured in his spirit, crossing it with the rigid spirit of Lenin, was already being recruited as the new "cadres" into the Communist Party.

The old man Tolstoy was as changeable as Nature itself—a "boundlessly varied, fairy-tale man." Now he acts the simple peasant, then suddenly draws himself up and stuns those who worship his simplicity: he is an aristocrat. Sometimes sharp, cunning, at other times he seems lost, as if just come from another world, hardly caring about this. He is a secretive plotter with forces beyond human surveillance.

And Gorky concludes his story:

Of wondering at him one never tires, but still it is hard to see him often, and I could not live with him in one house, not to speak of in one room. That would be like a desert, where all is burnt by the sun, and the sun itself also is burning up, threatening an endless dark night.

Yes, *three* bears in one den—God, Tolstoy, *and* Gorky—would really be too much.


The Tolstoy Gorky saw—Jehovah Sabaoth on his throne, arrogant, lovable, a wizard, self-contradictory, childishly willful, awesome—was a figure of Summer and Winter, of the great decisive extremes. The recollections of Chekhov, as Gorky paints him, bring us another, purer and lighter season: crisp, sad, poetic, all-encompassing Fall.

Gorky himself, as he saw himself, looking back, was the breaking Spring. He hardly said it, he muted his own notes; but the logic of the mosaic speaks for itself. The three of them—Tolstoy, Chekhov, Gorky— took care of the whole human year.

In the recollections of Tolstoy, Chekhov had appeared as an austere and rather gentle presence—a rather gentle, always gracious brother, who could be counted on. Now he comes forward, strongly, but still lightly, still with that modest step. The one portrait flows into the other, by the instrumentality of Gorky's love for both men, and the unity of the time, and of the mosaic form.

This is characteristic of the relation of Gorky's whole art and his life, and why they are so hard to disentangle. They are mosaic: the stones are interchangeable. Elements suppressed in art are found in life; a seeming gap in life is accounted for by a piece of his art. There is great freedom in this form. For him, a form like this, though he created it seemingly by chance, was a necessity.

The portrait of Chekhov is less even, and less penetrating, than that of Tolstoy. He had started it as a young man in 1905, resumed it several times, completing it only in his post-revolutionary exile. Still, because his memory of the man as a "pure" man was so pure, and because he must have finally worked hard for unity, it has unity. And it fits against the great portait of Tolstoy like its companion mosaic.

It begins:

It seems to me that every man, in the presence of Anton Pavlovich, involuntarily senses in himself a desire to be simpler, more truthful, to be more himself, and I have witnessed more than once how people threw off the motley ornamentation of book phrases, fashionable words and similar cheap tricks, with which the Russian, desiring to resemble a European, prettifies himself, like a savage with shells and fish-teeth.

This bears the mark of Gorky's style of the Capri period, but as he goes along his syntax grows dryer, simpler, in keeping with the artistic, austere simplicity of Anton Pavlovich Chekhov.

A forte of Chekhov's is finding out and rebuking vulgarity.

A lady, healthy, pretty, well-dressed, came to Chekhov and complained, like a character from one of his plays, that all seemed gray to her: people, sky, sea, flowers; and no desire—her heart lay in sorrow, "like a sicknesss." Chekhov agreed: "It is a sickness. In Latin, *morbus pritvorialis*" (concocted from the Russian word *pritvoryatsa*, to pretend).

But looking deeper, past the dry wit, "sometimes it seemed to me that in his attitude to people there was something of hopelessness, close to a cold, quiet despair."

Was Gorky looking into Chekhov, or himself? Surely both. For it is there in Chekhov's work, and it is also there in Gorky's nature—this cold, quiet despair.

He sees Chekhov looking with sad, hopeless compassion at people wasting their lives, not able to work and make the future of which they dream, and he sees Chekhov commenting, in a "beautiful, sincere voice," "you are living badly, gentlemen."

The relation with Tolstoy had always been uneasy, in spite of its warmth. It was like a stealthy movement in a circle—Tolstoy spying on God, while Gorky spied on Tolstoy. But Chekhov . . .

There is a touching reminiscence by Teleshov, which pictures a party given by the Moscow Art Theatre. Dancing started; only Chekhov and Gorky, the two stars, whose plays were now the main substance of the Art Theatre, did not dance—apparently neither could, or both were too shy. They sat fondly looking at each other, and joking about it, while everybody else danced.

His eyes were fine when he laughed [Gorky wrote], somehow like a woman's, caressing and gentle and soft. And his laugh, almost soundless, was somehow especially fine. Laughing, he actually took pleasure in laughter, he exulted in it; I don't know anyone else who could laugh so— let me say—"soulfully."

Coarse anecdotes, Gorky added approvingly, never provoked from Chekhov even a smile.

Death was approaching for the tubercular Chekhov; its constant nearing interweaves with the man's own sad clarity to give the whole essay an autumnal refrain. And the two "Reminiscences" are then woven together, toward the end, as if weaving the three men—Tolstoy, Gorky, Chekhov—together always, establishing a final unity, in the imminence of death.

One day Tolstoy was speaking with rapture about some tale of Chekhov's, I think it was *Dushenka* (literally, "Dear Little Soul"). "It is like lace," he said, "made by a chaste young girl; there were such lace-makers in olden times; they used to depict all their lives, all their dreams of happiness, into their lace design. They dreamt in designs of all that was dear to them, wove all their pure, uncertain love into their lace."

Tolstoy spoke with great agitation, his eyes full of tears. It happened that that very day Chekhov's temperature had gone up and he was sitting there with a high flush on his cheeks, his head bowed, carefully wiping the glasses of his spectacles. He was silent for a long time, then he sighed deeply and said in a low, bashful voice:

"There are many misprints in it . . ."

# CHAPTER 30

WHILE he wrote, his life was a series of restless moves about Europe: first a Berlin suburb, Gunsterstahl; then the town of Saarow near Fürstenwald; next Freiburg, the following winter snow-locked Marienbad. Then came Prague, then Rome, and finally Sorrento. There he settled in the late summer of 1924, and there he spent the next half-dozen years.

The isle of Capri had increased its fame because of Gorky. The drowsy town of Sorrento had once been Nietzsche's retreat; but it was really raised from obscurity largely because that strange, monumental and ambiguous figure, "the great revolutionary writer," made it his refuge against contradictions he could not resolve.

Gorky's companion, off and on, in his wanderings, and for the first year in Sorrento, was Khodasevich. That ill-assorted pair, the young skeptical refined aristocrat and the rugged, originally arch-romantic, shy, egalitarian, plebeian crier of the storm and now its disillusioned mourner (but still its defender), shared successive apartments and then a villa, living in close proximity—"in circumstances," Khodasevich was to write, "almost village-like, when the natural character of a man is not sheltered by the conditions of urban life." His testimony about Gorky's character, his mode of life, habits, quirks, outlook, is important.

The other companions multiplied with time, in a way characteristic of Gorky. To Sorrento came Moura Budberg, having run through a second Esthonian marriage, and became Gorky's secretary. Gorky's son Maxim came to stay, with his wife and children. Another fixture was Rakitsky, "an ailing and exceptionally sweet man." Back in Petrograd, in 1918, Khodasevich explained, Rakitsky "had stopped in on Gorky, to get warm, because he was sick—and somehow accidentally stayed in Gorky's home long years."

Besides this "basic population" there was a "floating" one: Ekaterina Pavlovna, now Gorky's oldest friend, and still his legal wife, began to visit him; Khodasevich's niece, a painter, stayed a while; so did various Russian writers and intellectuals—exiles and nonexiles.

One real service by Khodasevich was to dispel the rumors of "Gorky's opulent life." He made clear, as a demand of honor, the actual circumstances.

Gorky first leased "a big uncomfortable rundown villa"; when Khodasevich and his wife arrived, they started looking for a more permanent place together. Khodasevich and young Maxim, Gorky's son, found a villa, Il Sorito, a kilometer and a half outside Sorrento, on a tiny headland bluff, looking into space because of a recent landslide—which had taken a hundred lives. This was why part of the villa could be leased, cheap.

They had a fine view of the Bay of Naples, Vesuvius, and Castellamare. Inside, there was little furniture, and it was cold. During the winter of 1924–25 they huddled around a fire of olive branches. The rent was six thousand lira (about three hundred dollars) a year.

Young Maxim and his wife both liked to draw. They would fight over the equipment: "That's my pencil!" "No, mine!" Finally, Rakitsky would intervene, and command Maxim to give his wife the pencil. Maxim would sulk, lips thrust out; but would soon go around whistling and prancing.

"He was a fine lad," Khodasevich wrote, having already noted that at thirty Maxim seemed more like thirteen. "He was happy, full of life. He very much loved the bolsheviks, though not from any conviction but because he grew up among them [the boy had been raised by his mother], and they always humored him." Maxim spoke fondly of "Vladimir Ilyitch" (Lenin), and "Felix Edmundovich" (Dzerdzinski); Khodasevich kept expecting him to call them "Uncle Volodya," "Uncle Felix." He dreamed of going to the USSR, where a car had been promised him; he even dreamed about that car. He tended his motorcycle, collected stamps, read detective stories, and would retell for hours the movies he saw, imitating especially the comics. Khodasevich felt he had a remarkable talent for clowning, could have become a first class comedian. He does not speak of Maxim's drawings; some say there was real talent.

But all his life Max had done nothing practical. One Russian writer named him "the Soviet prince." Gorky loved him with his whole soul, said Khodasevich, but it was a kind of animal love, consisting of anxiety that Maxim should be alive, well, happy. He was convinced that Maxim's premature death, in Moscow in 1934, had "cut down Gorky."

(This memoir was written in 1936, after Gorky's death but long before the sudden "revelation" that Gorky, and Maxim too, had been done to death by "enemies of the people.")

Gorky rose daily at eight, drank coffee and swallowed two raw eggs, then worked until one. Dinner (lunch) stretched, with after-dinner talk, until two-thirty. "Then began an effort to drag Gorky out for a walk." After the walk, he again "threw himself at his writing desk," until seven. On the big desk were spread good paper, colored pencils, new quills and pens, cigarets, bright-colored cigaret holders, in ideal order. He never used a typewriter. He smoked heavily.

Manuscripts came in vast quantities. Whatever his own inner doubts, it had become a tradition in Soviet letters that manuscripts of forthcoming books be sent to Gorky, and young "would-bes" would also mail him their first offerings—all of which he read carefully, and sent back with long letters. He wrote in the margins with his colored pencils, corrected spellings, and even painstakingly copy edited the manuscripts. He did the same, Khodasevich added, with printed books; and also with newspapers, which he then at once threw out.

After seven, supper, and then tea and conversation, which usually ended with cards: penny ante or bridge. In bridge, wrote Khodasevich, it was just a matter of slamming cards down: Gorky could not see "combinations" and had no card memory. After a hand, he would sometimes glumly or bashfully inquire: "May I ask, what was trump?" The others found it necessary to set up "bridge duty"—they took turns being Gorky's partner.

Around midnight Gorky went off to his room, and either wrote, clad in his red bathrobe, or read in bed—his bed was always made up, "hospital-style." "He slept little and spent ten hours a day or more at work. Lazy-bones he did not like, and had a right not to."

Perhaps a common belief in the salvation of work bound these two such odd friends—as it had bound Gorky and others—more than anything else.

He had read "a colossal quantity of books," and remembered everything in them. "His memory was fantastic." When he would start to "rain" citations and statistics, and was asked how he knew this, he would shrug and say in surprise: "But how should one not know it? There was an article about it in the 'European Messenger' in 1887, in the October issue."

Every scientific article, Khodasevich wrote, Gorky considered holy. (His crucial talk with Blok showed this was not really so.) He was harder on works of literature, always suspecting them of distorting reality. Once, reading a three-volume novel, he showed Khodasevich, furiously, a "glaring inaccuracy." It seems that in the book a ship had arrived at Nizhni Novgorod for a regatta, and after the races dinner was served aboard. The younger man wondered why Gorky was so upset. Gorky shouted: "But this is *before* the races! *After* the races the buffet isn't open! You have to know such things!"

In general, Gorky was hale, strong, according to Khodasevich. The tuberculosis of his youth had healed long ago, and although it was reflected later in coughing, bronchitis and pleurisy, still the effects had been much less than the public usually thought. He used the legend of his heavy illness whenever he did not want to see someone or go somewhere, or, contrariwise, whenever he wanted to get away somewhere. But at home, among his own, he did not like to talk about illness even when it occurred.

"Physical pain he endured with extraordinary fortitude." In Marienbad, he had a tooth pulled without any anesthetic, and never complained. Once, in Petrograd, he stood on the bottom platform step of a jammed streetcar, and a soldier came down on the small toe of his foot, full tilt, with his heel. Gorky did not even go to a doctor; but for three years thereafter, from time to time, he indulged in "a strange evening occupation"—using his own fingers to dig bits of bone out of his wound.

Gorky's feelings about the Soviet Union, Khodasevich testifies, were sad and bitter; nor did he trouble to hide them. When he lived in Freiburg, two teams of spies followed Gorky: a German team, afraid he would start a revolution, and a Soviet team, afraid he would start a counterrevolution. He was chagrined, among other things, at the increasing literary censorship and political censorship of writers, in the Soviet Union. In a burst of anger, he wanted to sign, with Khodasevich, a joint protest. Khodasevich, knowing his real inner torment, prevailed on him not to do so.

Even more revealing of his state of mind are Gorky's own remarks, in his letters to Khodasevich in 1923 and 1924, before the poet joined him in Sorrento. Those which are supposed to be jokes hit even more poignantly than the others.

"Oh, I am sick of this century, and I would so like to have it over with as quickly as possible. For I am convinced that in the twenty-first century people will stop doing stupid things..."

"My head aches, and since my head is close to my soul, my soul aches."

The roar of the sea reminded him of the wise maxim of a certain Odessa Jew: "Our life is not worth a kopeck, like that stormy sea." (This was said by a character in one of the short stories of Isaac Babel: a writer whose work Gorky really admired, and whom he defended cunningly against inquisition. The sentiment of Babel's wise Jew—that life seemed so storm-tossed as to be of no value—Gorky clearly shared.)

When he heard of an index of banned books in the Soviet Union, set up by a committee co-chairmaned by Krupskaya, Lenin's wife, he wrote: "The first impression I experienced was so strong that I started writing to Moscow to announce my repudiation of Russian citizenship. What else can I do if this atrocity turns out to be true?"

From Sorrento: "Almost every day there are fireworks, processions, music, and popular celebrations. 'And at home?' I think. And—forgive me! —I am overcome to the point of tears and fury by envy and anguish and disgust and everything else."

"I am going to buy a pistol, hammer it barrel-first into the wall, and hang myself on the handle."

"I try to joke, and that too comes out badly. Jokes used to help me."

"I feel so discouraged that—if it were not so banal and ridiculous— I would shoot myself."

Yet the splendid essays continued in a stream, during those bitter years of exile. The memoir form kept his style clear, as if he were under an obligation to those he was writing about, to write with hard simplicity.

With chagrin had even come a certain humor, increasing the sense of "openness" in his style. It was more "airy," because the world was more airy—it had proved to have less substance, had become a tragicomic mummery, its reality held together by the memory of old relations, and—still —by hope.

One essay—characteristic of the man—was on Sofia Tolstoya, the Countess, wife and guardian lion of Tolstoy. She had never liked Gorky, and therefore he had never liked her. His essay was as fair to her as she had been unfair to him.

It was here that Gorky made his sober and famous statement of the dilemma of Tolstoy: that in him—"probably in agonized conflict"—dwelt the moral preacher and the brilliant skeptical artist.

This conflict was only too well known to Gorky himself: that of the moral man and the artist who sees the amoral reality. If the two are kept resolutely apart, there is an "agonized" split; if combined, as in Tolstoy's late novel "Resurrection" and in so much of Gorky's work, the artist trembles on the literary edge of the Beautiful Lie.

Side by side with the essays of reminiscence—the Populist Mikhailovsky, the Ukrainian writer Kotsubinsky, Leonid Andreyev—came more fragments of autobiography; they show the same solid clarity, and "openness," the same glinting passage of original ideas and judgments across the mind's retina, and the same sense of the preciousness of human warmth.

"My Universities" is the story of young Gorky in Kazan. Two essays on Korolenko are permeated with fond respect. "The Watchman" covers the post-Kazan period of odd jobs at whistle-stops. An essay "On the Harmfulness of Philosophy" describes his initiation, at the feet of the tragic barefoot populist Nikolai Vasiliev, into the system of Empedocles. This, under its "humorous" title, suddenly records one of the most lasting influences on Gorky—one that now, in the decade of mature despair, would rise again in all its unpitying philosophic power.

First, Vasiliev showed young Peshkov the atoms of Democritus. Then he cautioned the stripling: "The convictions of enlightened people are just as conservative as the usual ideas of the illiterate superstitious masses ...You just take this thought and keep remembering it."

Next, he spoke to the youth's confidence and integrity:

"You are a man of the kind I'd like you to remain to the end of your days. Remember what you already feel: freedom of thought is the only and most precious freedom attainable to man. Only he possesses it who, taking nothing on faith, examines everything..."

He added: "Live by your mind."

I well remember his words, probably the best and most sincerely friendly advice of all the advice anyone ever gave me.

What thoughts must have thronged the writer's head as his hand moved. Much, probably, of the anger in his past work was an anger at himself for not always being able to follow this "best of all advice," to be true to his mind and therefore to truth. But the need for faith and hope, during his youth, had proved too great.

That tortured skeptical seeker, Nikolai Vasiliev, then seemed to turn on the very belief in reason he had recommended. Mankind, he felt, would always either describe facts and then make unsuccessful guesses about the substance of truth, or else, ignoring facts, would create fantasies. "Aside from this—only ... God. But God is unacceptable to me ... There are people who consider idealism and materialism equivalent fallacies of reason..."

Young Peshkov "felt the pain in Nikolai's soul."

Taking each other's hands we stood a minute, silent. A good minute. Probably one of the best minutes of happiness experienced by me in life —that life which, sufficiently variegated, might have given me somewhat more such minutes.

Nikolai's thoughts had claws. He had already insinuated the "fallacies of reason." Now he paved the way for that tragic hypothesis, the Beautiful Lie: saying farewell, he recalled a friend who always said: "Truth is only the thinking about it." That thought would be hard to unroot.

And at their next "tutorial," he opened the world of Empedocles. What came, for the impressionable youth, of this insight into a gloom-filled, strife-ridden cosmos, where Love and Hate struggle in terrible implacable chaotic splendor, recalls vividly the hallucinatory paintings of Breughel and Hieronymus Bosch: men who, like Gorky, combined (in varying degrees of anguish) social vision with bitter pessimism.

I saw something indescribably terrifying: in the depths of a huge, bottomless bowl, turned on its side, float ears, eyes, the palms of hands and outspread fingers, roll faceless heads, walk human legs, each separate, leap lubberly hairy things that resemble bears, beat the roots of trees, like huge spiderwebs, while the branches and leaves have separated from them; fly varicolored birds, and mutely gaze at me the eyeless mugs of bulls, while their round eyes frightenedly leap behind them; here runs the winged leg of a camel, and behind him races the horned head of an owl—all this seen by me in the inside of the bowl filled with whirling movement of sundered human limbs, parts, pieces, sometimes combined with one another in outrageous irony.

Other hallucinations follow. Gorky was really retelling, in 1923, the collapse of his early efforts at faith, which forced him, by recoil, into the revolutionary movement. Now—after thirty years—because of the shattering effect of the Revolution, this same state of mind had returned (more complex, but also held in artistic balance): the world is either chaos, or emptiness.

He saw God, as in the ikons, sitting alone on a heavy throne, sewing with golden needle and blue thread a long white shirt, that reaches down to earth in a transparent cloud. Around Him is a boundlessly widening, deepening, emptiness, impossible to look at without horror.

The story he had already told, with lacquered surface, seeming humor, is now told in depth: the old night watchman begins to find him wandering and muttering incoherently late at night, leads him home by the sleeve. It is another account of the approaches to suicide, and who can tell whether it is not more true. The dates are not vital; Gorky transposed them at will.

On Capri, writing of his suicide try, he had urbanely explained his wrought-up state as that of a young man of prolonged sexual chastity. He was bolstered *then*, looking back at youth's unbelievable despair, by the belief that his essential vision, Vasska Buslayev's green-glowing world —the God-building vision—lay ahead.

But now nothing lay ahead for him. All had gone down the drain, in the fury of elemental strife, the steady "scientific" activities of the Cheka, the power struggle. The chaos of Empedocles—in which, at best, one could distinguish the guiding but implacable principles of Love and Hate —was supreme. This sense underlies all Gorky wrote in those years. If he masked it at all, this was because he still doggedly retained a final, hidden, tender hope.

# CHAPTER 31

WITHOUT the vision of Empedocles, the letters of despair, and
the whole vista of a ravaged Russia under dictatorship, it is easy
to miss the sense of the "Diary Notes" (or "Diary Fragments"), one of
the finest achievements of Gorky; to see in them only a quaint collection
of sketches, mainly of odd characters.

He mentioned them to Khodasevich, in those poignant letters: ". . . I
have written 10 of the Notes". . ."The Notes are very dull. . ." He was
writing, without wanting to know it, the most distilled, perhaps the most
unified and vibrant, of his works.

At first glance, they are quaint; the unity seems of a bright, interested,
amused regard turned on queer, strange people, in a queer strange life—
an alienated life. How amusing it is, how . . . sad it is, how . . . terrible it is.

The amusement often borders on delight. The reader chuckles, or
laughs out loud, then suddenly stops.

Gorky is very sure of himself. Like a magician, he shakes out of his
sleeve these bright-colored, multivaried people. He knows them all by
now—night watchmen, barefoot bums, landlords, factory owners, hunchbacked tramps . . . arsonists, spinsters, police chiefs—displaying them in
flashes, then making them disappear . . . a flick of the wrist, and another
image. He is really splendid. One delight follows another—one tart, bitter
delight after another. And behind the magic, the store of delights, lurks
the image of a goblet turned on its side, full of severed trunks and heads
. . . the horned head of an owl . . . ears, hands, eyes, combinations of outrageous irony . . . swimming in whirling chaos . . . all very amusing.

It is a bitter, bitter book—so clever and good one hardly knows it is
so bitter.

For example, there is a series of "Notes" about fires—fires big and small,
terrible and tiny, all described with a fascinated fondness, even "with
delight." This love of fires reached far down in Gorky's moot nature;
it was a psychological quirk, but one which he used to convey much
of importance in the "Notes."

A certain wealthy landlord keeps nail parings and throws them into
fires, along with copper pennies; he also reads Swedenborg and Boehme.
He comments, with fumbling wonder, on society. "It seems to me,"
Gorky finally tells him, "that you have expressed it all very clearly your-

self by saying: 'When one loses faith in one's own strength, one has to seek faith in something outside oneself.'"

Then there is a priest sentenced for heresy to thirty years of solitary confinement in a stone pit in a certain monastery. He becomes half-witted, animated only in front of fire. His horror on seeing his first electric light: "What! The fire imprisoned, too! . . . Oh you slaves of God, why do you do it? Imprison a sunbeam! Oh you sinful people, beware of the fire's wrath!" Then, sobbing, lightly touching the shoulders of those close to him, "Oh—let it go—set it free!"

There are "Notes" about Arzamas. The blue-painted town, where he had once lived "under surveillance," had long been for Gorky the symbol of a drab meanness in life; but now it became a symbol more dread—quintessence of a final senselessness: the "Arzamasian horror."

"The gray-blue sky pours on the earth an unseen molten pig-iron . . . The earth cracks, peels in the sun, like a dried fish . . . The town is covered with a cloud of some moot, yellowish dust . . .

"Strange people live in this town."

One of them, a storekeeper, tells Gorky: "It's from the mind that people are suffering, that's the chief culprit of all our blunderings. We've got no simplicity, we've lost simplicity. The heart is honest, but the mind's—a swindler."

Another, the town barber, thinks the scientists lie: they can't know the details of the sun's movement. Suppose it won't come up tomorrow? Suppose it gets caught on a comet, "or maybe it'll just stop on the other side of the earth, and there's a lid of eternal darkness for us . . ."

Then he confides: "Men need something unusual, something terrible. Terror for the soul is like a bath for the body, very wholesome . . ."

"God," says another Arzamasian, the local atheist, "is thought up. Above us isn't anything, only the blue air. And all our thoughts are from the blue air. Blue we live, blue we think—there's the riddle. The whole point of my life, and yours, is very simple: we were, and rotted."

The Arzamasian day draws to its end. "The dove-colored distance grows more dusky. Acquiring the color of glass burnt by the sun, and as if becoming denser, it approaches the city in a transparent but impenetrable wall."

These are New Testament colors, they are those of a Rouault—neo-Christian coloration and art-form, imposed on a tough contemporary theme: bitter chagrin, bewilderment; and only behind the veil, the transparent but impenetrable wall, lurks—hope.

Then there is Makov, with his spider. Gorky met Makov (so he says) on a Volga paddle wheeler. Makov was a man whose soul was taken away by his mistress, who was the wife of a dying man; she replaced it by a strange soul. He goes around with a spider sitting near him, strolling along beside him, always on watch. He has tried suicide, by throwing himself overboard; but the faithful spider caught on to him with some of its legs, to the ship's rail with the others, and prevented it.

"Does the spider talk to you?" Gorky asks.

"Are you joking? How can a spider talk? It was sent to keep me in fear, to remind me that I can't dispose of a stranger's soul, can't kill it. Don't forget that the soul I've got is not my own—it's as though I had stolen it."

What must be grasped is that these "fragments" are all fragments of Gorky. These stories may possibly have happened, these people may possibly have existed, but they are all—all—himself, and his own bewildered wonderment, bitter amusement, at how things had turned out, at the impenetrable wall, at the very good possibility the sun might get caught on a comet, at the heart being good, the mind a swindler . . . at the horror of imprisoning a sunbeam! How can a young man like Dzerdzinski not understand that you can't just kill people? Has he forgotten—or doesn't he even know—that we all carry around stolen souls, and that each soul is responsible for every other? And how awful to conclude that the spring of life, and successful government, is this: "Men need something unusual, something terrible. Terror for the soul is like a bath for the body, very wholesome . . ." And what is there left? "We were, and we rotted."

There is a "Note" about Anna Schmidt, who—if one is to believe Gorky —worked with him on the staff of the Nizhni-Novgorod "Leaf." This strange spinster headed a heretical little religious sect, who believed Christ was never slain, but lived in Moscow, on Arbatskoy Street. She was a devotee, too, of the mystic religious philosophy of Vladimir Soloviev.

She told Gorky: "In the turgid flow of life we swim, mute, like fish." And she recited to him "a poem she had composed." Of course the poem is Gorky's—and it states his dark idealism at its darkest.

> The soul in flesh from heaven came
> But earthly life grew to her dear.
> The soul got used to earth,
> And like a bee grown tired
> Drinks the sweet poison of earth's evil.

Gorky also remembered the last two lines of "her" poem, which she spoke loudly, with majestic threat, opening wide "her imperial eyes" and swinging her hand:

> Nor will an eternity of bells
> The soul once dead awaken.

And soon—conveniently soon—"I went away to the Crimea, and after then I never met Anna Schmidt, the Nizhni-Novgorod reincarnation of Sophia the Holy Wisdom."

But in his last days, when he was revealing his last view of things, very privately, in rewriting an old, old play, he would make her appear again— or does she appear without his willing her?—as his last vision of woman, his last vision of Russia: Sophia the Holy Wisdom, transcending terror and blood.

Another "fragment" describes the bad spirits that throng this life. The worst are like soap bubbles, on which a face keeps appearing, blue and transparent and sad, with question marks instead of eyebrows, round eyes without pupils. They whisper ceaselessly, like a man whispering to himself: "Perfect solitude will come for me after death, when my spirit shall fly away into fathomless space and there, chained motionless to one spot... I shall be doomed eternally to look into myself, remembering the sad folly of the past. And silence. And emptiness."

Such were the thoughts of the Stormy Petrel, aged fifty-four, meditating on the reality of the Promethean gale which, long ago, he had helped charm up from the deeps.

On this note of torment, question marks, of remembrance of past folly, silence and emptiness, we approach a crucial "fragment": the memorable conversation between Maxim Gorky and Alexander Blok. The two foremost Russian writers of their age sat on a bench in the Summer Gardens of besieged, cold, starving Petrograd. It was the beginning of April, 1919.

The time was one to provoke, or even force, men to search for what they believed existed beneath the chaos, alarums, blood. This essay tells how Blok, clutching for communion in the flux that soon carried him to death, forced Gorky to say, diffidently, glancingly, what he believed. This time Gorky was not the hunter but the quarry; and he didn't like it. But when he saw it was important to Blok, he told him what he could. There is in this essay "about Blok," as usual, a double revelation; and this time the revelation of Gorky is more than usually direct.

To protect himself, Gorky makes clear at the very start that he himself
is guided by Reason. Under this eternal sign he stands; his view is calm
and dispassionate. He is not led by emotions, or hope. He believes the
Russian soul is sick with fear of itself, and therefore resents reason and
is afraid of it. Tolstoy, he recalls, said that "consciousness is the greatest
moral evil"; Dostoyevsky called it a failing; Pisemsky said thinking was
"a mange of the soul." All such fear of the mind is unfortunate. It stems,
perhaps, Gorky suggests, from the Bible, where it is said:

"Azazel taught men to make knives and swords . . . he initiated them
into different arts . . . explained the ways of the sun and the moon. And
then came the time of great godlessness and corruption on earth, and the
ways of men became tortuous . . ."

This is not from the Bible "proper," but from the apocryphal Book of
Enoch, written at a time of vast revolution, chaos and despair, between
Old Testament and New, when the Jewish nation was perishing and the
world was being rent, old forms collapsing in blood and terror while the
new were not yet at hand. Gorky's instinct was sure. The talk with Blok
took place in a similar sign of apocalypse—a fine time to stand firm for the
supremacy of Reason.

They leave the office of World Literature together (Gorky had gotten
Blok a job there). They talk as they walk—a fine depiction of the crossing
of minds, not without its mysteries. Blok reminds Gorky of "a child in a
fairy tale, lost in the woods: a child sensing the approach of monsters out
of the darkness and muttering incoherent exorcisms in the hope that they
will frighten the monsters away." Blok has rejected the possibility of civilizing the masses; for this Gorky chides him, "as tactfully and gently as
I could." The thing that makes it hard to talk with Blok is that he does not
admit the world is ruled, nonetheless, by Reason.

Blok turns on Gorky. He refuses to believe that they are so far apart.
"I have always felt that this is not your real self. Already in 'Little Town
of Okurov' one can see that you are worried by 'childish questions'—the
most deep and terrible of all."

He was mistaken, but I did not protest, I let him think what he liked.

If this talk were not so serious, it would be funny at this point: Blok
was right, of course: the "childish, deep, terrible" questions were at the
bottom of everything for Gorky.

"Why do you not write on these questions?" Blok insists.

I told him that questions about the sense of life, of death, and love, were strictly intimate, personal matters, concerning only myself.

Besides, "To speak of oneself is a subtle art—I do not possess it."

They enter the Summer Gardens and sit down on a bench. There Blok, eyes shining "almost insanely," his "cold tormented face trembling," and trying to rub out a sunray on the gravel path with the sole of his boot, says reproachfully: "You are hiding your real self. You conceal your thoughts on the spirit, on truth. Why do you do it?"

Gorky hurriedly starts talking about something else: The Russian intelligentsia is "the packhorse of history." It has "lifted the proletariat to the heights of the revolution, unparalleled in the vastness and depth of the problems which it has placed before us." Blok sees through the ruse. He agrees the Russian intelligentsia was responsible for the Revolution; and for bolshevism too. Having evoked the spirit of destruction, it cannot now disclaim it. But then the poet suddenly returns to the "terrible, childish" questions—and this time it is all up with Gorky and his sense of the strictly intimate.

"What do you think," Blok demands, "of immortality?"

Gorky can dodge no more. All he can do is try to keep it matter-of-fact, light.

I replied that perhaps Lamennais was right; if we admit that the amount of matter in the universe is limited, it is to be presumed that its combinations are repeated in infinite variety in the infinity of time. This point of view makes it possible that in some millions of years, on a foggy spring afternoon in Petrograd, Blok and Gorky shall again be sitting on a bench in the Summer Gardens, talking of immortality.

Blok asks if he is serious. Gorky, "astonished and annoyed," says stiffly he does not consider Lamennais' point of view less convincing than others.

"But you, personally, what do you think of it?" He [Blok] stamped his foot impatiently. Until that evening he had always seemed to me so composed, so unwilling to talk.

"Personally [Gorky finally says], I prefer to imagine man as an apparatus, which transmutes in itself the so-called 'dead matter' into a psychical energy and will, in some faraway future, and transforms the whole world into a purely psychical one."

Blok cannot understand; is it panpsychism? Painful as all this is to Gorky, he explains: In the end, nothing will exist except pure thought, "incarnating the entire mind of humanity from the first flashes of it until the moment of the last explosion." All matter dissociates, giving off light, electricity, electromagnetic and hertzian waves, radioactivity ... It will all finally be absorbed by man, and transmuted by his brain into a sole energy—psychical.

"This energy shall discover harmony in itself and shall sink into self-contemplation—in a meditation over all the infinitely varied creative possibilities concealed in it."

Blok says he is glad the law of conservation of matter contradicts this dismal fantasy. Gorky replies the laws from laboratories are not the last word on the universe's unknown laws; he is sure if the world's weight could be measured, it would be shown to be gradually diminishing. Blok shakes his head: "It is all much simpler; the thing is that we have become too clever to believe in God and not strong enough to believe in our own selves."

Here ended Gorky's account of that wonderful, fantastic conversation.

He had offered Blok, shyly, reluctantly, two rather similar choices:

(1) Lamennais, starting as a fiery Catholic ultramontanist, ended as a religious heretic, speaking (like Berdyaev after him) for a kind of "Christian communism." He saw an inexorable destiny for man, no real rapport between God and the human universe. Yet nature is united by its maker; and faith in God as a trinity permits a final perfect union—or at least a perfect correspondence—of humanity with God. Rejecting the French Revolution's violence, he still saw the revolutionary wave as a movement toward a single family of humanity. The fate of all—or their final blessedness—is the same. "All arrive there (to God) with more or less toil, because God draws all to him, for God is love, and love is stronger than death."

(Thus would Grandma, too, have replied to Empedocles.)

Lamennais thought the stars in the immensity of space might be like the globules which make up the bloodstream, "immersed in the torrent of the universal circulation." This opens swinging doors into a limited universe, a total living being. It is both religious and materialistic. Gorky and Blok might indeed meet again, and converse on immortality, on another spring day, on a bench in the Summer Gardens.

(2) The second choice Gorky offered, which he called his own, is phrased in terms of science. It differs from the first mainly in that there is finally escape from all recurrence. The way seems to lead back toward

Gassendi and La Mettrie, and forward through radioactivity, the anti-electron, "un-matter"—themes familiar to Bogdanov. But actually it leads farther back, to the Ionian Greeks and from them Eastward. What for Lamennais was faith in a union in the all-embracing apparatus which is the body of God becomes, in Gorky's "own" choice, a Buddhistic hope (with scientific shellac) in the achieving of a final Nirvana—that of the total Mind. "This energy shall discover harmony in itself and shall sink into self-contemplation..."

Blok carried away from this meeting, and his whole contact with Gorky, some thoughts he put down before his death:

"Gorky is bigger than he wants to be... because his intuition is deeper than his intellect: inscrutably, by the fatal force of his talent, his blood, the nobility of his strivings, the infinity of his ideal, and the scope of his spiritual sufferings, Gorky is *a Russian writer*... I will even go so far as to say that if there exists in reality what is called 'Russia'... that great, boundless, spacious, melancholy and felicitous something which we are accustomed to combine under the name of *Rus*, then we must recognize Gorky as the man who expresses all this in the highest degree."

That cleft between knowledge by the "intellect" and the greater knowledge of the "intuition," which he attributed to Gorky, was not alien to Blok himself. His poem "The Twelve"—the first and possibly finest poem of the Soviet era—concludes its picture of the brawling, raping, looting progress of a Red Guard detachment through Petrograd's streets with the image of Jesus Christ marching at their head, leading them into the future. Blok himself was amazed. "Could I have really meant this?" he asked, when it was pointed out to him. "Yet I must have, for this is what I wrote..."

# CHAPTER 32

SOON after Gorky wrote of this talk in the Summer Gardens, Khodasevich was living with him, and thinking about what Gorky was, what he really believed. "His whole life," the younger man decided, "was permeated with sharp pity for mankind, whose fate seemed to him inexorable." Reality was senseless unless to it was added *hope*. "The creation of any thought whatever, capable of sustaining mankind" by giving it hope, "roused him to joy and trembling."

He insisted that therefore Gorky was forced to stay true all his life to the Beautiful Lie:

> "Sirs! If to holy truth
>  The world its way can't find,
>  Honor the madman, then, who spills
>  Gold sleep over mankind!"

Khodasevich saw Gorky at close range; but he was a "pure" artist, unable to grasp the problems, and dimensions, of the artist who is determined to stand with his feet in the mud of the earth; or to appreciate the idea of the union of society with God, in mutual love—the theme of Lamennais. He was honest about Gorky, but not quite fair to him.

Those lines that are his "key to Gorky," spoken by the Actor in "The Lower Depths," are from a poem by Béranger. That poem is actually a defense of three French reforming socialistic thinkers: Saint-Simon, who offered a New Christianity based on social justice; Fourier, who had created the theory of the workers' cooperatives; Esplandin, who had fought to give women the right to vote. These "dreamers" were also "madmen" only for the benighted; to men of good will, their dreams were both noble and practical. This was the meaning of the lines of Béranger, in context. The Russian translation, by adding "holy" and "golden" and other touches, had changed the lines into a quatrain recommending a "golden sleep," instilled by a madman, as a refuge from bitter reality.

No doubt Gorky was misled by the Russian version, and thus encouraged toward the tempting idea of the Beautiful Lie. But he knew the *whole* poem (Béranger was one of the most intense favorites of his youth), and therefore must have had a sense of its original intention: men who were called dreamers and madmen could, by their idealistic dreaming-thinking, lead the world to truth where more prosaic spirits had failed. This was what he really wanted to say.

It is true that reality for Gorky was inexorable, fated. But as he revealed it to Blok, on that bench in the Summer Gardens, it allowed for a faith, or a hope, that did not rest on the Beautiful Lie. Admittedly, he only broke through to that level at moments; and life would force him to descend again. "The soul . . . like a bee grown tired, drinks the sweet poison of earth's evil . . ."

At any rate, the tremendous universe of rational and mystical yearning and thinking, opened up in Gorky's answer to Blok, is at the farthest remove from the world as seen by Lenin. Lenin's "what I believe" is in his book "Materialism and Empirio-Criticism," written to refute Bogdanov and all those trying to use modern thought to give a modern frame of mind to the revolutionary movement. In a way, Gorky was Lenin's chief antagonist, although Lenin refused to name him, in his book, for he was determined Gorky would still be useful.

Anyone reading Lenin's book at all carefully has seen how stultified and truly "dead" is his whole notion of the world. And the sterile formulas, the use of demagoguery to stifle ideas and free inquiry, which was Lenin's method, aborted much that was pregnant in both Marxism and the whole revolutionary movement, and which therefore could not be realized.

Gorky, poet and thinker, had nothing in common with either Lenin's method or his view; and this the conversation with Blok makes clear.

The struggle between hope (or faith) and truth comes forward in each new fragment—and the bitterness of the fact that there is no real resolution. Nearly all the "conversations" that take place in the fragments, except the one with Blok, are really internal.

One takes place on a train, to the refrain of shafts and wheels, which seem to say: "Fellow-traveler, fellow-traveler." Besides its usual meaning, the phrase clearly has another, bitter one. The fellow-traveler is a man who goes along with something he does not believe in... reconciling himself to dreadful things... because of a vision?... weakness?... fear?

Gorky's fellow-traveler is a man "so colorless that in bright sunlight he would probably be invisible." "Truth," he remarks, "is a judgment, imbued with... hope." Then he tells a laconic story. He was one who had tried, against his better judgment, to believe in the "truth" of his son, who for Lenin's "truth" died a bolshevik in the Red Army's ranks. Later, the father was being questioned by a young, clean-cut agent of the Cheka.

He told the Chekist there was a contradiction between his heart and his reason. The Chekist said he knew this already, from reading the man's letters to his son, but "this doesn't help your situation." The man asked: "Will you shoot me?" The Chekist replied, "Very probably"; then added, brightly, "Maybe it would be better for you to die, isn't it true? Because to go on living with such a rip inside yourself... must be—agonizing."

The fellow-traveler yawned, looked out the window at the streams of rain running down the glass. The writer asked: "And still they freed you?"

"I helped them figure out certain questions of evidence."

"Fel-low trave-ler . . ." beat the wheels, ground the shaft. In this "frag-ment" is all the implacable horror of those years. Gorky could write no more than the fragment—a miniature, a Ring Lardner story ("Haircut") but more awful because of the more awful social vista. There was a rip inside. Any more would have destroyed him.

At the end of another fragment is a poem of course attributed to one of the characters. Its last stanza:

> How will we then go on living?
> What will this horror bring us?
> What will now save my soul
> From hatred against people?

Only in such cryptic symbols, senseless without their key, could he speak. Because there still must be "hope," no novel dealing with this horror directly, no play, nothing but such fragments, could ever be born.

One final "fragment"—or "Note"—throbs in a remembered voice: that of Grandma, transposed—a hurt, poetic reply to the refrain of the shaft and the wheels.

He spends a night (during some long-ago wandering) in the hut of a local "sorceress," a powerful Mordvin woman, the village bear-huntress. She tells him, suddenly: "You can't offer a man to God, as you offer a girl to an old man. You can't drag a man toward God against his own will. Such a marriage would be no good. There would be no truth in it."

She tells him about Keremet, her old pagan God. "Your God loves faith, but Keremet loves truth. Keremet knows that if God and man are friends, there will be truth."

In the night he is awakened by the wail of wind in chimney, and a heavy spluttering whisper. It is the Mordvin woman, on her knees, praying. (It is Grandma: even the details of that early memory are repeated.) She is scolding Christ, lovingly, hurtfully, for letting his priests wrong Keremet —who is the union of man and God, which is truth.

"O Christ, you are a bad God, a jealous God, an unkind God, not a human God at all . . . Whom are you serving, Christ? . . . Shame, oh shame, Christ, this is not the way to act . . . God does well when he listens to people, just as people do well when they listen to God . . . Listen to me . . . I know the truth better than you, before you, O Christ!"

The rain lashed the thatch of the roof with sharp whips, the wind squealed piercingly, inhumanly, trying to deafen the heart's complaint of a human being.

There may have been such a village, such a night, such a bear-huntress, daughter of an unconverted Mordvin father. But it is really all interior: Gorky's lament for Russia, dragged into a marriage without truth in it; his life's continuing outcry against the blindness of the "old God," his continued yearning for "a better God"; and his constant inner struggle, between the need for faith and the love of truth. To choose truth—Keremet—as the Mordvin woman did, meant to stay in exile; to ever return to Russia, he would need to give up truth, for faith.

"Childhood" and "Among People" were probably the first high peak of his art. The mosaic of the "Reminiscences" and the "Notes"—the great portraits and the great interior monologues and dialogues—forms the second.

# CHAPTER 33

HIS fame, at this time, was far beyond that of any other Russian writer. Enormous numbers of letters arrived in Sorrento, in all languages (Moura Budberg could read them); wherever he appeared, strangers surrounded him for his autograph. Correspondents came, took rooms at a nearby hotel, and hung around just to glimpse Gorky in his garden or at table.

This fame, wrote Khodasevich, brought Gorky over ten thousand dollars a year (in 1924, a large sum); he spent on himself an insignificant portion. In food, drink, clothing, he was "to a rare degree undemanding." Cigarets, a glass of vermouth at the corner café in Sorrento's only piazza, a cab home from town—the younger man could recall no other personal expenditures.

But *about* Gorky, dependent on him, was a permanent circle Khodasevich estimated at no less than fifteen, in Russia and abroad—ranging from titled émigrés to just plain parasites, from relatives to people on whom he had never laid eyes. "Whole families lived on his account much more freely than he himself lived." There were also "chance pensioners"; and writers-in-exile turned to him for help.

Gorky handed out money without realizing the actual need, or worrying about what it went for. Sometimes it got "stuck" in transmission; Gorky pretended not to notice. Some, in his entourage, even used his name and eminence, Khodasevich says, for purposes as miserable as plain "extortion." However they vied for his money, he adds rather cryptically, they united in directing his public activities and statements, to render them profitable.

Partly, Gorky let this go on simply because he wanted to be left in peace to write. He had written that Tolstoy urged his followers to believe in his religion only so Tolstoy might be left alone, to do his writing and ponder on death! Another reason, however, Khodasevich felt, was Gorky's confused attitude to truth and lies.

Raised in life's miseries, "among people forced to be sinners or sacrifices, usually both," Gorky—as Khodasevich saw it—had conceived an imaginary barefoot-bum hero, "twin brother of the traditional benevolent bandit," endowed him with a dream of a better life, "in a framework of natural and social truth, whose content he at first did not know himself, then sought in religion, then in social progress." In this process, he had created the ambiguous Luka—holy wanderer or charlatan. Luka is "pure Gorky." He concluded that Gorky had upheld the idea of revolution not because he believed deeply in it, but because he believed in the saving power of the very dream, and therefore became the rouser and defender of that dream, a Luka-holy wanderer. He pointed, of course, to the story of "The Siskin Who Lied"; and then to a letter written by Gorky (1929) to an old friend who upbraided him for defending a Soviet image untrue to life: "I most sincerely and unwaveringly hate truth." Khodasevich adds: "I seem to see him, as, with a furious face, bristling, with vein bulging on his neck, he brings out these words."

Much of what Khodasevich saw, and guessed, is accurate. But he neglects, or perhaps could not even see, these things: (1) The depth of the struggle in Gorky, between admiration for the amoral "benevolent" but bloody "heroes," and the moral injunction for quiet truth, instilled by Grandma; and (2) the fact that many of those who are very clear about "truth" and "lie" calmly weave their lives around lies of the past, and even live on their proceeds. A shaking moral issue at the start of a culture is often a habit at the end. For Khodasevich, in a way, there was no problem; for Gorky it was, as he repeatedly said, "a fist fight"—down below.

Each man sees by his own guiding image. Khodasevich, the fairest and most subtle of critics, was led by the image of Pushkin, the surrounding aristocratic values of Pushkin's age. The breadth and human warmth of Gorky he appreciated, and defended; the depth—where tortured issues of today, not yet resolved, fought and floundered—he could not take too seriously: Pushkin would not have cared.

At any rate, he believed that because Gorky could not help admiring the scoundrel, the successful con man, counterfeiter, outright bandit—while being morally the most upright of men himself—he permitted all kinds of things to others, and even winked at their deeds, looking away and hiding in his mustache a chuckle of admiration.

Italian holidays, with music and fireworks, he adored. In the evening, on the balcony, he would call for everyone to "come look." Watching the rockets and Roman candles, agitated, rubbing his hands, he kept crying out: "That's over at Torre Annunziata! And that's from Herculaneum! And that's by Naples! Ookh, ookh, ookh, they're really frying!"

"This 'mighty realist,'" comments Khodasevich, "in truth liked only that which embellished reality, led away from it, or took no account of it, or that simply added to it what was not in it."

Quite a few writers prided themselves on the fact that Gorky had cried over their work. Actually, there was nothing to pride oneself on; Khodasevich could hardly remember anything Gorky *didn't* cry over. What shook him was not the quality, but the very fact that it was something written, created, thought up. Mayakovsky, whom Gorky had helped to the top, even convincing a reluctant Lenin that the poet's hard-to-understand work was good, repaid Gorky by going around the cafés offering, for sale cheap, a coat "drenched by Gorky." Gorky was not ashamed (said Khodasevich) to cry over his own writings: "The second half of every new story, which he read to me, invariably was drowned in bawling, sobbing, and the wiping of clouded eyeglasses."

It was the beginnings of writers that he loved, Khodasevich felt; once they got established, he seemed to cool, for now it was no longer possible to dream about their future.

Again because of the difference in values, Khodasevich missed something. It was not just a matter of dreaming of the future of young writers; there was a national idealism, released by the Revolution, whose direction Gorky could still hope to affect. Until the creeping paralysis of dictatorship won out, there was a vibrancy in Soviet letters; the early twenties were a brief but genuine literary renascence.

These young men and women had emerged from the Civil War, that cauldron of horror and idealism. The voice of the trumpet still in their dreams, struggling in a Russia of reconstruction, having lost all the old models in the disruption, they turned to Gorky as the only discernible model. This could not but begin to exert a counterpull, by appealing to his sense of duty, while also saving him from being consumed by grief and despair. The price he paid was to let the myth grow of a wise, loyal hermit-in-exile, to whom the "church" sent young pilgrims.

To Khodasevich, conditioned in the rather febrile Pushkinian ideal of "the lazy poet," this whole social and civic aspect of Gorky—which gives both his life and his work a big part of their valence—could not help being quaintly amusing.

Ironically, it was the apolitical "pure poet" who saw everything in terms of contemporary politics. The older man, more intensely anguished over political repression, the brutal mistakes, the social suffering, yet saw Russian literature as a living medium for amelioration, the carrier of the highest values and life's last hope. In this sense he was the purer artist: he valued art more highly in relation to life.

He loved both fireworks and fires. He would talk for hours about arsonists, and saved clippings. During after-dinner talk, he would slyly heap matches in an ashtray, then, watching to see that nobody was looking, would quietly set the pile afire. Then he would sit as if nothing had happened, as if hoping the little blaze would escape attention until...  He was sheepish, or angry, when he was caught.

His admiration for anyone who could embellish reality, who could lie and get away with it, extended to the way he treated those who panhandled him. He demanded of a man boldness and evidence of hope. If the man asking money of him seemed fallen in spirit and complained, Gorky was relatively indifferent; but the bold liar got more than he asked, and Gorky defended his lies in every way possible, not wanting anyone to dispel the illusion. He never let a liar down, said Khodasevich.

He speaks of Gorky's concern for his "biography": doing things, and not doing them, writing things he did not want to write, keeping quiet when he wanted to speak out, saying things he did not believe, because of the image of Gorky the Self-Born, the Storm Messenger, the Revolution's Stormy Petrel, which had now grown into the skies and which he did not want to spoil. This concern, together with the great distance he had risen, might have been expected to exert an evil influence on his character. That had not happened.

"In contrast to very many, he did not chase after fame or tire himself with care about upholding it... He did not suffer from arrogance and did not, like many celebrities, play the spoiled child. I have not seen a man who bore his fame with more diffidence and nobility than did Gorky."

Gorky sometimes asked Khodasevich for advice and criticism; he would argue, defend himself, but often acknowledge the criticism, give in, and at once set to rewriting in accord with it.

Once, lying abed, he asked Khodasevich: "And tell me, please, what about my poems, are they very bad?"

"Bad, Alexey Maximovich," said the direct and honest Khodasevich.

"I'm sorry. Terribly sorry. All my life I dreamed of writing at least one good poem."

He looked up with sad, reddened eyes, then had to take out a handkerchief and wipe them.

It was a cause for wonder, and even of "a kind of trepidation," for Khodasevich to see how this man, such a consistent hater of "truth," wanted only truth when it came to his writing, not only accepted criticism but "in a manly way" sought it out.

Here again, in being honest by his lights Khodasevich was less than fair to Gorky. He himself was a sensitive lyric poet, in an old Russian classic tradition. Gorky, from the "fist fight" of life and conflict of ideals and realities, brought much wider scope to poetry; but could not achieve either the "smoothness" so important to the classic school or the imagery of the more modern. But in his scattered stanzas, in that prelude to "Vasska," in the duet in "Children of the Sun," in "The Young Girl and Death" (the poem Stalin so liked!), and in poems buried apologetically in his prose, beats the true urgency of lyric poetry.

When still in Germany, Gorky and Khodasevich together had founded a literary review, *Beseda* ("Discussion," or "Chat"), published in Berlin. Gorky hoped it would be a meeting ground (a place for chatting) for Russian writers in the Soviet Union and in the emigration. Much of his own fine work of the early twenties appeared there, including the "Reminiscences" and the "Notes." The Soviet authorities apparently promised him that a large quantity of each issue would be bought for Soviet distribution, then reneged, so that the publishing firm (Russian émigrés) went under.

While the two men were still together in Sorrento, Lenin died. His wife Krupskaya sent a letter asking Gorky to write an essay on Lenin.

According to Khodasevich, Moura Budberg made Gorky sit down to it, and he dashed it off; he was angry, and sent with it a harsh letter to Krupskaya, demanding that some issues of "Discussion" be admitted into the Soviet Union; and a token number were then actually ordered. But by that time the magazine was doomed.

Clearly his reaction to Lenin's death was not the kind of reaction Gorky had when he heard of Tolstoy's. But he did contribute the glory-sing.

And still, the glory-sing ends on a suddenly strange, challenging note: "In the end, that wins out which is honest and righteous, in what is created by man that wins out without which there is no man."

In later editions of Gorky's works, it was replaced: "Vladimir Lenin died: the heritage of his reason and will live on, are alive and work successfully as no one, nowhere in the world, ever worked." The editors say Gorky made the change in 1930; this is possible. However, on the basis of style and content, it seems more likely that the change, which perverts the essay's final statement, was made on Gorky's behalf, perhaps posthumously. The new text seems to be modelled on a rather perfunctory sentence Gorky once had written to somebody about Tolstoy's death; and the scary image of Lenin's reason and will working on, and on, and on, was a standard Party cliché.

As for Krupskaya requesting the essay, this is not in the records. There is, however, a letter from her, telling Gorky that "yesterday we buried Vladimir Ilyitch" (he was not exactly buried); then telling how Lenin, in his very last days, had her read to him Gorky's "My Universities" and his fond essay on Korolenko, listening with "deep attention." This sounds unmistakably like a plea, as if to tell him that Lenin had wanted to say: "I see better now. Please believe me." Lenin did make several gestures, in various directions, in those last days; perhaps he was capable of rethinking many things, now that the grip of determination had loosened.

Either Gorky—whose heart had hardly ever been able to withstand any plea—did not answer the widow; or his reply has not been preserved. The essay, however, especially as amended, besides helping Lenin toward immortality, got the myth under way of Gorky's and Lenin's resolute, enduring friendship.

## CHAPTER 34

THE complex, anguished state of Gorky's emotions and thoughts was reflected with unfailing, painful fidelity in his creative work. In a letter to Khodasevich, before the poet joined him in Sorrento, he had said: "I have decided to write a long story about a factory owner, and how they will curse me for it! I have written a short story in which a globe, a visual representation of the earth, by spinning on its axis plays the tune: "Siskin, siskin, where've you been? . . ."

(The jingle, widely known, goes:

> "Siskin, siskin, where've you been?"
> "At the bar, drinking vodka.
> Drank a glass, then drank two,
> and my head began to spin.")

The story of the siskin who got drunk and saw the whole world spinning and singing drunkenly has not been preserved, if actually written. It would have been a pitiful reincarnation for that siskin who had sung heroically about the free, bold life all could attain: young Gorky's dream.

The long story about a factory owner is certainly the novel "The Artamanov Business." It is supposed to be about the rise and fall ("decadence") of a powerful merchant family of Russia.

He had, long ago, really talked about such a novel. Savva Morozov had urged him. Tolstoy had taken him by the sleeve and said, "You must write this." But by the time he actually did, a cataclysm had taken place. The merchantry had not "fallen": they, and everything else, had simply been stamped under. A wider, more awful theme was needed.

Retribution on a whole nation is the theme: either divine (the wrath of God), or by a grim force of natural selection: the "unworthy" being trampled down by that which is stronger, no matter how barbaric.

The novel flows directly from the great and bitter "Notes." It is an indictment of a people, a culture, a nation; of God, and his world; of a drunken reality. When he wrote "they will curse me," he certainly did not mean the merchants; they no longer existed. He could only have meant the bolsheviks. The book is one of the bitterest statements ever made about the Bolshevik Revolution.

It begins as a good social novel should. In this genre Gorky was, at his best, fair: honest and colorful, but tedious, not nearly the peer of the good social writers like Balzac, Zola, Dreiser, George Eliot. He had no capacity for emotional distance.

By the time old Artamanov—the burly, amoral founder of a dynasty—dies, and the sons run the business, the story has changed its whole nature; if only the reader was not taken in by the idea that it was social realism, he finds himself behind the facade, in the tortured presence of the old Gorkian quandaries, the "childish questions," the disembodied psychological states and conflicts which make up the real creative germs of Gorky's living work. Then the interest is seized, the story grows.

Three main "states of the soul" emerge, as the main characters: that of Peter, the oldest Artamanov son, now head of the firm; that of the youngest son, Nikita, a cripple, who has become a saintly monk, to whom the Church sends pilgrims for advice and consolation, but who knows he has no answers and is only telling them Beautiful Lies, and who would like to run away and be a holy wanderer; and that of an old servant of the family, or factory foreman—his role is never clear, precisely because he is not a man but a state of soul—named Tikhon Vialov ("Tikhon" means "man of quiet"—like Grandma's ancient hermit).

One of them, however, Peter, is more than symbolic; and he is again the young Foma Gordeyev. A good part of the novel becomes, in fact, a rewrite, deepened by life, but less vibrant, of that early novel, still Gorky's best.

Foma had chosen (hopeless) rebellion; Peter chooses to be a Babbit—a man caught in life's machinery, struggling to understand, to live better, but unable. Like Babbit, he emerges with dimensions of passion and contrition, and thus as not only a state of soul but a real living figure of fiction, only the second Gorky ever managed to create—Foma, who was the same thing, was the first.

By the eve of the Revolution he has transformed the Artamanov merchant dynasty, somehow, into the torn, vacillating intelligentsia of Russia: all those who held a meaningful Russian future in their hands, and were too selfish, weak, or short-sighted to protect it; they squandered it and the nation, and deserved extinction, even if this meant darkness and a barbaric age for Russia. Gorky clearly included *himself* in this dread sentence: Peter, like every real figure he ever made, is autobiographical.

(Too many sins! It is time for a clearing-away, a shattering. Let night descend. Let you—and all of us—be wiped out.)

Said the mysterious Tikhon Vialov—who had bided his time, with a few cryptic words, all these years: "Men ought to have their memories destroyed. Memory breeds bad things. Things ought to be so that when one lot have had their lives and died, all their ill doings die with them. Then let a new lot be born, with no memory of evil, only good..."

Here again the reader is up against one of the cunning ambiguities of Gorky. It takes some reflection to see what old Tikhon Vialov, hermit-Teiresias, is talking about: the crimes done in the name of the Revolution. This is the "memory" that needs to be destroyed.

That, then, was Gorky's hope for Soviet Russia: Let the generation who did these things, and of those who suffered them, die away. Let the memory of the cruelty and killings be expunged. Let a new generation be born, with no memory of these sins of the immediate past. Let them know only good. Let them look into the future.

The finale is swift, drastic, dark and shocking. Whatever hope there is, or was, glimmers like a wraith, mockingly. Old Peter Artamanov, dying, awakes lying in the summer shed in the yard. October 1917. The house, and the firm, have been confiscated. Only because his son, Ilya, is "with them"—an ambiguous, queasy ray of hope in the dark novel—is the old man still alive, to die "naturally" (of hunger). His old wife has gone to find a crust of bread.

To him comes old Tikhon Vialov. He tells old Peter that the rest of the Artamanovs are dead; "this is war—against *you*." The boots of Red Army men, patrolling the house, stamp around them. So Tikhon Vialov is the conquering vengeance of the old servants, workers, peasantry? Then why is there no triumph—but only bitterness? Vialov says:

You called me a fool, but I saw the truth before anyone else did. Now you see how it's all turned out. I said it would be prison camp for every-body. And it's come...Satan used the tool—and you helped him. And all to what purpose? One long chain of wrong, no counting it... All you did, cast in lead...

The two old men fought it out, at the end, the one blaming the other for making him lose his faith in God, the other blaming him in turn for "infecting my son with folly"...and a country in ruins...and the only thing one could offer a loved one in torment, if even that—a crust of straw-filled bread...

"I don't want it!" cried Peter Artamanov. "Away!"

Well may the poor drunken siskin stagger around, singing. But at least when one is drunk the world seems to spin—even if it's only one's head—instead of hurtling, fragmented, into black chaos. It was soon after this novel was completed that Gorky, apparently, for the first time began to drink rather heavily.

In the sign of repudiation, and retribution, he had completed "The Artamanovs." To repudiate the Revolution itself—the vehicle of retribution—this he could not make himself do. And even if he could, there were others, who had emotional power over him, who would not let him, believing they knew what was best for him and feeling they knew him better than he knew himself.

One evening, in Marienbad, Moura Budberg had called Khodasevich in for a "chat." She explained that Gorky's earnings could barely support the numerous people he insisted on "carrying on his shoulders." She herself was a monarchist "to her marrow," but was keenly aware that the income from foreign editions alone would not support the whole entourage; Gorky could not help being dependent on continued income from Soviet sources. "And Alexey Maximovich himself will be unfortunate, if through some careless act he spoils his biography."

Then, in Sorrento, the now frequent visits of Ekaterina Pavlovna Peshkova—at that time a stalwart cultural emissary of the Soviets to foreign revolutionaries—exerted a further influence on Gorky. The two women seem to have understood each other despite their different perspectives, and plumped for the same thing.

The decisive visit by his wife was early in 1925. Long discussions took place in private. Afterward, he (Gorky) "walked literally on tiptoe, and tried to open his mouth as little as possible, while Ekaterina Pavlovna had the look of a mother who has returned home, and seen that without her the little boy has got into mischief, learned to smoke, got friendly with the wrong boys—and, willy-nilly, it was necessary to switch him." Sometimes the discussions included young Maxim.

Ekaterina Pavlovna had two strong cards: Gorky's "biography" and Max's future.

How long could "the great proletarian writer" stay abroad, in ambiguous exile, without risking the loss of the title of "the great proletarian writer?" She may even have brought to him what amounted to a Soviet ultimatum. And here was Max, doing nothing but running around on a motorcycle, while in the Soviet Union he could become a useful man. Gorky had doubts and forebodings, but ...

It was from this point that Khodasevich felt his path and Gorky's were parting. In the spring of 1925 the poet left for Paris. A correspondence continued for some time. He began to feel, as it went on, that Gorky was not being altogether truthful, that the need for the Beautiful Lie was becoming stronger. Gorky's letters show continued demoralization, bewilderment, and—an urge to drink.

So, sometime in 1925 may be taken as a turning point. Something was taking place; "logical" explanations usually are an overlay on more mysterious ones. He could not live indefinitely in the exile of despair.

Things that seem of little biographic importance may play a strong role: in 1925, for example, a letter arrived in Sorrento, addressed simply to "Italia: Massimo Gorky." It was from the Gorky Labor Colony near Poltava, where a man named Makarenko, inspired by a devoted reading of Gorky's works, was trying out educational theories in the rehabilitation of homeless waifs, mostly juvenile delinquents—Chelkashes and Malvas of a Russia torn by years of riot and upheaval. The emotional impact of such a stretching out of hands to him cannot be overlooked.

When Gorky wrote to Khodasevich that he was thinking of giving up Soviet citizenship—over the setting up of the index of "forbidden books"—Khodasevich did not believe him; Gorky may have actually thought he would do this, he wrote, but knew in his heart he could not.

Their correspondence ended. The younger man felt Gorky had by now, at least subconsciously, determined he would eventually return to the Soviet Union; and that it was too painful for him to face Khodasevich any longer, even in letters—or too compromising.

In 1926 Gorky burned another bridge connecting him with the possibility of living out his years in exile. He did it by means of a message of condolence, with a sentence of eulogy, upon the death of Dzerdzinski.

Even moderate émigrés were driven to hurt fury. It was a drastic thing to do—to eulogize the killer of so many, the head of the Cheka and the GPU. Many were aware of Dzerdzinski's "pure" and fanatical idealism, and that he had tormented himself—perhaps to his death—over his self-assigned role as the Revolution's executioner. But for Gorky ...!

Khodasevich pointed out that Gorky's wire stressed the fact Ekaterina

Pavlovna joined him in his grief; and this is undoubtedly the hint to the explanation. She had been fond of Dzerdzinski; and he must have been something of a father to Maxim, her son and Gorky's. Gorky was caught in a moral trap. A natural guess is that Ekaterina Pavlovna demanded a wire of condolence, and Gorky, again, submitted.

He was coming around, probably without knowing it himself, to a decision: that only by accepting the Russian reality, and somehow externalizing the blame, could he again make sense of life and banish the thought of suicide. He was thereby preparing the ground for a return to the Soviet Union.

The hope voiced so cryptically in the book of the Artamanovs—that the mutual sins and bloody memories of the recent past might begin to die—must have grown in him. The defeat of the Communist Opposition, which most Western scholars now see as the triumph of Party "apparatus" over the Revolution's "conscience," must have seemed to Gorky, then, the harbinger of unity. Zinoviev, one of the chiefs of the defeated group, had been among the most fanatical bolsheviks, and Gorky's archtormentor. The new man who had emerged, Stalin, seemed to be leading Party and country away from extremism, toward the moderate course desired by men like Bukharin and Rykov.

As for "democracy"—Gorky had bitterly decided, and made Tikhon Vialov say it for him, that until the Russian people were spiritually reconstructed they "could only run wild without a master." He saw this as bitter reality; and could not go on grieving over "the follies of the past."

Yet there was a terrible hurt anger, that choked him, that made the world seem chaotic and drunk. Who then was to blame for the cataclysm? Who and what must be repudiated? In "The Artamonovs" he had already shown where he was turning: Blame the past, and all those who had permitted the cataclysm to take place. They had all proved craven and ineffectual. Repudiate them all. Clear the deck!

And in this spirit he began, in 1926, a huge four-volume novel, "Klim Samghin."

It is a tedious, lumpish work, on a vast canvas—the world of the intelligentsia of Russia from the 1880's until Lenin's arrival in 1917 at the Finland Station. This world he knew least, and despised most—as a defense, and for many slights and hurts endured. The work's prevailing qualities are hatred and self-hatred; disgust that is clearly also self-disgust. This was how he meant it.

For he had a theory: everything negative, everything doomed to retribution, including much of his own past and even his character—for he must be merciless—was to be in that book. It would be a "receptacle," for all the sins of all the people against their own great possibilities, against truth, against God, against one another. The novel was to be an utter repudiation of the past, to help liberate the future.

Klim Samghin, the "anti-hero" of the work, by his very name shows that Gorky himself was prepared to be the first sacrifice on the pyre of the sinful past. Samghin (the Russian word for "self," the Greek for "born") is how Gorky had often thought of himself, and how others openly thought of him: Gorky the Self-Born, who came from nowhere, became everything by his own mind and heart and sweat. This proud name, in his great initial gesture of repudiation, he bestowed on a man who was everything he despised: irresolute, a cowardly twerp, mistrustful of the world and people, a snob, joyless, treacherous . . .

All, in this huge book, is dissatisfaction, hypocrisy, gnawing ennui . . . The book is studded with powerful ideas, but all end in a sneer; snatches of real poetry are then dismissed as insanity; love yearnings end in crass and disappointing acts of sex; women seemingly interested in idealism turn out to be police spies. Bloody Sunday, Savva Morozov, the Barricades of 1905, the joyful end of "The Confession," radical exiles abroad, praters about Marxism, secret believers in heretical truths of religion—all, seen through this venomous prism, are sullied, revealed as false and disgusting, cast aside. It is a real holocaust—of whatever was. And the epitome of all cowardice, banality, tedium, death-in-life, Klim Samghin, plods wearily through the story.

What is real? Lenin arrives at Finland Station; Klim is trampled by the cheering crowd of soldiers. But where there should, then, be triumph, there is only a final sick dying away . . . Lenin never is actually seen . . . In a trickle, the vast work trails off . . .

He couldn't face it. The last paragraphs—for which the whole giant thing was a buildup—were never written. He never returned to it. By the time he was doggedly working on the last of the four volumes, in the Soviet Union in 1932, he knew he had conceived a sick monster, because the whole "theory" on which it was founded was a perverse fantasy . . . and, besides, a Lie . . . For Hieronymus Bosch could claim to be afflicted with madness, but Gorky was desperately sane; there was no hiding place.

"Klim Samghin" is truly a tragic work, in the sense that a man so talented and noble could so becloud himself, in an effort to rationalize a terrible spiritual dilemma; and because so much splendid material of life and imagination, suitable for high art, perished, like entombed miners, in it. And yet, the misbegotten effort contained a certain greatness.

By the time Gorky had completed two volumes, he had already made his first triumphal return visit to the Soviet Union. Soon he would be returning to stay.

# BOOK VI

## *The Holy Wanderer in the Iron Age*

## *Second Apocalypse*

## *Flight's End*

## CHAPTER 35

THE return, ending the long ambiguous exile, was meant to end a tormenting inner conflict. Well prepared, it was nevertheless an act of desperation.

Many Russians, who lived out their lives (often shortened by grief and poverty) in exile, cursed Gorky as a man who had "caved in." They forgot that their psychological life was not his. To decide on permanent exile would have meant admitting a life largely misspent and mistaken; the question of suicide would have become really insistent.

He *had* come from a different class. *They* had lost loved ones, to the brutality—often vengeful or needless—of the Revolution. *He* had been torn from his own parents by the brutal callousness of the old Russia, and the only dear ones he ever actually knew—Grandpa and Grandma—had died begging in the streets of that Russia of the cultivated émigrés which the Revolution had overthrown.

They said he sold out. If he had ended his days in the cafés of Paris, or in New York, among them, most of them would have mocked him. It would not have been human not to rejoice at such a dismal end for "the Revolution's Stormy Petrel."

And he would have approached judgment staring into an accusation that he had *really* sold out: sold out the sacred memory of Grandma and his family, of all the castoffs and sacrifices of the old society, who had appointed him their champion, avenger, justifier before the throne of time.

On the Soviet side, Bukharin and Rykov led the public clamor—in *Pravda* and *Izvestia*—for Gorky's return; they also urged him in private letters. Ekaterina Pavlovna continued to work on him. Lunacharsky tried to convince Gorky their old common dream was still possible.

Even Stalin began to correspond with Gorky in Sorrento. To him Gorky finally broached some of his ineradicable dreams: to organize a newspaper which would deal with the life of Russians "beyond the frontiers," and make reconciliation possible; to get together writers and prepare popular handbooks about the Civil War—toward a pooling of memories and experiences, of that vast tragedy, which might knit enemies again into brothers; to "examine" the question of antireligious propaganda in the Soviet press (he must again have been dreaming of God-building!).

Stalin gave him assurances about the publications, and would "talk with the comrades specializing in antireligious propaganda about your proposals."

Gorky even went as far as to ask that Radek be put in charge of one of the contemplated magazines—a man who had joined Trotsky's opposition and was now in disgrace. Here Stalin rebuffed him:

...Not one of these enterprises can be entrusted to the leadership of Radek or someone among his friends. The issues are not the good intentions of Radek or his conscientiousness. The decisive point is the logic of his fractional struggle... The history of our Party (and not only the history of our Party) teaches that the logic of things is stronger than the logic of human intentions.

This might have been enough to tip off a man, even one with as much yearning as Gorky, about what still lay ahead for the Soviet Union. Still, Stalin's hard response, to his gentle effort to start the healing of wounds, was probably quite understandable to him. He himself had learned that the world spun drunkenly, that the logic of human intentions went down the drain. There was a terrible, dark logic in brutal things.

This man Stalin—one may try to follow Gorky's wishful thought—might be reasoned with; his belief in the dark logic of things might be tempered toward humanism. He was a member of a minority group, a Georgian; this was lucky for Russia. He was a practical man—Gorky's wishful thinking may have continued—not one of the intelligentsia snobs. He had even written poetry (unpublished). His meager education had been toward the priesthood; and these things went deep. Gorky undoubtedly was tipped off—and this was certainly true—that Stalin was no dogmatic theoretician. If, under him, "Marxism" in Russia was to be a state religion, a working myth toward a new and happier reality, then here was a man with whom Gorky could do business. He might well manage finally to wangle Radek and other nonconformists, now in trouble, onto one or another project after all. Hadn't he done as much with Lenin?

He had always been good at reading his own motives, and emotions, into others. And by now he was committed to going back.

Richard Hare, in his book about Gorky, believes Gorky "persuaded himself that, whatever their initial crimes and blunders, the Bolsheviks were vigorous educable people ... He flattered himself that the masters of the new Russia would be glad to learn from him, might benefit by his guidance."

Both points are undoubtedly true. But "logical" reasoning of this kind could only have been secondary, for someone like Gorky. Emotional reasoning—the stern shades of Grandpa and Grandma, of the little dead brothers—must have been primary; and the feeling that he should end his days on Russian soil.

All reasons, for his return, interlock: sense of duty to the shades; brutal economics; wishful thinking; a man's pride in his identity; his family. In the last year of his life, in a very private conversation, Gorky was asked why in the world he had come back to the Soviet Union. He replied: "I was put into a situation in which I could not fail to come back."

In the summer of 1928, and again in the summer of 1929, there were dummy runs—triumphally staged visits by Gorky to the Soviet Union. The very triumphal staging must have made final return inevitable. It would have taken not only great will power, but clarity, to repudiate this kind of obligation.

In 1928, he was escorted in glory through Minsk, Moscow, then down his Volga—Nizhni, of course, which staged a "jubilee" exposition for his sixtieth birthday, and which soon would be renamed Gorky; Kazan; Samara; Stalingrad, which he had known as Tsaritsyn; then Vladikavkas, Tiflis, Erivan. Each must have been meant to touch a chord of the old lyre, and undoubtedly did. The émigrés told bitter jokes: "Watch out, Volga—Gorky's tears will make you overflow your banks." It is quite possible that the river's level rose; he had always cried easily, and now he was getting old.

In 1929, the red-carpet route took in, besides these cities and others, the huge collective farm, Giant; and also Solovki—the brutal concentration camp on the Solovetsky Islands, where so many perished. Gorky's visit there was used by the Soviet government as testimony that Solovki was really a gentle place, where humans were "rehabilitated" through honest labor. A former inmate has given an account of the travesty by which Gorky was hoodwinked. The camp was spruced up frantically, new clothes issued, hours suddenly shortened, guards dressed up as prisoners to make a better impression, a library hastily installed . . . Gorky was paraded through with Cheka men beside him.

It would seem that only a determined decision to refuse to see could explain his failure to see, on this occasion. As Khodasevich had remarked, Gorky not only was naïve, but practiced appearing more naïve than he was.

There is evidence, although it is faint at first, that Gorky was not so readily hoodwinked. At one point in the first grand tour, he put on a disguise, including false wig and beard, and wandered about in the throngs gathered to greet him. One biographer, once a bolshevik but long bitterly hostile, comments that the secret police were undoubtedly a pace or two behind. It seems a pathetic effort, but shows a man trying to get through prearranged surfaces to the insights he needed. The garments he put on, including the wig and beard, may be viewed in the Gorky Museum in Moscow.

Fortunately, there is another source that tells more. A certain Moroz, a bolshevik commissar at the front in 1920, but by 1928 badly disillusioned, accompanied Gorky on that tour; later, in Paris exile, he wrote of the experience.

When Gorky arrived, wrote Moroz, "in very many citizens . . . a hope grew warm—of finding in him, at last, a savior. Everyone thought: Gorky, the stormy petrel of liberty, who fought so many years with such strength, with such passion, against violence and injustice, will not be silent."

But he was; only a glance at the existing situation would be needed to show that he had to be.

Yet as the tour went on, he confided—clearly, in desperation—in Moroz, a stranger but one whom he sounded out, in his naïve, cunning, Luka-like way.

In Moscow, after the greetings by the throngs, Gorky remarked to Moroz, ambiguously: "Such grandiose welcomes can take place only under two conditions: either when the people are living in material, political and spiritual satisfaction, or else when the people exist in absolute material, political and spiritual poverty and slavery."

Hundreds of letters came in the first mail in Moscow, from people in every walk of life, communists and noncommunists, "begging him to save arrested children, husbands, fathers and mothers." By the time Gorky got to the Caucasus and Rostov, says Moroz, he had the picture.

There Gorky called him aside for a talk. He asked him, "desperately," if he was an anarchist; Moroz said no. The talk continued. Gorky, suddenly, asked, "And can you keep quiet, when you have to?" Moroz said he had been doing so for seven years, having learned this with the aid of Lubyanka Prison. "I'd like to put one more question," said Gorky. "Tell me, please—and, if you can, frankly—how do you think, are there many who keep quiet in the Union?" Moroz asked if Gorky, in his turn, would respect his confidence. Gorky: "Well, of course. Otherwise there's no sense to our chat." Moroz then said he thought the percentage of quiet-keepers was about eighty per cent; that soon it would include all except the Party wheelhorses, "the hallelujah-boys." Gorky looked at him glumly, sat silent, then: "Yes, I suppose you're right ... But why is it so?"

At the Giant Collective Farm, and elsewhere, when the Party regulars asked for comment, he commented; but nobody could say, afterward, just what he had said. And in the hotel he started another discussion with Moroz: "If you think I understand anything from all this, about what's going on, you're mistaken. No matter how I stretch my brains, I cannot understand these things being done with peasants and workers and city people. The only thing that comes through clearly is that all this, taken together, takes us back to the fifties of the previous century, but in a more ruthless form."

He added: "In the mist of all events, about the only thing that emerges is suffering."

At a final dinner for him, Gorky insisted on talking about his youth. When A. A. Andreyev (later a Politburo luminary) finally pinned him with a direct question, he said: "The whole business of collectivization, I think, should be put on a voluntary basis, without any force being used."

As to whether he really was taken in by the tragic mummery at the Solovki concentration camp, the same Moroz, in a talk with him toward the end of Gorky's life, asked him why he had written an article lauding that institution. Gorky said simply: "Everything in it but my signature is absolutely the opposite of what I wrote."

And in spite of it all, he prepared to return, permanently. During these "casing" visits, he did manage to lay foundations for various magazines he would edit: "Our Achievements," "USSR in Construction," "The Collective Farmer," "Living Abroad" (literally, the Russian who is living abroad, in exile). For government and Party, these would be more propaganda organs; for Gorky, points of strength wherein he could operate a program of culture and humanization. It was clearly a gamble and, he must have thought, an implicit bargain.

The state of mind to which he was girding himself, to make a final wholehearted return possible, comes out well in a letter to an old friend, one of the most independent and humane of the original Russian Social Democrats. Kuskova had written him, from Paris, reproaching him for covering up hideous Soviet faults and repressions. To her he replied—and this is the letter Khodasevich mentioned, whose words he could imagine Gorky penning, with violent emotion, "the vein bulging on his neck":

The fact is that I hate, with the most sincere hate, the most utter, that truth which, for 99 per cent of the people, is an abomination and a lie ... I know that this reality is miserable for fifty million people who make up the mass of the Russian people, and that men have need of another truth which does not debase them but which lifts their energy in toil and creation ... What is important, for me, is the rapid and general development of the human personality, the birth of a new cultivated man; what is important for me is that the worker in a sugar refinery reads Shelley in the original; what is important for me is the man who shows a large and healthy interest in life, who understands that he is building a new State, the man who lives not only by words but by passion for work and action. This man I have observed not only during my stay in Russia last summer, I have been in touch with him for more than four years. He is an excellent man, full of fervor and confidence. He does not need this impoverished and lying truth in which he defeats himself, he has need of a truth which he creates in himself. He creates if and affirms it on earth. You say that I am an optimist, an idealist, a romantic, etc. Say it, that's your affair. Mine is to explain to you, as best I can, why I am "unilateral." And, in this connection, recall that I started being so thirty-five years ago.

This would take it back to 1894, the time of his very first published story; he was thinking of his total self, his total social idealism, with no reference to the Party's image of Russia or the bolshevik experiment.

Those who, from afar, watched Gorky making the great return could not imagine him serving as anything but a front—a sad bitter end for a man so noble. Few, certainly, anticipated that meaningful art could come of his last decade, out of a return to a dire confronting of earlier hopes in the light of later reality. Most were agreed that his contribution had been made. Nobody could have foreseen that at least one great late creative peak would follow.

Nor could anyone have foreseen the more terrible years at once to come —the lies, the tortures, the internecine murders, the millions of deaths from dislocation, protest, and brutal decision. If they had, they would surely have been convinced of Gorky's doom—either physical, or spiritual.

And so this man, approaching sixty-five, set out into the New World, which in a measure had been his creation, a world of great horizons, presumably inhabited already by the first generation of the New Man, presumably on its way to the construction of the New God, but shod in a strange iron darkness—the unexpected but now accepted iron day to which the "iron dawn" sung by Yesenin and others was the prelude. Straight into the heart of the greatest of our age's contradictions Gorky made his way, like a *strannik*—a gnarled, bitter, still hopeful holy wanderer.

Long after Gorky's return to Russia, and after his strange death, Khodasevich, who had once known him so well, would write:

He finally sold out—not for money, but to preserve the powerful illusion of his life, both for his own sake and for the sake of others. Stubborn and rebellious as he was, he knew that he could not hold out and would go running back to the USSR, because no matter how the Revolution had turned out, it was the only thing that could guarantee his reputation during his lifetime as the great proletarian writer and leader and after his death assure him a niche for his ashes in the Kremlin wall. In exchange for that, the Revolution required of him, as it requires of everyone, not honest service, but slavishness and sycophancy. He became a slave and a sycophant . . . He was transformed into a superintendent of writers. He acquiesced in that too . . . To put it briefly—he turned into the direct opposite of that lofty image of himself for the preservation of which he had made his peace with the Soviet regime. Whether he was aware of the whole tragic nature of this I won't venture to say. Probably . . . he tried to hide it from himself and from others with the help of new illusions, new uplifting deceptions, which he so loved and which, finally, doomed him.

This was harsh; only a closer look at the last years can show whether it was fair.

## CHAPTER 36

GORKY returned, for good. Again he was paraded, like a birthday king, through the towns of youth, and through evidences of
"socialist construction"... the great dam, Dnieprestroy, again the Giant
Collective Farm... Baku, Murmansk...

Then he settled down in Moscow. And, in accord with the rule of his
life, and that "lofty image of himself," he became useful.

The evidence about these last years must be pieced together: from
speeches (although some were clearly ghost-written)... letters (some
clearly falsified)... the memoirs and "recollections" of writers and friends
(scattered and guarded)... a multitude of books, largely hagiography—
the life of a Party-minded literary saint. But from each it is possible to
extract grains of the real Gorky. And his art, against his times, tells most
of all.

Here is the background against which Gorky returned, forever, and
against which his last works, thoughts, and actions must be set.

The Iron Age—so they called it themselves—was on in earnest. In 1928
the Party, now the hand of Stalin's will, had made a monumental decision: to collectivize all agriculture and to achieve heavy industrialization,
regardless of human cost. "We have ten years," Stalin told the Party congress. His conviction, and that of his Party faction, was that within that
time, if Communist Russia were not a strong industrial state, the capital-
ists would pounce and dismember it. Russia would become, at best, an
agricultural colony of the more advanced states of Europe.

It was to be a race against time, the people—an entire generation, it was
understood—to be the sacrifice.

By 1932 this social revolution bore first fruit: famine began. Millions
of kulaks (meaning wealthy peasants, or "fists," but actually including all
who resisted collectivization) were violently removed to Siberia, and
many of them perished. Sholokhov painted an indelible picture of this,
in his novel "Virgin Soil Upturned"; Stalin told Churchill, many years
later, that ten million had been "dealt with." In the famine itself that followed, as grain was taken from resisting peasants, in a year of bad harvest,
it is estimated that five to eight million died. This time, no plea for

American aid; to the outside world, the Soviets kept turned a face of strength and stone.

To enforce the vast and ruthless decision, the Party's hold on all levels of Russian life was clenched. The power of the internal police, the Cheka (renamed the GPU) waxed, and to them, largely, the responsibility of carrying out collectivization was given.

Hunger reached into the cities, striking the workers, on whom fell the weight of the other great program: industrialization. There was protest, and it was dealt with. The internal spy system flowered. Opposition from the trade unions was broken. Terror became a norm of government.

In 1932 the internal passport system—symbol, for the young Gorky, of Old Russia's stifling of freedom—was set up again; and peasant and worker were tied to farm and job. Piecework, which Marx called one of the prime means of capitalist exploitation, was introduced to increase production. The use of forced labor by convicts, many of whom were "political prisoners," was becoming a key part of the Soviet economy.

There was, inevitably, sabotage. Where it was imagined, where real, nobody can ever know fully; the land was shot with distrust, fear, secret agents, old and new injuries, motives for revenge. A trial of engineers, foreign and domestic, was staged in 1929, on charges of sabotaging social-ist construction: building plants in marshes, spoiling machinery, and so forth. Most went to concentration camps.

In 1931 took place the "trial of the mensheviks," on clearly framed charges of "counterrevolutionary conspiracy." It was a trial of scape-goats, necessary because of the terrible hardships of forced collectivization and industrialization. The mensheviks were not killed—the outright killing of former revolutionaries had not yet begun—but none survived the labor camps.

Though Gorky was no Marxist, these "left mensheviks" were men with whose thinking he had always had an affinity. One, Sukhanov, Gorky's old editor during war and revolution, was perhaps the Revolution's finest historian, whose writing speaks of a noble, incorruptible, if somewhat naïve, mind. In concentration camp, he was naïve enough to clamor for release, because it had been promised him promptly if he would make a false confession: needless to say, he did not get it, and is presumed to have perished.

It was in that same year, 1931, that Gorky returned to the Soviet Union on a permanent basis.

He surely knew his old friends too well to think they had suddenly become counterrevolutionaries. Probably, he thought if he was on the scene he could influence their trial; possibly, his presence may even have had something to do with the decision not to kill them on the spot. All is speculation.

The drastic state of the nation was reflected in the Party itself. To carry out the forced program, a new Party in effect had to be constructed. Party purges ("cleansings") swept the ranks. This meant driving from official posts, then from the Party, all the old bolsheviks Gorky had known except a few of the hardest or most subtle. Trotsky had been exiled in 1927; increasing numbers of his followers were taken to penal camps; from 1929, the pace of arrests and purges was stepped up. By 1932, men like Bukharin, Radek, Riazanov, now called "right oppositionists" because they opposed the forced measures of construction, besides men like Kamenev and Zinoviev, who had been allied with Trotsky, were already so fallen, so marked, that they were being ostracized, out of fear.

To deal with threat of mutiny, Stalin by 1931 had set up his own police "secretariat," within the GPU. That year he also proposed that capital punishment be made permissible to use against Party members. (This was something Lenin had outlawed.) The opposition to this, in the Politburo, was led by Kirov and Bukharin; Stalin withdrew his proposal, until 1936, when it was adopted. But already in the Soviet legal code was a law that made families and relatives accountable for the counterrevolutionary acts of any individuals.

Still, mimeographed sheets were circulated secretly, attacking Stalin and demanding a change in Party leadership as well as disbanding of the collective farms. This, called "the darkest moment of the upheaval," is placed by observers in late 1932. It was, therefore, gathering to its climax as Gorky was completing his play "Yegor Bulichev"—his last major work, his one tragedy.

It was a dark scene. No ray of light could come through. One who cared, straining his eyes, would have to say: "I can see nothing! . . ." There was no way of appealing, then, to the central committee from the Politburo, as Khrushchev did in 1957; the monolith was solid, the opposition was ground under.

It was in this crucial situation, too, that the image of Stalin as "Father" —the father of the new country and all its people—was introduced, and the Byzantine system of nauseating eulogies of him. This was not vainglory (he was not vainglorious), but brilliant politics. Each eulogy, once in print, was a "pledge of allegiance" in the vicious internal Party struggle, to Stalin and the dominant organization; it could be undone only by trickery, making a man a plotter; and it was also a temporary guarantee of physical safety. This is the primary meaning of "personality cult."

Yet it was an era of construction too; positives were being built, on brutality, as time has shown. The big question was what kind of image the "new man" would have, whether the brutal would triumph completely, or whether it was possible to create a human image. This was where Gorky apparently felt he should come in: to have a hand in the shaping, so that the stupid brutality and bloodiness might prove only a "dying truth," to give way in near future to a "living truth."

Against that fantastic and macabre background, with this fantastic hope, the indefatigable man—who defined genius as "the capacity for work"—set to work. The Soviet government gave him a house in the center of Moscow, and a villa in a suburb called The Hillocks. His son Maxim, with his wife and two children, lived with him. His wife, Ekaterina Pavlovna, lived in an apartment not far from his Moscow home. Moura Budberg had not returned to Russia with him; a bronze hand on his desk at The Hillocks is said to have been cast from her hand. It seems likely: she was probably the nearest he came to finding a Queen Margot. With Maria Feodorovna Andreyeva there seems to have been no close relation, though she received royalties from his works; nor does it seem that any further women were important in his life.

His work, as he spread it before him, was multiform—as if Vasska himself was trying, in old age, to make that "green-burning" world come true; there is pathos here, and a certain grandeur.

Franklin, sketching the proposed American Philosophical Society, seeking "an enlarged intellectual life" for his new land, listed all the various forms of knowledge to be accumulated: about plants, roots, juices, fossils, minerals, arts, trades ... "All philosophical Experiments that let Light into the Nature of Things, tend to increase the Power of Man over Matter, & Multiply the Conveniences or Pleasures of Life ..."

Gorky's perspective, in his "new land," was heartrendingly more difficult. Franklin, in a virgin land, with a fairly united, reasonably developed people, was able to aim direct at the conquest of nature. Gorky, in a long-besotted, blood-accustomed, superstition-filthy land, driven from above, seething below, was aiming at an inner conquest of man, to permit a start on the rational conquest of nature. This seems the burden of his late thinking, just as it had been at the time of "The Confession," and at the time of the Revolution. It may not have accorded with reality; it accorded with hope.

He must have seemed a fantastic apparition to Party fanatics promoting the Iron Age: an apparition out of the dim past, laughable and irritating. But he was such a work horse; and he was so useful . . .

Part of the price he paid was becoming a leader of official optimism. He had to let himself be hoodwinked; to hoodwink himself; to help others hoodwink themselves. He must have choked on that bitter "dying truth" he so hated, which he so wanted not to admit.

Only when he turned to his art, the anger and sorrow and pain got the upper hand. None of the works of his last period could be called works of optimism, not even by the most optimistic. And it is art that conveys the most of the man, the most of reality.

The first work of his last, the Soviet, period was a play, "Somov and Others." This strange, inferior work was actually finished early in 1931, before his permanent return to Russia from Sorrento. Its theme is the sabotage of Soviet industry by engineers. To read it is to trace a mind's half-hearted effort to convince itself, on the basis of third-hand and doctored evidence; to find Good Guys and Bad Guys in a new surrounding and taking the Party's word for what had happened. He could not do it; and so the play became an outlet for Gorky's general anger at the "unworthiness" of people.

It is possibly his only work as an artist to which one could point with shame: he violated in it the artist's necessity to judge for himself—that "best of all advice" given him, so many years back, by Nikolai Vasiliev: "Live by your mind. Examine everything."

Probably he felt he had no choice but to begin, at the start of a new relation, with Stalin, by accepting the Party's interpretation of the trial of the engineers. Probably he could only be made acceptable to Party fanatics, by his friends, on the premise that he would again write pro-bolshevik plays, as he had once done for Lenin; that he would become again the Stormy Petrel of a triumphant Bolshevik Revolution, rallying the people against cunning internal foes, who were responsible for the unhappy state of Soviet Russia.

He really knew the ailment of Russia went deeper; he had said as much, often. But in order to return, he had to shut awareness' eyes. Casting about for ways of resuming an old humanitarian role in new conditions, he failed to see there would be a moral conflict. The play represents a real moral lapse. The previous chapters have traced his growing demoralization, in those last years of exile, the rising despair and the temptation finally to lose that firm hold on values with which he left Grandma.

He was coming into a new situation, controlled by a man much cruder, and tougher, than Lenin. His bargaining power was that he was a world-known symbol; but he had little tangible backing where it would count once he came in and the gate fell behind him—among the Party's new leadership. A sixth sense must have warned him; and so, trying not to admit this to himself, he may have decided to propitiate Stalin and the Party machine with a sacrifice, a small one, a bit of his artistic integrity— a play.

Once the die was cast, he must have banked heavily on that correspondence with Stalin, and his wishful size-up of the man. The image of the relation of an older man of thought to a younger man of action, to whom the younger man sometimes listens, is one of the great images of national life. Aristotle had tutored, and (they say) restrained, Alexander . . . The situation was hard and dangerous, but it had room for dreams.

There is one especially strange thing in the play of "Somov." Really Good Guys there are none; but what half-heartedly were meant to pass for Good Guys are the GPU agents who come in at the end, to arrest the engineers. Gorky, who had written "The Man Nobody Needed," could not have been expected to admire men of this calling, even new-style. They are efficient but cheerful, gay and polite . . . and their faces are blanks.

What is so evocative about these ciphers? . . . There suddenly comes to mind a scene that took place in Sorrento, when Gorky's loved (too much loved) son Maxim—happy-go-lucky, cheerful, reader of juvenile detective stories, breakneck driver of motorcycles, gay, charming, polite—confided to Khodasevich his desire to go back to Soviet Russia and make a career in the Cheka (now the GPU). His mother had come from Moscow to Sorrento with a message from Dzerdzinski, that there was a job in the security police waiting for him, and after all it was time he thought of a career . . . and there was a promise of a real automobile, if he came, and he could just imagine himself driving it . . . whereupon he suddenly advanced on Khodasevich, squeezing an imaginary horn and giving out a great "HONK!"

It was at about the time of this episode that Gorky, after long private talks with Ekaterina Pavlovna and Max, began, it seemed to Khodasevich, to turn his psyche toward a permanent return. He never spoke about the possibility of a career for his son in the Cheka; it was as if he didn't know. He only told Khodasevich, once, he didn't want the boy to go back to Russia. The poet said, "Well, let him go, if he wants to." Gorky exclaimed: "And what if they finally cut him up, then what?" He was very much upset.

Gorky was a father; this foolish, happy boy was his only son. It is only in this frame that the pictures of those happy normal ciphers, the agents of the GPU, in the foolish play "Somov," make sense.

Complicated emotions and emotion-drenched reasoning must have led Gorky to return. How much more complex must have been his state of mind once it was irrevocable, and he saw the Iron Age not as a pampered visitor but from inside—with the sudden clarity that forces itself on a man only after what's done is done, and he can no longer play blind. What hurt, what fury at life. What sense of bafflement, betrayal, fraud, darkness.

It all had to come out somewhere.

He had always confided to his art things he could not to his life. In Sorrento he had begun (it is not known when), in Moscow in 1932 he finished, the play "Yegor Bulichev and Others."

# CHAPTER 37

"BULICHEV" is his great play. It rests solidly on its central figure, a man powerful, hurt, angry, dense. One of the few like him in literature is Lear.

It seems to be the story of a provincial merchant of Russia—a lesser Savva Morozov—who, in February of 1917, approaching death, curses his family and class and is half prepared to give his angry blessing to the rebels of society.

But the intuition grows quickly that it is not, ultimately, about either physical death or 1917; that these are symbols. And finally it is clear that "Bulichev" is, like "Lear," a drama of human betrayal, of struggle against psychic blindness, of the ability of Evil to defraud, and even destroy, the Good. The *real* time is—1932.

On the surface, the February Revolution is beginning; during the play's course, word comes that the Tsar has been overthrown. In the provincial town, there is failure of order and authority. War fortunes are still being made; but businesses that falter go under.

Yegor Bulichev, head of a strong local firm, is fatally ill, with cancer. Around him circle corrupted creatures: his old wife; his daughter and son-in-law; a wealthy abbess, Melania, his sister-in-law and once his mistress. They impatiently await his death, so they can divide the business.

But there is also a small gallery of the Good: Shura, Bulichev's red-headed illegitimate (natural) daughter; Jacob Laptev, his godson, of lower class origin, a leader of undefined rebel agitation; finally, Glafira, the veteran maidservant, Bulichev's physical and emotional partner.

Here is the late configuration of Gorky's sky: on the one side those with status, corrupted frauds; in opposition, the orphaned and natural, who care for Man—and this particular man, Bulichev—himself.

Bulichev knows true from false; but he cannot bring himself to unmask and repudiate the false . . . because he knows that without fraud life is impossible. So he exposes himself to their fraud; but then *refuses to be taken in.* In this final struggle for honesty is his despairing heroism.

In this is also a unifying simplicity. The result is a more unified play than "The Lower Depths." There is a gnarled ripeness, too; and surer structure. At last, by tortured paths, Gorky's symbolic art has reached its natural goal: symbolic tragedy.

The main action is the presentation to Bulichev of three faith healers. He may either believe in their fraud, or face the truth. The truth is that he must die; but on the play's deeper level, it is worse: a terrible bitter truth about . . . something.

The local priest, Pavlin, suggests to the dying Bulichev that, in some foreign sanatoria, music is used to heal. And locally, there is a fireman who employs a trumpet.

"Will it heal?" Bulichev wants to know.

Everything's possible, the priest assures him. "We live in mystery, in the gleam of innumerable and unresolvable mysteries. It seems to us there is light, and that the light springs from our reason, but the light is only for our corporeal sense, while the spirit, it may be, is only darkened by reason, and even—is extinguished." Bulichev sighs—"What a lot of words you have."

Only against the thirties in Russia—years of the hardening of state repression, in mockery of socialism's theory of freedom—do the priest's words take on meaning; and Bulichev's deep sigh.

Those years were a watershed of modern times. On that Russian field, as surely as at Agincourt, a whole age fell: rationalism—the faith in the ability of human reason, clothed in knightly socialistic theory, to build a noble world—received a great defeat. Here was one of rationalism's oldest knights, Gorky, surveying the field of slaughter ... and, with a deep sigh, questioning a lifetime's faith in Reason ...

Bulichev calls Glafira, the maidservant. Taking her hand, he asks: "Do you love me anyway? Even ailing?" Glafira falls on her knees: "My loved one, my Grief ... Yes ... Don't ail. Don't!" She tears herself away, runs from the room.

This earthy love, these warm people, the one dying, the other no longer young, recall vividly the pair On a Raft: Gorky's inner vision of the free companionship of men and women ... much of the root of the whole communist dream, for him and probably for many others.

Later, Bulichev tries to get vodka; the buffet is locked. "They stand guard," he mutters ... "It's as if—I'm under arrest." On this touch of mystery, the act ends.

In the second, Bulichev torments the hypocritical abbess, and the priest. He insists that God and the devil must be business partners; otherwise, why should Evil be allowed to make such a senseless mockery of Good? Then he suddenly declares: "No, the matter is not with the Tsar ... but in the very root." In other words, the Revolution—solved nothing.

In fury and despair, he sits downing glasses of vodka. Glafira begs, "Don't drink, don't harm yourself"; to come away with her, to Siberia. "Why do you want to stay here? ... They'll swallow you, like worms ... No one loves you, all wait for your death ..."

Bulichev: "Stop, Glakha ... I—know everything. I see everything ... Maybe I'll still get well ... Call the trumpeter, go ahead." The ghost of a last desire to believe, to be deceived, is still with him.

The fireman has been waiting in the kitchen. Sorry, gaunt, pants held up by bright suspenders, he carries a huge trumpet in a bag. The sardonic scene becomes marvelously grotesque. The trumpeter's name, sure enough, is Gavrilo (Gabriel). Bulichev wants to know whether he considers himself a fool or a swindler. Gabriel doggedly denies he is either, but ... "You yourself know; without fraud, one can't live." "There!" Bulichev cries. "True! Brother, that—is—bad—but true."

"Isn't it shameful to use fraud?" Shura demands. "Why shameful," says Gabriel, "if they believe you?" Greatly agitated, Bulichev roars: "That's right! That's—right!"

He commands Glafira to bring the trumpeter money. The grateful trumpeter begs Bulichev to give the trumpet a chance. "Who the bitch knows how it does it, but honest to God, it sometimes works!" Bulichev refuses, then laughs, changes his mind. "All right, show me—go ahead. But loud!"

The trumpeter lays on—and the blast is deafening. Glafira and Shura watch in agitation. Bulichev shouts: "Give it all you've got!" The trumpeter does. Everyone comes running. Shura cries: "Go away, trumpeter, go away!" But Bulichev roars: "No, don't stop! Blow on, Gabriel! Judgment Day! The end of the world! Blow ... ow ... ow ... !"

The raging irony of that act-ending has seldom been touched. No harsher cry of disillusionment, betrayal, was ever heard. What a contrast between this Archangel—Gabriel—and that Archangel of a quarter century earlier, Michael, in "The Confession." The one, a worker-archangel, friend of John the Baptist, brought a young God-seeker the message of a new, beautiful world. The other, a poor charlatan, blows for the old Bulichev Doomsday, and the end of that beautiful illusion. What a dreadful gulf across which this insane trumpet blast carries back to the land of the Stormy Petrel, the Flaming Heart of Danko.

Bitter fury and feigned madness hang over the play's last act. Bulichev is in great pain, talks wildly. Shura begs him to lie down ...

Bulichev: "To lie down—means to give up. This is—like a fist fight. And ... I need to tell you. You understand ... how it happened ... I'm living on the wrong street! I fell among strangers, thirty years I've been among strangers ... And here I am ... I can't express it to you."

"Thirty years"—within a year, give or take a few months, brings one back to when the young Gorky, after writing "The Lower Depths," started moving from impulsive revolutionary protest toward the bolshevik part of the spectrum, to see himself as "saved" by Lenin's salvation army. He had "moved to the wrong street" just about thirty years before he completed the play of Bulichev.

Bulichev: "To you—I never told stories, I always told the truth. See ... priests, tsars, governors ... what the devil do I need them for? ... In a God—I don't believe ... And there aren't any good people ... No, they're all false coins! ... Now they've all fallen to warring ... gone out of their heads! And what have I got to do with them? ... And you—how are you going to live among them?"

Nobody in the play had "gone out of their heads." The lines only make sense against the background of 1931–32, growing terror, paralysis of morality, the Party factions locked, warring, as if gone out of their heads . . . And Shura, the red-headed natural daughter, to whom the old man always told only the truth, is clearly also the inner Gorky: his soul, his conscience.

The trumpeter wasn't enough. Outside wait Zabunova, a local sorceress, and Prokopia (known as Propotey—"Sweated-Through"), a frenzied simpleton with a direct line to the divine. One of them, the abbess urges, may really save him. To Bulichev, everything now seems funny. "Call the sorceress."

She enters, singing: "Oy you, evil spirits, fleshly griefs! Unfasten yourselves, roll away, get away, from this slave of God! . . ." But the cunning Bulichev traps her: she admits that a malady as grave as his requires dealing with the Unclean Power.

Bulichev: "With Satan himself?"

Zabunova: "Well, not direct with Him, but still . . ."

He drives her out, roaring.

This, the briefest of the three temptations, lights up the man's new stubborn resolve: he will not traffic with Evil, pretend that fraud is faith, even to save his life. Fraud is not faith; it does not really heal. By now, he knows this.

"He's pretending madness," the abbess tells Bulichev's wife. "Let him play that game." If Bulichev's will favors Shura—if the testimony Gorky leaves behind favors his soul, his conscience, and not their false claims—they'll prove he was mad, using Zabunova and the trumpeter as witnesses.

The last shot in the locker of quackery, Sweated-Through, takes his turn: a bush-league Rasputin, in bast shoes, long linsey shirt, lead crosses and images on his breast, wild thick hair, long thin beard, the jerky movements of a syphilitic. While Shura protests, he comes up to Bulichev, and starts his song routine:

> No sleep—for the heretic.
> The little clock—goes tick tick tick.
> If God would—if he could—
> I'm pretty good—All the same
> Who's to blame?
> Play, Satan—Whee!
> You're free.
> Midnight beats—the rooster bleats:
> "Cock-a-doodle-doo!"
> The heretic's through!

Then the salvationist goes into a gruesome dance, twirling his staff, chanting, spinning more and more furiously.

Shura begs, "Chase him out! ... Father—why are you silent?" Bulichev waves his hand: "Wait ..." The abbess defends the "holy" simpleton. "You mustn't touch him. He's in ecstasy!" But this is too much even for the rest of the family; they tear Sweated-Through's staff out of his hand, and drag him out, hooting like the winter wind.

His weird words ... "Who's to blame?" ... and the frenzied hunting down of heretics ... cling to the mind.

There had been, in Gorky's life, one superhunter of heretics of the mind, a man with "the spirit of the watchman" (Rosa Luxemburg said that of him) ... a great salvationist, furiously active, with a direct line to final truths ... Here, briefly, in the grotesque guise of the lunatic Sweated-Through, Lenin has made his last appearance in Gorky's works of the imagination.

Shura and Glafira support Bulichev to the sofa. Outside, singing. He mumbles mootly: "... A sort of mass ... sung over a living man ..." Then he makes his final statement.

"And the Kingdom perishes where there is foulness. I can see nothing ... (He rises, holding on to the table, wipes his eyes.) ... Your Kingdom ... What kingdom? Beasts! Kingdom ... Our Father ... No ... Bad! ... What father are you to me, if you have not condemned death? For what? All die? Why? ..." He ends with hoarse incoherent shouting.

All run to him, and he stumbles toward them (all, even the bad ones—all are human). Shura opens the window. "Dense singing" bursts in.

Bulichev: "What is it? The mass again ...! Shura! Who is it?"

Shura: "Come here, come ... see!"

Bulichev: "Ekh, Shura ..."

The curtain.

To try to explain Bulichev's last dark speech as an outcry against God, the Father, for permitting death, does not really light up its darkness ... or the "Beasts!" ... Nor would heaven's kingdom perish through earthly foulness ...

Nor could "The Kingdom" possibly refer to Tsarist Russia. Nobody, for many years, had thought of it that way.

But that very word, "The Kingdom" (*Tsarstvo*), was used regularly— by friend in joy, by foe in mockery—as a statement of the Revolution's aim: the building of "The Kingdom," or even "The Kingdom of Heaven"

—those were Lunacharsky's words!—on earth. That Kingdom was to be the Soviet Union.

And from this flows the only possible meaning of that climactic line: "The Kingdom perishes where there is foulness."

And the singing at the end? Clearly, not the Orthodox liturgy. Here, in February of 1917, the Russian "Marseillaise" would have been in place —"Let us reject the world of the past, let us cast its remains from our feet ..." To it had marched Populists, the goers To the People, the idealist martyrs ... But, equally clearly, this could not be—in 1932. If Gorky had wanted the "Internationale"—the bolshevik hymn—that could easily have been arranged. There are no stage directions. There is no light. The view is tragic.

And the bitter old writer wrote, to the director assigned by the Party to produce his great tragic work: "... You have staged it interestingly, the public will laugh, and that is very important."

But the man to whom Gorky had read the first script of "The Lower Depths," and who had helped stage it, Nemirovich-Danchenko, wrote to Gorky:

"It is long since I have read a play as captivating. Truly, it's as if you have just struck the age of 32! ... Youthful ... alive ... simple ... And all that, in your sixties ... clever, clever, clever! Fearless, wide-souled ... Such a manly facing of the past, such brave truthfulness, speaks of the triumph, the utter and full triumph of the Revolution, more than scores of placards and demonstrations."

No letter was private. The old director said what he could. "The age of 32!"—that takes the mind back to the end of 1900, to the vibrant, searching, idealistic Gorky, telling Nemirovich his plans for "The Lower Depths."

"Thirty-two" is not "thirty," but close enough. Both men were thinking the same thoughts, about Gorky's life and what became of the dream, from slightly different perspectives.

The novelist Alexey Tolstoy wrote to Gorky: "You never before rose to such simplicity of art ... The presentation makes an enormous and lofty impression. It is astounding that, having traveled such a path, you have arrived at such a fresh and youthful art."

Astoundingly, on a darkened canvas, muting his anguished theme, he had still conveyed "such brave truthfulness." From the tragic darkness had risen a lofty unity, and a grave poetic communication.

Note: Apparently the original script, and possibly a limited edition of the play run off in December of 1932, concurrent with production, did really call for the "Marseillaise." It was to be sung as "a funeral march" for the dying Bulichev. This must have been both dramatic and provocative—and Gorky more reckless than one would have supposed—for then Bulichev's death was unmistakably also the death of the idealistic Revolution. The deletion of the "Marseillaise," and the wrangle over what should replace it, probably account for the dark confusion at the ending. As the play appears in Gorky's collected works, there are no stage directions.

# CHAPTER 38

"BULICHEV" did not mark a final turn. The dying shudders of faith were prolonged; besides, Gorky had probably gone too far, and needed to protect himself. A play written the following year, "Dostigaev and Others," was meant to be more acceptable to the Party. He managed to bring off a work ambiguous but with power and solidity. Whatever went on in his depths, and had burst out in "Bulichev," in everyday life he still defended the dream. Perhaps the strength to hang onto it was his chief strength.

There were things he himself had inspired into being, which demanded his loyalty. One such thing was the belief that it was possible to remake character. This was being done, among young vagabonds and orphans—like Gorky—by Makarenko.

The heart of Gorky's social belief was that a sharp changing of the psyche was necessary for Russia; and that restoring the collective soul could make man "a friend to man, comrade and brother." This kind of "psychic engineering" Makarenko was dutifully attempting. His waifs were formed into the Gorky Labor Colony; they were to live for the collective.

If Gorky was a melange of desperate yearning and a put-on naïveté masking a deep pessimism, Makarenko—as befits the disciple, born in the 1880's and weaned on Gorky's early romanticism—was trule naïve. His "theory," still a cornerstone of modern Soviet education, was mainly a fervent belief in his outcasts as human beings. What this bespectacled spindly ascetic had to offer was unsparing purity of dedication.

A kid himself, he pioneered with his kids, hacking out their "road to life" in unbelievably primitive conditions, until they raised all their own food, ran tractors, and had a six-crop rotation. They had grown up in Civil War; he organized them on military lines, in "detachments" with rotating leadership, complete with salute, procession on "proletarian holidays," bugle, drum. It was all imaginative training for a collective society—democratic, or totalitarian. Good and bad are inextricably mingled in this offshoot of Gorky's dreaming.

Gorky's letters Makarenko read aloud to their assemblies, during their "peaceful meditative poetic evenings" by campfires. "I would like my 'Childhood' to be read," Gorky wrote, "by the colonists in the autumn evenings. From it they will see that I was just like them, only from my early youth I had the sense to stick to my desire to study, and was never afraid of work. I have always believed 'It's dogged as does it!' "

It seems, somehow, as if a forking off had already taken place, between this fond letter and the program of the colony. Makarenko, forming his lads and lasses in disciplined, paramilitary ranks, to march toward ennoblement by meaningful work, could not but begin an engineering of souls rather different from Vasska Buslayev's dream of freedom.

Makarenko made a striking finding: that the young did not feel the greatest respect and love for those who were affectionate to them, but to those who showed knowledge, the ability to work, success. He made a real contribution to the world's educational theory, with these simple, rueful, hard conclusions. They also contain dangers. Possibilities of use and misuse lie together in their seemingly artless depths.

Glasses glittering, Makarenko plunged on. He saw a "profound analogy between industrial and educational processes." Many details of human personality and behavior could, thus, be made from dies, "simply stamped out en masse," though the dies must be the finest and most precise.

This was a natural step, for one brought up on the Leninesque worship of technology, the mechanistic theory of human nature. It was a step farther from Gorky's vision of the free individual.

The next stop was fateful, but probably inevitable, given the configuration of forces in Russia as it entered the Iron Age.

The professional educators had fought Makarenko. He found sudden financial and moral support from the dread internal police, the Cheka. And through Makarenko and his "Gorkyists," the internal police, killers out of idealism, also became crucially important for the climax of Gorky's own story.

All this is weird only if one forgets the double edge of the Cheka's role. Its men were the moral guardians of the Revolution, as well as its bloody cleansers. Because of the kind of Revolution it had made, the Party was forced to set this heroic image of the Chekists before the land.

In the Chekists, Makarenko somehow found for his young charges a model. Here were living personalities of the new, hoped-for stamp!—guided by principles, but not their slaves; terse of speech; disliking formulas; full of "gay, unlimited capacity for work."

The play of "Somov" showed that Gorky, too, made a brief, half-hearted effort to see in the terse, gay Cheka-men the new Russian ideal. Master and disciple exerted an unquestionable mutual influence.

The touching climax of Makarenko's "Road to Life"—his story of the Gorky Colony—is the long-awaited visit by Gorky.

The salute to the colors, the swish of boys' hands, their burning eyes, their open hearts—all those were laid at the feet of our guest like a carpet. Gorky moved along the ranks...

And as Gorky's visit ended, Makarenko sadly informed his young Gorkyists that he himself was being transferred, to run the Dzerdzinski Commune, in modern buildings built for him by the Cheka. Into the stream of his noble, poetic experiment in education would now flow, joining Gorky's vision, the rather different spirit of the security police.

And from now on, for Gorky to be in touch with Makarenko's work and use his influence to help the homeless kids—the bezprizornie—he had to work through the security police: the proper administrative channel. This meant constant and close contact with the GPU, and made surveillance over him, his contacts and correspondence, go more smoothly.

Old Bulichev had muttered: "It's as if—I'm under arrest."

The arrangements of his Soviet life therefore naturally included frequent contact with Yagoda, chief of the GPU, and his assistants. One of them, Pogrebnitsky, seems to have been really Gorky's friend; he was directly in charge of the work with homeless children. In the years of blood that began almost at once after Gorky's death, Pogrebnitsky was one of the many who killed themselves.

Attached to Gorky also, leechlike, was Kriuchkov, who by now seems to have controlled arrangements for all new editions of Gorky's works. It is hard to find someone who will say a good word for Kriuchkov.

Besides his GPU job, he apparently held a job in Stalin's private security police—which watched over the GPU.

A young writer who admired Gorky once asked the old writer: "What do you need fellows like *that* [Kriuchkov] around you for?" Gorky gave that diffident wave of his hand: "It's all nonsense. Forget it."

An old, bedraggled Danko blunders through desolate bogs, still bearing aloft his burning heart. It still crackles spurts of flame, but sometimes (for it is burning out) it emits a pall of smoke; he coughs, staggers, runs on . . . half-blinded by despair's smoke . . . some people, who believe in him, still following. Danko himself has long given up the milk-and-honey vision . . . but the myth is needed . . . without it, what will sustain Russia . . . ?

Trying to explain how Makarenko survived the bloody thirties, an American sociologist points out that his theories of education seemed to promise to produce the type of human needed for the Iron Age; but adds that, besides, Makarenko served "by sustaining the original fraternal vision of the Socialist Revolution, long after it became clouded by the realities of Soviet life."

This probably applies as much to Makarenko's mentor, Gorky. He was the carrier of the old sacred flame and creative myth into an age of bitter reality.

This was not all cynicism on the part of Stalin and others. Gorky's own desperate belief was that the myth of today might be the reality of tomorrow. Here was probably a real meeting point for him and Stalin—not in any "ideological loyalty," which was not in Gorky. It probably explains his survival until the terms of survival became intolerable.

Stalin, in his own morose and tortured way, clearly believed in the myth of Danko; and the idea of "engineering souls" was as much Gorky's as his—the term may even have been coined by Gorky.

The function of the myth for Stalin was shown by an incident long after Gorky was ashes in an urn, and after the ravages of World War II.

The Soviet film industry had at last moved from the powerful strident movies of revolution and civil war into its Hollywood phase. The first new-style major movie was "The Stone Flower": a beautiful old fairy-tale in color of a hero who finds an undersea elixir of happiness. Stalin invited the American ambassador to a private preview. After, as they walked out, he touched the American's elbow, looked up at him long and earnestly, and said: "You see, the people still need myths. Some day they will be able to accept the reality."

A great difference is shown, in this statement by the old theological student, between his view and Gorky's desperate faith in the transforming spiritual virtue of the myth, but the same belief in the need for the myth. For Stalin, there was no romantic human transformation; but the myth, the "gold sleep" that Gorky had sung, was a necessary anesthetic, for the terrible time of transition, until industrialization and education had done their engineering work. He considered himself not theory's, but history's, slave.

All roads seemed to lead to the security police.

One of Gorky's projects, as "superintendent of writers," was the creation of a panel of writers working on a "History of Factories and Industrial Enterprises." This effort to churn out history re-edited "from the point of view of the working class" employed many writers who otherwise might have had a hard time proving their loyalty and making a living. He was trying to repeat, as best he could, what he had done during the first years after the Revolution.

In 1931 the Soviet government decided to build the White Sea–Baltic Canal. This would link Leningrad with Archangelsk, Karelia with the rest of the Union, the rivers of Asia with the Baltic and Atlantic. It was one of the feats of construction which made a powerful modern state.

The job was done by "forced labor": that of imprisoned revolutionary idealists and democrats, of great numbers of the old-fashioned liberal intelligentsia, of recalcitrant peasants, of engineers convicted of sabotage, and of vagabonds, thieves, murderers.

"It was Stalin who started the idea of building the White Sea–Baltic Canal with prisoners, because under his leadership such a method of reform appeared possible." It was also on Stalin's direct initiative that the Party entrusted to the security police (the GPU, née Cheka) the managerial responsibility.

In August of 1933 the Party sent out a call for writers to make a trip to the site of the canal. At once Gorky called together the board of "The History of Factories." Four days later, one hundred and twenty writers, with Gorky in the lead, made the trip. Thirty-four of them then formed a committee for a "group writing project": a book, to be done at high speed, about the construction of the canal and the spiritual reconstruction of the "enemies of the state" who were constructing it.

These thirty-four included names known, and to be known, in Russian literature: Vyacheslav Ivanov, Kataev, Dmitry (once, Prince) Mirsky, Zoschenko, Zelinsky, Alexey Tolstoy, Vera Inber... These were not hacks; there was talent to burn. Most of them were still young; Gorky was old; the moral responsibility was his, and he must have known it.

The writers probably spent two to three weeks in actual contact with the construction camps. They interviewed members of the GPU—thirty-seven of these were said to be all that were used to supervise the many thousands of prisoners. They talked to probably a couple of dozen prisoners (carefully screened) at length; with others, on the run.

The book's plan was then drawn up and the work allotted; conferences were held to discuss the manuscript. All thirty-four took full responsibility: "They helped one another, corrected one another." It was like the putting together of the song by those two women in Arzamas—the cooperative creative effort. This makes it impossible to know who wrote what.

Only one section is set off, in direct quotes: the contribution of Zoschenko, that admirable satirist, whose mocking sketches of Soviet life would later give the Party's literary expert, Zhdanov, heartburn. It was as if Zoschenko wanted it clear he was vouching only for what he himself said. He had seen at close range, he wrote, the rehabilitation, through labor on the canal, of one highly picturesque Jewish gangster from Odessa.

Swiftly, in January 1934, a beautiful volume was published, "full of praise for agents of the GPU and miracles performed by prisoners." At once it was translated (ably) into English. It became an important means of convincing Westerners that Soviet labor camps were not like those of Nazi Germany; that "group effort"—by writers and prisoners alike—was a thrilling USSR patent; and that imprisoned engineers put in charge of the enormous and technical task had really been anti-Soviet plotters, but had been redeemed by good treatment, their own patriotism, and the redemptive value of useful work.

The book has been called, by two of the most knowledgeable critics of Soviet society, Dallin and Nicolaevsky, "a monumental hypocrisy, humiliating to Soviet writers." They go on: "No doubt, only a few of the authors believed what they wrote; as for the rest, they were merely carrying out orders... Maxim Gorky belonged to the first group. He was a strange mixture of great literary talent and childish naïveté. Almost until his death, he wanted to believe that the avowedly terroristic Soviet regime was in the process of establishing a community of human brotherhood." His name, they add, was used by the security police "to cover up many a crime and monstrous cruelty."

Yet the book has eloquence, the feel of sincerity. Of course much of these may have been supplied by Gorky, Averbakh and Firin, the final editors (the last two undoubtedly representing RAPP and the Party); but hardly all of it.

Were they all, then, naïve fools? ("What do you consider yourself," Bulichev asked the trumpeter, "a fool or a swindler?") The charge of naïveté must have been anticipated. Zoschenko, as if under instructions, expressly called attention to the fact he was never noted for being naïve; of course, by confining himself rigidly to one case of "conversion," he used his escape hatch.

Against accepting the book's eloquence as truth, there is too much direct and burning testimony, of what went on in Soviet labor camps in those years—when at least five million lived, and a good proportion died, in them. ("It's prison camp for everyone," Tikhon Vialov had said, prophetically, to the dying Artamanov.) A half a million were conscripted for the Baltic–White Sea Canal; at its completion, about 12,000 were amnestied, and sentence was shortened for about 60,000. But reliable evidence says that the majority of those "liberated" were quickly shipped to work on another epic project, the Moscow–Volga Canal. The chief of the prisoner-engineers who built the Baltic–White Sea Canal was arrested again in 1937, and disappeared. Most of the others who took outstanding parts in the work similarly perished.

Naïveté is one thing, lies another. There really was, as part of the Revolution's psychology, an image of the heroic security police. To young writers to whom the ash-gray coats, the leather jackets, the steady rifles, of the Chekists were a knightly thing, making heroes of these men was not dishonesty. These men "knew the truth," and sacrificed themselves and, if necessary, others for it. No man could do more.

The downright lies are mostly of omission. Reading the book, it is as if there were no imprisoned socialists and anarchists and innocent liberals, men and women, condemned to death—without amnesty—in the prison camps and on these "heroic" projects.

If it were possible to lay aside the lies, and the knightly image of the guardian-killers, there is in the book a magnificent idea, a poetic faith—the rebuilding of personality and character, through ennobling labor—Gorky's old dream. Only in reality's unwelcome daylight does it strike as chill, tragic, macabre.

Did Gorky know the reality of "the great Stalin canal" was different? This is probably the point at which to face the question of whether, in general, he knew what was going on or was a man of "childish naïveté," a constant weaver of "uplifting" self-deceptions and illusions. The evidence of the preceding chapters seems clear: he knew. The man who wrote "Bulichev" had never really been taken in. Playing dumb was Luka's favorite cunning defense.

Rolland or Zweig could plead ignorance; Brecht, youthful, and against the closer Nazi perspective, could shout foolishly: "Wallow in filth, embrace the butcher—but change the world!" But Gorky had never been an extremist; he was right there; and he knew. To say he was a naïve, unrealistic dupe is doing him no favors. He knew; did what he could; took on himself the sins he had to. This was what Grandma had advised, and what Grandpa had done.

He knew this also: that slaves had built great empires and civilizations in the past, and their brutal rulers were—and are—admired, deified, held up as models for humanity. Stalin, morose, literal-minded man, and his party paladins, were only putting lessons of history to use. One like Gorky could only take part in the inexorable process while ameliorating it and saving lives where he could, keeping the hope and dream of a different reality alive, in himself and others, as long as possible; or escape from where the kingdom had perished from foulness; or, in a final fist fight, die.

If he misled these young writers, maybe he thought he was protecting the lives of some of them; and maybe he was. Some of them certainly wanted to be misled—needed to be misled, to believe they were helping build a fairer land.

There is evidence, in all Gorky's late works, that he regarded himself as doing much sinning. "Of course I'm a sinner—I've injured people, and in general sinned in all kinds of ways," Bulichev said. "Without fraud, one can't live," the trumpeter told Bulichev, and the old man cried, "True, brother! ..." And before that, Stepan Razin had shouted that nobody could do any good without doing evil. This was one of the hard and terrible conclusions of Gorky's whole life. He never really accepted it, searched for an answer, never found one—until the final clarity, that ushered in death.

## CHAPTER 39

FRAGMENTARY and elusive are the insights into the aging, perplexed, doggedly active, unhappy Gorky. To Russians of today, that Gorky, like the earlier one, is almost unknown. As one critic says: "The ordinary Soviet mortal must now penetrate a dense adulatory barrage, if he ever wants to see the real Gorky face to face."

He continued getting and welcoming the offerings of beginning writers, sending them long critiques. The specific advice he gave was, on the whole, useless, and would only have made it harder for them to find their own styles. But that was unimportant. He cared; he "taught" them that somebody could care.

"Literacy is absolutely necessary for all people, especially those who occupy themselves with literature," he told them. They must approach literature "as a serious and difficult labor, love and respect that labor, display stubbornness in it, strive to make things as well as possible." Such remarks are permeated with his desire for Russia.

One who peers through the adulatory barrage may see him—in publications he himself controlled, not dedicated to the Beautiful Lie—outlining a proposal for a series of books to introduce children and young people to the physical and natural sciences; urging another series of comparative studies of peoples, depicting their essential unity in their diversity; directing young writers toward a study of the literatures of the non-Russian nationalities. He seems to have been trying to project the ideas and methods recommended by the old historian Buckle—of an integrated education, toward the discovery of "the one vast scheme of the universal order," physical and moral.

At the same time there was appearing, under his by-line, a stream of articles in the official press, lauding the Party as the natural leader of the people, speaking of "love of Party" as the source of the people's strength . . . These, by the evidence of style alone, as well as of Gorky's thought through the years, were undoubtedly ghost-written.

What Gorky really felt about love of Party comes fairly clear in an essay that is genuine with the unmistakable clear charm of his real writings. It is not about an intellectual-bolshevik, or a careerist, but about a worker-bolshevik, whose orientation could be the most readily justified. This was Kamo, the lovable gangster who had been Gorky's unrequested bodyguard on the eve of 1905; who had later carried out picturesque train robberies for Lenin and Stalin; who had survived Tsarist tortures; and had materialized again before Gorky in 1920, in Red Army uniform and wanting to become a student, to gain the know-how that would help construct bolshevism. Gorky's soft spot for him can be appreciated, Kamo was a barefoot bum whose faith in a Cause seemed (to Gorky) to promise that he might rise from banditry to idealism. Gorky hoped to make Kamo into a writer, and actually set him to work on his memoirs.

And now, in 1932, looking back at Kamo, Gorky wrote for an obscure magazine:

For me Kamo is one of those revolutionaries for whom the future is more real than the present. This does not at all mean that they are dreamers, no, it means that the strength of their emotional revolutionary class feelings is so harmoniously and strongly organized that it feeds the reason, serves as the base for its growth, goes—as it were—before them. Outside of revolutionary work all of the actuality in which their class lives seems to them something like a nightmare, a hallucination, while the real actuality, in which they live—that is the socialist future.

The balanced, realistic, dispassionate view of the old Gorky could not be clearer; nor the carefulness with which he had to work—like a lens-grinder; the method by which he communicated honestly and still survived in his role. The first sentence is his essential statement of the visionary nature of the best in bolshevism. The second ("This does not at all mean . . .") is for the Party, to make his essay on Kamo acceptable while keeping the kernel of his integrity. The third and last sentence, most carefully ground, with gentleness and sympathy expressed for socialism (in which he always believed), memorializes the touching, pathetic and hysterical quality of the worker-bolshevik at his noblest. Kamo was understandable, Gorky is saying; while his pointed use of the present tense throughout means that he is speaking of the bolshevik type—existing at the moment of writing, in 1932. Kamo was dead; but the type—with or without Kamo's crude idealism—was the apparatus of Stalin.

Dispassionate, realistic, calm, was the view Gorky was trying to achieve on everything, as a last defense in the vast darkness of disillusionment. It was at the farthest remove from the visions and delusions of the Party "hallelujah-shouters" and the Kamos. It was a logical step from the amused and tragic regard he had turned on reality in the "Notes."

To a friend, in an unguarded moment, he declared his ambition: simply to portray the world and man as they were, without the myth of love, "repudiating nothing, praising nothing"; repudiation was unjust, while praise was premature—"for we live in chaos and ourselves are fragments of chaos." He compared his desire with that of Einstein, "trying to alter radically our representation of the universe."

This effort to rise to the cosmic level, to pretend *not to care*, so as to reconcile intolerable reality with the need for continued life, is strong testimony to the inner desperation of the Holy Wanderer, in those last iron years; and to the continued constructive power of his yearning imagination.

And he was also holding down that other job, as "superintendent of writers."

Around his friendships with the writers who had broken through (not the "would-bes"), thick mists of hagiography have risen. It is hard to tell what his relation really was with men like Leonov, Sholokhov, Zoschenko, Gladkov, Furmanov, Fedin. Did he "reconcile" them—that word once hateful to him—to the reality, and to what the Party wanted? Did he help them keep their integrity? Protect them? Apparently, all three.

Leonov: "Few of us there are who do not have letters from him, received just when they were most needed. This friendly participation and support by an old master, whom we all believed absolutely, more than once gave us strength for our future work."

Babel, one of the century's most gifted stylists, wrote: "I owe everything to that meeting [with Gorky] and to this day speak the name of Alexey Maximovich with love and gratitude." Gorky made it possible for him to be published. Then, Babel's "Red Cavalry" stories, with their mordant searching look at the quality of humanity in the ranks of the glorious Red fighters, raised a violent Party protest. Gorky defended Babel on the preposterous grounds that he had portrayed moral heroes, since they were consecrated by their very cause. The most passionate story of his own childhood, the story of a Jewish boy during a pogrom, Babel dedicated to Gorky.

Sholokhov, powerful novelist who has always ultimately accepted the

Party's view of history, is another whose comments on Gorky, as adviser and conciliator among writers, ring very true. And the second volume of Sholokhov's classic, "The Quiet Don," was published only through Gorky's efforts; the Party did not want it to appear.

Even the words of the Party fanatic, Fadeyev, sound genuine: "... Among Soviet literary people there is hardly one who was not touched in large and small degree by the educational influence of Gorky."

Fadeyev not only emasculated his own work at the Party's request; he hounded "deviating" writers. After Gorky's death, he was the head of the Union of Soviet Writers; and the memoirs of Pasternak indicate he carried out what he considered his duty to the Party only too well. It is hardly likely he knew what he was doing; his own novels breathe idealism. After Khrushchev's 1956 speech revealing some of the murders of the Stalin era, Fadeyev passed from heavy drinking to suicide. Pasternak imagines him—"with that guilty smile"—looking into the mirror, taking leave of himself with, say, these words: "Well, there, all's finished. Goodby, Sasha."

There is known to have been severe correspondence between Gorky and Fadeyev. It seems only likely that it was over human rights versus duty to Party. It has not yet been made public. One can only guess Gorky tried, without much luck, to influence Fadeyev.

Occasionally, in the various "reminiscences" about Gorky, something else comes through—showing starkly the shame men who had long admired him felt watching Gorky as Stalin's "superintendent" ... but also conveying other things ...

Alexey Maximovich looked us in the eye with a severe gaze and stated: "The master and, let us add, the boss of the time, our Yosif Vissarianovich [Stalin]."

These words—Yosif Vissarianovich—he spoke so sharply, hotly, and at the same time without the slightest affectation, that to him these words as he pronounced them were not only pleasant, but also very beautiful. Sometimes, in minutes of special tenderness, he spoke another word, sounding almost inspired on his lips: "The Boss." His eyes gave out a sharp and strong gleam. He would take out his handkerchief, wipe his eyes and then smile, as if himself a little surprised, that it was possible to pronounce so well and tastily the word "boss" ...

While hating the property-owning bosses of old, the writer went on, in the same tone of mock lyricism, Gorky had always dreamed of a "true boss ... authentic, wise, beautiful and brave in all his deeds." And now, together with millions of others, he had won the right to see the authentic boss—the Soviet man—and specially that "first of the first bosses of in-spiration: the mighty revolutionary and scholar—Stalin."

This essay, with its transparent mocking irony, was published in Stalin's lifetime; that it got by the censor is a sorry reflection on the mental apparatus of the watchdogs of the Party apparatus. And its author had gone unerringly to the flaw in the center of Gorky's work of faith, "The Confession"—that dangerous longing for a "boss of life": a fantasy now come true.

Another momentary glimpse: Gorky sits reading a poem published by one of the really gifted young writers of the time. The young poet—and this was an indication of the spirit in which the young had been raised, and still lived, as the flame burned—spoke of the Iron Age, the muse presid-ing over their days, in which the Soviet Union stood girt by its foes:

> If it [the Iron Age] says lie—lie.
> If it says kill—kill.

Gorky takes up one of the thick, colored pencils he loved to use, circles these lines, and in the margin places a heavy **?** .

There is a scene of Gorky calling writers together, at The Hillocks. He was planning a new group writing project—biographies of the builders and engineers who had made the Dnieprestroy Dam. He had requested a budget of several million rubles for the book. This one they could put their hearts into without qualms.

The writers arrived by nine A.M., many rubbing away sleep. Gorky came downstairs in his now famous blue blouse, his hair wet. As they talked, Gorky's secretary glided over and said, "Yosif Vissarianovich is on the phone." Gorky got up and started hurriedly from the room. Then, says the writer who recalls this, "he remembered he was Gorky—and slowed down."

In a minute he returned, walking with assurance, looked around with "a cunning smile," and said, "The senior comrade advises us to be econom-ical and not throw money around." Cheerfully, they went on with their meeting.

But before our gallant band, with their gallant leader, could even start throwing money around, nearly all the engineers and builders who were to be their subjects were suddenly arrested as saboteurs and "liquidated."

Again the old Holy Wanderer had been "taken." For all his cunning smile, he was a credulous being, awandering in the senior comrade's incredible jungle.

The tangled strife and politicking by which the Party firmed its grip on literature was reflected first in efforts by RAPP (the Russian Association of Proletarian Writers, the Party's tool) to blacklist or pressure into conformity the non-Party writers, then in RAPP's sudden disbanding and its replacement by the all-inclusive Union of Soviet Writers.

Gorky was involved in the infighting against RAPP and within RAPP, and probably helped in its downfall. Actually the change seems to have been a further step in the use of literature as a tool of politics. Writers, Party and non-Party, were now to be conscious agents in pushing industrialization and collectivization. To what extent Gorky was a cat's-paw would be hard to determine.

But he had defended men like Babel against RAPP's efforts to blacklist them. When RAPP was dismembered, it was time for some of its leaders to be scapegoats; then Gorky defended the beaten RAPP-ists, like Averbakh, and got jobs for them on the staff of "The History of Factories."

He was made the head of the new Union of Soviet Writers, in 1934, made a keynote speech on a properly remote, properly inspiring level, and seems to have cut a sorry figure. But it was because of his personal insistence, to Stalin, that Bukharin and Radek, long on their way to ostracism and the Lubyanka Prison, were invited to speak at that congress; thus he prolonged their lives, and Bukharin gave a keen estimation of Soviet poetry. It was probably also due to Gorky that Babel was asked to speak, and thus hauled partway out of disfavor; on the rostrum, Babel explained to the assembled writers his current literary experiments—he was cultivating the literary genre of "silence."

The talented novelist Pilnyak had written a story about a Soviet general who, urged by a political boss to undergo an operation, died on the operating table. By one of those mad coincidences, Frunze, a top Red Army general, had failed to come through an operation urged on him by Stalin.

Frunze's ghost was mollified by the naming of the chief Soviet military academy after him; but apparently Gorky had to mollify Stalin. The price he paid is not known; but Pilnyak stayed alive and even free until after Gorky's death—some years of grace. This was more than Aristotle had been able to wring out of Alexander, for his own brother-in-law.

Zamyatin was a tormented writer of great talent. His book "We" was the first of the weird, powerful "negative utopias"—an outcry at the horror of a collectivized world, but also, by echo, against the whole trend of modern life. Huxley would unashamedly base his "Brave New World" on this novel. When "We" came out in Czechoslovakia, in Russian, Zamyatin was in bad trouble. Gorky went to Yosif Vissarianovich, and got permission for Zamyatin to emigrate. He lived out his life—though unproductive of literary achievement—in exile.

So, if Gorky was used, and a cat's-paw, he also got his price. If he naïvely thought he could really change anything, bring about some unity, avert the new horrors now rising ahead, that was the illusion, as always, of his kind of man. The men he put his mantle over lived on at least until after his death, when the time for mass fratricide set in. Many think it could not begin until Gorky was dead.

One Soviet critic says: "His attitude was always: 'We are all doing one work. We should not quarrel.' He considered group warfare unprincipled."

This deadly group warfare, among writers and through all the veins of the regime, is the subject of one short poem by Gorky that survived, of all the hundreds he must have written in those last years—one each morning. It ends:

> I bawl: All-Holy Mother!
> What can I hit them with
> Over the head, so they'll
> Stop and consider?

The moment when he gave up even the daydream that a good tap on the skull would cure anybody, Yosif Vissarianovich or anybody else— that moment of final despair, the extinguishing of the last spark of illusion breathed on by tender hope—is hard to pinpoint. But it came.

One Soviet "Gorky-scholar" insists that Gorky still "believed in" even the trials of 1934, following the assassination of Kirov.

If Gorky was credulous about this, at least at first, he had much company. Only after Khrushchev's 1956 speech has it become generally believed that Kirov was killed on Stalin's orders, and his killing then laid on mythical "plotters," as an excuse for all the trials and killings to follow.

Still, it seems only logical—given the peculiar way that killing was "investigated," and the fact that Gorky was, perforce, in close contact with leaders of the security police—that the inside story finally came to him; and with it a final turn in the long road. This was at the end of 1934.

And besides, it was in late 1934 that Gorky's son, Maxim, suddenly died (at the age of thirty-seven) of "pneumonia, complicated by intestinal disorder." At the graveside, friends had to hold up the weeping old writer, or he would have fallen.

Max had been a stalwart communist; but with a doting father to whom he was unusually attached, whose true feelings in politics ranged from private doubt to private despair, it is not likely that Max was a Stalinist. Nor was he one who could keep his mouth shut; and he had a talent for mimicry and caricature, verbally and in art. These factors were an excellent combination for nonsurvival.

It seems clear that for old Gorky—now, after Max's death, one has a right to call him old—by 1935 faith was no longer possible. The most convincing evidence, in his own creative writings, will follow. The time had come for the final and terrible despair, and whatever strength he could muster to meet it.

And the time was also coming when the great purges, long in blueprint, could no longer be postponed. The whole subject of the slaughter by a revolution of its children is mysterious. But it is clear that the group warfare, by the "logic of things," had opened into the next stage: the fanatical idealists of the 1880's and 1890's needed to be destroyed by the realists now in control of the Party, their younger fanatics of the apparatus, and their Calibans (a new breed). Some of the original revolutionaries had become disillusioned, and there is nothing worse than an ex-believer. Some were haunted by old romantic notions of "freedom," and therefore opposed the rough measures needed to forge a modern totalitarian state. Some probably still dreamed they could change the balance, and leadership, of the Party.

And, it seems fairly clear, the liquidation of many of them was also needed so as to free the government to move, if necessary, toward alliance with Nazi Germany. All the dread events of the years now beginning echo with the question that must have tormented the Party: whether a military-political rapprochement with Hitler would be brilliant, or fatal.

The decision to proceed with the purges must have gone deep into the psychology of the system. To dump it on Stalin alone is historically unsound.

To Gorky, whose main drinking companions in his despair must have been the top GPU officials—Yagoda, Pogrebnitsky, Menzhinsky—what was being planned could not but have become known. The question now rose: what would be his attitude? And, if it was negative, was his usefulness at an end? In the Boss's balance sheet, at what point would he become a liability?

## CHAPTER 40

GORKY by 1935 faced reality, and saw what lay ahead. That he was shattered by what he saw, and hardly knew where to turn, is clear.

What he felt is all spelled out in two plays, which he had first written more than twenty-five years earlier on Capri, and now, in his last year of life, worked over, inserting the grim contemporary story into the skin of the old one. They are not the unified achievements "Bulichev" was; the new content is too overwhelming. For that very reason, however, the stark and poignant words stand out unmistakably.

"The Zikovs" (the closest he ever came to duplicating the sound of his own name, Peshkov) is, on its face, his constant story again: of a middle-class family that runs a business. But the underlying plot, as in "Bulichev," beats its way to the surface: the effort of the spirit, besieged by darkness, to find a way.

Central figure is Sofia, capable widow, manager of the business. As the play goes on, it is seen that Sofia is, as her name says, the Holy Wisdom; and that she is also—Russia. Her brother is the violent but warm-hearted lumber merchant, Antipas. There is Paula, the too gentle girl: a spiritual-ized figure, the gentle Christian soul, the unworldly conscience. Antipas has taken her away from his too weak son, Mikhail. (Again, as "On a Raft," the theme of the strong, the natural, taking what they want; and also Gorky's vision of the freedom of men and women in their love.) But Paula, hurt, pure, idealistic thing, only wants to escape, to sleep "for a year . . . three years . . . and wake up—and everything will be different." Gorky, from exile, watching Russia with heartbreak, had written exactly the same thing in a letter—only he had wanted to sleep out the century!

"A German," suitor for Sofia's hand, gives her his findings about Russia, over a period of eighteen years. (From 1917, when Soviet history began, to 1935, when the play was rewritten, makes eighteen.) He tells Sofia: "Russia suffers from a shortage of healthy people, able to set clear goals . . . You have much metaphysics, little mathematics." Then, "You are a woman of mind and character . . . I even think of you allegorically: Sofia Ivanovna —the new healthy soul of Russia, who, in circumstances worthy of her, is capable of achieving everything, is able to do much cultural work."

Therefore he proposes a union. "When two strong figures understand their problems . . . that is very important, especially for Russia, on that day when she will have to, finally, throw aside all . . . dreamings . . . take in hand the simple matters of life."

Gorky's own view was that Russia needed to cast aside fanatical dreaming, Marxist metaphysics, and get to the hard work of building a cultured, happier nation. But the rub is that the German is also clearly speaking for those Russians who wanted a military alliance with Germany. Throughout the last, mysterious plays of Gorky is the echo of this inner struggle, that must have agitated Party and government. And the very next lines make clear Gorky's own stand.

For Sofia abruptly turns the German down, as a "thief." She has on her table documents showing his "crooked deals, forgeries, attempted bribes . . ." She bids him get out.

The play's mysterious heart, however, is Sofia's defiance of a man named Muratov: a man who once seemed honest ("Long ago—six years ago—I thought well of him"), but proved dishonest, in wielding his great power as the supervisor of Sofia's (Russia's) forests and estates. He had formerly done useful things for the peasants, but then suddenly got "blinded and mean" . . . He makes everyone quarrel, is a liar, and "not clean in regard to women." He lives terribly, Sofia tells Muratov to his face, "loving nothing and nobody."

This phrase, repeated, arrests the reader. The man at the center of Russia's history in Gorky's last days—and for years before and after—was a man against whom the chief accusation that makes sense is that he "loved nothing and nobody." There is only one portrait of Stalin in Soviet literature, and this is it, in "The Zikovs."

Muratov strikes back, mocking Sofia: "Such as I, are thousands; such as you, only solitary ones. You are completely superfluous. You don't even have anywhere to turn. Formerly you could go to the Revolution, but the Revolution is no longer needed by anyone."

The scene grows darker and more chaotic. Mad lines appear, that have no purpose in the plot. Paula suddenly cries out: "Dear ones—but you can't live without loving anyone, without pitying anyone . . . My dear people—can it really be that you are enemies to each other? . . . My God, my God . . . Somewhere there must be truth. You must search for truth." And Shokhin (Muratov's assistant, who once killed a man brutally, but is gnawed by remorse) says: "It's crowded. They can't see . . . who (kills) whose own . . ." A sense of blindness, and of tragic death-dealing, fills these mysterious discussions.

On various levels the soul's tormented dialogue goes on. Antipas and Shokhin talk of running away to a monastery, there to spend their last years and pray away their sins . . . Antipas' weak son suddenly tries to commit suicide. Antipas, in anguish, demands of Muratov an explanation: "Why? . . ." (These strange lines were undoubtedly written about a year after the sudden death of Gorky's son, Maxim.)

Antipas decides he must let Paula, the pure one, go. There is no room for pity, or even love. "Only Sofia I greatly respect. But to say I love— that's very dangerous." Is a translation needed? "To accomplish anything, for Russia, I cannot keep too pure a conscience. I cannot refuse to lend my name to lies, and even evil. If I spoke out, I could no longer do what little good I now can. I must only work on, in the sense of holy respect for Russia and her latent possibilities."

Then, a sudden shift. Over and over, Gorky's characters had insisted that without evil it is impossible to do good. Now, in this buried play near a life's end, appears a defiance absolutely new to Gorky, born either of old age or desperation. Antipas, tormented because Paula, the clean soul, now fears him insisted of loving him, suddenly shouts: "You won't get anywhere by removing yourself from evil . . . No, you've got to go to evil itself, strike at its heart, hurl it down, stamp on it, destroy it . . . I won't run away . . . Our life is a fist fight. I—won't run away." Shokhin says, cryptically, "We'll see." (What can it mean? Surely a decision by Gorky. What is the fist fight to come? "We'll see . . ." The time must have been late 1935. Gorky had perhaps nine months, perhaps ten, to live.)

To Paula, crying over lost "truth," Sofia says: "Truth can't be thought up, it has to be worked for . . . There's nothing for you to find—nothing has been lost . . ."

Paula: "I can't understand . . . anything . . ."

Sofia (sharply): " . . . You still haven't learned to love. When people love, all is clear . . . All happens by itself . . . On a sunny day one doesn't ask—why is it right? In your heart, it seems, the sun has not yet risen . . ." Gorky really could not abandon the notion of love; he raised it to a mystical level. To respect and work for Russia—that is the higher love.

And finally Sofia confronts Muratov and denounces him.

Sofia: "In your preserve in seven years (from 1928, the start of the

Iron Age, to 1935 makes seven) your Shokhins have killed and tortured some tens of people."

Muratov: "Well, not that many ..."

Sofia: "And how many have been put in prisons, how many families have been broken ...? Did you count that?"

Muratov: "No, of course not. And what business of yours are these statistics? Madam, all that is romanticism ..."

Sofia (rising): "Listen, Vasili Pavlovich: Yes, for me you are worse than Shokhin, worse than any drunken peasant—a peasant can be made into a man, but you—you are something hopeless ... It is not easy for me to tell you this ..."

It surely must have been far from easy to tell this to Stalin, even in masked form, in a play that never would be staged. And dangerous.

"Try being an honest man," Sofia adds.

Muratov: "But what is an honest man?"

"We have nothing to talk about!" she cries.

"That means," he tells her, "you cannot answer. You are terribly alone ... alone and powerless."

This, of course, was true. But Sofia then exclaims, to Muratov, who is Stalin—and this is perhaps the last outcry of the old romantic view that made the Revolution, and the continuing cry of a humanism which has always survived all the Muratovs:

"That's not true! There are, somewhere, people who feel life as I do ... In my soul there is light—that means, light also exists outside my soul; in my soul is faith in the possibility of a different life—that means, it exists in people, this blesssed faith. Much I do not understand, I am poorly educated, but I feel life is a blessing, and people—good ... And you always lie about people ... and even—against yourself ..."

Muratov (the unhappy, tormented man of steel): "I always speak the truth."

Sofia: " ... It is a dying truth!"

Muratov: "Till this day it has been considered immortal."

Sofia: "No—another truth lives and grows ... There is another Rus, not the one in whose name you speak! We—are strangers ... I am not a fellow-traveler of yours, and—we have finished, I trust?"

Muratov: "I'm confident that on the path to that other truth of yours you will break your neck."

They had, indeeed, just about finished. Late in 1935 Gorky interposed, without success, on behalf of Kamenev, at the first trial of the old bolsheviks—preliminary to their "show-trials" and slaughter. Muratov's parting words probably reproduce Stalin's last warning to Gorky.

For a moment, Sofia reveals, to her brother Antipas, the depths of her disappointment (this would be the last one): "If you only knew how agonizing it is to lose respect for a man . . . If you only knew how I have sought good people, how I believed . . . I would find one! I didn't . . . I'll still seek . . ."

But then she straightens. "Enough. We'll live alone. And it may be that good people will come, to teach us, help us. For there must be good people?" (This sentence, declarative, ends touchingly on a question mark.)

Antipas replies: "If we show that we are good, we'll find those who are good."

The final decision, by sister and brother, is one of strength. Antipas will not retreat to a monastery, but will *fight*, for what he believes in. Shokhin has agreed to stay too, and fight beside him. (Whoever Shokhin was in real life—Menzhinsky? Pogrebnitzky?—he went to his death as well.) Paula is sent away: farewell to naïve goodness, naïve idealism . . . Sofia is happy: we have not given way to grief; we fight on. She speaks as if from on high—like a goddess.

There is nobility in the whole ending. There is almost a happiness— that of, at last, an unambiguous decision, to do one's duty and struggle for values, even if it means . . . death. It is the closest thing to a happy ending in anything Gorky ever wrote, except "The Confesssion."

The other play, of Gorky's last tragic year, is "The Survivors"—literally, "The Last Ones." To give it this title, he disregarded the advice of friends, who feared for him. It can only mean the "last" of the idealists (like last leaves) who had believed in a humanistic revolution.

The form: outright Christian allegory. The main personae are the sisters Love and Faith; their brother Peter; Sofia (Wisdom, this time their despairing mother); the father, Ivan (John, who was once Yegudiil); John's brother Jacob (the ancient of days, unacknowledged father of Love).

The story—pasted over the plot of an old play of 1910—is undramatic, and hardly makes sense. The main theme, however, is clear: the betrayal of Love and Faith. And, through the parents' blindness, failure to meet moral issues, to stand up for their convictions . . . lack of strength to tell the truth . . . the whole family (the human soul) is destroyed.

The action is all internal dialogue, among the parts of the perplexed soul. And yet this allegory, this seemingly ethereal, Blake-like play of abstractions, is the vehicle for a dense, heartrending biographical statement: Gorky's horror at what has become of Russia; his despair at how he had compromised his own integrity; the continuation of the story of his betrayal by Stalin; his grief and guilt at his unwitting part in the destruction of his only son; his decision to flee, if he could, to the capitalist West; and—failing that—his realization that he had before him only one ultimate choice.

Faith prepares to sell herself to a rich man (the capitalist) to preserve something for the family (the soul) as it faces ruin. She can do nothing else; the man who claimed he loved her turned out to be a liar, dishonest, incapable of love (clearly, the man who "loved nothing and nobody": Muratov-Stalin). She realized this only after running away with him.

Sobbing with disillusionment, Faith describes to her mother, Sofia, her betrayal by "this villain." Sofia: "My own, my child..." Faith: "...My dear Mama, how did it happen? I joked, I played—tell me, is it not permitted to joke, to believe in the good?"

An awful vision, this late one of Gorky's: of Faith—the girl who lives in the human soul—in song and poetry playing, spelling out her dream, changing a land in accord with her happy yearning, creating a terrible world of fear and violence and terror.

Sofia (suddenly): "Peter, have you been drinking?" Peter: "Just a drop, Mama. Hardly any." Sofia: "Why? For you, that's suicide." Peter: "Suicide is stupid. It's terribly banal, when people of my age shoot themselves." (The temptation to suicide must have kept recurring to Gorky; and by now he was indeed drinking heavily.)

Peter has been at a gathering "at Kiril Alexandrovich's." (No such character appears; this can refer only to a meeting of the anti-Stalin Opposition.) He won't go there any more, "or, in general, over to that side. There... they demand of a man... understanding of life, respect for people, and so on, and I—I'm like an empty suitcase. Me they took along on the road by mistake, forgetting to fill me with the things necessary for a journey..."

(To Tolstoy, many years ago, Gorky had confided a dream that shook him, of an empty pair of boots marching along, on a long lonely road... It must have returned, charged with new dreadful emphasis. It is a dream of self-accusation: "I am a man without enough guts to risk joining the Opposition.")

Faith defends her father, who has been called dishonest; but Peter demands directly: "Father, are you an honest man?" (Gorky no longer had a son; but his grandchildren might some day look at him, asking him such questions.)

Sofia: "I can only say this. Forgive me, dear children, that I gave birth to you." Then, to her husband: "To beg their forgiveness, that is the only thing good that we can do ... I am guilty before you, before all, before each! What will become of you?"

The light this casts on the surrounding vista is—terrible.

The kindly Uncle Jacob—who had been sustaining the family—expires. They approach the dead man.

Love (quietly): "Only in this way can we leave this house. It is the only path ..."

Peter: "The other—is death of the soul."

This can only mean: "There are just two ways out of my situation. One is death, the other is dishonor." In these perhaps old-fashioned terms Gorky had always been accustomed to think. In these terms he must have made his final decisions ...

Death or dishonor. This was the choice, and 1936 was approaching.

One of the family says: "This (Jacob's death) was to be expected at any hour ... but still, death never arrives in time ..."

(Gorky had compromised himself, in many eyes, by those last six years of defending Stalin's Russia. His reputation as a writer and humanist was sullied. In this sense, death had not arrived in time.)

Now the father calls on the family, in the face of death's eternal mystery, to throw aside differences and quarrels, to embrace. "We are sacrifices of this awful time, its spirit poisons everything, destroys everything ..."

Fedosya, the old, old family nursemaid, angry, mutters in her corner.

The father continues desperately: "We need to remember ... the family is our security ... There is our strength, our protection ..." Sofia (quietly): "Stop it." Fedosya (her mumbling suddenly breaks into a sharp cry): "Heavenly Queen, take up your sorry slave ..." Peter: "If only I believed in God, I would go away to a monastery." (But the ending would be on earth, in the fist fight of life; for Gorky there could be no monastery of refuge again—Capri, Sorrento, or any other.)

Peter: "Wherein was I to blame? And Faith? And all of us?" Love: "Death faithfully serves the business of Life ... The weak—the unneces-

sary—perish . . ." Fedosya mumbles. Her words are indistinguishable. She
may fear to say them aloud.

So it ends. This play, and "The Zikovs," were probably his final statements in any depth. "The Survivors" has been dealt with after "The
Zikovs," but it is not known which he finished later. It would be nice to
think that "The Zikovs" was his last word, with its glimpse of Sofia and
her brother—the new dream-Russia and her Gorky—facing a better future,
transcending "this awful time" to which all are sacrifices; rather than the
utter terribleness of Peter's cry: "Wherein was I to blame? And Faith?
And all of us?"—and the heartbreaking muttering of the outraged old
nursemaid in her corner.

# CHAPTER 41

IN 1935 Gorky applied for a passport to attend an "international
        congress against war and fascism," in Paris; it was refused him.

Either late in 1935 or early in 1936 he applied for a passport again, to
go to Italy, on grounds of health. This was Luka's cunning trick, and it
had always worked before; but these were different times and "Muratov"
was a different kind of man. Gorky was told the climate in the Crimea
was as good for his health as in Italy.

There was no exit now, no refuge; it was, as he had predicted, physical
death or "death of the soul."

One who met him on the street in Moscow, early in 1936, was "shaken
by his appearance." He was an "unrecognizable skeleton." In intimate
company, it was said, he sat and "muttered"; during the nights, it was
said, he cried.

Gorky's position and importance are defined in a document often used
as a source for this period—the "Letter of an Old Bolshevik":

Gorky's influence had greatly fallen after the second Kamenev trial
[in the early spring of 1935], but . . . he remained until his death the only
person whom Stalin was compelled to take into consideration . . . It is
possible that had Gorky lived, the August 1936 trial (the first "show-
trial") might have had a different denouement . . .

Gorky went to the Crimea. There he was visited by the same Moroz to whom he had talked, after asking him if he knew how to "keep quiet," eight years earlier. Moroz was astonished and upset: Once tall and gaunt, Gorky had become "a completely hunched, tired man, no matter how bravely he tried to carry himself." Gorky, noticing his "agitation and tears," said soothingly: "You take everything too much to heart. Take everything with a certain coolness, and take care of your nerves and health. They'll still be useful to you in life. I understand you . . . It's hard and often even heavy on the soul but you have to remember that to stop with internal strength the wheel making the history of Russia is impossible. They've stepped in too far. Too powerful are the forces holding up and guarding reaction with the bayonet."

It was then that Moroz asked Gorky why in the world he had come back to Soviet Russia; and Gorky did state to him a justification. He said that Stalin's article (famous in history by its title: "Dizzy from Success"), which marked the dramatic reining in of brutal forced collectivization, was "the result of my insistence on making collectivization voluntary. This gives me a basis for looking more optimistically at the meaning of my coming to the USSR, although I really could not but come."

On May 26—suddenly, apparently—Gorky left Sevastopol for Moscow. On June 1, according to the official records, he fell ill. The first news was published on June 6. Bulletins began to appear in the press. On June 18, at 11:10 A.M., a bulletin, which was reprinted next day in *Pravda*, stated:

The Central Committee of the All-Russian Communist Party (bolshevik) and the Soviet of Peoples Commissars of the USSR with deep grief announce the death of the mighty Russian writer, the talented artist of the word, dedicated friend of the toilers, fighter for the victory of communism—Comrade Alexey Maximovich Gorky, which took place at The Hillocks, near Moscow, 18 June, 1936.

The medical conclusions were published: influenza, complicated by catarrh of the breathing passages and inflammation of the lungs; heavy infection on the base of chronic disease of the heart, vessels, and especially the lungs, "in connection with his old (contracted in childhood) tubercular process"; by the third day, weakened heart action, sharp blockage of breath. "By energetic application of all means . . . it was possible to keep up the action of the heart till the morning of 6/18. On the night

of 6/18 Alexey Maximovich fell into a coma, from 10 A.M. the heart's
activity began to fail, and at 11:10 death followed, in the 69th year of
life, with the appearance of paralysis of the heart and breathing."

A state funeral was at once announced, and the creation of a committee for "receiving the literary heritage and correspondence of Gorky."
Korin, an artist who had been a personal friend, did a sketch of him in
the casket. The sculptor Merkulov did a death mask. The casket was
brought to Moscow and placed in the Hall of Columns. Messages came,
not only from Soviet writers but from men like Romain Rolland ("We
share the grief of the whole Soviet people") and Wells ("One of the
mighty figures that moved forward the revolutionary process in Russia
has gone away into eternity").

On June 19 the Hall of Columns was open to the public. From 5:30
on, government and Party leaders stood vigil beside the casket: "Stalin,
Ordzhonikidze, Khrushchev, Mikoyan, Andreyev and others," to quote the
official record of Gorky's life. Cremation was between 7 and 8 that night.
On the 20th, a "meeting of mourning" in Red Square, an orchestra playing the "Internationale." Stalin, to the volleys of guns, carried the urn to
its niche. Molotov gave the speech:

"Comrades: Saying farewell today to Alexey Maximovich Gorky, we
... experience a feeling as if, for each of us, a certain bright part of our
own life is departing forever into the past ... Gorky was forced for many
years to wage a stubborn battle to tear himself away from heavy need and
grief ... He was thrown more than once into life's lower depths ... That
is why the workers and all toilers see in Gorky *themselves, their* man,
*their* life and fate, *their* future. That is why Gorky has been loved, is
loved, and will be loved by the toilers of our land and the toilers of other
lands."

Here was the image that would be projected—and one psychologically
sound; here was the "biography" that had long been ready, that needed
only his death.

"By the force of his influence on Russian literature," Molotov went
on, "Gorky stands with such giants as Pushkin, Gogol, Tolstoy ... Gorky
is the immortal friend of the toilers and the inspirer of the battle for
communism ... After the death of Lenin, the death of Gorky is the
heaviest loss for our land and for humanity."

One who apparently was present, as a youth, in the bright sun on Red
Square, says that Molotov's words sounded with "surprising sincerity."

Then, he writes, "under the slow and disturbing drum-roll the regiments of the Moscow division in steel helmets, with fixed bayonets, banners lowered toward the ground, began to march past the [Lenin] mausoleum with measured tread."

How treacherous is any reconstruction of that era is shown by the fact that this speech of Molotov's, the high point of the funeral, which "fixed" Gorky's image, is not even mentioned in the official record of Gorky's life and death; by the time that chronicle appeared, Molotov had fallen from power. The records of who bore the casket, who stood the vigil and so forth, are similarly doctored.

A man of finer quality than Molotov, who had no official part in the proceedings, the writer Paustovsky, also wrote, in his diary, about "The Day of Gorky's Death":

Death came on a summer day, when over Moscow noised warm thunders. He died facing the entire fullness of life, loved furiously and stubbornly, before the face of the naked leaf, the high sky, the grass of the fields, the sun glittering on the clouds and forests.

He died before the face of a new earth—rich, clean and beautiful. He ought not to have died at this hour.

Left is the sense of being orphaned, which strikes the heart.

Gorky's ashes were now in the Kremlin wall—that spot for which Khodasevich, who had held him dear, said he sold out.

The inscription on the marble plate marking his niche in that brooding wall:

ALEXEY MAXIMOVICH

28      GORKY      18

18 III 68        19 VI 36

His niche is flanked by the niches containing the ashes of Lenin's wife and Lenin's sister—two women he rather disliked. Presumably this helps establish his role: the gentle side of the Revolution.

But the story of Gorky's death was not to be that simple; like his life, it proved desperately complex, part of the very substance of the age's tragedy and drama.

Within a few weeks, rumors spread in Moscow, that he "had not died his own death." They were soon muted, however, by the din of the events that followed, for which his death may have been a signal. These events were the great "purges"—what has been called "the ritual of liquidation"—whereby the Party and the state were "cleansed" of outlived forms: the dreamers and doers of an outlived day.

There was a series of staged "show trials," followed by the killing of almost all of the old bolshevik revolutionaries who were, or had been, in opposition to Stalin and the dominant group in the Party machine. Some managed to commit suicide. At the same time, whole rows of men who had always served the apparatus faithfully, but who protested or opposed the purge of the "oppositionists," were destroyed *without* public trial, often following torture. It was as if "Muratov" and his machine were carrying out, in the only brutal way they knew how, the desperate recommendation of Tikhon Vialov: Let memory be destroyed; clear the deck!

Virtually all the fanatics and romantics of October still alive were killed on that sacrificial pyre, mainly by the men of the next two generations, whom they themselves had reared. The "head-cutting" was like a drummed roll call of October: Kamenev and Zinoviev . . . Bukharin and Rykov . . . Radek . . . Pyatakov . . . Menzhinsky . . . Ordzhonikidze (forced suicide) . . . Kuibyshev, Sokolnikov, Serebriakov . . . Tomsky (suicide) . . . Enukidze, Preobrazhensky, Mrachkovsky . . . Postyshev . . . Radzutak, Eikhe, Chubar, Kossior, Kosarev . . . A multitude of talents perished: Riazanov, Litvinov, Rakovsky . . . Gamarnik . . . Gifted writers like Pilnyak, Svetlov, Babel . . . The great director Meyerhold . . . The gentle poet Tsvetaeva, whose son was killed, killed herself . . .

The scythe went down the ranks, in cities and provinces, lopping the heads of the Party apparatuses, of intellectuals, activists. Nearly the entire Party Central Committee was killed; nearly the entire Soviet war council; nearly the entire Red Army command, starting with its head, Tukhachevsky; 35,000 officers; most Soviet ambassadors, almost the entire staffs of *Pravda* and *Izvestia*, most of the officials of the Cheka (including its head, Yagoda), most of the leaders of the Young Communist League . . .

From late 1936 into 1939 the slaughter went on. The tortures and shootings that took place in the basement of the Lubyanka, headquarters of the security police, must have set a world record for one building. All of this Gorky, with prophetic vision, had foreseen: "Dear ones!" Paula, the gentle Christian conscience, had cried, "But you can't live without pitying anyone!" The sense of blindness, and tragic death-dealing, that crowds the pages of "The Zikovs" now crowded every corner of the land.

"No longer able to bear barbaric tortures," Khrushchev would tell the Party twenty years later, one old bolshevik cried out—and his cry shows

the mentality against which no Paula, no Gorky, could have prevailed—
"I will die believing in the truth of Party policy as I have believed in it
during my whole life!" Says a scholar of that period: "The loyalty of
these men and many like them to the idea of 'The Party'... was in the
last resort the main reason for Stalin's victory."

Yezhov, who replaced Yagoda as head of the security police, killed
everyone in sight, cheerfully, like a loyal beast. Thus Eisenstein, the great
director, would portray him in the movie of "Ivan the Terrible"—Ivan's
(Stalin's) loyal beast, who after doing his Boss's work comes and rubs up
devotedly against the Boss, purring happily as the Boss scratches him
under the chin. For this movie Eisenstein died. But it was Gorky who, in
"The Zikovs," had coined the phrase "loyal beast," to describe the men
who did "Muratov's" killing for him. Yezhov (before he himself was
killed) received the Order of Lenin at the opening of the Moscow–Volga
Canal, built by the same forced laborers whose "moral rehabilitation"
(while building the Baltic–White Sea Canal) had been sung by the lyric
writers headed by Gorky.

And Gorky's ghost was finally invoked, for the last of the purge trials,
in 1938. In the dock were a medley of idealists and drabs: Bukharin,
Rykov, Rakovsky and Krestinsky; Yagoda; and sixteen others including
the two doctors who had treated Gorky and also including Kriuchkov,
Gorky's "literary manager." The indictment of course charged "Trotskyist conspiracy," spying for Germany and Japan. But there was a mysterious
passing reference: the criminals had also tried "to hinder the normalization
of relations between the USSR and Germany." This was the first official
hint of the coming Nazi–Soviet pact.

Finally, Yagoda, Kriuchkov, the two doctors, and Bukharin were
charged with murdering Gorky, as well as Gorky's son Maxim—and Kuibyshev and Menzhinsky for good measure.

Yagoda "confessed" carrying out the instructions of a mythical "unified
bloc of Rights and Trotskyists." This bloc's "center" had long "worked"
Gorky, trying to alienate him from Stalin—in vain. "Gorky remained, as
previously, faithful to Stalin and his Party." The traitors, "considering
that the overthrow of the Soviet government was a prospect of the near
future, regarded Gorky as a dangerous figure... In case the conspiracy
was carried into effect, he would undoubtedly raise his voice against the
conspirators." In view of Gorky's immense prestige, in and out of the
country, the "center" finally "made a categorical decision about Gorky
being physically put out of the way."

Bukharin, like the others, wanted at least some of his family and relatives to survive, and for this "confession" was usually required. Still, he
drew the line at "admitting" he had plotted to kill Gorky. He did "acknowledge" that Tomsky (who had already killed himself) had told him
that Trotsky, from abroad, was preparing a "hostile act" against Gorky.
"I think," said Bukharin cryptically, "that what Tomsky had in mind
was the great resonance that each word of Alexey Maximovich caused in
the international arena."

There was nothing cryptic about Kriuchkov's testimony. He declared
stoutly: "I perfidiously assassinated Maxim Gorky and his son Maxim
Peshkov, under orders from Yagoda." The son was done in first so that
Kriuchkov could become Gorky's literary executor; this would also help
"cut down" the father. Kriuchkov and the doctors got Max drunk, had
him sleep on a cold bench amid snow, then finished him off with huge
amounts of champagne.

Next, Kriuchkov, in the Crimea, urged Gorky to stand near bonfires
inhaling the smoke (many knew how Gorky loved fires; this must have
seemed a nice detail). Then he prevailed on Gorky to return hastily from
the warm Crimea to cold Moscow. Gorky got the flu; it turned to pneumonia. Digitalis was given, stimulating fatally an already overstimulated
heart. "Such is my second and horrible crime," ended Kriuchkov's script.

All the "conspirators" except Rakovsky and one of the doctors were
killed at once; neither of these two was again heard of among the living.

Although this trial, like all the rest, was a gruesome fake, there is no
real reason to be assured that Gorky was not indeed helped to depart—
not by order of a mythical Trotskyist center but following a command
decision by Stalin and the Party machine. Soviet officials today tell anyone who asks that Gorky's death was undoubtedly natural, that "penicillin
would have saved him"—although neither the fake trial nor the fake confession have ever been officially repudiated. The Russian government
understandably, would like to forget the matter for a few hundred years.
To consider the manner of Gorky's death again would be to risk a truthful examination of his life, and his writings ... and this would mean re-
examining ... Lenin ... the Revolution ... everything. Party and government are not ready for this.

Scholars outside Russia have decided that much of the "evidence" and
"confessions" of the purge trials were actually highly doctored and "reversed" accounts of real events and motives. By this technique, the doomed
men "confessed to," and were killed for, the very things Stalin and the

Party machine had done or planned to do. A transposition of key words in the testimony usually gives, in this way, a fairly true report.

Thus, the message from the mythical bloc to Yagoda, about killing Gorky, when reversed and interpreted becomes a message from Stalin to Yagoda: that, since the physical liquidation of the former Opposition leaders was now a near prospect, Gorky was a dangerous figure; if it was carried out, he undoubtedly would raise his voice against the leadership of Party and government; and that therefore, in view of Gorky's immense prestige in and out of the country, Stalin had made "'a categorical decision about Gorky being physically put out of the way."

These scholars add (basing themselves on an informant): "Stalin's feeling, in 1930, that it was necessary to humor Gorky, was presumably followed by the feeling, in 1936, that there was now 'no other way out' than to kill him." This feeling on the part of Stalin, with its shade of regret—that there might be "no other way out"—was exactly conveyed, by Gorky the poet, in describing "Muratov's" last warning to Sofia. Seldom has art led life so faithfully.

Souvarine, head of the French Communist Party who quit the Cause, states that Gorky, after being refused a passport, wrote critically about the regime to "a famous Western writer"; but the message was intercepted in Gorky's immediate entourage, where the security police had an agent. Gorky's silence worried his friend, who asked another Western writer, about to visit the Soviet Union, to be sure to look up Gorky. The second writer friend made known his intention to do so. Yagoda brought this before Stalin, who said to forbid the contact. "When Yagoda pointed out that this would, to the already wavering Western writer, be an admission of things having gone wrong, Stalin ordered Yagoda to have Gorky killed."

The first writer was probably Wells or Zweig, the second probably Romain Rolland.

Now, read "backwards," Bukharin's cryptic remark about "the great resonance that every word uttered by Alexey Maximovich found" makes sense, completing a fairly convincing documentation of motives for a preventive killing. Gorky, whose words carried great "resonance," had never spoken out; now there was real danger, for Stalin, that he would— to eminent foreign writers, and possibly even at home, in desperation—in view of the slaughter being planned. He was a menace. This overcame the admitted, sad mocking fondness "Muratov" had always had for Holy Sofia—that romantic.

It is possible, of course, that "the terrible time" simply sapped Gorky's will to live, that Max's death really "undercut" him.

It is also possible that, although "suicide at any age is banal," he voluntarily did away with himself. One can only speculate that, having once tried it, he would always at the last minute refuse this way out. Still, heavy drinking was, especially for him, a form of suicide (as Sofia pointed out to Peter, Glafira to Bulichev); it is said that there was a very heavy drinking bout after his return to Moscow, just before he went down.

But that time's awful logic points to the bitterer conclusion. Once Gorky decided it was "death of the body, or death of the soul," Stalin had no more to hope from him. A major national program, such as the purges, required an intricate timetable, in advance. It would have been unrealistic for Stalin and the Party machine to sit back and count on Gorky's voluntary suicide, or his death after a drinking orgy of despair. Gorky had to be dead for the trials and slaughter to start in full security. Logic dictated helping (gently but firmly) an obstinate and now dangerous old man pass away, into a beautiful and useful legend.

## CHAPTER 42

A MONTH before the end, with the bravery of one who knew all this and no longer cared, Gorky actually moved into action, like Holy Sofia and her brother Antipas: "You've got to go to Evil itself, strike at its heart, hurl it down, stamp on it, destroy it . . ."

Early in May, while he was "resting" in the Crimea, where one who saw him again after eight years looked at him with "agitation and tears," some documents were suddenly printed in *Pravda*. They were from a forthcoming book, "The Failure of the German Occupation of the Ukraine"—referring to the rather brutal occupation after World War I. The book itself, edited by Gorky (with a coeditor, the historian Isaac Mintz), was being published by the press of one of the many "writers projects" Gorky headed, that dedicated to publications concerning the Civil War. The book was strongly anti-Nazi and antifascist.

To put *this* before Party and people was clearly "hindering the normalization of relations with Germany"; and the last thing the machine could tolerate was a frank discussion of "who were the heroes of our Civil War?" since most of those still alive were slated for liquidation. If Gorky, under cover of the existing antifascist policy, and over the heads of the Party leadership, started whirling books off various presses—and using *Pravda*, on whose staff were many antifascists, to help him—linking current Nazi atrocities against the Jews with past German brutality against Ukrainians and Russians, the whole faked case against the "old bolsheviks" could be made a shambles; certainly one of its main supports, the anti-Semitism of the know-nothings in the Party, would be badly shaken. The purges could be aborted, a whole domestic and foreign policy imperiled.

And a campaign of this sort was clearly what Gorky had in mind. The hour was late; some of the doomed men were already in the Lubyanka, being "prepared" for "confession." The Party leadership apparently reacted violently to the sudden anti-German "exposé." *Pravda*'s editor, Mekhlis, frightened, wrote to Gorky about a "misunderstanding." Gorky tried to rally him: "We need to use more widely in *Pravda* the documents exposing German fascism." The last sentence of this letter—which is the last of all Gorky's known correspondence—is: "We must hurry, there is little time left."

With the "scoop" in Pravda, and that book about the German occupation, Gorky had advanced into foredoomed battle. It was surely the act of an old man grown reckless in his desperation. When he suddenly quit the Crimea and returned to Moscow, the last week in May, he had undoubtedly been summoned by the Boss, and as he prepared to board the train in Sevastopol he undoubteedly knew this would be the last long train ride. ("Our life is like a waiting at the station/Before departure to the world of darkness.") He had really left the Boss no choice; nor did he have one himself. Escape was surely impossible; and anyway, Ekaterina Pavlovna, his grandchildren, his son's widow, and other hostages were in Moscow; but it seems clear that he had long given up any thought of escape. He may have even dreamed, to the last, that there was a chance of carrying on the fight against Evil at close quarters.

If his brave, naïvely cunning effort to change destiny had prevailed, Russia would have been spared much agony. But this would have meant an internal revolution—twenty-five years before it could take place.

From the point at which that last letter to the editor of *Pravda* ended (May 23)—"there is little time left"—the trail of events is difficult; it must have been swift. The official "chronicle" of his life, compiled years later, does its best to provide the stately continuity proper for the legend of Gorky (working hard to the end, constructing the socialist reality). Yet some of the items, the peculiar wording, even the sequence, make one pause. End-of-May items: he compiled notes for a contemplated children's magazine; he discussed with the physician Burdenko the need for "a separate faculty of synthetic medical studies"; with writers, the need for a new youth magazine. On June 1, for some reason, he is supposed to have written "a negative answer" (the word rendered "negative" here connotes "refusal" or "rejection" of something) to a story submitted by a clumsy beginner, entitled "Vinegar" (acetic acid, in Russian, is "vinegar acid"); he "sent back the manuscript." Then, for that same day, June 1, there is the fatal entry: "At The Hillocks, falls ill of the flu." He is said to have continued working; on the 4th is said to have "approved the setting up of a committee for an international peace congress." Thus the official chronicle.

The artist Korin, a real friend, who had done a perceptive portrait of the old Gorky, was waiting for a phone call setting a time of meeting. He had waited at the train station on Gorky's return from the Crimea, but missed him because Gorky was "very much delayed by those there to meet him." On what must have been the last day of May or June 1, Korin's phone rang, but stopped before he could get to it. Later he was told Gorky's daughter-in-law had phoned, at Gorky's request; Gorky was going to visit his son's grave, and on his way wanted to drop in on Korin; she hung up—apparently, very quickly—"thinking nobody was home."

"Right from the cemetery Alexey Maximovich went out to The Hillocks, and on the following day fell ill." Korin phoned every day, and several times asked if he might come. "I was told that nobody was being admitted to him." Finally Korin got a phone call: "It's all over"; he was to come at once, with his equipment, to make a death sketch. The honest old man tried hard (writing his "reminiscences" in 1949, still under Stalin) to convey his suspicions.

It was probably during the last week, while Gorky was sinking, that Yagoda, with assistants, went through his manuscripts and destroyed them; they must have included the poems Gorky had long been writing, one a morning. Yagoda is said to have looked up from his perusal—if these were the poems, then surely this was one of the most touching readings of a manuscript of poetry in history—and remarked (an old Russian proverb): "No matter how you feed the wolf, he'll always keep looking away into the forest."

A diary is also said to have been found, by that "committee for bringing into order the literary remains of Gorky," which caused the members to panic when they started reading; an oath of silence was taken by all present, on pain of death. At once after Gorky's death all letters to him in the hands of private citizens were called in; whoever was known not to have complied was brought to the Lubyanka. All the magazines Gorky himself had controlled—such as "Our Achievements" and "The Soviet Collective Farmer"—were locked up, and all connected, down to typesetters, arrested. These reports come from men who were close to the scene and to Gorky; the magazines, certainly, were discontinued in 1936. To have kept a final diary, as a testimonial to history, is something a Gorky would have felt almost obligatory.

However Gorky, after stopping beside his son's grave, was brought into the presence of "Life's beloved sister" Death, the actual process of dying seems amply and poignantly shown—even in his own words. The problem is, again, to untwine truth from forgery. In particular, the counterplay of the official records of the last days and hours with the real background, and with fragmentary "unofficial" reports, is both fascinating and ironic.

At The Hillocks, during the terminal weeks, there were no "unofficial" visitors. Many Soviet writers who had a genuine affection, and even love, for him have written their "reminiscences of Gorky"; not one says he saw him in those last two and a half weeks.

On the 8th, says the official chronicle, leaders of Party and government visited him. He and they talked of Soviet literature, and particularly "of his work on 'The History of the Civil War.'" (This was the organization he had created and headed, which was bringing out the book about the German occupation.) Apparently right after that chummy visit, a doctor, Speransky, was admitted, and he tended Gorky during much of the last days and nights. His account is clearly a mingling of factual description, official legend, and nuances aimed at the truth.

By the time Speransky appeared, the issue must have been long decided. Gorky could not breathe lying down; he sat almost all day and night in an arm chair. Arterial changes had taken place, and "certain nervous symptoms" were noted, connected with the inability to breathe and also with "blood circulation in the brain." There were moments of "relief," when Gorky spoke "heartily and in his usual jocular way"; at other times he was upset by his illness; at still others, in a coma.

The doctor avers that Gorky spoke "not once" about himself. He spoke, however, "with delight" about the prospect of a new Soviet constitution—it was announced that same month, June, and is still a splendid document; the mass killings began in August. "Losing breath, interrupting his speech with forced pauses, he constantly returned to the paragraphs touching the rights of citizens, the reciprocal relations of nationality groups, and especially the part clearly and forever formulating the position of women." Several times he repeated, the doctor recalled—and possibly the good doctor was stretching his imagination—"Here you and I are concerning ourselves with trifles, unnecessary things, while there in the land perhaps the stones sing."

He spoke of the hard struggle against the "harmful vestiges of the past" (this was a formula Gorky had long used, when he wanted to refer—but couldn't directly—to brutality, fanaticism, repression). Several times he is supposed to have recalled Lenin, once—at night—to have started to talk about their first meeting. (The official legend has tried to fix the image of the Gorky–Lenin relation as it was in its first years; the rest is too difficult and disquieting.)

Greetings came from front organizations; letters from Chinese writers; from Romain Rolland—who had tried in vain to get in touch with Gorky while Gorky was well—a copy arrived of Rolland's book, "Fellow Traveller," inscribed "to Maxim Gorky with Deep Love." This is one of the nicest touches in the chronicle.

Two days before death there was a temporary improvement. "An illusory hope appeared." He is quoted: "It seems I'll jump clear." He shook hands strongly, endured his suffering stoically.

After that, apparently, began the last descent, and its record is preserved —one cannot help feeling this part is genuine—in pencil notes he himself managed to scribble on small slips of paper.

"Things are getting heavier: books, the pencil, the glass, and everything seems smaller than it was.

". . . No end to the night, and I cannot read.

". . . They forgot to give me a knife to sharpen the pencil.

". . . Slept almost 2 hours. It's growing light.

". . . Extremely complex sensation—

"Two processes in rivalry:

"Enervation of the life of the nerves—as if the cells of the nerves are being extinguished—becoming covered with ash, and all thoughts grow gray.

"At the same time—a stormy onrush of a desire to speak, and this comes prior to coma. I feel as if I speak incoherently, though phrases are still sensible.

"They think—inflammation of lungs—guessing: probably I won't live through it.

"Can't read or sleep."

A break in time, or in passage to a last slip of paper, is indicated in the chronicle by a line consisting of dots (. . . . .). Then:

"End of the novel—end of the hero—end of the author." (This, the chronicle explains, was dictated by Gorky.)

Another break is indicated by dots. Then finally, again in his own writing:

"The last blow."


As if to signal that the notes are genuine documents—his last creative words—whatever the rest of the account of his final days may be, there is no interruption in their sequence, in the official chronicle. After that, comes a different kind of entry:

On the last day, in a coma, he spoke of wars: fragmentarily, in short phrases, he said: "There will be wars ... We have to prepare ... We've got to button all our buttons," etc.

When this was published, in 1940, war was indeed approaching. These phrases attributed to the dying Gorky were used to help explain the need to tear apart the Red Army by killing its commanders and officers, for "plotting with Germany." "We've got to button all our buttons," the dying old writer, knowing the treacherous state of the military establishment, muttered in a coma.

Unfortunately for any belief in the genuineness of these dying mutterings, there had been no military plot with Germany; Tukhachevsky and the other generals and officers have been posthumously cleared; Gorky was not likely to have been aware of a military disorder, since it did not exist until after his death, when the commanders and officers of the Red Army were slaughtered as a step to making the German pact possible. These prophetic remarks can only be interpolation by Party legend-makers. Gorky the man was dead; Gorky the legend was now free to go to work—for Party and country.

"Gorky was tortured also by the thought," states the chronicle, just before the entry of his death, "that much still needed to be done by him for his land. Of this he spoke on the first day, and of this the fragmentary phrases burst out when the mighty writer was in a coma."

And now his spirit has been tortured enough, by this post-mortem as well as by the manner—whatever it was—and the processes of death. "The Last Blow" freed him from all perplexities, yearnings and disillusionments, the unanswered questions, the quandaries that could not then be resolved. That he died in the bitter ashes of mighty aspirations and dreams is not unique. There are no "eternal flames"—all die out, and some are again lighted.

# CHAPTER 43

THE spiritual quest and the inner anguish of Gorky are almost unknown in the West. He is vaguely thought of as the writer of "The Lower Depths" (which few have understood) and as one of those responsible for "socialist realism"—something (whatever it is) with which his own enduring work has nothing in common.

In Soviet Russia, a spiritual reaction has taken place against the "Party line" in literature. With this line the Party has always tried vigorously to identify Gorky. This means that most of his finest work is screened out—being religious in its morning, tormented and disillusioned in its afternoon and evening. What remains is his early romanticism and his "realism."

The land's youth, trying to find something in the past that explains the present and points to the future, fail to find that reality in Gorky—in whose work, actually, as has been seen, it is deep and rich. They see in that early romanticism, which is pushed at them, something nostalgic, from a dim, innocent and lost past. The "realistic" plays of his "Lenin" period only repel them.

They have no idea how far Gorky himself moved, of the bitter tormented inner battle—the whole struggle over the Beautiful Lie. "The Confession" has no place in Russian literary history. His life between the start of the Revolution and his return to Russia has been suppressed and edited. "Stepan Razin" is a buried scenario; the agonized "Notes" and "Fragments" a quaint puzzler. The terrible overtones which make "Yegor Bulichev" majestic are so muted that, apparently, they are not heard; "The Zikovs" is almost, "The Survivors" altogether, unknown; the last poetry was destroyed.

How Gorky is seen is conveyed poignantly by a young Soviet poet of today:

> O romanticism, blue smoke,
> O the burning heart of Danko!
> How much water, how much blood
> Has flowed under the Lubyanka...

This Gorky is a museum piece. The truer Gorky—the tormented, yearning and disenchanted symbolist, poet of the Russian soul in his times, poet of the human interior—awaits discovery.

The legend, which already was being shaped while he lived, which could hardly wait for his death, has some relation to reality; the great legends usually do. The torment and disillusionment are washed out. The Beautiful Lie is the Truth. And the Truth goes marching on. If only memory can be destroyed, the past can be seen as the glorious struggle of lofty men, possessing the Truth, for the highest dreams, with Gorky the resolute fighter for socialism, the humanist—which he was—seen as the Beautiful Vision (not a Lie) demands it; he laid down his life for the Russian people.

The land changes, as the old psychology, that had to be changed, and the old fanatical dream die together; while the reality emerges of a powerful industrial state. A new and more humane image is needed, and that image is Gorky's.

Today, with "Muratov's" vast image cast in shadow, his monument removed from the Kremlin burial ground, the image of Matvey the Godbuilder, the holy wanderer Luka, has been lifted, and it is second only to that of the man it would not be altogether fair to identify as Razin: Lenin.

A common formula now is: "As Lenin said: .... And as Gorky also said: ...."

If his image can only be lifted still further, it will be all the better for the so long unhappy, so powerfully unfolding land. A land cannot help shaping itself in accord with the guiding image put before it.

Lenin's, no matter how softened—as Gorky tried desperately to soften the character of Razin—is withdrawn, cold, fanatical. It is still too close to the image, in socialist garb, of the old masters of Russia. Far superior to the "heroic" images that for so long unhappily mesmerized people— the ambitious butchers, the Alexanders, Caesars, Ivan the Terribles and Charlemagnes—it still must be considered obsolete, "a dying truth," if the future is to be different from the past.

But Gorky remains: very human and warm, tormented in the good old human fashion, only more than most; romantic, as people are, but no fanatic; confused; virile enough for all his sensitivity; weak in the way thinking people too often are, and have a right to be; magnanimous; intelligent. A fairly complete man, though a strange and unhappy one.

Guiding images do change. There are historic cases of religions which, after their crusading barbarism was finished, moved into the background their more fanatical and violent founding fathers, and advanced the ones who represented a gentler humanism. This, it seems, Soviet Russia is already, in a clumsy way, trying to do. Gorky's movement to second place in the pantheon—a dark horse coming up along the rail—is such a movement.

This process is necessary, and full of hope.

The effort to heal old burning wounds, and bring together again all the rich and shattered streams that made up, originally, the great Russian revolutionary movement, and to give each its due, is needed for the successful nation Russia wants to be. To do this in the sterile sign of Lenin is impossible. In Gorky's sign it can be done, and in the sign of a modern version of his Holy Sofia.

One day soon, it is said, Lenin's tomb and the whole Kremlin burial ground—that gruesome waxworks, shrieking of blood—will be moved somewhere into the suburbs. The urn with Gorky's ashes can then, one may hope, be buried more privately, perhaps by the grave of his son, with a place beside it for the remains of Ekaterina Pavlovna. She blundered along with everybody else, making ghastly mistakes, but nevertheless she hung on, and shared the family's tragedy.

Then a real study of Gorky and his works will be more possible. This will enable new Soviet generations to know what they must, about their real past and their real heritage.

He is worth studying, by the world as well.

He is large. As an artist, he is one of those whose work must be taken together as a single vision, mainly symbolic and allegorical. Then the early romanticism, and even the mediocre "social" works, fall into place, while the stars—the great fragments, "Childhood" and the other autobiographical books, the literary reminiscences, the religious vision of Matvey, the dark star Bulichev—give the depth and splendor.

He is even larger than that. For this is one of those cases where the whole man, unique, never-to-be-repeated (as Molotov said, in puzzled awe, in that eulogy; as Chekhov had foreseen: "The man Gorky will not be forgotten in a thousand years"), is larger than the artist alone, and suggests new, larger definitions of the relation of art and life. He can hardly be contained in the term "writer." His place is with those timely, or special, figures who helped create, or shape, a changed view of the world: one of the crucial reforming thinkers, both highly original and eclectic. That he was also a bard and an unhappy creative spirit was his misfortune and our good luck: this made him able to sound back emotions that help us understand, and even be inspired by, a whole age and its ideals; understand, and even forgive, its dread realities.

That he destroyed himself in refusing to sever art from life makes him only the more contemporary. His need for hope, to the point of myth, was painful to see; but it was really the need for a moral life. His retreat from Reason was harrowing to trace; but it may have helped us know that reason is not an object to worship but to use. That bitter, fighting retreat was a signal of the opening of the modern age—our struggle. The "religion of man" was and is valid, and of plain necessity will be more valid as realities come clear. The "religion of work" may be done for, but it carried many people over an otherwise impassable stretch of road.

These are only some of his banners, his contributions.

There he stands, the old holy wanderer, staff in hand, at the Byelorussian Station in Moscow, facing the West. A resolute pilgrim in life with its fistfight, seeking answers beyond life, he saw himself; and this statue is not out of keeping.

Soviet artists have also tried to depict Gorky as a heroic, fierce Stormy Petrel, shod with Revolution's gale. This is a rough assignment—because of the kind of bird the petrel really is.

Not a large bird, it is a species of gull, or albatross. English sailors know it, unromantically, as "Mother Carey's chicken"—and this conveys the sense of its rather forlorn, hysterical flight. American sailors and marines, with the special American genius, call it a "gooney bird."

Usually sooty black or grayish blue, it has a tubed nose, through which it makes shrill trumpet noises. An archaic form, it flies largely over the North Atlantic and South Pacific: it is possible Gorky never really saw one, but small related gulls undoubtedly follow ships on the Caspian and the Black Sea, as they do on other inland seas, picking up garbage in the ship's wake.

The curious bird has great powers of flight; in fact it seems to be unable to do anything but fly, eternally and ceaselessly, unable to settle, driven over land only by winds of gale, or when it resorts to cliff holes to breed.

It often flies, especially when after food, close over the water, and suspends itself by extending its wings, thus seeming to run on the water. Thence its name: petrel, "Little Peter," recalling the apostle Peter when he walked on the water. And thence, probably, the belief that it is very unlucky to kill a petrel—it would be like killing the apostle. Failure to remember this cost Coleridge's Ancient Mariner dear.

So, essentially, we are in the presence of one of the timid, familiar birds little Alexey Peshkov so loved, whose minds and songs he learned, whom he and Grandma trapped so she could sell them at markets—goldfinch, bullfinch, titmouse, and above all the siskin!—with whose singing Matvey the God-seeker filled his house—the kind of birds Gorky meant when, in a revealing moment, he wrote that birds were the lovely beings in whose image man made the angels and cherubim ... for his own consolation.

There is no grandiose symbol here, but something small, dear, common, but unhappy: an unhappy siskin, torn from the familiar haunts of birds and men, doomed to live flying over desolate waters, veering and calling ceaselessly, separated by something in its nature, and its bird-fate, from the warm mass of the land-inhabiting cherubim. With this, we approach again the mystic base, from which the man and artist grew.

We might start with the first legend told by Old Isergil—about the son of the human tribe who, for his arrogance, was condemned to roam the universe, alone, forever. It brings us to the second legend, of Danko and His Flaming Heart. And Danko, as we have seen, was only the little, shy siskin grown bold and heroic, as we grow in dreams. And the growth of the dream brings us back to Grandma's dreamy ballad-legend, of the old hermit, kneeling in prayer for all human sins, while Ivan-Warrior, numbed in his eternal spell, waits, sword rusting in hand, and while the young oak grows till it overarches them. And the holy hermit, in a more complex age, takes to roaming and is the holy wanderer; and the holy wanderer, inspired by new energy from the West, carries his dream into life, becomes a rebel and a revolutionary. And so all the legends turn on one another, and are contained in the quaint, wing-fluttering figure of that wave-walking unhappy cherub of God and God's storm-messenger, the stormy petrel, the "Little Peter"–Mother Carey's chicken. This is the poet's starting, and circular, vision of the world.

The little petrel's frantic flight just before a storm makes it seem to "announce" the storm, and it is easy for the human mind to merge the idea of "announcing" with that of "invoking." Thus the timid, strange bird, upset and stirred as it senses the coming gale–being more sensitive than other beings, for it is more like the angels, and solitary and maladjusted to boot–ends up being seen as a demonic thing, which calls up the very gale from the deep.

There is even a legend that when the petrel has flown a long time over the gale, and the gale does not abate, the bird–finally grown mortally weary–alights atop the angry cloud, folds its pointy wings, tucks up its little webbed feet, and goes to sleep on the back of the gale.

So let us leave him, asleep on his gale.

The following writings of Gorky are discussed in the course of this study: